WILD LILY, PRAIRIE FIRE

Wild Lily, Prairie Fire

CHINA'S ROAD TO DEMOCRACY,
YAN'AN TO TIAN'ANMEN,
1942–1989

EDITED BY

GREGOR BENTON AND
ALAN HUNTER

PRINCETON UNIVERSITY PRESS

PRINCETON, NEW JERSEY

#3190006/

Copyright © 1995 by Princeton University Press
Published by Princeton University Press, 41 William Street,
Princeton, New Jersey 08540
In the United Kingdom: Princeton University Press,
Chichester, West Sussex

Library of Congress Cataloging-in-Publication Data

Wild lily, prairie fire : China's road to democracy,
Yan'an to Tian'anmen, 1942–1989 /
edited by Gregor Benton and Alan Hunter.
p.   cm.
Translated with abridgement from various sources in Chinese.
Includes bibliographical references and index.
ISBN 0-691-04359-0 (acid-free paper) — ISBN 0-691-04358-2
(pbk. acid-free paper)
1. China—Politics and government—1949- —Sources.
2. Dissenters—China—Sources. I. Benton, Gregor.
II. Hunter, Alan, 1951- .
DS777.75.W54   1995
951.05—dc20   95-5200

This book has been composed in Sabon

Princeton University Press books are printed on
acid-free paper and meet the guidelines
for permanence and durability of the Committee
on Production Guidelines for Book Longevity
of the Council on Library Resources

Printed in the United States of America
by Princeton Academic Press

2   4   6   8   10   9   7   5   3   1

CONTENTS

FOREWORD, BY LIU BINYAN   ix

PREFACE   xi

ACKNOWLEDGMENTS   xiii

A NOTE ON PRONUNCIATION   xiv

ABBREVIATIONS   xv

INTRODUCTION   3
   NOTES TO THE INTRODUCTION   63

CHAPTER ONE
WILD LILY, 1942   69
   Document 1 WANG SHIWEI: *Wild Lily*   69
   Document 2 WANG SHIWEI: *Politicians, Artists*   75
   Document 3 DING LING: *Thoughts on March 8 (Women's Day)* 78
   Document 4 LUO FENG: *It Is Still the Age of the Zawen* 82
   NOTES TO CHAPTER ONE   84

CHAPTER TWO
THE HUNDRED FLOWERS, 1957   85
   Document 5 *Forum of Democratic Parties and Groups on the Rectification Movement* 85
   Document 6 *Symposium of Scientists*   88
   Document 7 *What Is the Fundamental Cause of the Trade Union Crisis?* 89
   Document 8 LUO YUWEN: *Distressing Contradiction*   92
   Document 9 *Liu Binyan and Tai Huang: Rebellious Journalists* 93
   Document 10 LIN XILING: *Excerpts from a Speech Made at a Debate Held at People's University on May 30, 1957* 94
   Document 11 *On the New Development of "Class"*   98
   Document 12 HEAVEN, WATER, HEART: *Democracy? Party Rule?* 99
   Document 13 *I Accuse, I Protest*   100
   Document 14 WANG FANXI: *Seven Theses on Socialism and Democracy* 101

CHAPTER THREE

CULTURAL REVOLUTION, 1966–1976   104

Document 15 NIE YUANZI: *What Have Song Shuo, Lu Ping, and Peng Peiyun Done in the Cultural Revolution?*   104
Document 16 *Red Guard Statements, 1966–1967*   108
Document 17 *"Revolutionary" Power-holders*   120
Document 18 SHENGWULIAN: *Whither China?*   124
Document 19 LI YI ZHE: *On Socialist Democracy and the Legal System*   134
Document 20 WANG FANXI: *On the "Great Proletarian Cultural Revolution"*   145
NOTES TO CHAPTER THREE   156

CHAPTER FOUR

CHINA SPRING, 1979–1981   157

Document 21 WANG XIZHE: *Mao Zedong and the Cultural Revolution*   157
Document 22 YI MING: *China: A History That Must Be Told*   175
Document 23 WEI JINGSHENG: *Democracy or a New Dictatorship?*   180
Document 24 *Interview with Xu Wenli*   185
Document 25 XU WENLI: *A Reform Program for the Eighties*   189
Document 26 EDITORIAL BOARD, *RENMINZHI LU: A Statement of Clarification*   194
Document 27 COMMENTATOR, *ZEREN: Democracy and Legality Are Safeguards of Stability and Unity*   196
Document 28 GE TIAN: *A Guangdong Youth Forum on Wall Posters*   199
Document 29 GONG BO: *The Wind Rises from among the Duckweed: Elections at Beijing University*   202
Document 30 HE NONG: *Election Scandal in a Rural Commune*   210
Document 31 ZHENG XING: *The Election Movement Is in the Ascendant*   213
Document 32 *The Student Movement in Hunan*   217
Document 33 CHEN DING: *Youth Disturbances in China's Far West*   221
Document 34 *Advertisement: Modern Clothes*   227
Document 35 FENGFAN: *The Reawakening of the Chinese Working Class*   228
Document 36 FU SHENQI: *In Memory of Wang Shenyou, Pioneer of the Democratic Movement, Teacher, Comrade*   229
Document 37 *Interview with Yang Jing*   234

Document 38   XIAO RUI: *Eyewitness Account of the Arrest of Liu
  Qing*   239
Document 39   THE FAMILY OF LIU QING: *Liu Qing Is Innocent!*   244
Document 40   LIU QING: *Sad Memories and Prospects: My Appeal
  to the Tribunal of the People*   247
Document 41   *Women Are Human Beings Too*   257
Document 42   *China and Solidarnosc*   259
NOTES TO CHAPTER FOUR   263

CHAPTER FIVE

PRAIRIE FIRE, 1989   264

Document 43   *Proposal to Resign from the Party and Prepare an
  "Association to Promote China's Democracy Movement"*   264
Document 44   *Letter of Petition*   266
Document 45   REN WANDING: *Speech in Tian'anmen Square*   266
Document 46   *A Worker's Letter to the Students*   269
Document 47   *A Choice Made on the Basis of Conscience and Party
  Spirit: An Open Letter to All Party Members*   270
Document 48   *Hoist High the Flag of Reason*   271
Document 49   *Where I Stand*   274
Document 50   YANG XX: *The Socialist Multiparty System and China*   275
Document 51   *A Letter to the People*   278
Document 52   *Preparatory Program of the Autonomous Federation
  of Workers of the Capital*   279
Document 53   *Workers' Declaration*   280
Document 54   *Open Letter to the Students from an Army Veteran*   281
Document 55   *Smart Thieves' Voice*   282
Document 56   *Provisional Statutes of the Autonomous Federation
  of Workers of the Capital*   283
Document 57   LIN XILING: *Statement*   284
Document 58   WANG FANXI: *Statement*   285
Document 59   AN EYEWITNESS: *The Massacre in Tian'anmen Square*   286
Document 60   CHAI LING: *Account of the Beijing Massacre*   291
Document 61   YANG LIAN: *The Square*   295
Document 62   *Open Letter to the Chinese Communist Party*   296

CHAPTER SIX

THE INTELLECTUALS' CRITIQUE   299

Document 63   SU SHAOZHI: *Proposals for Reform of the Political
  Structure, 1986*   299

Document 64   YAN JIAQI: *The Theory of Two Cultural Factors*   305
Document 65   FANG LIZHI: *Problems of Modernization*   307
Document 66   WANG RUOSHUI: *In Defense of Humanism*   312
Document 67   WANG RUOWANG: *On Political Reform*   317
Document 68   LIU BINYAN: *The Bureaucratic Paradise*   327

APPENDIX: SOURCES OF THE TEXTS   333

INDEX   343

FOREWORD

THIS book provides a rather complete collection of materials on the bitter historical experience of Chinese intellectuals over the past fifty years. It is a most valuable contribution toward understanding the Chinese revolution in the twentieth century in its passage from glorious victory to tragic failure—an as yet unfinished tragedy.

For the past eighty years, successive generations of Chinese intellectuals have chosen the road of the Chinese Communist Party. The leaders and core members of the Party in its formative period were almost all intellectuals; in 1949, however, those communist leaders and cadres who proclaimed the victory of the Party and the establishment of the People's Republic from the rostrum of Beijing's Tian'anmen were for the most part soldiers and peasants. Very few Chinese people know the true history of the Communist Party and of China between the years 1921 and 1949. Even though a few are familiar with the name Wang Shiwei, whom they identify as a "Trotskyist," until now the communists have carefully concealed the terrible cruelties of the so-called "anti-Trotskyist campaign" of the 1940s and 1950s, which engulfed hundreds of thousands of innocent victims. This deception was one of the main reasons why three generations of intellectuals, from the 1950s to the 1970s, continued to act as faithful servants of the Party.

Mao Zedong dominated the intellectuals more effectively than any other communist leader anywhere. First he destroyed their independent status; then he successfully killed off their critical spirit. During the Cultural Revolution, the Gang of Four held a splendid ceremony every year on May 24 to commemorate the publication of the "Talks at the Yan'an Forum on Literature and Art." Why was this piece, of all Mao's works, singled out for such special treatment? Because in it, Mao delivered his severest blow at intellectuals, and pronounced the death sentence on their independence and their critical spirit. At that time, "Wild Lily" came under attack, and Wang Shiwei's tragedy started to unfold. Between 1942 and 1956, it was impossible in any sphere of communist control to exercise criticism in literature, journalism, philosophy, social science, or any other form of social activity: one could only endorse and praise the status quo. After the brief revival of independent thought in 1956 and 1957, China again fell silent for many years. In other communist countries, people were rarely classified as heretics on account of just one single utterance, and then sentenced to decades of loss of rights or even to death.

In China, this was the fate of many millions of people. The Communist Party's fear of language and the written word became an obsessive illness.

The fundamental reason for the weakness of Chinese intellectuals was the long-term and sometimes fanatical support given Mao Zedong and the Communist Party by the Chinese people. As soon as intellectuals came under attack by the Party, they found that they were totally isolated. So changes in the status and subjective feelings of intellectuals moved in tandem with the awakening of popular awareness during the Cultural Revolution. Unfortunately, from then on, intellectuals became alienated from workers and peasants.

Five years after the defeat of the Tian'anmen movement of 1989, Chinese intellectuals have undergone a split. Some have become apologists for the regime; others have gone into business. Liberal intellectuals, under great pressure and at a time when the democratic tide is at low ebb, are weak and powerless. But it is encouraging that some young intellectuals born in the 1960s are choosing a different path from that of the "intellectual elite" of the 1980s, and are turning toward the lower levels of Chinese society, conscientiously investigating the reality of life in China, and seeking a way forward that accords with China's specific national conditions.

Liu Binyan

PREFACE

THIS collection of documents is meant primarily as source material, with special reference to dissent and protest against the Communist Party, for students of Chinese politics. Our aim has been to provide readable translations of the original documents, and we have considerably shortened many of the texts. Cuts and deletions are mainly of repetitions, passages that we found excessively declamatory or rhetorical, redundant verbiage, long quotations from Marx or Mao, and allusions that might help a Chinese reader but simply nonplus a Western one. David Joravsky, justifying his editing of Roy A. Medvedev's *Let History Judge* (New York: Knopf, 1972, p. xix), said that the reason he changed Medvedev's style was because he saw him not as "an exotic or antique source that must be translated verbatim to preserve its special flavor," but as a serious thinker whose work deserved the best English its editor could give. We have approached these Chinese writings in the same spirit as Medvedev. In most cases, we have retained all the substantive argument, and simply changed the voice. However, several texts, for example those by Shengwulian and Li Yi Zhe, are extracts from much longer works. For reasons of space, in these cases we necessarily dropped some of the argument as well as editing the style; but those parts of the argument that we retained are faithfully given.

Many of the introductions to documents provide brief information about the authors and texts. For full bibliographic information, readers should consult the Appendix, which provides references to original Chinese texts and indicates to what extent each document has been abridged or edited. The Appendix also provides details, wherever possible, of fuller English translations of documents here abridged.

ACKNOWLEDGMENTS

Documents 10 to 13 are excerpted from Dennis J. Doolin, *Communist China: The Politics of Student Opposition*, Stanford: The Hoover Institution on War, Revolution and Peace, 1964, with the permission of the Hoover Institution Press. © 1964 by the Board of Trustees of the Leland Stanford, Jr., University.

Part of Document 16, "On Collective Boarding Schools," translated in Victor Nee, *The Cultural Revolution at Peking University*, New York: Monthly Review Press, 1969, is reprinted with the permission of the publishers.

Document 61 is excerpted from Yang Lian, *The Dead in Exile*, Tian'anmen Publications (P.O. Box 4100, Kingston ACT 2604 Australia), 1990, with the permission of the publishers.

Document 63 is reprinted with permission from Su Shaozhi, *Democratization and Reform*, Nottingham: Spokesman, 1988, © Su Shaozhi.

Document 68 is reprinted with the permission of the publishers from Liu Binyan, *China's Crisis, China's Hope*, translated by Howard Greenblatt, Cambridge, Mass.: Harvard University Press, 1990. Copyright © by the President and Fellows of Harvard College.

The editors would like to thank Wang Fanxi for providing materials and ideas, Flemming Christiansen for a careful reading of the Introduction, and those Hong Kong supporters of recent democracy movements who have collected and disseminated writings by Chinese activists and dissidents.

We are also grateful to our colleagues Delia Davin and Brian Hook for their encouragement and support during the early stages of this project. Finally, we wish to acknowledge the expertise and cordial assistance of editorial staff at Princeton University Press, especially Heidi Sheehan and Bill Laznovsky, and we thank Bob Palmer for his meticulous preparation of the index.

A NOTE ON PRONUNCIATION

THIS book uses the Hanyu pinyin system of romanizing Chinese. Most letters in the pinyin alphabet can be pronounced more or less as in English, but readers should note the following sounds:

c	is "ts"
chi	is roughly like the "ch" in "chuff"
ci	is like the "ts" in "rats"
g	is always hard, as in "go"
i	is "ee" after all consonants except c, ch, s, z, and zh
q	is like "ch"
si	is like the "su" in "sum"
u	after j, q, and x is like the French "u"; otherwise it is like the English "oo"
x	is something like the "sh" in "she"
zh	is roughly like the English "j"

ABBREVIATIONS

APD   Association to Promote Democracy

CAD   China Alliance for Democracy

CCP   Chinese Communist Party

CPPCC   Chinese People's Political Consultative Conference

FDC   Federation for a Democratic China

GMD   Guomindang

NPC   National People's Congress

Party is used as an abbreviation for the Chinese Communist Party.

WILD LILY, PRAIRIE FIRE

INTRODUCTION

Here on the baked back,
quicked by no other tree or flower,
of the dread rock,
Vesuvius exterminator,
you strew your lonely tufts, lithe broom,
you who with fragrant brakes adorn these stripped slopes,
you too will soon succumb to the cruel power of the buried fire,
edging its greedy fringe into your soft clumps.
And you will bend your guiltless head,
never before bent in cowardly petition to the future oppressor.[1]

Giacomo Leopardi, "La ginestra"

WANG SHIWEI'S wild lily is frail yet enduring, a Chinese echo of Leopardi's flowering broom. "The wild lily is the most beautiful of the flowers in the hills and countryside around Yan'an" wrote Wang in 1942 in his slight, fateful, deathless essay. "Though its bulbs are similar to those of other lilies, they are rather bitter to the taste and of greater medicinal value." Wang dedicated "Wild Lily" to the woman Communist Li Fen, martyred in 1928 and the object of his unrequited love. For him, it symbolized the lost purity and innocence of the revolution, its prophylactic, cathartic, and elixir.

Why did the Communist leaders let Wang publish his radical criticism of them? In answer to a later brief, brave flowering of dissent, *Renmin ribao* (People's Daily) said (on July 1, 1957) that "poisonous weeds are easier to uproot if they are allowed to grow; they can be used as fertilizer." Some Party leaders even in Yan'an undoubtedly held similar views, yet in 1942 Mao was probably at first banking on his own and the Party's moral authority to keep the criticism within acceptable bounds. Still, there is no instrument for measuring sincerity, and whatever Mao's intentions, the practice of encouraging intellectuals to reveal themselves and then pulverizing them *pour encourager les autres* was repeated on several occasions thereafter.

In 1947, five years after writing "Wild Lily," Wang was hacked to death, bending under the killer's sword his innocent head "never before bent in cowardly petition." But for all the Party's efforts to isolate and discredit him in 1942 and ever since, his ideas have captured the imagination of consecutive generations of Chinese youth, and today—more than half a century after he wrote "Wild Lily"—they are as much in vogue as ever, while the platform that he was murdered on is in ruins.

"A single spark can start a prairie fire," Mao liked to say. Traditionally this cliché spelled both a warning (that small mistakes can multiply into a catastrophe) and a hope (that a mighty force can grow from small beginnings). In Mao's construction, the emphasis is on its second, positive meaning: that a handful of dedicated Communists can create a revolution "Prairie fire" refers to the revolution that Mao intended, but it images even more aptly the sudden conflagration that engulfed Tian'anmen Square in April, May, and early June 1989, raining down fire over all China.

A single spark? Is there a link between Wang's lonely stand in 1942 and the great people's movement of 1989? Yes, and on two planes. First there is a direct, explicit link, for Wang was an issue in the crisis, as he always has been in similar movements in "People's" China. In 1989 Dai Qing, one of China's best-known investigative journalists, arrested after the June massacre in Tian'anmen Square on suspicion of "taking part in the turmoil," published a major study of Wang Shiwei that defended his libertarian stand and denounced his murder.[2] In 1957, during the Hundred Flowers campaign, Wang's article had also been cited, and it was cited again in 1979. In fact there has probably never been a period since 1942 in which Wang's ideas, kept in the public eye by Stalinist politicians as "negative teaching materials," have not continued—as symbols of libertarian dissent—to unsettle and undermine the bureaucrats who killed him.

The "Bolshevizing" of the Chinese Communists

Some people hold that revolution and democracy are mutually exclusive, yet China's Communist tradition was born of a movement for democracy and science. At first the Chinese Communist Party (CCP), founded by Chen Duxiu in 1921, tolerated a wide range of radical viewpoints. "When we founded the Party," said Mao in 1959, "those who joined it were all young people who had taken part in or come under the influence of the May Fourth movement. After the October Revolution, when Lenin was still alive, when the class struggle was acute, and before Stalin had come to power, they too were lively. . . . Generally speaking there was no dogmatism in this period, despite the mistakes of Chen Duxiu-ism."[3]

As Wang Fanxi has shown,[4] before Chen became a Communist his project was to save China by learning humanism, democracy, individualism, and scientific method from the West, just as Europe's early Enlighteners had sought their light in China. But unlike the *philosophes*, who had a century to prepare and spread their thinking, Chen learned these things in artificially compressed time, and although democracy was more rooted in his thinking than the other doctrines, even it was no match for the Bolshevizers who ousted him.

Bolshevization, which had its source in Moscow, meant the imposition on the CCP (and on Communist Parties everywhere in the mid to late 1920s) of iron discipline, blind obedience, doglike loyalty, and extreme centralism of the sort that Stalin had already started to impose on the Soviet Union. In 1925 a first team of Chinese Bolshevizers set out from Moscow to supplement Chen's leadership. In 1930 a second, stronger team returned, this time to supplant it. The transition reflected changes in the intervening five years in Moscow's role in the world Communist movement: from meddler in it to master over it. The expulsion from the Party in 1929 of Chen Duxiu prepared the way for this second and more decisive "Bolshevik" injection. Chen reminded his old comrades in 1929 that "democracy is a necessary instrument for any class that seeks to win the majority to its side," and warned them that suppressing dissident views would lead to a regime of bureaucratic centralism in the Party, but they ignored his criticisms. Chen's expulsion could only speed the Party's bureaucratization, for he was the main champion in it of democracy, and a leader of uniquely independent stature who had no need of Moscow's backing.

In 1927 the CCP, defeated in the towns, began its descent (completed in 1931) into the villages, where peasants lacked the plastic power of city workers to press their interests and values on it and contain its authority. The Soviets that Mao and others set up in the mountains were directed almost exclusively from above. During land revolution the main political say in the villages went only briefly to the poor, within the local communities that formed the horizons of their lives. The changes were earth-shaking for those at their center, but they formed no basis for wider democracy: and once the initial tumult had died down and the changes had been fixed from the top in formal institutions, even the small element of local democracy evaporated. The villagers were unable to criticize and constrain those above them; their lateral ties to other villages were controlled by higher Party authorities.

The Party's new leaders after 1927 used methods learned from Moscow to crush their rivals. To win Stalin's favor, they tailored their policies to his dictates, and so became increasingly irresponsible and unaccountable. In 1935, however, on the Long March, they briefly lost touch with Moscow, and Mao Zedong began his ascent—completed in 1938—as Party boss. Mao, leader of the Party's main "outsider" faction in the early 1930s, had never been to Moscow, nor would he go there until after the victory. He represented the return of power in the Party to China, and in the new Red capital at Yan'an he attended more to the real interests of the revolution than to Stalin (though he was careful always to appear loyal to him). He also won the gratitude and support of Communist veterans by moderating the old regime of violent purges, which had created a general mood of terror both inside and outside the Party. That is not to say that

Mao was even remotely libertarian. The Party under him became more rather than less dirigiste and disciplinarian. The Red Army generals had reached North China at the end of the Long March as outsiders, conquerors even. Among the first things they did there was to purge indigenous Communists from power. "Everything in Yan'an has been built up by the gun," said Mao in 1938. His was a party geared for war. Though his army was less cruel and corrupt than Chiang Kai-shek's, it insisted like any other military establishment on discipline, regimentation, secrecy, top-down command, and the concentration of power at the center. Over the years these qualities rubbed off thickly on the Party, and combined easily with the Stalinist view—absorbed by Mao no less than by his more orthodox Moscow-trained rivals—of the Party as a machine run "from behind the curtain" by revolutionary professionals. So the idea held by some socialists that "the longer the liberation war, the better the social-ism" is quite wrong, for long wars exhaust not only people and things, but also democracy.

The party that took Beijing and Shanghai in the late 1940s had long been used to viewing itself as the sole fount of wisdom, authority, honors, and reward. Its essential strategy in power—and at first even its main tactics—were modeled on those of Stalin's Russia. Even had its leaders been fully on their guard against the dangers of political regimentation and autocracy, they would have been hard pressed to prevent them, given their own experience and the absence in China's political culture of a tradition of democracy. As it was, they failed almost completely to do so. They jealously guarded their monopoly on political decision-making, even against the proletarian class that they feigned to represent (and to which for twenty years they had lacked all ties). Though they spread wealth more evenly—and in that sense made a revolution—they kept po-litical power wholly to themselves. Far from stirring up the workers, they systematically damped them down. They not only controlled industry and the state but set themselves up as arbiters over all spheres of life, from sex to science.

Even so, it was some time before they lost their strong base in society and acquired a more complete set of Stalinist features. In Russia after the revolution, social solidarity was obliterated by purges, forced collectivi-zation, Stakhanovism, and war. The cohesion of the classes that had helped to make the revolution was shattered by these catastrophes, atom-izing civil society in the Soviet Union. Though Mao had followed what was in many ways a Stalinist course before 1949, his party depended in the struggle for power on the political mobilization of large numbers of supporters, so it was necessarily less repressive. It was only through the crises that punctuated Chinese political life in the 1950s and 1960s that the Party lost its ties first to the intellectuals (in the aftermath of the Hundred Flowers campaign), then to the peasants (with the Great Leap Forward), and finally to the workers and even to the great mass of its own members (with the Cultural Revolution).

Mao believed that he could put his own reputation and popularity among ordinary Chinese to productive use by directing outside social pressures onto the revolutionary state, and thus prevent its Soviet-style bureaucratization. Who would police and discipline the Party? The masses, said Mao and the Maoists, though they kept a tight grip on how the term was defined. This strategy, a defining characteristic of the Maoist variant of Stalinism, inevitably failed. The social groups and classes mobilized to exert such pressure and weed out "bad elements" were never content to stay within the limits set by the Party, and when they expressed themselves in ways of which the Party leaders disapproved, they were suppressed. In any case, governments can only be brought properly under control if the people are sovereign over them: sporadic pressuring from outside is no substitute.

But this occasional resort—unique in world Stalinism—by Mao and other Chinese Communist leaders to "the masses" as a scourge of the administration incidentally opened the door—normally shut tight—to the expression of unorthodox and dissenting views. The reason that the Maoists, and for a while Deng Xiaoping too after his return to power in the late 1970s, could afford this consultative style (which Stalin would never have dared adopt) was mainly because their authority and self-confidence was greater than that of other ruling Communists and they had seen in Eastern Europe that too much repression can lead to dangerous social tensions. The Party's division into factions in the early 1940s (between Mao and the Russia-returned "dogmatists") and after 1959 (between Mao and "capitalist-roaders" like Liu Shaoqi and Deng Xiaoping) also resulted in a greater role in politics for ordinary Chinese, who have now and then been fetched onto the streets by Party leaders wanting to bring pressure on their rivals. Such excursions are the exception not the rule, and Mao and Deng's system of "consultation" demanded of Chinese not so much "participation" as "involvement" (heartfelt or not), for to stand aside would imply disagreement, and spell great danger.[5] All the same, they have created brief interludes in which the Party's old tradition of radical democracy, and—more recently—a new tradition of Western-style bourgeois democracy, could assert themselves.

YAN'AN, 1942

Wang Shiwei was never a big name in Chinese Communism, nor—we suspect—would he ever have wanted to be. Up there with Marx, he is surely looking down in puzzlement at his posthumous fame. Gifted as a translator and a writer of fiction, he hardly shone as a theoretician, and he spoke more to the heart than to the brain. So the main value of his 1942 articles lies less in their analytical depth than in what they reveal of the mood of the only audible part of Yan'an opinion still outside direct Party control in early 1942: the writers and intellectuals. Wang's articles stirringly reflect the concerns of these people. For writing them, he was eventually beheaded.

Wang was one of many city intellectuals who, as patriots and socialists, went by secret and dangerous paths to the Communist headquarters at Yan'an after the outbreak of war with Japan in 1937. Many radical writers joined this migration, and their work soon began to appear in the Yan'an press.

In early 1942, shortly after Mao had started a Rectification Campaign against "bureaucratic tendencies" in the Party, some of these writers began to voice their own disquiet about life in Yan'an. They denounced the growth of a privileged elite, removed from the concerns of ordinary Chinese, in the comparative security of the capital of the Communist bases. Their criticisms alarmed the authorities, who quickly moved to silence them.

The woman writer Ding Ling attacked the lack of sexual equality in Yan'an, the privileged position of the wives of some leaders, and the sexism of Yan'an males. Xiao Jun, a talented Manchurian writer, denounced leading cadres for their high-handed ways, and argued that the Communists should inject the spirit of religious fervor and idealism into their work. Others too were disturbed by what they saw as symptoms of moral degeneration among Party leaders. Wang Shiwei voiced his disgust at the selfishness of some leaders, the widening of income differentials, the suppression of free speech, the lack of democratic rights, and the growing alienation of young people from the Party. The 1942 writers were united against the lack of "true human feeling" in the Party, and wanted a return to the revolutionary ideals of equality and solidarity, an end to authoritarian methods, and an end to the unnecessary elaboration of ranks and distinctions.

The writers dealt too in their essays with the role of literature in a revolutionary society. They argued that writing must be free from direct political control, and that a main function of revolutionary writing must be to monitor tendencies toward bureaucracy and privilege in the revolutionary state. In support they cited arguments of Lu Xun, modern China's best-known writer and a sympathizer with the Communists, who held that "politics wants to preserve the status quo, and thus places itself in an opposite direction to literature as a symbol of discontent."[6]

Another reason why the writers thought that literature should be free was because it dealt intimately and inevitably with questions of human spirit, to which politics has no answers. Wang Shiwei decribed writing's task as to change people's "hearts, spirit, thinking, consciousness," and to remake the human soul, "starting with ourselves and our own camp." For the poet Ai Qing, the writer is the "recorder of emotions, the nerve or the eye of wisdom of a nation, i.e., in the sphere of emotions, impressions, thoughts, and mental action, the loyal soldier who protects the nation or class to which he belongs."[7]

The writers were out to strengthen the revolution and not, as their critics claimed, to weaken it. They stressed the moral superiority of Yan'an, with all its shortcomings, over Chiang Kai-shek's Guomindang (GMD) areas. Most had proud records of revolutionary work. Ding Ling, who had reached Yan'an in 1936, had been a revolutionary since the mid 1920s, and had spent three years in prison after the execution of her husband, the Communist writer Hu Yepin, in 1931. Xiao Jun had fought in the Manchurian resistance to Japan before coming to Yan'an.

Wang Shiwei, the most outspoken and consistent of the Yan'an dissidents and their only martyr, was at the time the least known of the writers. Born in Huangchuan Henan Province, in 1907, he enrolled at Beijing University in 1925, though he never graduated.[8] In 1926 he joined the underground Communist Party in Beijing at the behest of his fellow-provincial Chen Qichang and classmate Wang Fanxi, both later leaders of Chinese Trotskyism.[9] He was a man of strong emotion, quick to lose his temper and fired by a strong sense of justice.

In Beijing Wang Shiwei had his first taste of Party criticism, in an episode that foreshadowed his later tormented relationship with the Party establishment and reveals something of his stubborn and impulsive character. He had fallen unhappily in love with his fellow student and Party member Li Fen, to whom "Wild Lily" is dedicated. He wrote her an unending stream of love letters, but she always rejected his advances. The secretary of the Party branch, also infatuated with Li Fen, called a meeting to criticize Wang Shiwei's relentless pursuit of her. Shiwei's friend Wang Fanxi spoke up in his defense, on the grounds that love is a private matter, and that the Party had more important things to do during the grave political crisis in the capital after the arrest of Communist leaders in early 1927 than criticize people's personal lives.

Wang Shiwei's biographer Dai Qing says that Shiwei quit the Party as a result of this criticism, but Wang Fanxi believes that he lost his membership only in 1928, when Chiang Kai-shek's White terror reached Beijing and Communist organization in the city was disbanded. If so, he neither left the Party nor was expelled from it, but was simply cut adrift like many thousands of other Party members in the crisis years after 1927. In 1930 he tried, unsuccessfully, to get back in touch with the Party in Shanghai. While he was living in extreme poverty there, his closest friends (in particular Wang Fanxi) were driven from the Party as Oppositionists, and he too became an Oppositionist of sorts. He stayed in touch with his friends and translated various political writings for them. But he passionately believed that social revolution was never so radical as revolution in the soul, since unreformed human nature—the source of Stalinism—would taint any future revolution that failed to deal with it. So his Trotskyist friends considered him an emotional revolutionary rather than a hardened Bolshevik, and he never joined their ranks. He probably rejoined the Party after going to Yan'an in 1937.

1942 was a tough year for the Communists' war effort in China. Their bases were in deep economic and military crisis due to the tightening GMD blockade to the south and intensified pressure from the Japanese to the east. In this crisis the Party desperately needed support, but it did not always go skillfully and tactfully about getting it. Many of its officials acted more like mandarins than like revolutionaries: they had fallen into set routines, put their own interests first and showed scant concern for the welfare of the people under them. This, then, was the background to Mao's Rectification Campaign, which singled out as its main targets bureaucratism, dogmatism, sectarianism, and a failure to cherish the masses. In starting it, Mao was incidentally preparing the way for the last step in the political destruction of the "right opportunist" tendency led by the Party's main Russia-returned leader, Wang Ming, and so for the further strengthening of Mao's own position as Party Chief.

The dissident writers were at first heartened by Mao's attacks on bureaucracy. They enthusiastically repeated his criticisms and added some of their own. Wang Shiwei saw the Rectification Campaign as a struggle between Mao's "orthodox" group, which he supported, and the "unorthodox" faction.[10] He may even have hoped that Mao would back his libertarian manifesto. He was to be rudely disillusioned.

At first the writers were widely applauded, notably by young people in Yan'an. Democratic views were particularly strong in the Central Research Institute where Wang worked, and which was one of the first units to join Mao's Rectification Campaign. On March 18, 1942, at a conference, Wang clashed with the Institute's leadership on how to set up a Rectification Inspection Committee. The leaders had decided that cadres above a certain grade should join the Committee automatically, while others should be chosen from among the "masses." Wang disagreed. He thought that the entire committee should be elected directly, and a majority backed him. Wall newspapers, which the leaders of the Institute proposed as a way of backing up the campaign, were also a contentious issue. Wang Shiwei argued that their contributors should be allowed to stay anonymous so as to "guarantee their democratic rights," and again the majority agreed. One wall newspaper, called *Shi yu di* (Arrow and Target), proclaimed "democracy as the arrow, evil habits as the target." According to an article published in 1984,[11] it "turned the spearhead of rectification against the 'big shots'" in the movement. Large crowds gathered to read it, "like at a temple fair," and it gained much support. One evening Mao Zedong went along to take a look at it and pronounced: "The ideological struggle has found a target."

On March 30 Mao criticized the movement started by Wang, marking the start of the "ideological struggle" against him. But the criticism was as yet restrained. On April 6 Mao said that steps should be taken to resolve young people's legitimate grievances, and even that some points in "Wild Lily" were reasonable. The Communist leader Hu Qiaomu visited Wang and wrote letters to him criticizing his "mistakes" and saying that Mao hoped that he would correct his wrong standpoint.[12]

The official press complained of resistance to Party policies by groups with ultra-democratic and ultra-egalitarian ideas, and many spectators at Wang Shiwei's later trial initially dissented from the condemnation of him and were "sympathetic to his arguments and proposals."[13] Such was the depth of feeling that Mao called a temporary halt to his campaign against bureaucracy and turned his attention instead to the writers. In May 1942, in his famous Talks on Art and Literature, he went out of his way to rebut their view of literature as social criticism, advancing the thesis that literature's task was not to light up the "dark side" of revolutionary society but to reflect its "bright side" and extol the masses.

The writers were far from being a tightly knit group, and under this pressure their common stand collapsed. All but Wang Shiwei and Xiao Jun disavowed their earlier views, and Ding Ling was even prepared to announce Wang's expulsion from the Anti-Japanese Writers' Association.[14] During the next two years she gave up creative writing and became a journalist. Others lost the urge to write altogether, fearful of further attacks from the purists. The literary scene in Yan'an now resembled more than ever that in the Soviet Union under Stalin. An all-powerful Party machine decided what could be published, sold, and read. The temporary license for criticism had been withdrawn.

Wang Shiwei alone among the writers was put on show trial for his views. Why was he chosen as the scapegoat? Because he was the least known of the writers, so he would attract the least outside attention; because he took his criticisms of Yan'an society furthest; because of his past Trotskyist associations; and because he refused to eat his words.

Wang Ming's campaign to smear Chen Duxiu and the Trotskyists as agents of Japan had achieved its end, so the charge of "Trotskyism" leveled against Wang Shiwei was damaging and helped swing public opinion against him. Evidence of various sorts was offered at Wang Shiwei's "trial" to "prove" his Trotskyism: he had called Stalin boorish and unattractive; he had condemned the Moscow purges and the sentencing of Zinoviev; he had refused to brand the Russian Oppositionists as fascists, and continued to insist that Trotskyists like Wang Fanxi and Chen Qichang were "Communists of humanity"; he had made a distinction between a political party of the workers and a peasant party with proletarian leaders; and he was allegedly negative about the wartime united front with the GMD. But "Wild Lily" suggests that his position on the united front was in fact quite orthodox. As for his other opinions, Mao himself is reported to have said similar things about the Moscow purges and the Trotskyists, and Wang Ming had made a similar assessment of the class nature of the CCP as late as 1941.[15] In fact Wang never belonged to any Trotskyist organization, though he had been close to the Trotskyists on many questions and agreed with Trotsky's polemic against the idea of "proletarian literature" (but so did Lu Xun, the Chinese Communists' main literary hero).

Wang Shiwei stuck to his views even though he was attacked and humiliated in front of an audience that at times numbered more than one thousand. On the fifth day of his trial he asked to be allowed to resign from the Party and "go his own way," since he no longer felt able to "reconcile himself with the Party's utilitarianism." On the seventh day, "touched by the love of comrades," he withdrew this request, "made in an abnormal state of mind."[16] Eventually he was dismissed from his translating job and sent to work in a matchbox factory in Yan'an.[17] In March 1947, while Party leaders were temporarily retreating from Yan'an during the civil war, he was executed, allegedly without the Central Committee's authorization.[18] However, it is hard to believe that the execution was not officially premeditated, for Wang's killer was probably not some simple soldier but Li Kenong, the Party's security boss, who had succeeded Kang Sheng as chief of Yan'an's political police in 1944.[19] In 1962 Mao said that it had been wrong to kill Wang, though he approved of the other penal sanctions against him.[20] Curiously, Mao then remembered Wang as a "Guomindang agent."

In the 1980s the slanders against Wang were openly retracted, and in 1990 he was rehabilitated.[21] Once "democracy and legality" had been officially approved after Mao's death, most Party veterans clearly thought that the time had come to reopen his case, which had haunted the conscience of some of them for decades. The role played by Kang Sheng in the persecution of Wang probably helped Wang's posthumous exoneration, for Kang had been Mao's main henchman in the Cultural Revolution, and his memory is deeply hated by his highly placed victims now back in power. At the time of Wang's rehabilitation, two members of the

Public Security Bureau tried to give his widow ten thousand yuan "as an expression of sympathy," but she refused to accept the money for herself and instead donated it to endow a literary prize.[22]

Wang Shiwei was the CCP's first real dissident, and the writers' opposition was a forerunner and prototype of the democracy movements of 1957, 1978–81, and 1989. True, the writers were not free from strong Party ties: in that sense they were the democracy movement in its infancy, not to say in embryo. Even so, they shared or foreshadowed most of the concerns of the later, freer movements of dissent. Wang Shiwei in particular wanted to infuse rectification with an antielitist, democratic content, and proposed specific measures to protect civil rights. Like their present-day imitators and admirers, the writers were distressed by official corruption, truculence, manipulation, bullying, and hypocrisy. Their arguments, their examples, their very tenor, even their turns of phrase, have echoed time and again in the leaflets, posters, pamphlets, and journals of their political progeny. They took bold advantage of the brief relaxation of controls in the spring of 1942, and ended up as victims—the first of many—of what was to become a staple tactic of the Chinese Communists in power: "tempting the snake from its pit" in order to crush it.[23]

THE HUNDRED FLOWERS, 1957

"Let a hundred schools of thought contend," said Mao in May 1956, seven years after founding the People's Republic: "let a hundred flowers bloom."[24] "Among the people," explicated Lu Dingyi, his propaganda chief, "there is freedom to spread materialism but also to propagate idealism." So started the main phase of the Hundred Flowers, a campaign of cultural and political liberalization that ran from January 1956 to early June 1957. The Hundred Flowers slogan was a reference to the proliferation of philosophical teachings—the Hundred Schools—in China's Spring and Autumn and Warring States periods, several centuries before the common era. But on the minds of many people preyed a more obvious and ominous contemporary analogy: that of 1942. Few were quick to take up the novel offer of free thought, for experience had shown that policy could change suddenly, with today's license becoming tomorrow's sentence. Of the surviving Yan'an writers, none save Ai Qing dared bloom and contend.

Why this sudden relaxation of controls under a regime noted for its intolerance of dissent? The Hundred Flowers were designed, primarily by Mao, to win back to the Party the loyalty of China's intellectuals organized in the small "democratic parties," who had started out in 1949 with high hopes of the revolution but soon lost them. The permit to think freely and critically was extended to scientists, writers, technicians, and professionals of all sorts. These people had been main targets of the movements of the early 1950s to "reform thoughts" and "remold ideologies." Under constant criticism and self-criticism, they had become alienated and demoralized. Mao planned through the Hundred Flowers to restore their faith in the Party and in themselves, and to persuade them to play a more active role in speeding up national construction (by that time slowing after a quick start in the early 1950s). He hoped that they would help him ease various problems that (like in Yan'an) had begun to plague the Party, namely dogmatism, bureaucratism, and a growing gap between government and society. The risings against Party rule in Poland and Hungary in late 1956 confirmed him in his decision to tackle these things, and in his belief that "democracy" was needed in China to resolve social "contradictions" and forestall similar rebellions. He also hoped that ending the estrangement between intellectuals and the state would reduce China's dependence on Soviet experts.

For several months the campaign evoked little positive response outside the natural sciences (which unlike literature and art had been declared free of class character). A few writers did begin in 1956 to criticize the evils of bureaucracy, and some philosophers—forerunners of the critical Marxists of the 1980s—drew attention to Marx' suppressed humanist writings. But they met with a tide of hostility from conservative bureaucrats. The intellectuals' reluctance to take Mao at his word was hardly surprising, and not just because of 1942. Mao's message about the need for a freer climate of thought and criticism was by no mean unambiguous, even though in January 1956 Zhou Enlai had pronounced the intellectuals' "overwhelming majority . . . members of the working class." Mao continued to draw attention to the intellectuals' "bourgeois" faults and to show that he still suspected and resented them. Yes, China needed their skill and know-how, but still they must learn to conform to Party ideology: the difference now being that they could apparently be persuaded rather than forced to do so. And his tolerance was selective. He encouraged criticism by some writers but not by others. For example, he attacked the writer Liu Binyan, a loyal Communist, for his "contentious nature" and for "provoking disunity" by criticizing senior leaders.[25] (In the 1980s, after his return to public life, Liu was soon back in trouble.) One writer who had least reason to believe in Mao's good faith was the Communist Hu Feng, jailed in 1955 for calling—like Mao a year later—for more openness and less bureaucracy.

Mao had failed as yet to convince the intelligentsia that it was safe to act: and most Party leaders and officials had convinced themselves that it was safe not to act. They did all they could to prevent the free expression of opinion, which they feared would undermine their power and privileges. Instead of taking bureaucratic abuse as their target, for a while they turned Mao's campaign on its head by identifying "extreme democracy" as the real danger. By early 1957 the campaign as Mao envisaged it had come to a stop as a result of the timidity of the intellectuals and the obstruction of the bureaucrats, and the first small crop of flowers was withering on the stem.

Starting in February 1957, however, Mao struck back with a series of talks that breathed new life into the campaign, despite continuing sabotage by officials at all levels. On February 27 he made his famous speech "On the Correct Handling of Contradictions among the People," which blamed bureaucrats for discontent among the people and again invited nonparty intellectuals to criticize the Party. "There is nothing terrifying about great democracy," he told his audience. Just because some Party cadres are quite senior, he added, they think that "they have the right to freedom from criticism," but they are wrong. He was even prepared to justify workers' strikes on the grounds that they are caused by "bureaucratism" in the leadership. "Non-antagonistic contradictions," he concluded, will persist even under Communism and must be resolved by peaceful persuasion, including by intellectuals criticizing Party cadres. Though the doctrine of "non-antagonistic contradictions" was not new in the Stalinist ideological canon, Mao's emphasis on the contradiction between the people and the Party, and on the fallibility of the Party, was new, and for the bureaucrats quite threatening.

When the criticism eventually did take off, in May 1957, it was not at all as Mao, captured by confident error, had expected. Nonparty intellectuals made it clear that for them the problems of bureaucratic abuse, corruption, and the suppression of free speech had structural roots in the Party's monopoly of power; some called for its end, others for its reform. Many called for "socialist legality" and a fair trial for Hu Feng. Writers too started—though more gingerly—to speak out in larger numbers, and echoed many of the themes of the 1942 writers' opposition on the role of literature in society.

In mid-May students and teachers in the universities also overcame their initial caution and began passionately, vehemently, and exuberantly to criticize the authorities. "What really shook the Party," said René Goldman, who was at Beijing University in 1957, "was a feeling that it faced the loss of its control over the youth. Young people brought up under Communist rule had become the loudest in denouncing the Party which had vested its hopes in them."[26] A Democracy Wall—child of 1942, father of 1979—was created on the campus of Beijing University, and so too was a Democracy Square, precursor of the one of 1989. One student, quoting Heraclitus, said that adults should die and the beardless young should rule. Most, like Lin Xiling, then twenty-one, used Marxist arguments to call for true socialism with democracy, an end to the privileges of the "new class," and a system of legal rights and guarantees. Lin reminded her listeners that "Beijing University inherits the true tradition of May 4," and like the radicals of 1919 some students tried to "go to the people" and organize them. In 1957 Lin's radical-socialist ideas represented the mainstream in Chinese dissent. According to *Zhongguo qingnian bao* (China Youth), they "were for a time all the rage among young people throughout the country, particularly university students." A few voices were raised calling for a "new interpretation of capitalism" and proposing that the Party "learn from the democracy and freedom of the capitalist countries."[27] This development foreshadowed the more pronounced forking of dissent into "left" and "right" in 1979, and again in 1989, when the "right" finally started to preponderate: a discussion that is developed further in the final section of this introduction.

On June 8, 1957, with the campaign becoming more and more disorderly and "seditious," Mao conceded defeat in his battle with the Party, though never in so many words. His strategy had been founded in the belief that the license to criticize would not be abused, that the intellectuals were patriots who would "serve their flourishing socialist motherland," that grievances could be expressed without discrediting the Party, and that the Party and the people were solidly behind him. The bitter and sometimes inflammatory outpourings of the five weeks of freedom stunned him into recognizing the limits of his authority. The students were the last straw. If even the children of 1949 were no longer prepared to do his bidding and wanted to put the Party—the "new mandarinate"—under real democratic supervision, he had no choice but to drop his plans for regulated dissonance and to back the clampdown. Clearly he had been wrong to think that class struggle was at an end and that free debate would automatically produce "correct" ideas: for though the economy was socialist, old attitudes lived on in the minds of the "bourgeois," as their "wild attacks" and anarchic behavior showed. The solution would have to be a return to "class dictatorship."

The flowers were declared weeds, and the number of schools was brought back summarily to two (bourgeois and proletarian). Mao had launched the Hundred Flowers to get the cooperation of the intellectuals in righting the economy: now he blamed its failings on the "harmful effects of their criticism." Deng Xiaoping took charge of the campaign to rectify the rectifiers (though Mao approved it). A few leaders of the usually tame "democratic parties" who had spoken out against the Communists were reinstated into public life only after repeatedly delivering abject self-denunciations. Most of the student "rightists" were let off lightly and allowed—under strict supervision—to continue with their studies (though a few like Lin Xiling were sent to the countryside for "reform through labor"). But more than half a million "rightists" were sentenced to jail, hard labor, or internal exile, where many of them remained for the next twenty-odd years until the verdicts on them were reversed after Mao's death. Even those not jailed or rusticated were ostracized by society. Among the most harshly criticized and treated were left-wing writers, including several members of the 1942 group, whose comparative silence in 1957 failed to win them immunity from the crackdown on truthful writing. In February 1958 the Yan'an texts were republished in *Wenyibao* (Literary Gazette) to show "how our enemies work." Liu Binyan was likened to the executed Wang Shiwei.[28]

The Cultural Revolution, 1966–1969

What did the Hundred Flowers teach Mao and the Party? That the intellectuals are unreliable, and that criticism is hard to keep in bounds. Yet the experience barely dented Mao's vast optimism and self-confidence. He still dreamed of representing the "masses," this time against the bulk of the intellectual establishment and those bureaucrats who in the wake of his disastrous Great Leap Forward rallied around the pragmatists in the leadership represented by Liu Shaoqi and Deng Xiaoping. All he needed were new "masses" and new methods, which ten years later he believed he had found. During the Cultural Revolution the following that he mobilized in the schools and universities was young and "blank," ready for the "newest and most beautiful characters" to be written on it, unlike the intellectuals, who had "read too many books" and by 1966 were no longer his main tool but his main target. The youngsters, it was predicted, would blindly conform to the "directives" of the deified Mao and take as their sole guide the "thoughts" in the Chairman's Red Book of Quotations, which provided the Cultural Revolution with its simple ideology. But just in case his "little generals" stepped too far out of line, Mao kept the army—newly indoctrinated along Maoist lines by Lin Biao—in reserve, ready to intervene if called on. By choosing young and unformed people as his instrument, Mao hoped to preclude a repetition of 1957. In the event, the Red Guards of the late 1960s got even more out of hand than the activists of the Hundred Flowers, and had to be suppressed.

The Cultural Revolution of 1966–68 was critical in three main ways for the evolution of political dissent. It plunged China into a terror that traumatized all social classes, not least the political elite—parts of which began to question their commitment to the methods of dictatorship. It gravely weakened the Party's institutional base and threw open to lasting question the legitimacy of its rule. And it spawned the Red Guards, who swept China for a time and got an appetizing taste for political independence.

It is necessary to ask whether the Cultural Revolution was a genuine movement of protest or dissidence. This is a rather complex question, and the answer to it is not as clear cut as in the case of the other movements represented in this collection. The Cultural Revolution still leaves much room for differing interpretations, even now, almost thirty years after its start. Most analysts agree that it was initiated by Mao Zedong and various cliques around him in a bid to oust Liu Shaoqi and his supporters. Behind the facade of Mao, some have discerned the shadowy chief of security Kang Sheng and Mao's ambitious secretary Chen Boda; others have stressed the role played by Jiang Qing and her faction. In this sense it was political maneuvering by one faction of the elite, which felt threatened and excluded from power and privilege.

On the other hand, the chaos that ensued, the mobilization of millions of young people, the attacks on cadres, and the shake-up in the military and the security apparatus permitted demonstrations and political activities that matched in scale even those of 1989. The participants were to some extent orchestrated and manipulated, and eventually they were suppressed by the military, but the depth of dissent and conflict inherent in Chinese society was plainly visible. Many Red Guard publications clearly served the interests of particular factions in the CCP leadership; others were heartfelt, sometimes naive, denunciations of privilege, corruption, and abuse of power. So the Cultural Revolution also brought to light genuine popular grievances. Finally, a few groups and individuals moved beyond personal complaints and factional intrigue, and attempted to produce serious political analyses of the condition of China twenty years after the revolution. Couched in language that now sounds ridiculous, still burdened by the worship of Mao Zedong, they are nevertheless thought-provoking: for example, the suggestion that if there is a restoration of capitalism in China, it will have a "social-Fascist" character, managed by corrupt former Party cadres and a new class of entrepreneurs, since the former landlords and capitalists had been eliminated.

A large group of top political leaders, managers, intellectuals, Party cadres, and others in the official world suffered in the chaos of the Cultural Revolution, when the search for "class enemies" grew ever more frenetic and the established norms of political behavior (such as they were) collapsed utterly. Throughout the mid- to late 1970s these people—said to number more than 2.7 million—trickled back into office as the administration, smashed by the Cultural Revolutionaries, was slowly restored. Many of them were far from being the hacks and stooges their Maoist critics said they were. A good few had joined the revolution in the 1930s and 1940s, and even more had surreptitiously or openly resisted Mao's excesses in the 1950s and 1960s, often at great personal cost.

Luckily, Mao was no Stalin, in the sense that while he never scrupled at purging his rivals, he normally stuck at killing them, for once dead how could they be reformed? So some of those who returned to power after his death in 1976 were not career bureaucrats, like in Russia after Stalin, but independent-minded people and experienced revolutionaries. Naturally they were unlikely to question the ultimate foundations of their own power, but some were prepared to tolerate new thinking about the relationship between democracy and socialism, and for a while the fruits of this rethinking enlivened the pages of China's main theoretical journals. From "returnees" like these came the strongest official pressure for the democratization—within limits—of Chinese politics and the strengthening of legal rights and guarantees.

The few hundred activists in the unofficial movement for democracy that started up in late 1978 would have been eliminated much sooner had they not been connected to the hundreds of thousands who in varying degrees represented the democracy movement in the official world, and who were deeply questioning and doubting Maoist methods and values. These unofficial activists had first entered politics as Mao's storm troopers in the faction fight of 1966 to 1967, but they soon exceeded the limits that Mao's group had set for them. In analyzing the Cultural Revolution it is necessary to distinguish sharply between the antibureaucratic, egalitarian impulses that motivated many of its activists and the efforts of Party leaders to manipulate it from above. True, most Red Guards became bogged down under the influence of competing leadership groups in an increasingly violent power struggle, and consequently factional ties overwhelmed political principle, but still a minority successfully resisted the meddlers and developed independent political ideas.

After 1967 the victorious new group around Mao, having managed to oust from power many of its rivals, began suppressing these troublesome "little generals" and consolidating its position. But it lacked a broad, stable base in society or in the Party, so to stay in power it had to resort more and more to crude dictatorship. The betrayed Red Guards reacted in varying ways. Some retreated into cynicism, apathy, or the individual pursuit of self-improvement and self-interest. Others wallowed in a melancholy romanticism of the sort exemplified by the new-wave "scarred literature" or "literature of the wounded,"[29] whose themes of tragedy, betrayal, and sacrifice became popular among educated young Chinese in the late 1970s. After the "ten years of chaos and catastrophe," Chinese of all classes and ages spat out their bitterness, but the most moving accounts of suffering and disappointment were by these intellectual youth. The experience of the Cultural Revolution had been deeply disillusioning. Their heroes had been unmasked as villains, their cause had turned into a nightmare. "Scarred literature" mapped out the mental and spiritual route that they had followed: their childlike faith in Marx and Mao, their enthusiasm and idealism, their total commitment to "revolutionary practice," their contempt for the class enemy, and their willingness to "go down to the villages, migrate to the remote borders, climb the high mountains, and live wherever the fatherland requires." But its end destination turned out to be the fall of the Maoist leaders, the virtual collapse of Chinese society and economy, the restoration to power of the "capitalist roaders," and the wholesale negation of the Cultural Revolution in which they had played the role of shock troops. By the late 1970s many of Mao's Red Guards felt that they had lost everything: their youth, their security, their chance to find love, and their opportunity to study: in return they had been painted by society as the villains of the "ten years' terror." History, it seemed, was mocking them: not surprisingly, they mocked back.

As a reaction to abstract collectivism of the sort that negates human individuality, some promoted the idea of "free competition" under the standard of extreme individualism.[30] Others, alienated by the constant tension of political struggle and campaigns, sought solace in religion and the freeing of the spirit.[31] Still others looked to sexual love as a refuge and fulfillment[32] and to existentialism and "free choice," or they reacted against the vulgar enslavements of society by promoting a cult of the Nietzschean superman. No few tried to find their way to the true, original form of Marxism by poring over the works of Marx, where they discovered dangerous concepts like humanism and alienation;[33] and some of these persisted with the political critique of bureaucracy that they had begun in the Cultural Revolution.

For this minority, the Cultural Revolution was by no means all bad. It had taken them the length and breadth of China and vastly stretched their mental horizons. It had taught them the value of "linking up to exchange revolutionary experiences"—a lesson that they put to excellent effect in 1979. It had also taught them how to write, edit, and mimeograph. Above all it had taught them that dissent is thinkable and "to rebel is justified." And although the Maoist leaders tried to manipulate this rebellion to their own ends and eventually cracked down on it when it departed too radically from its prescribed course, this lesson was not the sort that you could easily forget.

What had 1957 taught the intellectuals and the students? It had taught most of them the virtues of conformity and compliance, but it had confirmed a few in the belief that socialism needs democracy and that the battle for truth and personal integrity is worth fighting. What did the "ten years of chaos" teach? Far more than the earlier movement, it taught organizational skills, and the strength to withstand hardship. It also taught the most profound distrust of politicians. On their release from labor camps and exile after 1976, intransigent survivors of 1957, together with disillusioned Red Guards, were the pinch of yeast that helped bring the generations of 1979 and 1989 into ferment.

DEMOCRACY WALL, 1979

In late 1978 a new democracy movement sprang up in China's main cities. For several months the movement had the protection of Deng Xiaoping's "liberalizing" faction in the leadership and the strong approval of senior figures in the media, the universities, and the academies, so it was able to win ground and widen its support. It had many and varied points of intellectual reference, from Christ, Dada, and Montesquieu to Trotsky, Tito, and the humanist writings of the young Marx. The bifurcation of the democracy movement into left and right evident in 1957 continued and widened in this new phase of it. Wei Jingsheng, the movement's first prominent casualty, whose ideas were widely reported and translated in the Western press, argued forcefully for free enterprise as the only economic system compatible with political democracy (though he also called himself a socialist). Wang Xizhe and Chen Erjin, veteran dissenters whose writings in the mid 1970s[34] had marked the start of the unofficial movement, distilled from the Marxist classics the elements for a powerful and original critique of bureaucracy. Others lie somewhere between these two poles.

The democracy movement of 1978–81 was made up in large part of state-employed manual workers and technicians who identified with the workers and peasants' cause. Some were the offspring of influential Party officials and army officers or of foreign-educated scientists and technologists, but even many of these people worked in manual occupations. In the 1970s it was quite common in China for people to seek "backdoor entry" for their children to jobs in industry. Factory work had high social status, and for a generation that had missed out on formal education it was always better than the chief alternative: transfer to a village under the *xiafang* (down to the countryside) program. The result was that many young people well informed through family connections about political struggles at the highest levels worked in urban industry; and the leaders of the democracy movement came largely from among them. This is important for understanding the nature of dissent in China in the late 1970s, and the differences between it and dissent in the Soviet Union in the same period, which was mainly practiced by intellectuals, many of them highly placed. In China in this period even dissidents from well-off backgrounds distanced themselves from their origins by wearing patched clothes of coarse peasant-style cloth and eschewed the elitism common among their Soviet counterparts.

China's democracy movement activists were under no illusion about their strength in the winter of 1978–79, and were aware that they owed their freedom to publish and to organize solely to the benign disposition of some Party leaders. True, a popular movement—the demonstrations in Tian'anmen Square on April 5, 1976, generally taken to mark the beginning of the end of Maoist dictatorship—had been the main factor behind the rapid collapse of the "Gang of Four," and the democracy movement was directly descended from those events. But for the time being, the broader social forces mobilized in the Square had withdrawn from active political roles and were ready to entrust the affairs of state to the new Deng government. Although Deng had shown no enthusiasm for throwing the Party open to criticism in 1957 and Mao had had no difficulty in turning the Red Guards against Deng and Liu Shaoqi as symbols of bureaucratic corruption in 1966, Deng had been both a main opponent and a main victim of the Cultural Revolution, and—so one hoped—had emerged wiser from the trauma. Others supported Deng because they were tired of struggling, or because the alternatives looked worse, or because they feared to rock the boat while it was changing course and all sorts of perils—especially economic ones—lay ahead. But some of the democracy movement's bolder activists, not content to hold their tongues, strove to break from their isolation, and relentlessly exposed the gap between Deng's promise and his practice.

In 1979 sections of the movement tried to forge links to broader social bases, especially to the returned *xiafang* youth and the *shangfang* petitioners. The conditions of the millions of young people sent out to the villages (*xiafang*) before and after the Cultural Revolution were often harsh, and many of them believed that the procedures by which they had been chosen were arbitrary or discriminatory. After the fall of the Gang of Four, the government took steps to improve the conditions of these youth and allowed many to return home. The effect was to set in motion a huge influx of other young people into the cities, where they petitioned for relocation to their original homes. These *xiafang* youth were joined by crowds of peasants who came to the cities to demand redress of wrongs done them by officials under Mao. Together these two groups were known as the *shangfang* or "up to petition" movement. In many cities they staged demonstrations and even riots. According to a Beijing wall poster written by Zhang Xifeng, an agricultural worker from Shanxi, at one time there were ten thousand such "refugees" sleeping rough on the streets of the capital, where they lived by begging, theft, and prostitution. According to Zhang, these people were harassed, beaten, and occasionally rounded up and interned by the city authorities. Even had they wanted to, the authorities were in no position to put a quick end to the political and social grievances of the petitioners. The injustices were too many and originated mainly at the local level, to which the new "liberal" norms had seldom sunk. Largely unorganized and voiceless, the petitioners were an ideal target for proselytizing by the articulate but puny democracy movement. When peasants wrote about their troubles on Democracy Wall, dissidents copied their statements and published them in their journals to give them a wider airing. Some activists organized and led demonstrations of poor peasants and other petitioners in front of the government buildings at Zhongnanhai.

Students were the main force in the Red Guard movement of the Cultural Revolution, but in the decade after 1968 they had played practically no independent political role. Students in the early 1970s had been educated according to the norms and standards of the Mao group, so after 1976 they were poorly suited to the goals of the new pragmatic leaders, which stressed science and technology. Not surprisingly they showed no great enthusiasm for the program of the new government, though they did not actively oppose the changes after Mao's death. The classes of students recruited after 1976 could be expected to identify closely with the new leaders' goals, in which they were destined to play a star role. So students at first played no great part in the struggles and debates at Democracy Wall. In late 1979, however, this calm on the campuses was shattered by strikes and militant demonstrations, and the ferment sometimes took overtly political forms.

Nonconformist poets, painters, writers, and sculptors were an inseparable part of the unofficial movement, whose journals regularly carried their poems and stories and advertised their exhibitions. When Wei Jingsheng was jailed in October 1979, several hundred poets met in public to declare their support for him. In a system where art and literature are normally under tight control there is inevitably a link between cultural and political dissidence. Even after the clampdown on unofficial art and the reimposition in the early 1980s of censorship, many cultural leaders continued to make clear that they approved of the experimentation in new literary and artistic forms and did their best to encourage and protect it.

Deng's strategic goal in the late 1970s was to create the conditions—political, cultural, social, and economic—for modernizing China before the end of the century. This meant streamlining the administration, releasing the energies of the managers and the technocrats, and throwing out the old class shibboleths, which for Deng were a source of social tension and an artificial constraint on talent. After Deng's return to office, hundreds of thousands of officials returned to their posts at all levels of the administration, and large numbers of purged thinkers, writers, teachers, and artists were rehabilitated (some posthumously). The cases of millions of citizens denounced or persecuted over the previous thirty years were put under review, and the "class enemy" label was removed from all but a handful of "unreformed" landlords, capitalists, and others. Many of these rehabilitated "rightists" were scientists and intellectuals whose skills and knowledge could now be mobilized for the good of China. New legal procedures were introduced to replace the old ad hoc methods that had caused such widespread dissatisfaction under the Gang of Four.

But the new government stipulated the limits beyond which this liberalization would not go. Yes, a measure of democracy and intellectual freedom was indispensable for promoting scientific progress, but it must respect Party power. Yes, legal guarantees were necessary to protect common citizens against the arbitrary exercise of official power, but the judiciary should still bow where necessary to the Party. So when Deng saw the unofficial movement begin to go too far, he took steps to curb it and then to crush it.

But for a while Democracy Wall was extremely useful to Deng and his supporters, who still faced opposition from Maoists who had survived the fall of the Gang of Four and from the centrists around Mao's successor, Hua Guofeng. Deng Xiaoping, having spent the Cultural Revolution "in the cowshed," could hardly be blamed for its crises, and for a time he enjoyed great prestige among ordinary citizens. He was perhaps the only remaining leader who, like Mao in his time, could risk whipping up mass movements on the streets in order to influence decisions in the Politburo. By conjuring up the specter of popular discontent he could frighten into submission his opponents in the leadership, who were too compromised by the Cultural Revolution to feel comfortable about protest rallies and calls for human rights, democratic reform, and the bringing to account those responsible for the "decade of catastrophe." And so he finally won out in the policy debate. Meanwhile, the movement that he had earlier encouraged was threatening to get out of hand. Sections of it took their criticism of Mao to unacceptable lengths, and raised questions about the whole system of Party rule in China. Disorder broke out on the streets of the capital at a time when China's generals were fighting a difficult war against the Vietnamese.

On March 16, 1979, Deng Xiaoping made a speech setting narrower limits to the expression of political opinion. When Wei Jingsheng and others protested, they were seized by the police, and Wei was later jailed for fifteen years. In November further arrests followed at Democracy Wall, and shortly afterward the Wall was closed down. In February 1980 the Four Great Freedoms—to contend, to bloom, to put up wall posters, and to debate—were excised from the Constitution, and subsequently it was forbidden to sell unofficial journals in public.

These measures hit the democracy movement hard. Most unofficial journals stopped appearing, though a few continued to circulate by mail to circumvent the ban on public sales. Ties between groups in different parts of China were loose, and it was not easy for the groups to mount a coordinated response to the crackdown. But there were local protests. Mu Changqing, a leader of the Nameless Association, committed suicide in protest against Deng's speech announcing the repression, so giving the movement its first martyr; and in Guangzhou, Wang Xizhe and his friends caused a stir by standing up at a public meeting of the Communist Youth League and criticizing the suppression of the Four Greats. These were acts of individual heroism; they gave the movement moral stature. What the movement needed next was the quieter heroism of the collective: that is, hard organization. And it almost came within their grasp. In January 1980 three unofficial journals in Guangzhou launched the first national appeal for freedom of the press, and others throughout China soon joined them. In May representatives of various groups issued a joint protest against the arrest of Liu Qing; and on August 29 dissidents from Guangzhou, Wuhan, Changsha, and Shaoguan got together to discuss setting up a committee to defend Liu Qing. Two days later He Qiu and three others implicated in this action were arrested and held by the police for several days. But despite this pressure from the authorities the moves toward greater cooperation continued, and a month later twenty-one unofficial groups finally joined together in a national federation and appointed He Qiu to edit their all-China unofficial journal *Zeren* (Responsibility). The birth of this federation was a major achievement that, given time, would have greatly strengthened the movement by providing a vehicle for the practical expression of solidarity across provinces, and by quickening the flow of information and ideas.

At the same time the movement took steps to strengthen its external ties. In some areas its constituent groups began to win friends among disaffected factory workers. Though China's dissidents were themselves mostly workers, few of the factory rank and file had up to then actively identified with their positions, though many may have passively sympathized with them. Now this slowly began to change. Here and there the movement started to break from its isolation and to find new allies outside the fickle elite. In Shanghai, Fu Shenqi, editor of *Renminzhi sheng* (Voice of the People), ran for election in an engineering works after the government had announced that candidates no longer needed Party approval. Fu headed the factory poll at the first count, despite strong Party pressure on the electors to vote for the official candidates. In Changsha too a dissident student (married to an American woman) collected money from local factory workers to finance his election campaign in the face of official harassment. In Wuhan oppositionists managed to lead a strike. And in Beijing, Xu Wenli, editor of *Siwu luntan* (April Fifth Forum), wrote an open letter to Lech Walesa praising him as a "shining example for working classes in socialist countries the world over." Even in the vast countryside pinpricks of democratic agitation began to appear.

It would be foolish to exaggerate the victories that the democracy movement won among the workers, but these small successes showed that it was not impossible to make ties with them. The democracy movement, which had imbued from Maoist rhetoric a principled aversion to privilege and inequality, was strategically placed to intervene in social conflicts in the factories and on the farms and to win broader support for its political program. Had it done so more widely and systematically, the government would have found it much harder to suppress.

In late 1980 the trial began in Beijing of the Gang of Four (led by Mao's widow Jiang Qing) and the "Lin Biao clique," crushed after allegedly trying to overthrow Mao in 1971. Jiang Qing, found guilty of persecuting Communist leaders and conspiring to subvert the nation, was given a suspended death sentence, as was her fellow-Maoist Zhang Chunqiao; the other defendants in the case were sent to prison for long periods. This trial, repeatedly postponed, signaled a resolution of the power struggle and a temporary stabilization of the leadership. As long as cleavages continued at the top, the democracy movement had some slight space in which to work. But once Deng had succeeded in imposing his will on the refractory remnants of the Maoist old guard and in overcoming the last obstacle to a (limited) criticism of Mao, the space closed.

The trial of the anti-Deng leaders signaled a definitive return to "class justice" and so paved the way for extra-legal measures against political deviants. Officially, it was billed as a symbol of the return to "socialist legality" under Deng, but by any normal standards of justice it was a contemptible fraud. Whatever Jiang Qing's crimes, she had done nothing that her accusers would not also have done to keep power, and in that sense her only real crime was to have been defeated. The verdict against her was reached before the trial, and the trial itself was heavily censored and marked by a raucous and squalid campaign of sexist smears and innuendoes. Judges and prosecutors sat together, distinguished only by the color of their tunics. The defense lawyers based their cases entirely on evidence compiled by the prosecution. They objected to none of the prosecutors' questions, cross-examined no prosecution witnesses, and called no witnesses of their own.[35] Shortly after Jiang's sentencing, Amnesty International said that it was "concerned that the standards applied at the trial . . . might have an adverse effect for the conduct of other political trials in the People's Republic." Unfortunately, Amnesty was right. It was widely said in China before Jiang's trial that through it Deng wanted to convince skeptical Chinese that the courts "attack tigers as well as flies." But if seditious tigers get only the semblance of a public trial, it should surprise no one when the flies are sent to prison with no public trial at all.

The Hundred Flowers had sunk almost without trace under the waves of Party intolerance in 1957 and taken twenty years to resurface. Though the 1957 campaign was followed within ten years by an even more massive explosion of discontent in the Cultural Revolution, democracy was hardly a concern of Mao's Red Guards, and legality even less so. The course of the criticism movements in 1942, 1957, and the late 1960s was tragically predictable: the Party leaders urge the people to speak out; sooner or later the critics overstep the mark; the Party leaders reassert control by repressing the critics; and criticism lies dormant until the next sponsored round of "blossoming and contending." Or so it was until the Cultural Revolution. And here the first big difference between earlier and later forms of dissent becomes apparent. For whereas the clampdowns of 1942 and 1957 were more or less complete, so that the next generation of contenders was forced to start out with a largely blank sheet, the effects of a political earthquake like the Cultural Revolution could not so easily be wiped away. The Cultural Revolution was a movement of unprecedented proportions: even today its shock waves have still not died down. And so the democracy movement started out not with a blank sheet but with a positive as well as negative legacy of theory and experience.

As for the Hundred Flowers campaign of 1957, there are many parallels and ties between it and Democracy Wall. In the late 1970s, while the Wall was up, the repression of the Hundred Flowers was widely admitted by Party leaders to have marked the start of the "left" tendency and of China's troubles, and victims of the 1957 clampdown were not only being rehabilitated in their tens of thousands but were saying many of the same things they had said before their arrest nearly twenty-five years earlier. Yet the differences between China in 1957 and in the late 1970s, after the Cultural Revolution, were striking. In 1957 all sections of the Party were united behind their historic leader, Mao. The Party had stabilized its rule and had radically restructured the Chinese economy. However, the Great Leap Forward of 1959 plunged China's economy into crisis and destroyed much of Mao's support in the Party hierarchy. By 1979 the combined effects of time's tooth and repeated power struggles had led to the shedding of many old leaders, and China's economy and society were emerging from a period of debilitating chaos. In 1957 Mao had launched the Hundred Flowers to curb bureaucratic conservatism in the Party and

forestall "a Hungarian-style incident." The forces he mobilized were intellectuals newly emerged from the furnace of thought reform. The democracy movement of the late 1970s, by contrast, developed largely independently of the Party, over a long period of intellectual ferment and
experimentation. It was made up mainly of young workers hardened by
years of personal privation and political struggle. It shared some notions
with the students of 1957, but on the whole its programs had greater
theoretical depth and articulation.

A comparison with the Cultural Revolution is also instructive. In 1966
the Party leadership was badly split. The students and young people who
formed the mass base of the Cultural Revolution were politically raw and
easy prey for manipulators. The rival factions in the Party hierarchy vied
with one another to recruit a following from among the Red Guards,
most of whom lost sight of substantive issues and became hopelessly em-
broiled in factionalism and violence. But though some of the dissidents of
1979 were at one time open to pressure from Deng Xiaoping, most were
all along independent of him and followed their own lights, with no more
than a token nod in Deng's direction every now and then. Unlike the Red
Guards, they succeeded in avoiding a gross personalization of their politics despite the Party's stridently personal campaign against the Gang of
Four, and they argued that one should look not at the shortcomings of
this or that individual leader but at the underlying social system.

The two great planks on which Deng Xiaoping had been hoisted into
power after 1976 were modernization and democracy. It was unthink-
able that he would risk backtracking entirely on his promises of reform.
The "antifascist" mood among the Chinese people, particularly the intellectuals and the workers, was too strong, the memory of the "lawlessness" of the Cultural Revolution was too fresh in people's minds, and the
new leaders' authority was far weaker than had been Mao's in 1957,
when he cracked down violently on the "rightists" exposed by the Hundred Flowers campaign. And so the prospect of a Chinese spring remained. But on 16 March 1979 Deng Xiaoping made a speech setting
narrower limits to the political ferment. When Wei Jingsheng and others
protested, they were seized by the police and many were later given harsh
prison sentences . In November there was another spate of arrests, and
Democracy Wall was soon closed down altogether. In February 1980 the
Four Great Freedoms—including the freedom to put up wall posters—
were excised from the Constitution, and subsequently it was forbidden to
sell unofficial journals. The destruction of Democracy Wall showed only
too clearly that Party leaders would not tolerate bolder forms of independent politics or open up the system to the fresh gusts of mass dissent.
Their goal was the creation of a comparatively well-ordered society in
which "democracy" was carefully modulated to reinforce and stabilize

the regime. The sponsored revival in the early 1980s of the "democratic parties" that had supported the government since 1949 was entirely compatible with that project. The further growth of a nonconformist democracy movement was not.

DEMOCRACY SQUARE, 1989

China's latest, wildest proliferation of flowers and schools came about in the spring and early summer of 1989, ten years after the start of Deng's reforms, twenty years after the end of the Cultural Revolution, forty years after the founding of the People's Republic, seventy years after the birth of contemporary China in the May 4 Movement, and two hundred years after the French Revolution. How could a year of such bright ancestry fail to be extraordinary? The movement of 1989 marked the passage to autonomy and the first maturing of China's democracy movement, which in its previous incarnations between 1942 and 1979 had not yet broken the cord that bound it to the Party: it ended on June 4 in a sea of blood sprayed electronically into living rooms everywhere.

The Beijing spring of 1989 did not come suddenly into being, but took several years to prepare and bring forth. In late 1986 students in dozens of Chinese cities demonstrated for democracy, leading in January 1987 to the dismissal from the government of Hu Yaobang, a reformer who failed to crack down on the protesters; and from the Party of Fang Lizhi, Wang Ruowang, and Liu Binyan, as "agents and elements" of "bourgeois liberalization." For a few months the students quieted down, but they continued to discuss politics in their newly formed "democratic salons" or open-air discussion groups on the university campuses.

In February 1989 Fang Lizhi petitioned for the release from prison of Wei Jingsheng, the best-known victim of 1979's Democracy Wall; dozens of other intellectuals soon joined Fang. On April 15 Hu Yaobang died, and though he was hardly a leader of light and learning while alive, students and teachers in the capital used his death to demonstrate in Tian'anmen Square for democracy and against bureaucracy. "He who should live died," wrote the students, "they who should die live." They called for a reevaluation of Hu Yaobang, the repudiation of the campaigns against "spiritual pollution" and "bourgeois liberalization," and the rehabilitation of Fang, Wang, and Liu. On April 21, some two hundred thousand of them sat down in the Square in defiance of a curfew announced to coincide with Hu's memorial meeting in the adjacent Great Hall of the People. On April 24 they started a lecture boycott in support of their demand for fair press treatment and direct talks with the authorities, and they took the first steps toward setting up a Solidarity-style autonomous students' union. On April 25 Deng Xiaoping denounced them

as rebels and plotters, and the next day an editorial in *People's Daily*
called them counterrevolutionaries. But the editorial missed its intended
effect, for on April 27 Beijing again filled with students cheered on by a
crowd of more than one million.

May 4 is an important day in the modern Chinese calendar, for on
May 4, 1919, a movement in Tian'anmen Square for science and democracy triggered forces that created the Chinese Revolution. In 1989, on the
anniversary of this movement, three hundred thousand students gathered
in the Square to demand democracy. On May 15, Gorbachev and the
world media arrived in Beijing, and around this time the protest movement peaked and became a permanent carnival. On May 13, two hundred students went on hunger strike in the Square in support of their
demand for dialogue with the government and a retraction of the charge
of "counterrevolutionary rebellion"; they soon reached three thousand,
backed by a far greater number of supporters. After the start of the hunger strike the authorities lost control of the capital to the students. Protesters took over the center of Beijing, forcing Gorbachev and the Chinese
Party leaders to enter the Great Hall of the People by the back door, and
they usurped functions of the police in large parts of the capital. With the
police gone and the students in control, Beijing became more rather than
less safe and orderly. By May 17 the crowds had swollen to three million,
including contingents of intellectuals, government and ministry officials,
writers, scholars, five hundred editors and journalists (who inaugurated
five unprecedented days of press freedom), and hundreds of thousands of
workers. On May 19 a tearful Zhao Ziyang, the Communist Party's General Secretary and its main reformer, visited the Square to apologize to the
students for having come too late. After that he was dismissed from office,
ending ten days of struggle in the Party top, and real power came to reside
in a clique of senior patriarchs known irreverently as the "Gang of Elders": Deng Xiaoping (born 1904), Chen Yun (born 1900), Wang Zhen
(born 1909), and Yang Shangkun (born 1905). On May 20, Yang
Shangkun and Li Peng declared martial law in Beijing, though for the
time being they forbade bloodshed. But the occupation of the Square and
the demonstrations in support of it continued. Troops trying to advance
into the Square were blocked and forced to retreat. By the end of May, the
occupation was weakening and arrests started (on May 29), but crowds
surged back onto the streets on June 2 to stop troop columns marching to
the Square. On June 3 a huge army massed around the capital. The killing
started in the afternoon, and in the early hours of June 4 it reached a
climax. For the moment, the democracy movement had been driven underground. In the ensuing repression, between ten thousand and thirty
thousand people were arrested.[36]

"The Chinese people will need a new Cultural Revolution every few
years," Mao once said. Today, more than twenty years after the end of

the Cultural Revolution, his prediction seems to have been borne out, for China appears doomed to pass at regular intervals into political crisis. The events of May and June 1989 were the most recent and extraordinary in a string of upsurges against the Chinese government: the Hundred Flowers campaign of 1957, the upheavals of the Cultural Revolution, the mass protests in Tian'anmen Square in April 1976, the stormy emergence of an unofficial opposition in 1978, and the growth of a strong democratic trend of opinion in the CCP in the 1980s, all culminating in 1989's "Beijing Commune," which shook the regime to its foundations and (according to *People's Daily*) spread to eighty cities and 60 percent of China's universities and colleges.

It is instructive to consider the similarities and contrasts between this latest movement and Mao's Cultural Revolution. Many of the protesters of 1989, if asked their opinion of the movement of 1966–1969, would probably have condemned it, for it had become synonymous in Deng's demonology with anarchy and murder. But its parallels with their own campaign are quite striking. The Cultural Revolution began as a student protest against privilege and corruption, it was inspired by the idea of national self-reliance, and its Red Guards thought that China's salvation lay in "extensive democracy." These three planks—egalitarianism, patriotism, and democracy—were also in the platform of the students of 1989. The students' methods too owed much to the Cultural Revolution, whose veterans were reported to have been acting behind the scenes in the Square. Even many of the songs sung by the protesters in the Square were Red Guard songs from the 1960s. The Cultural Revolution taught millions of young Chinese self-discipline and self-organization, though today it is usually associated with violence and terror. The Party leaders could not but see the analogy between 1989 and 1966–69, but naturally they put a negative gloss on it, likening the people's movement to "power seizures" in the Cultural Revolution and to "the exchange of revolutionary experience and the establishment of revolutionary ties" by Red Guards.

But the differences between the two movements are equally striking. At the time of the Cultural Revolution, opinion was divided on its meaning. Some held that it was a drama written and directed by the Maoists, others saw it as a spontaneous product of high social tensions. In 1989, however, few people believed that the tumult in Beijing and other cities had been orchestrated by a faction in the Party, and serious observers sought its roots instead in the strains and conflicts of the society that Deng Xiaoping had engendered in the preceding ten years. It was Chinese Communism's first truly independent opposition, by nature indifferent to and even contemptuous of the ploys and intrigues of those bent on embroiling it in Party factionalism.

Even Mao's Red Guards of the 1960s cannot be wholly dismissed as his mindless creatures. True, they were cynically used by the Maoist faction in its struggle to win control of the Party. Their activities were generally stage-managed and they were punished if they strayed too far from the rough but obligatory script. Yet they had been mobilized by genuine discontents. Many, like the radical libertarians of Hunan's Shengwulian organization, refused to accept the limits that Mao imposed on them, and some (as we saw earlier) reemerged to lead movements of democratic dissent in the 1970s. So to that extent there is no absolute distinction between the movement that toppled Deng Xiaoping in 1966 and the one that tried to topple him in 1989.

While most of the 1989 generation of protesters had little apparent sense of their affinity with the Red Guards, some had privately begun to assess the legacy of the Cultural Revolution. They noted that Chinese students in the 1960s had succeeded in throwing out a corrupt bureaucracy; and that thanks to them the Party was no longer all-powerful and had been forced to institute reforms. In the late 1980s some students in Beijing took heart from this, and set out to achieve the same goal.[37] This interest in the 1960s extended far beyond the capital, and far beyond the universities. According to a report from Sichuan, students in Chongqing "fastened on the view that Mao Zedong had deliberately instigated the oppressed during the Cultural Revolution to rise up and struggle against the privileged and the powerful. . . . They envisioned the Red Guard movement, despite its excesses, as a righteous movement."[38] Workers too demonstrated in Beijing carrying Mao posters and wearing Mao badges, and peasants wore them in the countryside, where in some places temples have been put up in Mao's honor.[39]

In 1979 Chinese society was poor, immobile, closed, orderly, and stable. The economy had barely emerged from the shambles of the Cultural Revolution. Against this background, Deng set about reforming agriculture and the urban economy. He broke up the communes, parceled out the land, freed some prices, and slashed the welfare budget. He made Chinese people personally freer than ever before. But he failed to emulate Gorbachev's political reforms (just as Gorbachev failed to emulate Deng's economic reforms). At first, to discomfit the last Maoist remnants in the leadership, he supported the tiny movement for democratic reform that briefly hit the streets in 1978–79, but he crushed it once it had served his end.

Through Deng's measures, China by 1989 was twice as rich as in 1979, but it was also disorderly and unstable. A great tide of people, loosed from the villages by the rise in rural productivity, had reached the cities; between 1985 and 1987 this population of sojourners and would-be migrants (including a large minority of *mangliu*, i.e., "blind migrants" without job contracts) had grown from fifty to seventy million. Urban workers, once the regime's staunchest supporters, were angry and rebellious. The students had turned against Deng's government in the course of the 1980s, and in 1989 they spearheaded the insurrection against it. The defiance spread to all sections of the population, including Chinese overseas, and to most provinces. Chinese in Hong Kong supported it with the colony's largest ever demonstration.

The conventional explanation in the West, and among some senior Chinese intellectuals, for the emergence in 1989 of people's power in China was that economic reform had produced a middle class that wanted political freedom as well as prosperity. It was part of an "inexorable move toward freedom and free enterprise," said President Bush in Washington. This view was largely wishful thinking. The China crisis did not represent a mass conversion to the position of the Nationalists on Taiwan, as Taiwan's Lee Teng-hui claimed.[40] On the contrary, it was largely fueled by disgust at the greed and corruption exacerbated by the import into China of capitalist goods. It was only later, after the movement in the Square had begun to differentiate, that some of its supporters started openly questioning the relevance to China of socialism.

Another frequent explanation of the May–June crisis is that it reflected the growing influence in Chinese society of Western ideas, as a result of Deng's open door and of study abroad. This is the view of many foreign observers, and also—from an opposite perspective—of China's Gang of Elders, who see the West as the source of China's "spiritual pollution." But while it is true that increasing exposure to Western culture helped spread democratic thinking in Chinese society, the crisis and movement of 1989 were essentially homegrown: "the inevitable result of a fundamental breakdown in China's internal political, economic, and social structure."[41] Wuer Kaixi, leader of the autonomous student movement, also denied that the call for democracy originated from foreign sources rather than from the students' feelings of patriotism and Chinese society's own natural and inevitable evolution. Wuer himself had never been abroad,[42] and the same went for many of the movement's other leading activists. Lee Feigon, who was in Beijing throughout the crisis, living at People's University, understood better than most foreign observers that "fascination with the West" was not a main cause of the ferment: on the contrary, "slavish fascination with Western goods" was among its targets. People's University has close relations with the highest leadership of the CCP. Its students played a leading role in initiating the protests. "They acted," says Feigon, "because they felt deeply about the CCP and were upset by the corruption and bureaucracy they saw undermining it. They hoped to introduce democratic principles to the Party and make it more responsible to the people. It is tempting to say that this stance was a result of worldly influence, but in fact it had been a current in the Party from its founding. . . . Among both older and younger students, the leadership came from those least knowledgeable about the West, not from those who had studied abroad."[43]

Deng's strategy for the economy is to "let part of the population get rich first," as opposed to Mao's prescription of shared poverty and eating from a common pot (at least by "the masses"); to create a stable base for his government by cultivating a broad, prosperous, open class of new-rich entrepreneurs that the poor would (in theory) emulate and try to join. But to the extent that he succeeded, this new class of private traders quickly became impatient with his government. They considered his reforms too timid and too few, and they were hard hit and aggrieved by the credit squeeze started in 1988 to curb inflation. It was clear to them—and to others—that the government was split on how to react to the loss of popular confidence. Some leaders wanted to rein the economy back in, others to free it up even more. On price reform, reform of the labor system, political reform, and how to end corruption they were unable to reach a consensus.[44] This disunity at the top encouraged Deng's critics outside the government to take their grievances onto the streets and to try to help swing the balance against him and the old guard.

This new class of entrepreneurs became a mainstay of support for the student strikers in Beijing (and elsewhere too). They put at the students' disposal a fleet of pedicabs and three hundred motorbikes that were used to form a team of "flying tigers." China's privately owned Stone Company and various other businesses are said to have financed the protest movement to the tune of 40,000 yuan a day.[45]

Another consequence of Deng's reform was to create a new breed of gangsters, cheats, racketeers, and parasites who by manipulating Party ties monopolize access to the new wealth and "hegemonize the market." China has a tradition of endemic official corruption that the revolution barely stemmed. The switch under Deng to new economic policies after years of Maoist austerity sowed confusion, disillusion, and cynicism among the cadres, who—seeing those around them get rich with Deng's approval—began to practice their own form of private enterprise by filling their pockets at public cost. In the urban economy, opportunities to get rich by fraud are legion. The reforms created a hybrid economy in which fixed state prices exist alongside far higher market prices, and a hybrid class of party-mafiosi who use their political power to prey on the resulting chaos. Cadres and their relatives take advantage of the two-track system to buy goods cheap through official channels and resell them at a huge profit on the open market. The key to wealth in Deng's China is as likely to be connections and low cunning as innovative skills and entrepreneurial flair.

The reforms have led to a rapid and marked differentiation of classes throughout Chinese society. Some people became fabulously rich in the process, though many are now starting to get poorer. In the villages land, money, and power is accumulating in the hands of a new class of exploiters born of the liquidation of collective property in the early 1980s, when those with influence, connections, and "the presence of mind to put their lips to the trough in time" made a quick kill by buying up collective assets at bargain prices.[46] At the same time, local Party bosses are enriching themselves by extracting exorbitant taxes from local people.

Many young people expected reform to smash the system of "ownership by officialdom" and put power and productive resources back into the hands of the people, who could then truly begin to play an active role as "masters of society" and invest their energy in developing the economy. They hoped that economic competition would provide the material basis for political competition, that is, democracy. But because a "market mechanism" had been grafted onto a bureaucratic state, the resulting "commodity economy" turned into a Pandora's box of egoism, deceit, violence, graft, and all the other evils that infest Chinese society today. So well-meaning people who saw reform as the key to overcoming privilege and who believed that commodities and cash would equalize and democratize Chinese society were disappointed, for instead the privilege was compounded and ran rampant.

The jobbery and cronyism is worst at the top. Sons and daughters of Party leaders (including Deng Xiaoping and—in his day—Zhao Ziyang) go abroad on lucrative missions and start up import-export businesses using family ties. As the old leaders die, this new generation of "cadre-princes" is poised to take political power in China, like a hereditary aristocracy. (Li Peng, the adopted son of Zhou Enlai, is the prime example.) Everyone in China knows this. It was not just arrogance but a deep sense of shame at their personal exposure that prevented Party leaders, Zhao Ziyang included, from going to meet the students at the start of the troubles in 1989, as Zhou Enlai would have done.

The frugal majority of Chinese, shut out from the world of privilege, despise this new class of well-connected "feudal" jobbers, moneygrubbers, and "official-speculators." The contempt and hatred is universal. People of all classes are appalled by the colossal corruption generated in the Party by the reforms. Alerted by the wave of anger, the government sought out a few scapegoats, but this did little to stop the graft and served only to make it even more conspicuous. Even most Party members and many functionaries, including army officers, deeply hate the new luxury class of Party entrepreneurs, which they have little hope of joining. The striking students articulated the anger and dissatisfaction. This is why the police, the media, and even sections of the army showed solidarity with them before the final crackdown on their protest.

When martial law was imposed on Lhasa in March 1989 after clashes between Tibetan nationalists and Chinese police, Eastern European observers in China described it as "killing a chicken to scare the monkeys," meaning that its real purpose was as an example to the cities of China. The events in Lhasa were part of a wider pattern of ethnic unrest in Central Asia for which Chinese liberals (with a few honorable exceptions like Fang Lizhi and Wang Ruowang) have shown little or no sympathy. In the end, they paid dearly for this. The dictum that no people can be free as long as it keeps another people in chains applies to China too.

At first it seemed to many that the Chinese army was insufficiently united or resolved to treat Beijing like Lhasa, for it had a different style and tradition from (say) the South Korean army, which is habitually used to repress demonstrators. The Chinese Communists took power by the gun, but until 1989 they stayed in power mainly thanks to popular support or acquiescence. Soldiers played an active role in suppressing rebellious youngsters in the final stages of the Cultural Revolution in the late 1960s, but for most of the 1980s they were rarely employed to maintain internal security. Many believed that though there probably were hard divisions—perhaps in Tibet and along the Northern border—prepared to act against protesters, those stationed around Beijing were not. And it is true that the armed forces were split on whether or not to support the protests.

But on the night of June 3 to 4, divisions of seasoned troops shot their way into the heart of Beijing and fanned back through the suburbs and the campuses rooting out "counter-revolutionaries." Official Chinese sources claimed that those killed numbered "nearly three hundred," including "more than one hundred soldiers." ("This figure alone," noted Fang Lizhi,[47] "is higher than that of all the people killed in all the student movements of the last hundred years in China.") But according to Beijing hospital sources, fourteen hundred died and ten thousand were injured, and a Red Cross official said that thousands died in the atrocity.[48] Potentially, all China's urban youth were now Tibetans. China was plunged into the worst crisis since the founding of the People's Republic in 1949, described by Beijing officials as a "glorious victory" over "counterrevolutionary turmoil."

In the immediate wake of the massacre, it seemed for a moment that far from crushing the movement for democracy, the Beijing coup would spread it. Far from cowing the citizens of Beijing, it would outrage them and spur them on to new acts of defiance. Offices and factories closed down in several cities, either through strikes or because bridges, roads, and railways were blocked. A week before the massacre, the protests in Beijing had lost their momentum and the movement elsewhere had died down. But around June 4 reports from all over China suggested that big cities outside Beijing were back on the boil. The regime too appeared to believe that it had a long fight on its hands. "The offensive is not yet over," it said on Sunday, the day of the massacre: the invasion of Tian'anmen was "a first victory in a long struggle against dregs of society." On Monday it warned that "white [i.e., counterrevolutionary] terror" might engulf all China. It was some time before the authorities felt confident enough to start relaxing their military control, and handed operations over to the security forces. As after earlier protest movements, the prisons, labor camps, and firing squads were the rulers' ultimate response to challenge.

PEOPLE'S ARMY, PARTY POLITICS

By bringing the army into politics, Deng brought politics into the army. The Chinese Communist army, as a Party instrument, has always been political, yet its generals have rarely entertained independent political ambitions and have generally been content to submit to Party direction and supervision. China under the Communists has never been a Ghana or an Argentina, where soldiers vie for power with politicians.

Most Chinese officers have no experience in, or stomach for, quelling popular unrest, and were probably shocked by the large number of civilian casualties caused by invading the capital. The abiding image in the Beijing massacre is of a young man facing down a tank on Chang'an Avenue and leaping up onto the turret to confront its commander. The incident showed two things: the courage of China's roused youth, and the conscience of a soldier. ("There's only one thing wrong with tanks," wrote Bertolt Brecht: "they need drivers.") The spearhead of the democracy movement was formed by students from China's top universities. China is a society deeply rooted in kinship. Sons and daughters of China's elite, including its military elite, were almost certainly among the casualties in and around Tian'anmen Square, even if most were workers. It is not surprising that officers were loath to send in troops against the children of members of their class. By using the army to crush protest, Deng probably did it more harm than even Mao in his time, for while Mao too used the army against his rivals, he never dishonored it to the extent that Deng did. For weeks Deng's surrogates had been promising that the "people's own" army would never use violence against the people. He forfeited much popular confidence and moral authority when he spectacularly betrayed that promise by starting the bloodbath.

In the early twentieth century China disintegrated into fiefdoms ruled by competing warlords who destroyed the Chinese economy and colluded with foreign powers. The memory of this nightmare period in modern Chinese history has helped to stay the hand of generals tempted to dabble in politics on their own account. But the decade of reforms created a new dynamic of economic regionalism. Some of the fastest economic growth was in provinces—particularly Guangdong—where regional identities are strongest. This uneven development of the regions created a new economic base for regionalism in China. It strengthened the hand of China's regional Party bosses and lent them confidence to ignore unpopular proposals from Beijing. It may also, if it goes far enough, create islands of greater prosperity and freedom in China that will permit today's exiled democrats to return and work.[49] Yet it is unlikely ever to foster warlordism of the old sort, especially because the military reforms of the 1980s led to a new system of officer rotation and reassignment that has greatly weakened the regional identification of younger field-grade officers.[50]

Fear of chaos and national collapse prevented a slide into inter-army conflict in the crisis, and in any case coups and countercoups do not belong to the Chinese Communist military tradition. Yet more differences of view and interest divide the Chinese military than any other Communist-controlled army in recent times. The declaration of martial law in Beijing reproduced in the army splits similar to those in China's political life. In the Party, "liberals" like Zhao Ziyang wanted to conciliate the students, while hardliners like Li Peng, President Yang Shangkun, and Deng Xiaoping wanted to confront and crush them. Identical divisions appeared simultaneously in the army. Seven top retired military leaders made public a letter opposing the suppression of the students, and at least three of the eight military regions were reluctant to support martial law. When Li Peng declared martial law, even Defense Minister Qin Jiwei was said to have opposed him (though Qin later changed his stance), and a group of retired revolutionaries around Nie Rongzhen and Xu Xiangqian called the students patriots. Veterans like Nie and Xu had supporters throughout China's seven military regions. Their caution and moderation were probably a main reason why some commands apparently failed to send people to Beijing to help plan the crackdown. Deng eventually managed to bring the commanders round to his point of view, especially after the ousting of Zhao Ziyang, for though in crises of this sort China's generals usually fall out, their majority has always ended up supporting the Party's majority. However, the divisions required careful management, and it is interesting to note that China's rulers thought it necessary to draw from a wide range of group armies the force that eventually cleared the streets of the capital.[51] Since most soldiers think that it is only a matter of time before the verdicts on the Tian'anmen Square incident are reversed, it is not surprising that none apparently owned up to ordering the troops to open fire.

But the wish for democracy is not widespread in the Chinese army. Most generals want technical and economic progress, but politically they are far from liberal. Their reluctance to kill unarmed civilians in 1989 should not be confused with support for the protests. After all, they belong to China's privileged elite, and they are by training disciplinarian, secretive, and centralist. They do perfectly well out of the system, and they are up to their necks in cronyism, nepotism, and racketeering. In the absence of a foreign threat, they have started to invest heavily in industry and services, which they milk shamelessly.[52]

THE CHINESE LEADERSHIP AFTER TIAN'ANMEN

Now that the dissidents and protesters have been driven underground or into jail or exile, what are the chances of a revival and eventual victory of their movement? How is the Party likely to develop? Will China have a people's movement to match Poland's Solidarity? In addressing these questions, bear in mind that the boundaries between the Party top, the democracy movement, and the workers, the peasants, the minor bureaucrats, and the great mass of Party members are not easy to descry, and developments in one impinge on the rest.

The Party over which Deng Xiaoping has presided for the last ten years is probably less monochrome than any other Communist Party in power in recent times save Gorbachev's. It is deeply divided into what are commonly called "conservative" and "moderate" wings. But these terms correspond only partly to wider usage, so they are in many ways more confusing than helpful for understanding Chinese factionalism.

One group of conservatives (also called the "left") are led by semiretired Party veterans whose idea of socialism harks back to the early 1950s, when China followed a Soviet model. Another conservative constituency is the bulk of those estimated eighteen million members who joined the Party in the decade of the Cultural Revolution. Conservatives of both strains are opposed to a deepening of the reforms, which threaten to erode their powers, and to the market's growing role in China's economy, which they fear could revert to capitalism. But nor are they interested in wholesale abolition of the changes that have already taken place, for they are in a position to exploit them through illicit dealings.

The main body of moderate reformers, now in power, comprises some of those in the Party like Deng Xiaoping who were main targets of Mao's Cultural Revolution, plus others recruited to this faction since Mao's death. Before 1989 they were prepared to suffer a measure of liberalization, including some democracy, in order to create the conditions for China's modernization, though the democracy necessary for "emancipating the mind" was never meant to go so far as to challenge the Party's monopoly on political power. They promised a system that was stable, predictable, remunerative, and relatively clement. They are still more prepared than the conservatives to let the market modify central planning, but within stricter limits than before. Their decision to repress the people's movement has done little or nothing to resolve the problems that produced it. Though the Party elders are not yet dead, they are already brain-dead and incapable of rethinking their policy, which today combines the worst features of Stalinism and primitive capitalism. If these reformers are to achieve their aims, they must keep open the door to the foreign winds that they hope will bring China's economy to strength. But through the door come rushing not only investment and know-how but values of a more directly corrosive kind. Conservatives and mainstream reformers alike are alarmed by what they see as a great flood of bourgeois depravity and feudal debauchery that has hit China.

Finally there are the radical reformers like Zhao Ziyang, and others still in office. They favor extensive privatization of the economy and the further introduction of a labor market, and are criticized by their opponents for wanting to restore capitalism to China. They have also spoken out for more democracy and for human and civil rights, though for them these take second place to economic reform and are expendable.

Chinese politics in the 1980s seemed to many optimists to have institutionalized and rendered less disruptive the factional strife that in earlier decades had torn society apart, but 1989 threw this assumption into doubt.[53] The competition between China's different factions now seems likely to generate strains and tensions that could paralyze decision-making or erupt in open strife and a fierce battle for power. It is impossible to say who would win such a contest. Yet few can doubt that if the new clique of younger leaders, including Deng's heir Jiang Zemin, tries after the elders' death to preserve a regime of bureaucratic "socialism," they will generate the same discontents that exploded in revolution in 1989, and they lack the charisma and the loyal following in the Party that are a minimal condition for containing such unrest.

When linchpin figures like Deng die, it is conceivable as Liu Binyan noted in *China Focus*,[54] but not likely, that Zhao Ziyang may be allowed back into public life in an effort to conciliate the public. But if by some chance Zhao emerges as the new strongman, preposterously recast as Mr. Clean (actually he is one of China's best-known nepotists and probably more corrupt than many other Chinese leaders), there is no evidence that he could provide a fresh direction for Chinese economy and society. If he returns to power, he will probably try to combine economic liberalization with some measure of political reform. Here his problem is the opposite of Mao's. Mao created a China that was captive, desperately poor, but largely equal (except at the very top, where people lived in fabulous luxury). Zhao (like Deng) envisages a China that is less poor, and a little freer, but outrageously unequal.

CHINESE YOUTH

So much for the rulers. What of their subjects? Students, young and idealistic, are a sensitive mirror of Chinese opinion and keepers of the national conscience, which they felt Deng's policies had offended. Students pioneered and led the movement of 1989. Most were children of Party officials and professionals—not the high-placed few who have grown fat on the reforms, but those on small fixed incomes. Their ultimate aim was greater freedom and openness, but in the shorter term they wanted corrupt officials punished, and their immediate demands included the rehabilitation of Hu Yaobang,[55] a dialogue with the government, and a retraction of the charge that they were promoting "counterrevolutionary turmoil." Like the other constituents of the coalition that sustained the people's movement, they had their own special interests and proposals to defend. They were affronted by the neglect of education under Deng, by their own poor prospects on Deng's market, and by their diminishing prestige in society. They often live in terrible squalor on the campuses. Many of those without much social pull end up being assigned to poorly paid jobs in far-off places; and now there is the chance that they may get no job whatsoever, for the government plans to have done away with job allocations by 1993. Even their professors earn less in a month than many a hotel waitress or stall-holder at the market, let alone an "official-speculator." Mao despised intellectuals as the "stinking ninth category," but when Deng returned to power he won their support by promising them prosperity and respect, and assured them that their know-how was indispensable for China's modernization. He broke his promise. Instead of building his new China on knowledge, science, and hard work, he built it on greed and fraud.

Among the students, there was at first little evidence of a wish for capitalism. Their movement was the spontaneous product of widespread and deep-rooted popular discontent, a simple reaction to repression. They had no definite and positive program, but only a negative common goal: bring down the tyrannical and corrupt regime. Most seemed to have no clear idea of the sort of political and economic system that they wanted to see in China, and were prepared to be ruled by a Communist government as long as it listened to them and recognized their needs (though they learned their lesson from the massacre and have now shed their illusions). For some, singing the *Internationale* may have been a noise to hide their true voice, but for most it probably represented a vote (however qualified and muddled) for some form of socialism and against bureaucracy. Capitalism for many of these students was inseparable from the avarice and social atomization that is destroying China; and from the Japanese and

Western businessmen who are stealing China's autonomy and threatening to turn China into a new Brazil, open to exploitation by the rich countries. Which is why Gorbachev, who embodied the idea that renewal is possible within socialism, was a potent rallying symbol for the Chinese opposition in 1989, in a way that Reagan and Bush could never be.

What do Chinese youth today believe?[56] Some people call them the "thinking generation" on account of their commitment to the search for truth in science, society, and human affairs. It was young people of this description—typically graduate students of People's University—who ignited the protest in 1989. Another group is solely dedicated to material wealth: their ideal is to work for a foreign company, to become partner in a private business or to head for the gold-paved streets of Tokyo or Los Angeles. Then there is the group known as the "collapsed" or "lost" generation: a group that lacks ideals, personal integrity, altruism, and selflessness, and tends toward nihilism or the uncritical embrace of anything that is new, with eyes only for today. Those known as the "playful" or "leisure" generation wear outlandish clothes, or form up on the campus into a "mahjong faction" and a "dancing faction." If they believe in anything, it is nothing. They have developed to its extreme the cynicism that characterized part of the generation of the Cultural Revolution. They ridicule the old Maoist moral preaching, with its selfless toilers for the common good.[57] They hate wooden conformity and society's plethora of rules and regulations, which they do their best to thwart and subvert.[58] They neglect themselves, they burst out crying for no reason, they burst out laughing for no reason, they scream and shout; life, love, work—these are a game with no rules; only that which is "new" and "strange" impresses them.[59] They are contemptuous of old forms of fame, achievement, morality, status, and authority, but they also scorn the unscrupulous maneuvering and enslavement to cash and vulgarity that in their view characterizes Chinese society now. They feel that their lives are completely void of meaning: that they lack theme and target, that though they are dissatisfied with everything about them, they are unable to decide what they really want.[60]

Intellectual and cultural soul-searching by these children of the reforms created an "antipolitical politics"[61] that typified the mood in the Square after its early anonymous leaders—men and women in their late twenties and early thirties—had faded into the background. It found expression in an amorphous, iconoclastic "people's power" born of a search by younger students for personal space as much as for collective political solutions to China's crisis. "A long process of cultural reflection and activity," wrote Lee Ou-fan Lee, "had paved the way for the emergence of a new mentality, which the students also embodied—a new view of life centered on the provenance of the self, a new view of society as the sphere of public life separated from and even opposed to the party-state, and a new view of the Chinese nation as no longer identifiable with the party-state but defined instead as a larger entity trying to transform itself into a state of modernity."[62] This later movement—less disciplined, cheekier, more colorful, keener on the limelight—split into rival groups that at times "drew swords and bent bows" at one another, managed their finances chaotically and sometimes corruptly, and alternately idolized and purged their leaders.

THE INTELLECTUALS

The intellectual scene in China in the 1980s was characterized by a new diversity and ideological pluralism. Not only were different streams of thought considered, but intellectuals were beginning to abandon their allotted role as spokespersons for the ruling class. Moreover, many professionals and higher intellectuals, unlike the students, had quite specific ideas about how to change China. Their two best-known representatives were Yan Jiaqi (a top adviser to Zhao Ziyang) and the dissident astrophysicist Fang Lizhi. Both reached the conclusion—not all at once but gradually, before and after the people's movement—that Marxism is wrong, that socialism should be abandoned, and that freedom and democracy can only be achieved in Anglo-American-style capitalism.[63] Alienated by continuing bureaucratic controls, many critical thinkers came to believe that China's salvation lies in "Westernization" and an end to socialism. Some even admired Margaret Thatcher and Milton Friedman. Even before 1989 Fang Lizhi held that in China "the Communist Party has never had any success. Over the past thirty years it has produced no positive results."[64]

The thinking of people like Yan and Fang, which had developed over the years into a substantial critique of bureaucracy and Mao-Marxism, was reflected and popularized in the hit (not to say cult) television series *Heshang* (River Elegy), scripted by a group of people around Su Xiaokang and first shown in 1988. *River Elegy*, though widely criticized even by opponents of the regime as a dilettantish and superficial mishmash, played a major role in preparing a climate of public support for the veteran dissenters. In September 1988 the National Vice-Chairman Wang Zhen petulantly and comically denounced it for "insulting the Yellow River and the Great Wall," and in July 1989 officials accused it of inspiring the turmoil. *River Elegy* argued that Chinese civilization is dead, and strongly implied that China's way to rebirth lies in all-out Westernization. "Sea power is the key to democratic revolution," said Su Xiaokang; democracy is proper not to China's introverted continental culture but to the "azure," seaward-looking civilization of the West. Among Su's main theses was that Plekhanov had been right in his dispute with Lenin to argue that it is inappropriate for socialists to seize power in backward countries like China, for history's "stages" cannot be skipped; and that China's future rests not with the workers but with the intellectuals and the new class of private entrepreneurs. The implication was that had China followed the capitalist rather than the socialist path, the hardships of the last half century could have been avoided and China today would be rich and powerful.

Party leaders tried hard to portray the student movement as a creature of the older Party democrats like Fang Lizhi, Wang Ruowang, and Liu Binyan, who were said to have masterminded it from behind the scenes.[65] The idea that the students had been inspired by "black hands" in the academic establishment bent on overthrowing socialism was repeated in the trials of student activists held in January 1991. But actually a distinction must be made between the veteran dissenters and the student strikers. Though Fang and the others were repeatedly in the news in 1989, their contribution to the movement took quite another form: a petition (started on January 6, 1989) for the release of all China's political prisoners, and in particular Wei Jingsheng. True, on May 17 a group of senior intellectuals, led by Yan Jiaqi, supported the protesters with a manifesto, but their positions were far milder than the student radicals'. Some intellectuals who tried to end the hunger strike were denounced by the students as "new authoritarians." The exact relationship between the intellectuals and the students remains to be determined: it is not just the Chinese leaders who have called the demonstrators pawns.[66] But though some activists may have been advised or manipulated from behind screens, the protest movement sprang up without any sign of secret orchestration and in its most developed stage was too broad and spontaneous to be reduced to an artifact of "backstage bosses."

The consensus among the older democrats, including victims of the 1957 crackdown, was that democracy was not immediately realizable in China, and that it would only be so once economic reform had produced an autonomous middle class. They believed that the reform process had been, and would continue to be, led from above, rather than flowing from a people's movement. So they were anxious not to undermine the reformers in the Party leadership on whom they had pinned their hopes. This anxiety explains why they chose the petition tactic instead of promoting autonomous bodies such as trade unions.

The students on the whole favored a different strategy. They largely ignored the petition movement (according to Fang Lizhi, many had never even heard of Wei Jingsheng) and instead threw out a challenge to Party leaders of whatever ideological stripe by encouraging the principle of self-organization and calling for its official recognition. The main link between their movement and Fang's was temporal, in the sense that the one came after the other. Most students had been influenced to some extent by the ideas of people like Fang, but in the Square those under his direct influence were a small minority, and a tiny minority of those from outside the capital.

In his talks and writings Fang Lizhi developed a more sustained and coherent critique of the Party leadership than did the students, whose forte was practical not theoretical. This forking of the democracy movement into generations, and into thinkers and doers, disabled it, for the courage and vitality of its youth lacked articulation; and the organizational networks built up over the years by the veteran dissenters rarely operated beyond the academies and the press.

Why were the students of 1989 so mistrustful of and even hostile toward the veterans with their connections in the Party? Some critics blame this alienation on the students' "leftism," on their "fight-to-the-death mentality," on their inflexibility and tactical incompetence. The lack of contact, says Liu Binyan, "provided a key into understanding . . . the brutal ending" of their movement,[67] for the CCP is far from monolithic, and the crucial and progressive dynamic of 1979's Democracy Wall had been the productive alliance of democrats within and outside the Party. Why was this alliance not repeated in 1989? Why was the example of the veterans not followed? Mainly because pro-reform Party leaders like Zhao Ziyang vacillated for too long, abandoned the initiative to Li Peng, failed to make use of legal procedures (despite their support among sections of the army and the Party), abstained from taking advantage of the interlude of free press, and so lost the chance to influence the students' movement and nullified the strategy of the senior dissidents. The pro-reform leaders were neither organized nor united. Zhao Ziyang in particular was paralyzed by his sense of indebtedness to Deng, his patron. Hatched, reared, and pinioned under a regime of Stalinism, Zhao and the others were incapable of sustaining their opposition to the Party fathers.[68]

In any case, the students had little cause to take seriously Zhao Ziyang's commitment to democracy. Even had Zhao persuaded the protesters to hitch their wagon to his star, he would probably have crushed them once they had served their purpose, just as Deng did in 1979. In late 1988 and early 1989 members of think-tanks associated with Zhao Ziyang were prepared to drop democracy altogether from their political program in an attempt to forestall by stealing half their clothes the conservatives' plans to bring both the economy and society back under greater state control. Instead they put forward the theory of "new authoritarianism," invented in the 1960s by the American political scientist Samuel Huntington, who argued that in Third World countries the essential condition for modernization is a strong government capable of keeping society orderly and stable.[69] The sort of government China's new authoritarians had in mind was one modeled on autocratic free-market regimes like that of South Korea. Zhao soon moved away from this position, but still it showed that for him democracy—in as far as he ever called for it—was a means rather than an end.

Zhao's failure to make overtures to the students was matched in the academies by the failure of the overwhelming majority of intellectuals, even social scientists, to address the issues that engaged the people's movement, or to foresee this inevitable consequence of China's crisis. Why so? Because they had become professionally introverted, too narrowly specialized, disillusioned with politics and even life in the course of the 1980s, too obsessed with deadlines, meetings, and engagements in China and abroad, and content to restrict themselves to giving policy advice within the system.[70] In 1979, intellectuals' link to society was still vibrant: they had suffered and they were concerned to prevent a return to lawlessness, so they had a living tie to the activists at Democracy Wall. They knew society's lower depths, and they fellow-felt with its victims. But by 1989 their social status had been upgraded and a career ladder had opened up before them. They no longer knew how the workers, peasants, or even students lived, and some of them no longer even cared. Mao's campaign to "send them down to the grass-roots" to learn from the toilers had turned them against the very idea (says Hu Ping[71]) of "joining a united front with workers, farmers, and soldiers." So all but a handful played no part in the brewing of the people's movement.

This is one reason for the absence from the Square of inspired writing of the sort stuck up ten years earlier on the Wall. But in any case the intellectual climate and political context had changed radically over the ten years. In 1979 dissident thinkers—even Wei Jingsheng—were still wrestling with the legacy of Marxism, of which they considered themselves heirs, and some produced robust and thoughtful critiques of its Stalinist garbling. But the generation of 1989 no longer took Marxism seriously and so felt no need to rethink it. Their movement was more practical than reflecting, more sloganeering than theorizing, broader than it was deep. The generation of 1979 fought its struggles on the mental plane: that of 1989, on the Square. This, then, is why its tracts and manifestos lacked the depth and theoretical engagement of a Wang Xizhe or Wei Jingsheng, and why many of its ideas rang hollow.

Though the older group of veteran dissenters was by no means of one mind, its members were closely associated in the public eye and also by Party leaders, who by simultaneously expelling Fang Lizhi, Wang Ruowang, and Liu Binyan commixed in a promiscuous alloy thinkers of quite varying luster. Fang, Yan Jiaqi, and Su Xiaokang's *River Elegy* group wholeheartedly welcomed the "azure" civilization of an undifferentiated "West" and rejected the "primitive" culture of their own country. Like the later Hu Shi (1891–1962), modern China's most influential liberal scholar, they saw only the progressive role of Western capitalism or "global culture," glibly symbolized in *River Elegy* by computer banks, high-heeled shoes, and skyscrapers, and they regarded the concept of imperialism as an irrelevance. Their attitude offended the conservative "nativists" or Sinophiles—analogous to Russia's nineteenth-century Slavophiles—in the Party top, who revile it as "national nihilism." But it also angered China's more critical selective modernizers, who believed that China must both embrace and resist things foreign: embrace science and democracy, resist exploitation and subjugation.[72]

The parallels between Fang Lizhi and Hu Shi extend to their basic doctrine, which is "the doctrine of no doctrine at all."[73] Hu Shi was a pragmatist who favored the study of specific, practical problems: liberation drop by drop, bit by bit, inch by inch. Fang Lizhi shares this approach, but his grounding in the old culture that he rejects cannot compare with Hu's, and his modern thinking too is shallower and narrower. He believes not only that China's greatest hope lies with the intellectuals but that within the intelligentsia it is the scientists, and in particular the natural scientists, who will spearhead China's modern development, for "almost invariably it has been the natural scientists who have been the first to become conscious of the emergence of each social crisis."[74] But Fang is a far braver and more heroic figure than Hu Shi, and in that sense he is rightly known as China's Sakharov.

Quite different from people like Fang and Yan, though constantly linked to them, are Wang Ruowang and Liu Binyan, two of China's most distinguished living writer-journalists, known on the mainland as "South Wang and North Liu." Both joined the CCP at the age of nineteen, Wang in 1937 (after three years in prison) and Liu in 1944. For thirty-odd years Wang has been in endless trouble with the Party, for while loyally supporting it, he has also insisted on his right to disagree with and oppose it. Liu too combines the qualities of one of the old-style "literati of independent conscience who criticized China's political leaders when they did not live up to their ideals"[75] and of a Marxist believer who—like Yang Youde, the hero of Liu's first dissenting article—"is not afraid to differ." Unlike Fang and Yan, Wang and Liu, being products of the Party in its revolutionary phase, see themselves as its loyal opposition, scourges of its apogees. Both have spent more than twenty years in internal exile for fearlessly championing human rights, and have twice (in 1957 and 1987) been expelled from the Party; but both believe that the Communist regime benefited China in the early years after 1949, though it later changed for the worse.

For Fang Lizhi, the prospects for change in China are now grim: democracy will take at least twenty to thirty years to come. Liu Binyan's perspective is far more optimistic and short-term. Whereas Fang looks for change to the elite, Liu sees it brewing—now—among the workers and peasants, whom he knows well from his long years in the villages; and he expects a "genuine popular force" to emerge soon from China's present discontents.[76] Another important difference between Liu and Fang is in their view of the impact of the West on China. Liu does not share Fang's optimism about the benefits that world finance would bestow on China, and sees instead the danger of a loss of independence. According to Liu, "A large number of Chinese worry that on the mainland there will appear a group that uses its official position to become a comprador class."[77] In 1993 Liu Binyan joined with other prominent Chinese journalists, reformers, and writers in exile to publish *China Watch*, a journal sponsored by the Princeton China Initiative. As ever, Liu was scathing and outspoken in his attacks on corruption and abuse of power in the CCP; he seemed to have little new to offer by way of a political program, reflecting the apparent lack of credible alternatives on the Chinese political scene.

Others too in the official world developed a left-wing critique of Chinese state ideology in the 1980s. A handful of Party freethinkers campaigned whenever conditions allowed for a widening of the Party's idea of Marxism to include humanist concepts like alienation and human nature as "free, self-conscious activity," and they took as their chief reference Marx' writings of around 1844. They were partly influenced in their thinking by Chinese translations produced in this period of writings by Western Marxists (like Gramsci and Lukács) and other more recent foreign Marxist writings, the reading of which just a few years earlier would have invited terrible persecution. They have also drawn on the work of revolutionary Marxists like Bukharin and Rosa Luxemburg and of "revisionists" like Bernstein and Kautsky. The main representatives of this critical school of Chinese Marxism (crushed during the 1989 repression) are Wang Ruoshui and Su Shaozhi.

CHINA IN THE 1990s

Deng's sternest critics in the democracy movement have concluded from his failure that only all-out capitalism can save China and secure the passage to greater freedom. They take as their model Hong Kong, Taiwan, Singapore, and South Korea, which in capitalism have achieved the prosperity that eluded "socialist" China. But the model is inappropriate, and any attempt to implement it will only produce new crises. The economies of East Asia's "four small dragons" took off for quite special reasons that cannot apply to China. They developed in a period of world expansion, and they benefited in various ways from the fact of the Chinese Revolution: through an outflow of funds and expertise from China, and through an American presence designed to contain China's radical dynamic. In any case they are small and their output was easily absorbed by an expanding world economy, whereas future markets will impose severe restrictions on the export of China's vast product. There are also the rice-bowl obstacles to the development of capitalism in China, summarized by William Hinton as "bright, hard, and brittle." The bright (or golden) rice bowl is that of the bureaucrats, who will not easily surrender to market forces control over the economy that fattens them. The hard (or iron) rice bowl is that of the workers, who want safety first. The brittle (or clay) rice bowl is that of the peasants, who prefer self-sufficiency at subsistence levels to giving up their newly acquired strips of land to specialists who might develop their land's potential.[78] Capitalism is rising strongly in China now, but if it is restored completely, it will be at the cost of conflicts and instabilities that only dictatorship backed by the financial and military might of the U.S. could contain.

By 1993, some strains were already apparent. China's economy was growing extremely fast—perhaps at 15 percent per annum in some provinces—at a time of world recession, and the economic miracle still seemed a reality. But the problems were becoming far more acute: how to finance the foreign debt that had been incurred; how to deal with unemployment and underemployment; how to limit the outflow of capital in fraudulent transactions; how to control a boom-bust cycle of massive proportions; how to pacify the peasants. The leadership was well aware that it might not survive another outburst of civil disturbances. Its strategy has been to avoid them by generating nationwide economic growth and raising living standards, but this strategy in itself has created tremendous social pressures.

Deng Xiaoping said in the early stages of the 1989 crisis that the Party need not fear the students, for the army, the workers, and the peasants supported it. But events showed that the anger and indignation were virtually universal, and found expression in a coalition of students, thinkers, workers, and officials of all sorts, together with members of the huge new "floating class" of casual laborers and the unemployed. There have been numerous popular upsurges against Chinese governments since 1949, but 1989 was the first time that large numbers of factory workers have joined in one. Under Mao the proletariat was protected and respected. Life was hard but equal in the factories. The workers were better off than most other classes and enjoyed unprecedented security. Today in absolute terms they are more prosperous and personally freer than ever before, but still they have many grievances. By 1989 their iron rice-bowls (symbolizing job security) had been dented and the big pot (symbolizing collective welfare) was being smashed. Deng's labor reform is attractive to younger, fitter, highly skilled workers, for it gives them greater control over their lives and the chance to move about and earn high wages. But it is a threat to most workers, even young workers, who welcome the improvement in personal income since 1979 but still value security more.

Over the years workers have reached deals with their managers and Party bosses whereby in exchange for cooperating and keeping quiet they get security and welfare. They benefit less than other classes from the new policies—far less than many peasants and traders, who can get rich—and they suffer most from the inflation, unlike officials and intellectuals, who are relatively secure. Their perception of a decline in all forms of social security in the 1980s was a main cause of the political protests of 1989. They know what reform means, and they resent it.[79] Today, unlike in the past, workers' wages in the state sector are often far lower than those in the private or collective sector. So industrial workers—once Mao's aristocracy—resent the threat posed to them by Deng's market philosophy. While old capitalists and new rich parade their wealth more openly than at any time since 1949, weaker or less favorably placed groups are dropping progressively behind.

Many workers hanker after the days of Mao and Zhou Enlai, when they were poor but safe and equal, and when the gap between the great mass of people and the tiny handful of privileged was far less conspicuous (though probably not much smaller) than that between rich and poor today. Traders and senior intellectuals criticize the reforms for not going far enough, but most workers find that they have gone too far and threaten what for them are the revolution's main achievements. Few want a return to Maoist controls on thought and behavior, but many perceive the old leaders as purer and more honest than the present ones. Those disturbed by what they see as relinquishments of national sovereignty look back nostalgically on Mao's policy of self-reliance. Some of the workers who carried Mao posters onto the Square were using them to taunt Deng, Mao's apogee; others, to avoid incrimination as "counterrevolutionaries." But for many, the posters represented a vote for redness against expertise, solidarity over difference, benevolence over unconcern.

Workers alienated by the reforms found allies among Party managers worried that their role as planners will be scrapped if market forces are allowed to determine economic decisions. But at the same time many of these Party managers were suspicious of a movement that called so strongly for democracy, accountability, and an end to corruption. Some observers distinguish rather too strictly between book-trained protesters who want democracy and workers who want material things. But aspects of the struggle for democracy—in particular the demands for freedom of expression, press, assembly, and strike—are also relevant to the wider movement, and are closely connected to the fight against privilege and corruption.

China's factory proletariat is today many times bigger than when the Communists came to power, and quite different in character. Before 1949 Chinese factory workers were largely illiterate: now most are graduates at least of secondary school. In the 1980s, notes the dissident thinker Su Wei,[80] they "evolved into a new class that possesses contemporary self-consciousness." For the overwhelming majority of them daily toil and bare living are still the main preoccupations, but among them a tiny number of particularly brave and high-minded idealists are becoming directly concerned with critical politics, and some of these people were present in the Square.

At first the workers' role in the demonstrations of 1989 was a subordinate one, as bodyguards (through the Workers' Picket Teams) and providers of food and clothing. In May students called on workers to demonstrate and even to strike, but the assumption was that they would play second fiddle to the self-important students. In late April 1989, however, a small group of workers in the Square had begun to discuss what role other than that of passive spectators or ancillaries they could play in the protest, and on May 13 they decided to organize their own Workers' Autonomous Federation (WAF) outside the official unions.[81] At first they received only verbal support and were told to stay out of the Square so as to keep the protest "pure" and avoid a clampdown. This attitude was not confined to Beijing. In Chongqing, and probably elsewhere too, the students tried to keep the workers at arm's length (though they complained when they felt that the workers were not giving them enough support).[82] Only a handful of intellectuals (including the indomitable Ren Wanding) saw the importance of an independent workers' movement, and only a few dissenting students tried to help the new workers' body in Beijing. Most workers too were frightened by the autonomous unions, which looked dangerously like "nailing a flea to the tiger's head."

By June, however, Beijing's WAF had more than ten thousand members committed to "overseeing the Communist Party" and becoming real masters of the nationalized firms and factories; and the principle of workers' self-organization had spread to other cities. According to Lee Feigon, an eyewitness to the demonstrations, the members of Beijing's WAF hung Mao pictures round their tents in the Square and "talked openly and boldly about the good old days of the Cultural Revolution."[83] WAF early on became the prime target of government suppression. On the night of June 3 the Workers' Dare-to-Die Brigades suffered more casualties than any other group. The crackdown on dissenting workers was far more ruthless and violent than on the students, and imprisoned workers were more likely to be tortured or ill treated.[84] "No students or intellectuals have been executed," announced the government in late June 1989, implying that only workers had been executed. The crackdown spread to Shanghai, where by December 1989, seventy-two of the Shanghai WAF's ninety organizers had been seized.

Were there classes of Chinese other than the top bureaucrats who in the spring of 1989 were satisfied with the state of the reforms and prepared to support the government? Yes, but mainly in the countryside, where people are rarely organized or heard beyond their separate small communities. Many peasants have enriched themselves under Deng, yet the tens of millions of rural casualties of reform—pitched from farming into vagrancy, crime, or unemployment—will probably have a more conspicuous impact on Chinese politics than the tens of millions of its main beneficiaries.

By 1993, the situation in the countryside had deteriorated considerably, causing predictions of a "peasant revolt."[85] In 1992 and 1993 there were reports of more than two hundred peasant uprisings in a dozen provinces. The issues that most enraged farmers were spiraling prices, tax extortions, and payment by IOUs instead of cash. After a short-term boost to rural incomes and living standards in the early 1980s, farmers' standard of living fell way behind urban workers' after 1986. To make matters worse, cadres in many rural areas began to extort money from local peasants under the guise of taxation, a symptom of widespread official corruption and decadence. As a final insult, in 1993 cadres began to requisition agricultural produce for which they paid only by IOUs of doubtful legitimacy. The Communist Party's reputation used to be extremely high in much of the countryside, partly for historical reasons and partly owing to the success of the 1980s reforms. That reputation is now tarnished, and may be irrevocably lost.

Here it is worth asking whether socialism and a free peasantry are not congenitally incompatible in China. Would not the peasants by their very numbers overwhelm the urban bases of the collective economy and cause China to "change color"? Would village democracy not lead to the restoration of capitalism? These questions prey on the mind of some who otherwise would have no sympathy with China's Stalinist regime. The answer to them is no. Collectivism is doomed not if but unless the peasants get their political say. When the Party first began collectivizing in the 1950s, it largely used methods of example and persuasion, and it was rewarded with success. Only when it switched to a "commandist" style of collectivization during the commune movement of 1958 did it lose the peasants' confidence. Had the peasants wielded some political power, they could have checked the Party's urge to extend its control to the maximum, contained its reforming zeal, and engaged it in constructive dialogue. Then they might have continued along the slower but only sure path of collectivization by consent, instead of abandoning collectives altogether, as they now have. In the long run democracy for the peasants is the only guarantee of acceptable collectivism; without it, the Party is inevitably tempted along shortcuts where the peasants will not follow, and ends up going to the opposite extreme like Deng.

We must also ask how prepared the peasants are for democracy. Before 1949 most had only a vague idea of China: since then, many have come to see themselves as citizens of the Chinese state. Administration has penetrated to the villages, and most peasants have had contact (albeit passive) with forms of modern political organization, which quite a few have had experience in leading. For a while Mao's "rustication" campaign brought large numbers of urban youth into the villages, and now tens of millions of peasants sojourn where possible in the cities (while some hundred million others have gone to work in rural industries). Vastly more peasants (roughly half of them, mainly men) than in the old China can now read and write to a reasonable standard, and the spread of mass media is quickening rural modernization. So the preconditions for democracy are today present even in the villages. However, it seems unlikely that any political movement will start from, or even draw much support in, the countless villages where the great majority of the Chinese population lives. For the foreseeable future, political events will be determined in the cities, probably in Beijing, and only gradually be influenced by the demands of the countryside.

Many of those now on the right-wing of the democracy movement were at one time hopeful about China's prospects under Deng Xiaoping, but today they oppose his rule. How does their new economic policy differ from his old one, which ended up alienating many sections of the broad social coalition that greeted his original return to power? Deng was not unaware of what the results would be for society of his reforms, yet he had no choice but to push on with them. He knew that it was not possible to carry on down the old Maoist path of autarchy, puritanism, and egalitarianism, which would produce only despotism, terrible poverty, and perhaps even a collapse of the regime. But he would stop short of permitting the full restoration of capitalism in China, and so could only pursue his new line in fits and starts, alternately applying gas and brakes.

Deng also aimed to reinvigorate the economy by opening doors to the world for investment and fresh winds of change to rush through. His plan was to use Japan and the West to help China, but by the late 1980s more and more people saw that China's officials were becoming parasites on foreign capital, like nineteenth-century compradors. The start of the unrest in China was the seventieth anniversary of the May Fourth movement of 1919, when radical students raised the call for science and democracy to save China from being cut up like a melon by foreign encroachers. The issue at stake in 1919 was the Japanese claim to a slice of Shandong Province. But seventy years later the government was prepared of its own free will to lease large parts of the island-province of Hainan to the Japanese (for eighty years), which to many Chinese appeared as an act of national betrayal. "What a loss of sovereignty," students told the *Guardian*'s John Gittings, "when we used to make such a fuss about little scraps along our borders." Even before the announcement of this plan Hainan was notorious for speculation and corruption through its foreign contacts.

In the 1980s several incidents attested to a dangerous current of xenophobia in Chinese society. Since the fall of the Maoist "Gang of Four" in 1976, Chinese leaders have steered clear of difficult issues on which to rally support, and have been left with nothing but vacuous nationalism to combat the crisis of faith. At street level this took the uglier form of riots against the Hong Kong football team and the persecution of African students in China. But at the same time as beating the nationalist drum on matters of no consequence, Deng and his government have bent over backwards to avoid upsetting foreign investors. As a result, true patriotism in China now has become tantamount to dissent. In the early 1970s, Beijing vied with Taiwan to demand the recognition of Chinese sovereignty over the oil-rich Diaoyu reefs and islands, occupied by Japan. But in 1990 it lamely and belatedly trailed behind the campaigns on Diaoyu in Taiwan and Hong Kong, and took no real action.[86] Likewise, in 1985 it forbade demonstrations to mark the anniversary of the Japanese seizure of Shenyang in 1931 and of the anti-Japanese demonstrations of 1935—partly to please its Japanese creditors and trading partners, partly for fear of student unrest. In the 1930s the policy of Chiang Kai-shek's GMD government was to attend to the disease of the limbs (Japan) only after he had cured the disease of the heart (the Communists). Today under the Communists the affliction of the limbs has been forgotten almost entirely, so great is the perceived danger to the heart.

The Dengites have abandoned the old Maoist ethos but have nothing to put in its place save "socialism with Chinese features," which some young Chinese critics of the regime interpret as a mixture of Stalinist politics and capitalist economics garnished with a dash of Chinese "feudal" ideology. For a while in the mid- to late 1980s China's youth were in the grip of pessimistic despair, but in 1989 they found a new sense of social responsibility and moral cohesion in the Square. Chauvinism was superseded by patriotism and internationalism. The students saw themselves as part of a worldwide movement for people's power of the sort (pictured on Chinese television) that had led in Manila to the fall of Marcos. Hence too their headbands, popularized in China by television coverage of student demonstrations in South Korea.[87] For a while public resentment was diverted away from scapegoats and red herrings onto the true cause of China's loss of national dignity.

Events in Eastern Europe show that extra-party oppositions can play a central role in overthrowing entrenched regimes. In Eastern Europe, where there is a tradition—only partly quelled by Stalinism—of social and cultural pluralism (including a strong church), most opposition has been wholly independent of the ruling party. In China, however, elite dissenters (who commonly find themselves in opposition only after a change in the political climate) are more likely to seek consensus with sections of the political establishment than to contest it wholesale. Until 1989 they were closely allied to reformers in the Party, and indeed some of them were former advisers to Zhao Ziyang and beneficiaries of his policies. One reason for this connection is that the Chinese Communist Party, being perennially divided, offers a wider political choice than the old Eastern European Communist Parties. Another is that China's experiment in economic reform (which outside Hungary and Yugoslavia lacks parallels in Eastern Europe) has created affinal groups within and outside the Party.

In Eastern Europe and Russia, the end of Stalinism has resulted in new governments, all of which have espoused a rapid transition to a market economy. The pervasive despair with the old regimes meant that this program was endorsed almost universally, despite the desperate crises that the new governments faced. The collapse of central authorities also exposed ethnic rivalries and hatreds that had previously been suppressed, and which in many places were more virulent even than conflicts of economic interests. If this pattern is a reliable guide, counterrevolution may well happen in China. But China is unlikely to "change color" with the ease of Poland or Hungary. The Communist governments of East Europe, imposed by the Soviet military, were viewed as alien imports. China's revolution, in contrast, was homegrown: far from being incompatible with patriotism, it has been for many the main focus of nationalist identification. Also, the Han Chinese constitute the overwhelming majority of the population. There may well be outbreaks of opposition to Han rule in some areas, but they have little chance of escalating into serious military challenges.

So it seems possible that the Communist Party government may survive for a few more years, even after the death of Deng Xiaoping, and its demise may not be exactly comparable to that of the old Soviet regimes. But observers think that whatever form the succession to Deng takes—an attempt to stabilize a regime of bureaucratic conservatism, a successful return to office of reform-minded revisionists, or an insurmountable leadership crisis for example[88]—China before the end of the century will no longer be under Communist Party rule. In 1993 it seemed as though the

Chinese elite, especially in the south, had in fact decided to simply go its own way. A coalition of entrepreneurs, in some cases revitalized clan networks, abetted by mutant absconders from the bureaucracy, staged what may be one of most massive asset-stripping raids in history. State-owned capital was converted into private capital through the Hong Kong financial markets, and deposited in overseas accounts. The total amount is unknown, but reaches many tens of billions of U.S. dollars.[89] The political elite in Beijing has occasionally tried to interfere with this disaster, but its sons and daughters are themselves deeply implicated, and its officials always ready for the payoff.

Liu Binyan has commented: "The opening of stock and real estate markets since 1992 has allowed a number of well-placed people to reap staggering profits from speculation—as high as tens of millions of yuan. Even more shocking is the increasing difficulty of distinguishing officials and criminals. . . . It is not too much to say that nearly every type of crime that the Communists publicly oppose—smuggling, the drug market, organized prostitution, arms sales, manufacture of fraudulent commodities, and the kidnapping and sale of women and children—are in varying degrees carried out through the collusion of Communist Party officials with the criminal underworld."[90] Party rule may eventually end in squalid racketeering.

The absence from the Chinese mainland of a credible, effective democratic organization on the left or a strong conservative organization on the right of the sort that could end the Communist Party's monopoly on power may well open the way to a return to the center stage of Chinese politics by Taiwan's GMD. Taiwan was for many years a central pillar in Washington's Asia policy, and was only abandoned in the late 1970s when Beijing seemed to offer a surer way of securing U.S. interests in the region. Even now, Washington and Beijing by no means trust one another entirely, and the U.S. keeps strong ties to Taiwan that it could activate if necessary. Today the GMD's credibility on the mainland is high. For bureaucrats, Taiwan is a model of economic vitality and political stability. Ordinary Chinese dream of it as a consumers' paradise. And a steady stream of dissident Chinese thinkers, writers, and politicians have visited Taiwan and pronounced themselves impressed by its prosperity and new liberalism. The government in Taibei is anything but moribund. It actively seeks out political collaborators in China and abroad, and has powerful means to put at the disposal of those who win its approval. Its new democratic rhetoric has helped blur its old autocratic image. Above all it is a government of Chinese, and thus a legitimate choice for patriots to fasten on. So though China lacks a church and a tradition of political contestation, it does have the GMD, which after decades in the wilderness may stage a comeback if the Beijing government collapses, the army becomes disorganized, and a section of the Party leadership declares for economic counterrevolution.

Perhaps the greatest disservice that Mao and Deng did China was to strip the great mass of its citizens of a sustained capacity for independent thought. The vast protest movement of 1989 lacked a strong leadership and a comprehensive political program that could provide the basis for an alternative government. The only ground on which the demonstrators could agree was that Deng and Li Peng must go. They apparently produced no new theory (unless reporters on the movement missed substantial thinking that future research will bring to light). The declarations of the emerging WAF, comparable to those of the early Solidarity, attest to considerable intellectual activity among dissident workers,[91] but these workers failed to win the support of writers and publicists committed to setting out their case before a wider public.

It is important to ask what the prospects are in China for the emergence of an independent workers' organization. The democracy movement is in no sense a political party, let alone one with a single program and uniform thinking. Insofar as it can be viewed as a single movement, it consists of people from across a wide spectrum of beliefs, including a radical minority of students and intellectuals who see the workers and peasants as their political constituency and the engine of future change. These people are unlikely to be co-opted by a reformist or restorationist regime. Some understand the main lesson of the Beijing Commune: one section of society—however well supported, and however popular its cause—cannot by itself make China free. Civil society in China under the Communists has always been deeply compartmentalized: its main overarching identity has been provided by the Party and the state. This sectionalization has been reflected even in China's occasional interludes of "mass politics," which have rarely featured more than one social group at a time. In this sense the people's movement of 1989 was a rare transforming moment in Chinese history, for it encompassed all sections of China's urban society. Even so, its leading activists were drawn mainly from a narrow stratum of the educated and well connected, who for most of the time tried to keep Square and Street apart. "The maturity of a democratic movement," said the dissenting intellectual Su Wei, "depends on the maturity of all the classes in society. Although intellectuals are society's pioneers, we did not consciously join the growing process of other classes. In Poland, there are many theoreticians who are also labor activists, and the intellectual participation in the Solidarity movement was very effective. . . . In a social movement, the burden should be evenly distributed throughout society. Yet this time, students and intellectuals bore more than 90 percent of the burden."[92] By the time the students had overcome their exclusionist instincts, broadened their focus to include wider social issues, and realized the need to extend the principle of self-organization to the rest of society, it was too late.

So the movement to support them, though vast, lacked cohesion and quickly fell apart. However, it could quickly solidify again under the right conditions. Though the government solved the crisis by repression, it now knows that in future Chinese people will not always follow its dictates. After previous crackdowns on unofficial movements, most Chinese were cowed into submission and even cooperated in the repression. After the massacre, by contrast, there were few recantings and mutual denunciations. Most people—in the factories, schools, ministries, and offices—feigned compliance, covered up for one another, and are set to return to the streets once the Party starts showing new signs of weakness. So the attempt to establish a climate of fear in society has failed. Instead, today the government itself is frightened: that someday soon the people will once again get out of hand.

China's conservative fundamentalists claim to speak to the workers' social concerns, the reformers to the wish for more rights, greater freedom, and some form of democracy. Neither claim any longer inspires much confidence, but neither is wholly groundless.

The conservatives want to restore to strength the command economy, which Deng modified and Zhao would like to end. The command economy at its peak under Mao was the acme of irrationality and wastefulness. For workers, industrialization under Mao meant regimentation bordering on a sort of slavery, exposure to bureaucratic arbitrariness and corruption, and the drastic curtailment of leisure and consumption in favor of capital accumulation and quick growth. Its outcome in the mid 1970s was near economic catastrophe. Even so, it had certain compensations. It normally guaranteed employment for urban school-leavers and jobs for life for members of the state workforce and of the larger "collective" firms.

That does not mean that workers are interested only in safety and reward and not in democracy. True, there was little evidence in 1989 of a strong commitment by workers to a comprehensive program of democratization, yet their partial demands—for the right to organize and strike, for an end to corruption, for accurate press reporting, for more openness in government—add up to a large part of the content of such a program. When Deng Xiaoping first returned to power in the late 1970s promising "democracy and legality," the workers supported him, for they felt that as the main casualty of Mao's "fascist lawlessness" he could be depended on not to repeat it. For ordinary Chinese citizens, democracy meant safeguards against everyday oppression, a say in the distribution of the national product, and a better life all round. Unfortunately not much of this was realized, and Deng's reforms ended in a bloodbath.

Democratic Currents

China's democracy movement began for uninformed observers in 1989, but actually it has a long and tragic history. Its present post-Maoist phase started on April 5, 1976, when thousands demonstrated in Tian'anmen Square against the Maoist dictatorship and were harshly suppressed. In 1976, and at Democracy Wall in 1979, the main call was for true and democratic socialism, and probably only a handful wished for capitalist restoration. Dissidents of both left and right were repressed by Deng between 1979 and 1981, though foreign journalists paid most attention to Wei Jingsheng, a champion (sentenced to fifteen years in jail) of "free enterprise," and showed little interest in Deng's left-wing victims like Wang Xizhe, sentenced to fourteen years (his third term of imprisonment for speaking out).

Before June 4, there was a marked divide between the students and the increasingly right-wing group of senior thinkers around Fang and Yan, but the massacre partly rubbed it out. For the most part, the two sorts of dissenters have begun to merge in one camp. The Western press and academy, together with their counterparts in Taiwan and Hong Kong, have mainly cultivated those dissenters who are most to their taste, and they have also influenced the radical ones. This is the pull factor behind the new consensus. The push has been provided by developments in the CCP over the last fifteen years. One reason for the strong left element present until recently in Chinese dissent was the continuing vigor of the official party, which inadvertently seeded an unkempt fringe of thought. But now the vigor is spent, and the party is in the stiff grip of its dying fathers. So independent thinkers who in the past continued to look to it, or to factions in it, for inspiration and protection are now likely to look instead to "world culture," meaning American-style democracy and capitalism.

In the wake of June 4 and the collapse of "socialism" in Eastern Europe and the Soviet Union, the pro-Western, pro-capitalist orientation gained ascendancy in China's movement for democracy. Fang Lizhi, Yan Jiaqi, and the mainstream in the Federation for a Democratic China (FDC) set up in Paris to represent the democracy movement in exile wanted some form of capitalism in China (though for tactical reasons they did not always say so openly),[93] and they hoped for U.S. support in their endeavor. Many FDC supporters saw it at one time as the nucleus of a future Chinese government that would reactivate Deng's reforms, while realists in the organization hoped for "reform within the system," that is, they expected a moderate faction to rise to power in Beijing and institute reform. In that sense they were less extreme than the New York–based China Alliance for Democracy (CAD), which wanted "reform outside the system."[94] They even included in their ranks a man like Chen Yizi, then the most senior politician to have fled China and another of Zhao Ziyang's top advisers. Chen had never been a dissident, and believed that Zhao's reform would have worked but for the students and dissidents.[95]

Wan Runnan, founder of the non-state Stone Group, said that the future of democracy in China depended on the support of companies like Stone and also of foreign capitalists.[96] Even theoreticians like Su Shaozhi were disillusioned at least in part with Marxist ideology and became champions of free enterprise and a market economy, for according to them only when the middle class has grown more powerful will the democracy movement stand a chance of achieving victory. Such is their disillusion in socialism that those few who favor a convergence between socialism and capitalism, rather than the replacement of the former by the latter, now seem positively left-wing.

By the mid 1990s, the overseas dissident groups appeared to have lost their impetus, although the two main organizations, the CAD and the FDC, had attempted to unite in 1993. In part they suffered from factionalism and lack of leadership. More important, the Chinese government had succeeded in normalizing relations with the West, and had recovered from the worst shock of the Soviet collapse. The Party leadership showed considerable skill in controlling dissident intellectuals inside China, releasing some, detaining others, harassing their families, or offering inducements for good behavior by dissidents. The rise in living standards in China's cities in the early 1990s also helped the government avert a repeat of the unrest of 1989.[97]

According to reports in 1994, the democracy movement was firmly rooted in China, while exiled activists had become irrelevant. Dissidents were establishing links with factory workers, for they believed that the failure of the 1989 uprising had been due in part to the narrow social base of the movement, almost all of whose leaders had been students or intellectuals. "Now they are organising opposition among workers and even farmers, capitalising on the economic grievances spread by 15 years of reform and social dislocation. The core of the democracy movement now is 'workers' and peasants' issues'. . . . The issues may be economic, but the lack of effective channels to pursue them make the demands political," wrote John Gittings in London's *Guardian*. In 1994, the CCP general secretary Jiang Zemin named strikes in cities as the most serious peril facing the regime.[98]

Is there in Chinese politics a force capable of uniting under a single banner the concerns for social equity and freedom that are now disjoined? Or will "socialism" and democracy continue in polar opposition, the one tied to a discredited bureaucracy, the other to an impotent intelligentsia? Certainly it is still too early to pronounce dead the old-style dissent that sees socialism and democracy as linked. This view continues to have its exponents in China (a minority of students, radical workers, and some veteran dissenters). All China's democrats agree that the postulates of Marxism must be rethought in the light of June 4 and the collapse of Stalinism in the Soviet Union and Eastern Europe, but while most have concluded that capitalism is everlasting and socialism an illusion, some (like Liu Binyan) are trying to reconcile their old faith with the new ideas to which exile has exposed them. So among the exiles the struggle has not yet been resolved, and even those now wavering may be swayed back to their old beliefs as they learn more about the West and as the nature of the post-Stalinist crisis in Eastern Europe and the Soviet Union becomes clearer. In China itself the question of the relationship between socialism and democracy was addressed at length in the 1980s, including by the critical school of Marxist philosophers around Wang Ruoshui,[99] who endorse Marx the humanist, Marx the liberal, Marx the democrat. These veterans—some in China, some in exile—have a long history of struggle against the Mao-Deng dictatorship, and of persecution by it. They are the doyens of Chinese dissent, respected by democrats of all political persuasions for their sincerity and integrity. In this respect the situation in China is somewhat different from that in Eastern Europe, where Marxism has been discredited and dropped. Even some Chinese anti-Marxists like Fang Lizhi are by no means committed to full-blooded capitalism, but favor a Swedish-type compromise (though the idea—also entertained by Zhao Ziyang—is exceedingly naive).

The attachment to bureaucratic "socialism" of China's workers is hardly strong: it has brought them grinding poverty and reduced them to dependency on "patrons" who squeeze them hard in return for small "favors" and control much of their personal as well as working lives. But weak too is their attachment to reform, which along with some rewards has brought new afflictions. A main difference between China now and Eastern Europe on the eve of the Stalinist collapse is that in China capitalist-style reform is already a known quantity, with few attractions for those without connections. The workers are today the students' natural allies: unlike the intellectuals, they have no links with or illusions in any faction in the Communist Party, and they did not support Zhao Ziyang in 1989. But to realize such an alliance the students must articulate their ideas about society more strongly and convincingly, specify more precisely what democracy means to them, and above all cast off their ingrained elitism and learn to speak the language of the people.

One theme that runs through this introduction is that dissent or protest in China has many strands and many colors. In 1989 Western media generally represented the student movement as something wholly new, and as self-evidently in favor of a Western-style capitalist democracy. A reading of the following documents illustrates that neither representation is accurate. There is a tradition of dissent and protest against the Communist Party—or at least against its excesses and corruption—dating back to the early 1940s. And this tradition itself is differentiated. Terminological shorthand may identify certain dissidents as "leftists" or "rightists," but these terms were always of doubtful accuracy even in Europe; in China, the need for caution is even greater.

"Left" generally refers to ideas and movements that are radical, egalitarian, libertarian, and directed against exploitation and bureaucracy. Yet because of the way in which the Soviet Union and its satellites developed, communist parties came to represent bureaucratic despotism, supported by military power and police terror, running obsolete industries and inefficient agricultural systems. Hence the almost synonymous usage of "leftist" and "conservative" to refer to factions such as the old guard around Li Peng in China of the early 1990s. On the other hand, "rightist" in the West describes people like Margaret Thatcher and Ronald Reagan who were keen to preserve the vestiges of Anglo-American hegemony, were largely indifferent to human rights in their client states, and aimed at a free-market economy with sharp distinctions between rich and poor and little social welfare. People like Zhao Ziyang are in some sense rightists, for they want fairly radical economic reforms and personal enrichment; yet Fang Lizhi and Wei Jingsheng, who fight for human rights, a legal system, and democracy founded on universal suffrage might be considered rightists too, at least in China, since they appear to favor a market economy. But while Zhao was a power-holder and even in disgrace lives in comfortable house arrest, Fang is exiled and Wei languished for fourteen years in prison.

Readers will find all shades of left, right, and even ultra-left in the following pages. One demand common to nearly all of the documents is an end to special privileges for Party leaders and their children, to the abuse of power for personal gain that seems to be endemic in the CCP. Many others demand greater freedom of expression and a curb on censorship and the regimentation of thought. But there are also striking differences among the texts. The rebels of the Cultural Revolution rage against decadent bourgeois haircuts, while the students of 1989—just twenty years later—live in a China where Coca Cola and Kentucky Fried Chicken have made their appearance.

NOTES TO THE INTRODUCTION

1. Qui su l'arida schiena/ Del formidabil monte/ Sterminator Vesevo,/ La qual null'altra allegra arbor né fiore, / Tuoi cespi solitari intorno spargi,/ . . . lenta ginestra,/ Che di selve odorate/ Queste campagne dispogliate adorni,/ Anche tu presto alla crudel possanza/ Soccomberai del sotterraneo foco,/ Che . . . stenderà l'avaro lembo/ Su tue molle foreste. E piegherai. . ./ Il tuo capo innocente:/ Ma non piegato insino allora indarno/ Codardamente supplicando innanzi/ Al futuro oppressor. The English translation is by Gregor Benton.
2. Dai Qing, *Xiandai Zhongguo zhishifenzi qun: Liang Shuming, Wang Shiwei, Chu Anping* (Contemporary Chinese intellectuals: Liang Shuming, Wang Shiwei, and Chu Anping), (Nanjing: Jiangsu wenyi chubanshe, 1989). Some months earlier these three studies had appeared as separate articles in Shanghai's *Wenhui yuebao*. The section on Wang Shiwei, together with other documents, is translated in Dai Qing, *Wang Shiwei and "Wild Lilies": Rectification and Purges in the Chinese Communist Party, 1942–1944*, translated by Nancy Liu and Lawrence Sullivan (Armonk, N.Y.: M. E. Sharpe, 1994).
3. *Mao Zedong sixiang wansui* (Long live the thought of Mao Zedong), (Beijing: n.p., 1969), p. 160.
4. Wang Fanxi, "Chen Duxiu, Father of Chinese Communism," in *Wild Lilies, Poisonous Weeds: Dissident Voices from People's China*, edited by Gregor Benton (London: Pluto, 1982), pp. 157–67.
5. See James D. Seymour, *China: The Politics of Revolutionary Reintegration* (New York: Thomas Y. Crowell, 1976), p. 133.
6. Quoted in Tsi-an Hsia, *The Gate of Darkness: Studies on the Leftist Literary Movement in China* (Seattle: University of Washington Press, 1968), p. 253.
7. Quoted in D. W. Fokkema, *Literary Doctrine in China and Soviet Influence, 1956–1960* (The Hague, 1965), p. 13.
8. The following biographical sketch of Wang Shiwei is based on recollections of Wang Fanxi.
9. The Chinese Trotskyists formed the first and weightiest movement of radical democratic dissent within Chinese communism, but they scarcely feature in this study. For a study on and documents of the Chinese Trotskyists, see Gregor Benton, *China's Urban Revolutionaries: Explorations in the History of Chinese Trotskyism, 1921–1952*, (Atlantic Highlands, N.J.: Humanities Press, 1995), and Gregor Benton, ed., *Chen Duxiu's Last Articles and Letters, 1937–1942* (Amsterdam: International Institute for Social History, 1995). See also Wang Fan-hsi (Wang Fanxi), *Memoirs of a Chinese Revolutionary*, translated and edited by Gregor Benton (New York: Columbia University Press, 1991), and Zheng Chaolin, *Memoirs*, translated and edited by Gregor Benton (Atlantic Highlands, N.J.: Humanities Press, in press).
10. Fan Wenlan, *Lun Wang Shiweide sixiang yishi* (On Wang Shiwei's ideology), (Ji-Lu-Yu Bookstore, n.p., 1944), pp. 21 and 61.

11. The article, based on "historical materials" and interviews with Communist veterans, was published in *Dangshi tongxun*, August 1984.

12. *Dangshi tongxun*, August 1984.

13. See Fan Wenlan, *Lun Wang Shiwei sixiang yishi*, pp. 59–60, and Hu Hua (a top party historian), quoted in *Mingbao yuekan* (Hong Kong), February 1966, p. 92.

14. Lin Yü-t'ang, *Vigil of a Nation* (London, 1946), p. 238 fn.

15. See Zhang Guotao's memoirs in *Mingbao yuekan*, January 1971, pp. 90–92.

16. Fan Wenlan, *Lun Wang Shiweide sixiang yishi*, pp. 61–69.

17. Lin Yü-t'ang, *Ni ming* (Anonymous), (Taibei, 1958), p. 134.

18. *Dangshi tongxun*, August 1984.

19. Guilhem Fabre, *Genèse du Pouvoir et de l'Opposition en Chine: Le Printemps de Yanan, 1942* (Paris: Éditions l'Harmattan, 1990), pp. 117–18. Dai Qing believes the order to kill Wang Shiwei came from He Long. See Dai Qing, *Wang Shiwei and "Wild Lilies,"* pp. 67–69.

20. *Mao Zedong sixiang wansui*, p. 421. (Received into the official canon of Mao's writings in July 1978: see *Peking Review*, 1978, no. 27, p. 21.)

21. Lin Cuifeng, "Zhonggong rencuo, Wang Shiwei pingfan" (The CCP admits error, Wang Shiwei is rehabilitated), *Mingbao* (Hong Kong), May 25, 1991.

22. See *Wenhuibao* (Shanghai), February 22, 1993.

23. Among Wang's persecutors was Yang Shangkun, who despised his "sheer rotten liberalism." Dai Qing, *Wang Shiwei and "Wild Lilies,"* p. 59. Almost fifty years later, Yang was directly responsible for the Tian'anmen massacre.

24. The Hundred Flowers are analyzed in a number of special studies and general studies. They include Roderick MacFarquhar, ed., *The Hundred Flowers Campaign and the Chinese Intellectuals* (New York: Praeger, 1960); Dennis Doolin, ed., *Chinese Communism: The Politics of Student Opposition* (Stanford: The Hooever Institute on War, Revolution, and Peace, 1964); Merle Goldman, *Literary Dissent in Communist China* (Cambridge, Mass.: Harvard University Press, 1967); Roderick MacFarquhar, *The Origins of the Cultural Revolution*, vol. 1. *Contradictions Among the People, 1956–1957* (London: Oxford University Press, 1974); Maurice Meisner, *Mao's China: A History of the People's Republic* (New York: The Free Press, 1977), chap. 11; and Roderick MacFarquhar et al., eds., *The Secret Speeches of Chairman Mao: From the Hundred Flowers to the Great Leap Forward* (Cambridge, Mass.: The Council on East Asian Studies, 1989). Because of the wealth of studies on this period, we have kept this section of the paper relatively brief and omitted references for most of the data we use in it.

25. Merle Goldman, "Mao's Obsession with the Political Role of Literature and the Intellectuals," in MacFarquhar et al., eds., *The Secret Speeches*, pp. 39–58, at p. 49.

26. Quoted in Doolin, ed., *Chinese Communism*, p. 12.

27. Ibid., pp. 14–17.

28. Goldman, "Mao's Obsession," p. 54.

29. Called after "Shanghen" (Scar), by Lu Xinhua *Wenhuibao* (Shanghai), August 11, 1978.

30. Zhang Xinxin, "Zai tongyi diping xianshang" (On the same horizon), *Shouhuo* 1981, no. 6.

31. Li Ping, "Wanxia xiaoshide shihou" (When the evening mist fades), *Shouhuo* 1981, no. 6.

32. Zhang Jie, "Ai shi buneng wangjide" (Love, something that cannot be forgotten), *Beijing wenyi* 1979, no. 11.

33. Wang Ruoshui, *Wei rendaozhuyi bianhu* (In defense of humanism), (Beijing: Sanlian shudian, 1986). Wang Ruoshui is in his sixties, but most members of the group of Marxist humanists are young people.

34. See Anita Chan et al., eds., *On Socialist Democracy and the Chinese Legal System* (Armonk, N.Y.: M. E. Sharpe, 1985); and Chen Erjin, *China: Crossroads Socialism*, translated by Robin Munro (London: Verso, 1984).

35. See the account by Ma Rongqie, Jiang Qing's defense lawyer, reported in *International Herald Tribune*, January 8, 1982.

36. Asia Watch, "Punishment Season: Human Rights in China After Martial Law," in George Hicks, ed., *The Broken Mirror: China After Tiananmen* (Harlow: Longman, 1990), pp. 369–89, at p. 371.

37. This is a main thesis of Lee Feigon, *China Rising: The Meaning of Tiananmen* (Chicago: Ivan R. Dee, 1990).

38. Anita Chan and Jonathan Unger, "Voices from the Protest Movement, Chongqing, Sichuan," *Australian Journal of Chinese Affairs*, no. 24, July 1990, pp. 259–79, at p. 271.

39. Lecture by Su Xiaokang, translated in W. L. Chong, "Su Xiaokang on his Film 'River Elegy,'" *China Information*, vol. 4, no. 3, Winter 1989–90, pp. 44–55, at p. 45.

40. For a long time the Taiwan government said nothing about the events on the mainland. This was (*a*) to protect its growing relations with Beijing and (*b*) to avoid encouraging its own students to follow the Tian'anmen example. See Byron S. J. Weng, "Taiwan's Mainland Policy Before and After June 4," in Hicks, ed., *The Broken Mirror*, pp. 257–77, at pp. 266–67.

41. Liu Binyan, *China's Crisis, China's Hope*, translated by Howard Goldblatt (Cambridge, Mass.: Harvard University Press, 1990), p. 122.

42. W. L. Chong, "Fang Lizhi, Li Shuxian, and the 1989 Student Demonstrations: The Supposed Connection," *China Information*, vol. 4, no. 1, Summer 1989, pp. 1–16, at p. 8; W. L. Chong, "The Chicago Congress: Recent Activities of the 'Front for a Democratic China,'" *China Information*, vol. 4, no. 2, Autumn 1989, pp. 1–27, at p. 17.

43. Feigon, *China Rising*, pp. 130 and 142.

44. See Flemming Christiansen, "The 1989 Student Demonstrations and the Limits of the Chinese Political Bargaining Machine: An Essay," *China Information*, vol. 4, no. 1, Summer 1989, pp. 17–27.

45. Liu Binyan with Ruan Ming and Xu Gang, *"Tell the World": What Happened in China and Why*, translated by Henry L. Epstein (New York: Pantheon, 1989), p. 47; Chong, "The Chicago Congress," p. 9.

46. William Hinton, *The Great Reversal: The Privatization of China, 1978–1989* (New York: Monthly Review Press, 1990), p. 50.

47. Tiziano Terzani, interview with Fang Lizhi, "Free to Speak," *Far Eastern Economic Review*, August 2, 1990, p. 21.

48. Amnesty International, *China: The Massacre of June 1989 and Its Aftermath* (London: Amnesty International Publications, 1990), p. 31.

49. This is Liu Binyan's hope (see Chong, "Fang Lizhi," p. 13).

50. Harlan W. Jencks, "Party Authority and Military Power: Chinese Communism's Continuing Crisis," *Issues and Studies*, vol. 26, no. 7, July 1990, pp. 11–39, at pp. 30 and 39.

51. See Gerald Segal and John Phipps, "Why Communist Armies Defend Their Parties," *Asian Survey*, vol. 30, no. 10, October 1990, pp. 959–76.

52. Jencks, "Party Authority," pp. 26–29.

53. See Lowell Dittmer, "Patterns of Elite Strife and Succession in Chinese Politics," *China Quarterly*, no. 123, September 1990, pp. 405–30.

54. Liu Binyan, "Will Zhao Ziyang Stage a Comeback?" *China Focus*, vol. 2, no. 7, July 1, 1994, p. 1.

55. Actually Hu Yaobang had only been demoted from his posts, not expelled from the party.

56. Thanks to Feng Chongyi for help with this section on Chinese youth.

57. Tan Li, "Yige xingqiliude wanshang" (One Saturday evening), *Qingnian zuojia* 1981, inaugural edition.

58. Xu Jun, "Jinde yun" (Near clouds), *Sichuan wenxue* 1982, no. 1.

59. Liu Suola, *Ni bie wu xuanze* (You have no other choice), (Beijing: Zuojia chubanshe, 1986).

60. Xu Xing, "Wu zhuti bianzou" (Variations without a theme), *Renmin wenxue* 1985, no. 7.

61. The phrase is Vaclav Havel's, quoted in Lee Ou-fan Lee, "The Crisis of Culture," in Anthony J. Kane, ed., *China Briefing, 1990* (Boulder: Westview, 1990), pp. 83–105, at p. 85.

62. Lee, "The Crisis of Culture," p. 101.

63. Selections of Yan's writings are now available in English. *Yan Jiaqi and China's Struggle for Democracy*, edited and translated, with an introductory essay, by David Bachman and Dali L. Yang (Armonk, N.Y.: M. E. Sharpe, 1991); and Yan Jiaqi, *Towards a Democratic China: The Intellectual Autobiography of Yan Jiaqi*, translated by David S. K. Hong and Denis C. Mair (Honolulu: University of Hawaii Press, 1992).

64. Quoted in Orville Schell, "China's Andrei Sakharov," *The Atlantic Monthly*, May 1988, pp. 35–52, at p. 50.

65. See W. L. Chong's excellent "Twee generaties democraten" (Two generations of democrats) in Vincent Menzel et al., *Hemelse Vrede: De Lente van Peking* (Amsterdam: Balans, 1989), pp. 77– 92.

66. See for contrasting views on this Jane Macartney, "The Students: Heroes, Pawns, or Power-Brokers?" in Hicks, ed., *The Broken Mirror*, pp. 3–23; and David Kelly, "Chinese Intellectuals in the 1989 Democracy Movement," in ibid., pp. 24–51.

67. Liu Binyan, *Tell the World*, p. 85.

68. Ibid., pp. 104 ff. See also the views of Yan Jiaqi and Chen Yizi (another of

Zhao Ziyang's top advisers) as discussed in Chong, "The Chicago Congress," pp. 19–22.

69. Ma Shu Yun, "The Rise and Fall of Neo-Authoritarianism in China," *China Information*, vol. 5, no. 3, Winter 1990–91, pp. 1–18.

70. Liu Binyan, *China's Crisis, China's Hope*, pp. 135 ff. Kelly, "Chinese Intellectuals," p. 40.

71. Quoted in Trini Leung, "Vanguards and Bodyguards," *NaHan*, no. 4, 1990, pp. 14–17.

72. The naivete of the official view on this is nicely illustrated by Feng Youlan's "dialectic" of the changing relationship between China and imperialism. Thesis: The imperialists force their way into China aboard gunboats. Antithesis: The Chinese people drive them out through revolution. Synthesis: China welcomes Western and Japanese capitalists back in order to make use of them. The "dialectic" reads like a satire, but it is meant in earnest.

73. Fang Lizhi claims to have consistently avoided the term "wholesale Westernization" and to have talked instead of "all-round openness." (Quoted in Schell, "China's Andrei Sakharov," p. 42.) Similarly, around 1934 Hu Shi changed his slogan "wholesale Westernization" to "wholehearted modernization."

74. Quoted in Schell, "China's Andrei Sakharov," p. 37.

75. Merle Goldman, "Foreword," in Liu Binyan, *China's Crisis, China's Hope*.

76. Chong, "Fang Lizhi," pp. 12–13.

77. Quoted in Hinton, *The Great Reversal*, p. 29.

78. Ibid., pp. 164–74.

79. Gordon White, "Restructuring the Working Class: Labor Reform in Post-Mao China," in Arif Dirlik and Maurice Meisner, eds., *Marxism and the Chinese Experience: Issues in Contemporary Chinese Socialism* (Armonk, N.Y.: M. E. Sharpe, 1989), pp. 152–68. Carsten Hermann-Pillath, *Lebensrisiken, soziale Sicherung und Krise der Reformpolitik der VR China* (Cologne: Bundesinstitut für ostwissenschaftliche und internationale Studien, 1990).

80. Quoted in Trini Leung, "Vanguards and Bodyguards."

81. This paragraph is based partly on Trini Leung, "Vanguards and Bodyguards." The best source of information on the WAF is Hong Kong Trade Union Education Centre, *A Moment of Truth* (Hong Kong: Asia Monitor Resource Center, 1990).

82. Chan and Unger, "Voices From the Protest Movement," p. 272.

83. Feigon, *China Rising*, p. 211.

84. Asia Watch, "Punishment Season," pp. 378–79.

85. *Far Eastern Economic Review*, July 15, 1993, pp. 68–70.

86. See "Diaoyudao shijian" (The Diaoyu incident), *Zhengming* 1990, no. 11, pp. 6–14. Leaflets secretly circulated in Beijing demanded, "We want the Diaoyu, not the yen!"

87. However, some people explain them as a reference by the hunger strikers to traditional Chinese funeral dress, or the headbands worn by peasant rebels as portrayed in Chinese comic strips.

88. Jurgen Domes, "Four Ways Communism Could Die in China," in Hicks, ed., *The Broken Mirror*, pp. 466–72.

89. Some mechanisms of the privatization are revealed in Shang Hai and Wan Runnan, "Magical Chinese 'Privatization' Schemes," *China Focus*, vol. 1, no. 5, June 30, 1993, p. 1. See also *Far Eastern Economic Review*, July 15, 1993, p. 72.

90. Liu Binyan, "The Regime Goes Tiger-Hunting?" *China Focus*, vol. 1, no. 5, June 30, 1993, p. 1.

91. John Gittings, "Why There Is Hope for China," *Forum for a Better China* 1, September 1990, pp. 7–9.

92. Quoted in Trini Leung, "Vanguards and Bodyguards."

93. FDC's "guiding principles," announced on September 22, 1989, are: abolition of the one-party dictatorship, maintenance of basic human rights, development of a market economy, and the promotion of democracy.

94. Chong, "The Chicago Congress," pp. 2–3.

95. *NaHan*, vol. 4, 1990, p. 48.

96. Chong, "The Chicago Congress," pp. 7–9.

97. See K. K. Leung, "The Pro-Democracy Movement in the People's Republic of China and Overseas," in Joseph Cheng Yu-shek and Maurice Brosseau, eds., *China Review, 1993* (Hong Kong: Chinese University Press, 1993), chap. 21. A careful survey of political prisoners is Asia Watch, *Detained in China and Tibet: A Directory of Political and Religious Prisoners* (New York: Human Rights Watch, 1994).

98. John Gittings, *The Guardian* (London), June 4, 1994, p. 15.

99. See for a discussion of this issue Bill Brugger and David Kelly, *Chinese Marxism in the Post-Mao Era* (Stanford: Stanford University Press, 1990).

CHAPTER ONE

WILD LILY, 1942

DOCUMENT 1

WANG SHIWEI
Wild Lily

WHILE I was walking alone along the riverbank, I saw a comrade wearing a pair of old-style padded cotton shoes. I immediately fell to thinking of Comrade Li Fen, who also wore such shoes. Li Fen, my dearest and very first friend. As usual my blood began to race. Li Fen was a student in 1926 on the preparatory course in literature at Beijing University. In the same year she joined the Party. In the spring of 1928 she sacrificed her life in her home district of Baoqing in Hunan Province. Her own uncle tied her up and sent her to the local garrison—a good illustration of the barbarity of old China. Before going to her death, she put on all her three sets of underclothes and sewed them tightly together at the top and the bottom. This was because the troops in Baoqing often incited riff-raff to defile the corpses of the young women Communists they had shot—yet another example of the brutality, the evil, the filth, and the darkness of the old society. When I got news of her death, I was consumed with feelings of deep love and hatred. Whenever I think of her, I have a vision of her pure, sacred martyrdom, with her three layers of underclothes sewn tightly together, tied up and sent by her very own uncle to meet her death with dignity. (It seems rather out of place to talk of such things in tranquil Yan'an, against the warbled background of "Yu tang chun" and the swirling steps of the golden lotus dance;[1] but the whole atmosphere in Yan'an does not seem particularly appropriate to the conditions of the day—close your eyes and think for a moment of our dear comrades dying every minute in a sea of carnage.)

In the interest of the nation, I will not reckon up old scores of class hatred. We are genuinely selfless. With all our might we are dragging the representatives of old China along the road with us toward the light. But in the process the filth and dirt is rubbing off on us, spreading its diseases.

On scores of occasions I have drawn strength from the memory of Li

Fen—vital and militant strength. Thinking back on her on this occasion, I was moved to write a *zawen* under the title "Wild Lily." This name has a twofold significance. First, the wild lily is the most beautiful of the wild flowers in the hills and countryside around Yan'an, and is therefore a fitting dedication to her memory. Secondly, although its bulbs are similar to those of other lilies, they are said to be slightly bitter to the taste, and of greater medicinal value, but I myself am not sure of this.

What Is Lacking in Our Lives?

Recently young people here in Yan'an seem to have lost some of their enthusiasm, and to have become inwardly ill at ease.

Why is this? What is lacking in our lives? Some would answer that it is because we are badly nourished and short of vitamins. Others, that it is because the ratio of men to women is eighteen to one, and many young men are unable to find girlfriends. Or because life in Yan'an is dreary and lacks amusements.

There is some truth in all these answers. It is true that there is need for better food, for partners of the opposite sex, and for more interest in life. That is only natural. But one must also recognize that young people here in Yan'an came with a spirit of sacrifice to make revolution, and not for food, sex, and an enjoyable life. I cannot agree with those who say that their lack of enthusiasm, their inward disquiet even, are a result of our inability to resolve these problems. So what is lacking in our lives? Perhaps the following conversation holds some clues.

During the New Year holiday I was walking home in the dark one evening from a friend's place. Ahead of me were two women comrades talking in animated whispers. We were some way apart so I quietly moved closer to hear what they were saying.

"He keeps on talking about other people's petty-bourgeois egalitarianism; but the truth is that he thinks he is something special. He always looks after his own interests. As for the comrades underneath him, he doesn't care whether they're sick or well, he doesn't even care if they die, he hardly gives a damn! . . . Crows are black wherever they are. Even Comrade XXX acts like that."

"You're right! All this bullshit about loving your own class. They don't even show ordinary human sympathy! You often see people pretending to smile and be friendly, but it's all on the surface, it doesn't mean anything. And if you offend them, they glare at you, pull their rank and start lecturing you."

"It's not only the big shots who act that way, the small fry are just the same. Our section leader XXX crawls when he's talking to his superiors, but he behaves very arrogantly towards us. Often comrades have been ill and he hasn't even dropped in to see how they are. But when an eagle stole one of his chickens, you should have seen the fuss he made! After that, every time he saw an eagle he'd start screaming and throwing clods of earth at it—the self-seeking bastard!"

There was a long silence. In one way, I admired the comrade's sharp tongue. But I also suddenly felt depressed.

"It's sad that so many comrades are falling ill. Nobody wants people like that to visit them when they fall ill, they just make you feel worse. Their tone of voice, their whole attitude they don't make you feel they care about you."

"Right. They don't care about others, and others don't care about them. If they did mass work, they'd be bound to fail."

They carried on their conversation in animated whispers. At this point our ways parted, and I heard no more of what they had to say. In many ways their views were one-sided and exaggerated. Perhaps the picture they drew does not apply widely; but there is no denying that it is useful as a mirror.

Running into "Running into Difficulties"

On "Youth Page" no. 12 of this paper [*Liberation Daily*, the paper in which Wang Shiwei's article first appeared], I read an article titled "Running into difficulties" which aroused my interest. Here are two passages from that article.

Recently a middle-aged friend arrived from the Guomindang rear. When he saw that young people in Yan'an were incapable of putting up with anything and were constantly grumbling he raised his voice: "What's all this about? We people in the outside world have run into countless difficulties and suffered constant ill-treatment . . ."

He was right. Life in Yan'an may anger or offend you. But in the eyes of someone who has run up against countless difficulties and who has experienced the hardships of life, they are mere trifles. But it is an entirely different matter in the case of immature young people, especially those of student origin. Their parents and teachers coddle them into adulthood, whispering to them about life with love and warmth and teaching them to imitate pure and beautiful emotions. The ugliness and bleakness of their present situation is entirely new to them, and it is not surprising that as soon as they come up against difficulty they begin to bawl and to feel upset.

I have no idea what sort of person this author's "middle-aged friend" is, but in my view his sort of philosophy, which is based on the principle of being contented with one's lot, is positively harmful. Young people should be treasured for their purity, their perceptiveness, their ardor, their courage, and their energy. They experience the darkness before others experience it, they see the filth before others see it; what others do not wish or dare to say, they say. Because of this they are more critical, but this is by no means "grumbling." What they say is not always well balanced, but it is by no means "bawling." We should inquire into problems that give rise to "grumbling," "bawling," and "disquiet," and set about removing their causes in a rational way. (Yes, rational! It is completely untrue that young people are always engaged in "thoughtless clamor.") To say that Yan'an is superior to the "outside world," to tell young people not to "grumble," to describe Yan'an's dark side as some "slight disappointment" will solve no problems. Yes, Yan'an is superior to the "outside world," but it should and can be better still.

Of course, young people are often hot-headed and impatient—an observation that appears to be the main theme of "Running into difficulties." But if all young people were to be mature before their time, how desolate this world would be! In reality, young people in Yan'an have already seen a great deal of the world—after all, the grumbling conversation between the two women comrades that I quoted earlier was held in whispers in the dark. So far from resenting "grumbling" of this sort, we should use it as a mirror in which to inspect ourselves. To say that youth "of student origin" are "coddled into adulthood, whispered to about life with love and warmth and taught to imitate pure and beautiful emotions" is very subjectivist. Even though most Yan'an youth come from "a student background," are "inexperienced," and have not "seen more than enough of life's hardships," most arrived in Yan'an after a whole series of struggles and it is not true to say that they experienced nothing but "love and warmth"; on the contrary, it was precisely because they knew all about "hatred and cold" that they joined the revolutionary camp in the first place. From what the author of "Running into difficulties" says, all the young people in Yan'an were brought up pampered, and only "grumble" because they miss their candied fruit. But it was because of "evil and coldness" that they came to Yan'an in search of "beauty and warmth," that they identified the "evil and coldness" here in Yan'an and insisted on "grumbling" about it in the hope of alerting people's attention and reducing it to a minimum.

In the winter of 1938 our Party carried out a large-scale investigation of our work and summoned comrades to "unfold a lively criticism" and to "give full vent to their criticisms, no matter whether they were right or wrong." I hope we have another such investigation, and listen to the "grumbles" of the youth.

"Inevitability," "The Heavens Won't Fall In," and "Small Things"

"Our camp exists amidst the darkness of the old society, and therefore there is inevitably darkness in it too." Of course, that's "marxism"! But that is only one-sided marxism. There is an even more important side which the "masters of subjectivist factionalism" have forgotten, that is, the need, after having recognized the inevitability of such darkness, through Bolshevik activism to prevent its emergence, to reduce its growth, and to give full play to the ability of consciousness to transform objective reality. Given present conditions, to clean out all traces of darkness from our camp is impossible. But to destroy as much of it as we can is not only possible, but necessary. The "great masters," however, have not only failed to emphasize this point, but have scarcely even mentioned it. All they do is point out that it is "inevitable" and then doze off to sleep. They use "inevitability" as an excuse for self-indulgence. In their dreams they tell themselves: "Comrade, you are a product of the old society, and there is a tiny spot of darkness in your soul. But that is inevitable, no need to get embarrassed about it."

After the "theory" of "inevitability" comes the "national form theory" known as "the heavens won't fall in." Yes, it is impossible for the heavens to fall in. But what of our work and our cause? Will they suffer as a result? The "great masters" have given little or no thought to this problem. If this "inevitability" is "inevitably" allowed to pursue its course, then the heavens—the heavens of our revolutionary cause—will "inevitably" fall in. I suggest we should not be so complacent.

The so-called "small things" theory is linked with this. A criticizes B. B tells A he shouldn't waste his time on "small things." Some "great masters" even say: "Damn it! It's bad enough with the women comrades, now the men are spending all their time on trivia too!" It is true that there is probably no danger in Yan'an of such big problems as treason against the Party or the nation. But each individual through the small things he does in the course of his everyday life, either helps the light or helps the darkness. And the "small things" in the lives of "great men" are even more capable of calling forth warmth or desolation.

Egalitarianism and the System of Ranks

According to what I heard, one comrade wrote an article with a similar title for his departmental wall newspaper, and as a result was criticized and attacked by his department "head" and driven half-mad. I hope this story is untrue. But since there have been genuine cases of madness even among the "little devils" [orphan children who acted as personal assistants to the Communist cadres], I fear there may be some madness among adults. Even though the state of my nerves is not as "healthy" as some people's, I still have enough life in me not to go mad under any circumstances. I therefore intend to follow in the footsteps of that comrade and discuss the question of equality and the ranking system.

Communism is not the same as egalitarianism, and we are not at present at the stage of Communist revolution. There is no need for me to write an eight-legged essay on that question, since there is no cook crazy enough to want to live in the same style as one of the "heads." (I don't dare write "kitchen operative," since it sounds like a caricature; but whenever I speak to cooks I always address them in the warmest possible way as "comrade kitchen-operatives"—what a pitiful example of warmth!) The question of a system of ranks is rather more difficult.

Those who say that a system of ranks is reasonable use roughly the following arguments: (1) they base themselves on the principle of "from each according to their ability, to each according to their worth," which means that those with more responsibilities should consume more; (2) in the near future the three-thirds government [the "tripartite system" under which the Communists nominally shared power with the "petit bourgeoisie and the enlightened gentry" in the areas under their control] intends to carry out a new salary system, and naturally there will be pay differentials; and (3) the Soviet Union also has a system of ranks.

In my opinion all these arguments are open to debate. As for (1), we are still in the midst of the revolution, with all its hardships and difficulties; all of us, despite fatigue, are laboring to surmount the present crisis, and many comrades have ruined their precious health. Because of this it does not yet seem the right time for anyone, no matter who, to start talking about "to each according to their worth." On the contrary, all the more reason why those with greater responsibilities should show themselves willing to share weal and woe with the rank and file. (This is a national virtue that should be encouraged.) In so doing, they would win the profound love of the lower ranks. Only then would it be possible to create ironlike unity. It goes without saying that it is not only reasonable but necessary that those with big responsibilities who need special treatment for their health should get such treatment. The same goes for those with positions of medium responsibility. As for (2), the pay system of the three-thirds government should also avoid excessive differentials; it is right that non-party officials should get slightly better treatment, but those officials who are Party members should uphold our excellent traditions of frugal struggle so that we are in a position to mobilize even more non-party people to join us and cooperate with us. As for (3), excuse my rudeness, but I would beg those "great masters" who can't open their mouths without talking about "Ancient Greece" to hold their tongues.

I am not an egalitarian, but to divide clothing into three and food into five grades is neither necessary nor rational, especially with regard to clothes. (I myself am graded as "cadres' clothes and private kitchen," so this is not just a case of sour grapes.) All such problems should be resolved on the basis of need and reason. At present there is no noodle soup for sick comrades to eat and young students only get two meals of thin congee a day (when they are asked whether they have had enough to eat, Party members are expected to lead the rest in a chorus of "Yes, we're full"). Relatively healthy "big shots" get far more than they need to eat and drink, with the result that their subordinates look upon them as a race apart, and not only do not love them, but even. . . . This makes me most uneasy. But perhaps it is a "petty bourgeois emotion" to always be talking about "love" and "warmth"? I await your verdict.

DOCUMENT 2

WANG SHIWEI
Politicians, Artists

This article appeared in the journal of the Yan'an Literary Resistance Association in February 1942. In June of that year, it was cited in a condemnation of Wang Shiwei by the Yan'an Forum on Literature and Art: "We unanimously agree that Wang Shiwei's fundamental thought and activities are Trotskyite. They are antiproletarian and harmful to the Communist Party and the revolutionary cause. . . . Wang Shiwei's "Wild Lily" and "Politicians, Artists" are propaganda reflecting his incorrect thought. It is inappropriate for the Literature and Art column of the *Jiefang ribao* (Liberation Daily) and *Guyu* (Spring Rain) to print them instead of exposing and criticizing them." [2]

THERE are two sides to the revolution: changing the social system, and changing people. Politicians are the revolution's strategists and tacticians; they unite, organize, and lead the revolution. Their main task is to transform the social system. Artists are the "engineers of the soul," and their main task is to transform people's heart, spirit, thinking, and consciousness. The filth and darkness in people's souls are the product of an irrational social system, and the soul's fundamental transformation is impossible until the social system has been fundamentally transformed. In the process of transforming the social system the soul too is transformed. . . . The tasks of the politician and the artist are complementary.

The politicians command the revolution's material forces; the artists arouse the revolution's spiritual forces. The politicians are generally cool, collected people, good at waging practical struggles to eliminate filth and darkness, and to bring about cleanliness and light. The artists are generally more emotional and more sensitive, good at exposing filth and darkness, and at pointing out cleanliness and light. . . .

The politicians understand that during the revolution the people in their own camp will be less than perfect, and things will rarely be done ideally. They take the broad view, making sure that the wheel of history advances and that the light wins. The artists, more passionate and more sensitive, long for people to be more lovable and things to be more splendid. When they write they take small things as their starting points: they hope to eliminate the darkness as far as they can so that the wheel of history can advance as fast as possible. As the practical transformers of the social system, the politicians take things more seriously; the artists as the soul's engineers, go even further in demanding perfection of people. In uniting, organizing, and leading the revolution and waging practical struggles, the politicians are superior. But the artists are better at plunging into the depths of the soul to change it—transforming our side in order to strengthen it, and transforming the enemies so as to undermine them.

The politicians and the artists each have their weak points. If the politicians are to attack the enemy successfully, establish links with allied forces, and strengthen our side, they must understand human nature and the ways of the world, be masters of tricks and devices, and be skilled in making and breaking alliances. Their weakness springs from these very strengths. When they use them for the revolutionary cause they become the most beautiful and exquisite "revolutionary art," but unless they are truly great politicians they are bound to make use of them for their own fame, position, and interest, thus harming the revolution. In this respect we must insist that cat's claws be used only for catching rats and not for seizing chickens. Here we must distinguish politicians from artists; and we must be ever on our guard against cats that are good not at catching rats but at taking chickens. The main weaknesses of most artists are pride, narrowness, isolation, inability to unite with others, and mutual suspicion and exclusion. Here we must ask the engineers of the soul to start by making their own souls clean and bright. This is hard and painful, but it is the only way to greatness.

The Chinese revolution is especially hard. The difficulties of changing the social system are well known, but few realize that changing people's souls is even harder. "The further east you go, the darker society becomes." Old China is full of gore and pus, darkness and filth, all of which have inevitably stained the Chinese who grew up in it. Even we, the revolutionary fighters creating a new China, cannot escape this cruel fact. Only if we have the courage to look it in the face can we understand why we must be even more rigorous in our efforts to transform souls, so as to accelerate and win the struggle to change the social system.

Lu Xun was a fighter all his life, but anyone who understands him will know that at heart he was lonely. He struggled because he recognized the laws of social development and believed that the future was bound to be better than the present; he was lonely because he saw that even in the souls of his own comrades there was filth and darkness. He knew that the task of transforming old China could only be carried out by the sons and daughters of old China, despite their filth and darkness. But his great heart could not help yearning for his comrades to be more lovable.

The revolutionary camp exists in old China, and the revolution's fighters have grown up in old China, which means that our souls are inevitably stained. The present revolution requires that we ally not only with the peasants and the urban petty bourgeoisie, but with even more backward classes and strata, and that we make concessions to them, thus becoming contaminated with yet more filth and darkness. This makes the artist's task of transforming the soul even more important, difficult, and urgent. To boldly expose and wash away all that is filthy and dark is as important as praising the light, if not more important. Exposing and cleansing is not merely negative, because when darkness is eliminated the light can shine even brighter. Some people think that revolutionary artists must "direct their fire outside," and that if we expose our weaknesses we give the enemy easy targets. But this is a short-sighted view. Though our camp is now strong enough for us to have no fears about exposing our shortcomings, it is not yet fully consolidated; self-criticism is the best way of consolidating it. As for the maggots and traitors in anti-Communist secret service organs, they would concoct rumors and slanders even if we were flawless; they even hope that we will hush up our faults and shun those who might cure them, so that the darkness grows.

Some who think highly of themselves as politicians smile sarcastically when they speak of artists. Others who pride themselves on being artists shrug their shoulders when they mention politicians. But there is always some truth in objective reflections: each would do well to use the other as a mirror. They should not forget that they are both children of old China.

A truly great politician must have a soul great enough to move the souls of others and cleanse them; thus a great politician is a great artist. An artist who has a truly great soul is bound to have a part to play in uniting, organizing, and leading the forces of revolution; thus a great artist is also a great politician.

Finally I would like to appeal warmly to artist comrades: be even more effective in transforming the soul, and aim in the first place at ourselves and our own camp. In China transforming the soul will have an even greater effect on transforming society. It will determine not only how soon but even whether the revolution succeeds.

DOCUMENT 3

DING LING
Thoughts on March 8 (Women's Day)

Ding Ling's (1904–1986) famous essay, condemned in 1942 as "narrowly feminist," is remarkable for the light it throws on relations between men and women in Yan'an. Like Wang Shiwei, Ding Ling had been active in the revolution since the mid-1920s. After the execution of her husband by the Guomindang in 1931 she spent three years behind bars. She achieved early renown as a revolutionary writer, and was one of modern China's best-known women authors. She and the other writers, unlike Wang, quickly gave in to party pressure in 1942 and disavowed their heresies, so they escaped more lightly from the affair. But Ding Ling was back in trouble during the "anti-rightist" drive of 1957–1958: by then a member of the literary establishment, she was criticized and purged as an "inveterate anti-party element." She was rehabilitated in 1979, when she became a senior member of the Writers' Association.

WHEN will it no longer be necessary to attach special weight to the word "woman" and to raise it specially?

Each year this day comes round. Every year on this day meetings are held all over the world where women muster their forces. Even though things have not been as lively these last two years in Yan'an as they were in previous years, it appears that at least a few people are busy at work here. And there will certainly be a congress, speeches, circular telegrams, and articles.

Women in Yan'an are happier than women elsewhere in China. So much so that many people ask enviously: "How come the women comrades get so rosy and fat on millet?" It doesn't seem to surprise anyone that women make up a big proportion of the staff in hospitals, sanatoria, and clinics, but they are inevitably the subject of conversation, as a fascinating problem, on every conceivable occasion. What's more, all kinds of women comrades are often the target of deserved criticism. In my view these reproaches are serious and justifiable.

People are always interested when women comrades get married, but that is not enough for them. It is impossible for women comrades to get onto friendly terms with a man comrade, even more so with more than one. Cartoonists ridicule them: "A departmental head getting married too?" The poets say: "All the leaders in Yan'an are horsemen, and none of them are artists. In Yan'an it's impossible for an artist to find a pretty sweetheart." In other situations they are lectured at: "Damn it, you look down on us old cadres and say we're country bumpkins. But if it wasn't for us country bumpkins, you wouldn't be coming to Yan'an to eat millet!" Yet women invariably want to get married. (It's even more of a sin not to marry, and single women are even more of a target for rumors and slanderous gossip.) So they can't afford to be choosy, anyone will do: whether he rides horses or wears straw sandals, whether he's an artist or a supervisor. After marriage, they inevitably have children. The fate of such children is various. Some are wrapped in soft baby wool and patterned felt and looked after by governesses. Others are wrapped in soiled cloth and left crying in their parents' beds, while their parents consume much of the child's allowance. But for this allowance (25 yuan a month, equivalent to just over three pounds of pork), many would probably never get a taste of meat. Whoever they marry, those women who are compelled to bear children will probably be publicly derided as "Noras who have returned home."[3] Those women comrades in a position to employ governesses can go out once a week to a prim get-together and dance. Behind their backs there will also be the most incredible gossip and whispering campaigns, but wherever they go they cause a great stir and all eyes are glued to them. This has nothing to do with our theories, our doctrines, and the speeches we make at meetings. We all know this to be a fact, a fact that is right before our eyes, but it is never mentioned.

It is the same with divorce. In general there are three conditions to observe when getting married. These are (1) political purity; (2) similar age and comparable looks; and (3) mutual help. Even though everyone is said to fulfill these conditions—as for (1), there are no open traitors in Yan'an; as for (3), you can call anything "mutual help," including darning socks, patching shoes, and even feminine comfort—everyone nevertheless makes a great show of giving thoughtful attention to them. And yet the pretext for divorce is invariably the wife's political backwardness. I am the first to admit that it is a shame when a man's wife is not progressive and retards his progress. But let us consider how backward they really are. Before marrying, they were inspired by the desire to soar in the heavenly heights and lead a life of bitter struggle. They got married partly through physiological necessity and partly as a response to sweet talk about "mutual help." After that they are forced to toil away and become "Noras returned home." Afraid of being thought "backward," those who are a bit more daring rush round begging nurseries to take their children. They ask for abortions and risk punishment and even death by secretly swallowing potions to induce them. But the answer comes back:

"Isn't giving birth to children also work? You're just after an easy life, you want to be in the limelight. After all, what indispensable political work have you performed? Since you are so frightened of having children and so unwilling to take responsibility once you have had them, why did you get married in the first place? No one forced you to." Under these conditions how can women escape the destiny of "backwardness"? When women capable of working sacrifice their career for the joys of motherhood, people always sing their praises. But after ten years or so, they inevitably pay the tragic price (i.e., divorce) of "backwardness." Even from my point of view, as a woman, there is nothing attractive about such "backward" elements. Their skin is beginning to wrinkle, their hair is growing thin, and fatigue is robbing them of their last traces of attractiveness. It should be self-evident that they are caught up in a tragedy. But whereas in the old society they would probably have been pitied and considered unfortunate, nowadays their tragedy is seen as something self-inflicted, as their just deserts. Is there not a discussion going on in legal circles about whether divorce should be granted simply on the petition of one party or on the basis of mutual agreement? In the great majority of cases it is the husband who petitions for divorce. If the wife does so, she must be leading an immoral life, so of course she deserves to be cursed!

I myself am a woman, so I understand the failings of women better than others. But I also have a deeper understanding of what they suffer. Women are incapable of transcending the age they live in, of being perfect, or of being hard as steel. They are incapable of resisting all the temptations of society or all the silent oppression they suffer here in Yan'an. They each have their own past written in blood and tears, they have experienced great emotions—in elation as in depression, in the lone battle of life or in the humdrum stream of life. This is even truer of the women comrades who come to Yan'an, so I have much sympathy for those fallen and classed as criminals. What's more, I hope that men, especially those in top positions, and women themselves will consider women's mistakes in their social context. It would be better if there were less empty theorizing and more talk about real problems, so that theory and practice are not divorced, and if each Communist Party member were more responsible for his own moral conduct.

But we must also hope for a little more from our women comrades, especially those in Yan'an. We must urge ourselves on and develop our comradely feeling.

People without ability have never been in a position to seize all. So if women want equality, they must first strengthen themselves. There is no need to stress this, we all know it. Today there are certain to be people who make fine speeches about the need first to acquire political power. I would simply mention a few things that any frontliner, whether a proletarian, a fighter in the war of resistance, or a woman, should pay attention to in his or her everyday life:

1. Don't allow yourself to fall ill. A wild life can at times appear romantic, poetic, and attractive, but in today's conditions it is inappropriate. You are the best keeper of your life. There is nothing more unfortunate nowadays than to lose your health. It is nearest to your heart. Keep a close watch on it, pay careful attention to it, cherish it.

2. Make sure that you are happy. Only when you are happy can you be youthful, active, fulfilled in your life, and steadfast in the face of every difficulty; only then will you see a future ahead of you and know how to enjoy yourself. This sort of happiness is not a life of contentment, but a life of struggle and of advance. All of us should every day do some meaningful work and some reading, so that each of us is in a position to give something to others. Loafing about simply encourages the feeling that life is hollow, feeble, and in decay.

3. Use your brain, and make a habit of doing so. Correct any tendency not to think and ponder, or to swim with the tide. Before you say or do anything, think whether what you are saying is right, whether that is the most suitable way of dealing with the problem, whether it goes against your own principles, whether you feel you can take responsibility for it. Then you will have no cause to regret your actions later. This is what is known as acting rationally. It is the best way of avoiding the pitfalls of sweet words and honeyed phrases, of being side-tracked by petty gains, of wasting our emotions and wasting our lives.

4. Resolution in hardship, perseverance to the end. Aware, modern women should identify and cast off all their rosy, compliant illusions. Happiness is to take up the struggle in the midst of the raging storm and not to pluck the lute in the moonlight or to recite poetry among the blossoms. In the absence of the greatest resolution, it is all too easy to falter in mid-path. Not to suffer is to become degenerate. The strength to carry on should be nurtured through the quality of "perseverance." People without great aims and ambitions rarely have the firmness of purpose that scorns petty advantages and a comfortable existence. Only those who have aims and ambitions for the benefit not of the individual but of humanity as a whole can persevere to the end.

Dawn, August 3, 1942

Postscript

On rereading this article, it seems to me that there is much room for improvement in the passage about what we should expect from women, but because I have to meet a deadline, I have no time to revise it. Yet I also feel that there are some things that, said by a leader before a big audience, would probably evoke satisfaction. But when written by a woman, they are more than likely to be demolished. However, since I have written it, I offer it as I always intended, for the perusal of those with similar views.

DOCUMENT 4
_____

Luo Feng

It Is Still the Age of the *Zawen*

Luo Feng, a writer from Manchuria, argues here that the *zawen*—a laconic and fiercely critical essay form perfected by Lu Xun—is a useful tool for exposing the "dark side" of life in the Communist base areas of northern China, and should not just be reserved for attacking the Guomindang. Like Ding Ling, he quickly gave in to the criticism to which he was subjected for writing this essay. Of the 1942 *zawen*, Luo's is closest in style to the original model. In 1957 Luo fell from grace a second time—mainly because of his activities in 1942—after the crushing of the Hundred Flowers movement.

IN OUR glorious border areas there are some people who claim that we are no longer in the age of the *zawen*. I too wish that there were no need for the *zawen* to stage a comeback, for if there were no *zawen*, there would be no more of that dreadful darkness or of those evil, nauseating abscesses. If there were no *zawen* all the world would be at peace and we would be certain of final victory in the anti-Japanese war of resistance. But facts are rarely as rounded as hopes, and however much effort we expend on making our thought as brilliant as the sun, it will still be easy as the years go by to find dark, dank corners, full of decaying curios.

Experts in the study of historical evolution point out that the old-fashioned ideas and forms of behavior handed down across the millennia are not easy to uproot at one go. Certain clever gentlemen exploit the gap opened up by this theory as a bolt-hole in which to indulge themselves, happily wallowing and submerging like pigs in a stinking, filthy pool of mud. Themselves not afraid of getting dirty, they see nothing wrong with smearing passers-by. In actual fact there is nothing at all "clever" about such crude behavior. Then there is the other sort of person who, though lurking in the same hole, is always bandying around phrases and making dazzlingly brilliant speeches. It would never occur to natural intelligence that inside that lustrous and armored shell there hides a lump of boneless, sluggardly, timorous flesh!

Generally speaking, it is easier to deal with things that are out in the open. For example, there are ways and means of removing an obstacle that impedes the road to progress. But if you are caught in a thick fog that completely obscures your vision, you will inevitably feel confused and unsure of your footing. Those who have lived for a long time in the desolate mountains should realize that fogs of this sort not only appear frequently over Chongqing, but here in Yan'an too.

Yes, "Yan'an is the place with the highest level of political awareness." But if you constantly wear the same elegant clothes and are too lazy to wash them, sooner or later they are bound to get dirty. It is a basic principle of human behavior to practice what you preach, and a revolutionary should pay even more attention to this principle. Why hang a sign round your neck saying "vigilance" if you are going along the wrong road? Your own fate may not be so important, but have some consideration for those following you!

I often think of Mr. Lu Xun when I am on this subject. The dagger he used to cut through the darkness and point the road ahead is already buried underground and rusty, and few know how to use it. But it is still the age of the *zawen*.

Comrade Ding Ling, editor of the Literature Column, plans to revive the *zawen*. She has already presented her own efforts in that column, though they lack strength. As a reader, I hope that from now on the column will change into a dagger to make people tremble with fear, and at the same time to gladden them.

1. "Yu tang chun" (Spring in the Jade Hall) was a well-known Beijing opera aria. The phrase may simply be a sarcastic comment on living conditions in Yan'an. Dai Qing reports that it may also be a veiled attack on Mao, who married the actress Jiang Qing in 1939. See Dai Qing, *Wang Shiwei and "Wild Lilies,"* p. 36.
2. See Dai Qing, *Wang Shiwei and "Wild Lilies,"* p. 114.
3. A reference to the heroine of Ibsen's *Doll's House,* who left home to achieve her freedom.

CHAPTER TWO

THE HUNDRED FLOWERS,
1957

DOCUMENT 5

Forum of Democratic Parties and Groups on
the Rectification Movement

A forum of the leaders of democratic parties and groups was convened by the
United Front Work Department in Beijing between May 8 and May 16, 1957, at
which they were invited by senior CCP leaders to comment on and even criticize
the Party and the government. Thirty-six non-communist leaders spoke, discussing the work of the united front and the leadership of the Communist Party.
Among the most forthright speakers were Li Boqiu (China Workers' and Peasants' Democratic Party), Liu Qingyang (China Democratic League), Huang
Shaohong (Guomindang Revolutionary Committee), Chen Shutong ("non-party
element"), and Jin Zhixuan (China Association for the Promotion of Democracy). The democratic parties and groups have functioned since 1949 as a kind of
ornament or facade, "having posts but no authority," whose role is to endorse the
policies of the CCP. This week in 1957 was perhaps the only occasion in more
than forty years on which they expressed reservations about Party rule, and revealed the frustrations of their positions. It may be noted that they strongly criticize bureaucratic despotism and the lack of differentiation between Party and
government, but show no inclination to drop collectivism or argue for a market
economy.

LI BOQIU severely criticized certain members of the Communist Party
for hankering after special privileges. The democratic parties held posts
but no authority, and there was a contradictory relationship between the
Communist Party and the government. Li considered that these questions
reflected the sectarian tendency within the Communist Party: "This sectarianism on the one hand has its source in the class feeling of Party members. They grew up in a class different from that of the democratic parties
and in the past they were engaged in a long struggle against their class
enemies. This point is understandable. On the other hand sectarianism
also has its origins in the desire for special privileges on the part of some
Party members. This is without doubt a reflection of the mentality of the
old ruling class. The Communist Party educates its members to fulfill

their obligations to the people, to endure hardship first and to enjoy good fortune later. How is it that some Party members have forgotten this?"

Li stated that certain members of the Communist Party mechanically stress the principle of class struggle to cover up their desire for special privileges. Certain members simply rely on the prestige of Chairman Mao and the Party. They have forgotten the principle of collective leadership, of popular democracy. The desire for special privileges is the most deep-rooted cause of sectarianism. Li also criticized the work of the National Committee of the Chinese People's Political Consultative Conference (CPPCC). According to him, the CPPCC neglects the activities of the different parties and groups. The work of the CPPCC lacks political and ideological significance.

Liu Qingyang raised the difficulties encountered by the Red Cross and in women's work, and criticized the Communist Party for not attaching full importance to the people's organizations. She stated that views had been expressed on all questions except that of work among women, which did not attract attention. United front work had been criticized for uniting only with upper echelons and not with the lower levels; she would add that it had the defect of uniting only with men, but not with women. She gave the example of the Women's Association, the cadres of which have all been working hard and successfully. She felt that their efforts would all be unrecognized, and that the Association would not be granted resources. Sometimes the neighborhood women's groups would even refer to the Women's Association as a bourgeois organization.

Liu also severely criticized certain undesirable phenomena concerning marriage. She stated that in Hebei province, some agricultural coopera-tives took the trouble to train a number of women tractor drivers. But after they were married to army officers stationed in the area, they would no longer work as tractor drivers, were cut off from their cooperatives, and lived in army camps. They began to wear leather shoes and silk clothes, and went about in cars. This produced an unfavorable impres-sion among the peasants. Liu stated that this is not the road toward women's emancipation, but a case of ideological retrogression.

Huang Shaohong spoke on relations between the Party and the govern-ment, the rectification movement in relation to the legal system, and other questions. He did not question the leadership authority of the Party. But he said that in the past, in certain areas and in certain tasks, the Party issued orders directly to the people and to the government without first going through the proper channels. Decisions issued jointly by the Party and the government did not distinguish between directives from the Party leadership to its lower-level organs, and directives from the government to the people. This might lead some people or Party members into think-ing that the leadership method of the Party was to issue orders to the people directly. This would obstruct the mobilization and unity of the people, and hinder the tasks of the transition period. It would lead to serious bureaucratism, sectarianism, and subjectivism. He hoped that in the course of the rectification movement, the relations between Party and government would be scrutinized and clearly defined.

Huang said that the establishment of the legal system was as important as the rectification movement. The country's legislative machinery is not perfect and lags behind the development of the objective situation. Neither a criminal code, a civil code, police regulations, nor regulations for the punishment of public functionaries have yet been promulgated. Economic laws and regulations are especially inadequate. The first five-year plan is about to be fulfilled, yet the country still has not enacted regulations governing weights and measures. Huang stated that regulations such as those governing the punishment of public functionaries, the organization of various government departments, and rules for their conduct of business are closely related to the rectification movement, and must therefore be enacted as soon as possible. He also recommended a timely prosecution of cases involving leaders whose bureaucratism and subjectivism had inflicted serious damage to the people's life and property. He suggested drawing up a set of measures to deal with people who had undergone corrective labor, and hoped for a thorough review of some cases in which heavy sentences were passed on the accused.

Chen Shutong stated that some CCP members discriminate against people outside the Party. They look upon people outside the Party as "contemptible, disagreeable, and untouchable." They consider that you know nothing about politics, and even if you have some talent, your ignorance of politics turns your talent into poison, and so you are contemptible. Why are you "untouchable"? They consider that the class question is involved in relations between the working class and industrialists, and merchants and the petty bourgeoisie: if they have dealings with these groups they will be attacked, and so some people become "untouchable." Chen stated that if the Party is to be near the non-party people, the Party must first stretch out its hand. Finally Chen commented on the question of joint directives issued by the CCP Central Committee and the State Council. He recommended that the Party and the government should be separated.

Concerning the promotion of cadres, Jin Zhixuan considered that some Party members and cadres, once promoted, become separated from the masses and no longer care whether they discharge the duties expected of them. When young cadres take up their posts they are often subjective and doctrinaire, and feel that the government will simply take care of all their needs. When they are appointed to government posts they start to make complaints, and nobody dares to interfere with them. Non-party

people would not dare to cross them. And so they begin to cultivate bureaucratism. Jin stated that the rectification movement should not be restricted to the small fry, nor to the "young mistresses of the house."
Rather, it should begin with the "old ladies of the house" in the central
government departments, the ministers in various ministries who are
members of the Communist Party. In the past, the central government
seldom inspected their work, and the lower ranks did not dare to criticize
them.

DOCUMENT 6

Symposium of Scientists

Scientists too were encouraged to speak their mind and raise problems for discussion. The following is adapted from a New China News Agency press release,
reporting a symposium held on May 12, 1957.

MORE than 160 professors and representatives from scientific and tech-
nological circles held a symposium in Beijing this afternoon to discuss the
policy of "let a hundred flowers bloom, let a hundred schools of thought
contend" and other questions.

A number of scientists complained that the state does not allow them
sufficient time for their research. Scientists are often obliged to spend too
much time on political activities. The ideological transformation of scientists should be carried out in the course of academic research rather than
through political activities standardized by the state throughout the country. They hoped that responsible organs would see their way to relaxing
security control measures to a certain degree to create better conditions
for research work. For example, a geographer can hardly develop his
research work without the benefit of maps of 1:10,000 scale.

The symposium participants sharply criticized the CCP Beijing Committee, the Beijing People's Council, and a number of other related organizations for clamping down on academic associations. A number of
agricultural specialists expressed dissatisfaction with doctrinaire and
closed-door practices in academic work. Tai Songsi stated that in the
United States the use of hybrid corn to increase corn production by 65
percent is widely practiced, yet this achievement has been totally ignored
by some people on the pretext of idealism. Many scientists considered it
improper to refer to Morgan's theory of heredity as idealist. A few years
ago a responsible comrade in the Agricultural Ministry announced at a
symposium that seed selection was taboo, so the shortage of wheat was
never solved. Engineer Li Kouzi charged that in 1956 the responsible state

organ arbitrarily decided to manufacture double-share wheel plows for use in South China without consulting technical personnel. As these plows are designed for dry land and are unsuitable for the wet soil of South China, some 600,000 plows are lying idle.

Many people criticized the crude application of Soviet and other foreign experiences without taking into consideration the actual conditions in China. This has resulted in huge losses to the Chinese national economy. Professor Chang Sucheng of Beijing Normal University stated that in the past the textbooks for mathematics in middle schools had been quite good, but the Ministry of Education decided to replace them with a Soviet textbook. Later, when a member of the Soviet Ministry of Education visited China, he revealed that the textbook was about sixty years old, and far less advanced than books used in Britain and the United States.

A number of scientists are of the opinion that the Communist Party has not provided adequate leadership to academic organizations. At present, many academic association members are also members of the CCP, or of other democratic parties and groups. These members, however, are poorly qualified. Many intellectuals in China know very little or even nothing about Marxism-Leninism.

DOCUMENT 7

What Is the Fundamental Cause of
the Trade Union Crisis?

The following article by Jiang Mingdao and nine other members of the Shanghai Trade Union Council appeared in the *Gongren ribao* (Worker's Daily) Beijing, on May 21, 1957. It was written in response to an article titled "On an 8,000-li Tour of Hurried Observation" by Li Xiuren, a high-ranking trade union official. The article by Luo Yuwen appeared in the same newspaper on the next day. They reveal the despair felt by grass-roots trade union cadres, who were expected to defend the CCP, its policies and appointees in all circumstances, and never allowed to defend the interests of the workers whom they were supposed to represent.

THERE is indeed a crisis in trade union work at present, with the result that trade unions fail to play their due part in handling contradictions within the ranks of the people. Trade union officials face many difficulties. Party committees and the administration criticize them, the worker masses criticize them, and they even criticize themselves. Some of them complain that they have become "bean-cake cadres"—pressed on both sides; others call themselves "rubber cadres"—they can be stretched or pressed according to other people's whims.

Trade union cadres have encountered, and are still encountering, considerable resistance in the course of following the mass line. This resistance comes from various sides. Some people do not give the unions even minimum support or cooperation, using pretexts such as "the higher body has not made arrangements," or "no system has been instituted for this," or "who is to decide, you or I?" Some often blame the unions for making trouble, or for "routinism." Some even accuse union cadres of "unprincipled compromise with the masses." They bind the hands of trade union cadres with regulations, systems, and administrative measures, hindering them from following the mass line when solving the workers' problems. From our experience, we consider the demands raised by the workers in connection with their livelihood are, in most cases, not too high and should be given support. Those who "enter communist society ahead of schedule" are, in the main, not the union cadres or workers, but those "A class" cadres who believe they are "meritorious" and think they deserve privileges. After they have got modern flats, they want cars; after they have got dining rooms they want cadres' canteens. They do not like to queue up for meals, and they take tonics at the state's expense when they are perfectly healthy.

Comrade Li says, "Many workers want living quarters for their families and want to bring their families to cities . . . if all these demands are to be met, then house building and housing shortages will develop like a snowball." But if one probes the problem, one will find many factors behind it. Some leading cadres, as soon as they are transferred to factories or mines, or when they are promoted to senior positions, try to get houses and bring their families from rural areas to cities. Some of them take advantage of their power to register their wives, relatives, and friends in the factories and provide them with houses.

It is true that some trade union cadres call themselves "fourth-rate cadres." But the main issue at stake is not that they wish to have privileges equal to higher ranks, still less that they want to command and put on airs (of course there are such trade union cadres, but they are isolated cases). The majority of trade union cadres work hard and bear hardship without complaint. They feel they are fourth-rate cadres mainly because they are convinced that they cannot promote the legitimate demands of the masses. Reasonable demands may be arbitrarily rejected by managing directors, department heads, Party committee secretaries, branch secretaries, section heads, or workshop heads. Once a managing director or Party committee has made a decision, nothing can be done about it, even if it is clearly unreasonable. And trade union cadres, even if they do not agree with the decision, can do nothing except persuade the masses to accept it. They can only keep silent and show a smiling face, otherwise they will be accused of "fomenting discord," of "failing to implement the will of the leadership."

As to mass supervision, it is out of the question for the trade unions. Even today, when Chairman Mao's report on correct handling of contradictions is widely relayed, if the trade unions publish any criticisms put forward by the workers concerning the management, or present the views of the workers to the administration and Party committees, we would be interrogated: "Are you not mobilizing the masses to open a struggle meeting and criticize the leadership?" Trade union cadres have lost their guts. Union leadership emphasizes identity with the administration, but does not mention the contradiction between trade unions and the administration. It emphasizes acceptance of Party leadership, but does not make it clear that trade unions have a unique part to play in representing the masses. Trade union cadres dare not make decisions lest they should be accused of "economism," "syndicalism," and "tailism." And no one backs them up against such accusations. Besides, trade union cadres themselves are arbitrarily appointed or transferred by higher levels. "A clay idol cannot save itself when crossing a river"; how dare trade union cadres fight for proper demands on behalf of the workers?

Trade union cadres have shortcomings, and many shortcomings at that. We must actively join the rectification movement and overcome our shortcomings. But this cannot eliminate the root of the crisis in trade union work. During the recent labor disputes in some factories in Shanghai, the workers asked trade unions to support their proper demands, but trade union cadres had to seek the agreement of managing directors and Party committee secretaries on every point. A number of issues that gave rise to the dispute were referred by the unions to the relevant authorities, but they only dragged on with no solution. The workers knew this and said, "The trade union chairman is a good person but he has no power and cannot solve the problem."

The solution to this divorce between unions and the masses, and the end to the crisis in trade union work, lies in clarifying the function, character, and role of this mass organization—the trade union—under the proletarian dictatorship. We should solve the problem of how we may play a supervisory role, how to support the proper demands of the masses, and how to combat bureaucracy. We should ensure that the unions are not afraid of any pressure applied by the bureaucracy. Thus with their supervisory power increased, trade unions can fully play their unique role and can build close ties with the masses. And this point should be made clear not only in trade union work but, what is more important, to the whole Party.

DOCUMENT 8
_____

Luo Yuwen

Distressing Contradiction

I AM a new trade union member and was elected an official of the primary trade union only this year. I earnestly hope that I can do something for the workers and employees. I wish to say something about the problems I have encountered.

The workers and employees here have not as yet accused the trade unions of being "hand in glove with the administration" or "tails of the administration," but such a crisis may arise someday. For the officials and even the Party branches here expect trade unions and the administration to work "hand in glove" and expect trade unions to act "in accordance with the wishes of the administration." If trade unions hold different opinions on certain matters, then the majority of Party officials (none of whom are willing to join the unions) shout: "trade unions fight with the administration over power and money," "the trade unions are agitating for special positions," "the trade unions are trying to become independent of the administration." Does it mean that unions are supposed to be subordinate to the administration? I am really at a loss to understand why some local leadership, and even some Party organizations, do not give due importance to trade unions, although the Party Center does attach great importance to the unions.

Being a Party member, I must undoubtedly obey Party discipline and resolutions. On the other hand, being elected by the masses as a trade union cadre, I should listen to the voice of the masses, particularly the voice of the majority of the masses. I am required to be familiar with their conditions and study their problems. Further, I should explain to them certain questions they do not understand, and ask for their views and opinions. However the result is that the Party branch criticizes me for "enlisting the masses to fight the leadership, sowing discord between the masses and the leaders." I am told that I should study the problems with the leadership and not with the masses, and that to discuss issues with the masses means "becoming a tail of the masses." In short they hold that any decision made by the administration should be implemented whether it is right or wrong, that trade unions should unconditionally support the administration and explain to the masses the "correctness of some unfair measures." I am regarded as a trouble-making Party member. My views run counter to reality—that is the distressing contradiction in which I find myself.

DOCUMENT 9

Liu Binyan and Tai Huang: Rebellious Journalists

The views of many dissidents were never published, and our knowledge of them comes from official denunciations. It is hard to know how accurately these attacks reflect the original statements made by the people concerned, and to what extent they are misrepresentations. The two following passages were published during the clampdown on dissidents in July and August 1957. Liu Binyan maintained a principled stand against corruption and abuse of power since his youth, and is still active in the mid-1990s.

LIU BINYAN, editorial department of *Chinese Youth*, joined the Party in September 1944, but he refused again and again to devote all his strength to the Party. According to him, in the whole Communist Party with the unique exception of Chairman Mao, the top consisted of a number of conservative forces—the "privileged class" of ranking cadres; the middle was in the hands of a group of outwardly submissive but inwardly rebellious "local emperors"—the leading Party cadres at provincial and municipal level; and the bottom was a crowd of unsuspecting and ignorant "fools." He further opined that the formation of this "privileged class" within the Party was brought about by the system in its entirety. He frantically expressed his disagreement with Premier Zhou Enlai who said that bureaucratism had its origin in history. He considered this to be an excuse. He more than once sardonically and sarcastically described the Party cadres to other people as a group of characters who played cards all day long, who read light publications, but not literary books, and who had no interest in literature.

Liu Binyan's estimate of the present conditions inside the Party was embodied in the words "a mess." He opined that there was little democracy in the Party, that there were few criticisms in the Party, that elections in the Party were a formality. He said, "For the past few years, the Party has been increasingly estranged from the masses. Most of the people absorbed by the Party have been flatterers, sycophants, and yes-men."

In a report which he made last year in the course of a forum called by the People's Broadcasting Station in Shanghai, he said, "The mistakes were even more flagrant during the suppression of the counterrevolutionaries. The movement did not respect man and regarded human dignity as negligible." He ascribed certain defects in commercial work to the fact that the state "was trying every means to extort something from the masses."

TAI HUANG is a correspondent of the New China News Agency. He joined the Communist Party in 1944. In November last year, Tai Huang started to write his 10,000-word letter to the Communist Party Central

Committee and Chairman Mao to slander and maliciously attack the Central Committee and Chairman Mao. In the letter he affirmed: "There is a privileged class in existence. Even if a national united class has not yet been formed, the embryo of this class is forming and developing."

According to the preposterous allegation of Tai Huang, the "privileged class" had become an "exploiting class" which should be brought down. He asserted that there was a "sharp difference in livelihood" between his so-called "class" and the people. To prove this fallacy, he shamelessly fabricated "facts" like: "With the exception of rice, more goods are consumed by the revolutionaries who make up 5 percent of the population than the peasants who make up 80 percent of the population." He maliciously sought to provoke people by saying, "All the pork and edible oil have been consumed by members of the Communist Party and the cadres." He shouted, "The lot of our peasants is too hard!" The ordinary people had been "grievously disappointed." He even clamored, "The old ruling class has been overthrown but a new ruling class has arisen. The evolution of this will lead to an amalgamation with Taiwan!"

Tai Huang slanderously alleged that from the Central Government down to the local authorities, the leadership at all levels thought that "they themselves are above everything" and sought to "deify themselves." He tried to kill all the cadres in the country at a blow by asserting, "The high-ranking cadres violate the law and discipline while the cadres of the lower echelons have little regard for the law. They do not hesitate to perpetrate any evil save manslaughter and arson." He emphasized that the Central Committee should be held responsible for this.

After the outbreak of the Hungarian Incident, Tai Huang disapproved of the dispatch of Soviet troops to help Hungary suppress its counterrevolutionary rebellion. He said that "there was no case" for the Soviet Union to send in troops "on the ground of justice and morality" . . . . "If it was right for the Soviet Union to send its troops, then it would be also right for the United States to help Chiang Kai-shek." He slandered the people's journalistic enterprise as a "policy to make the people ignorant."

DOCUMENT 10

LIN XILING

Excerpts from a Speech Made at a Debate Held
at People's University on May 30, 1957

Lin Xiling joined the People's Liberation Army around 1949 and was discharged in 1953, with the rank of "cultural teacher." She then entered the People's University, set up in 1950 to train peasants and workers as Party cadres. Aged twenty-one and a fourth-year law student, she became a prominent leader of the unofficial movement that rose up in 1957 during the Hundred Flowers campaign, and, according to *Zhongguo qingnian bao* (China Youth), for a time "her rightist utterances were all the rage among young people throughout the country." She was jailed for fifteen years during the ensuing crackdown for denouncing the Party as a "bureaucratic apparatus that governs the people without democracy" and calling for a "full mobilization and upheaval" of the people to effect a "total transformation" of the state. She continued for some years to be held up as the epitome of a "counterrevolutionary." She was finally freed in 1979, and went abroad (see Document 57).

Documents 10 to 13 have an interesting history. In late May and early June 1957, at the height of the Hundred Flowers movement, members of the Beijing Student Union (a Party body) copied wall posters and took notes of speeches made on campuses. This material was rapidly assembled into a pamphlet titled *Kan! Zhe shi shenme yanlun?* (Look! What kind of talk is this?), dated June 14, 1957, that was used as incriminating evidence during the subsequent "struggle sessions" against the dissidents. Probably only one copy of this pamphlet ever reached the West. A student who fled China in 1962 smuggled it to Hong Kong, and it was later deposited in the Union Research Institute. Our documents are abridged translations from the pamphlet; the full texts can be found in Dennis J. Doolin, *Communist China: The Politics of Student Opposition* (Stanford: The Hoover Institution on War, Revolution and Peace, 1964).

AT PRESENT the economic foundation of our country is basically one of public ownership, and this is unshakable. From the point of view of development, public ownership is an improvement over private ownership. So the suggestion of some people that a fixed rate of interest be granted to business owners on their original investment over a period of twenty years should be resolutely opposed, because this is a continuation of private ownership. The time for abolishing fixed interest is completely ripe. Things should be publicly owned.

Personnel System: Irrational phenomena and sectarianism are clearly reflected here. A man is judged not by his virtues and abilities, but by whether or not he is a Party member or a (Communist Youth) League member. It is necessary not only to look into the many irrational phenomena themselves, but also to look at what stimulates them and what caused them to arise. Some people think bad things belonged only to the old society, yet even in the new society young persons have been given little chance for advancement. They want (the right) to seek knowledge, to listen to reports, and read materials, but here there are restrictions based on rank. Why are vainglory, fame, and profit in the thoughts of the young? This has something to do with the existing system. Some Party members rushed to join the Party in order to enjoy the resultant privileges; those who do not join the Party have no future. Someone asked me to join the League, saying that if I did not join the Party or the League, how could I manage to settle my future, marriage, and rank? Hearing this, I was very angry. I will *never* join the League for this reason.

Systems of Ranks: The cadres even distribute desks and wastepaper baskets according to ranks. The ranking system has permeated every aspect of life. Once I was ill and wanted medical care, but I had to be of the thirteenth rank to qualify. How could I climb to the thirteenth rank? Anyway, I was not willing to do so. Someone advised me to see the doctor through private connections, but I was not willing to do this.

THE rule of dogmatism in our country only propagandizes the bright side. So innocent youths are astounded to discover these problems when they enter society, and they knit their brows and drown themselves in disappointment. It is not the least bit strange that dogmatism hurts people.

The foundation has changed, but the ideology remains the same. The "three evils" are related to feudalism, compradorism, and fascism of the past. For instance, sectarianism is connected with feudalism and fascism, and dogmatism with compradorism. The compradors toadied to foreigners and worshipped America; (now) our learning from the Soviet Union is just like that. Of course, the Soviet Union is the first socialist country and Sino-Soviet friendship is indestructible, but wild copying of the Soviet Union is too dogmatic. Someone said, "The People's University is a great beehive of dogmatism." I think that it is the source and headquarters of dogmatism.

The Soviet Union is the source of dogmatism. The teachers lecture like typewriters; Soviet medical studies have not surpassed those at the Beijing Medical College; organized therapeutics have done much harm; the painless childbirth method is no longer in use—all this has resulted from a state of superstition.

There are many bad effects arising from the armed forces' copying the Soviet Union. Originally, the army was dearly loved and honored by the people, but now it has adopted a military-rank system which provides better salaries for officers and doesn't permit women comrades. I object to copying the Soviet Union in this manner. The rank system makes for very bad relations between officers and soldiers. There are numerous examples to prove this, and now the veterans in the army units (the professional soldiers) are grumbling. Communism should be based on national characteristics, and there must be national self-respect.

IN THE present socialist society, the interests of the working class coincide with those of the people. But there are still contradictions among the people that are expressed in relations between the ruler and the ruled (the leadership and the led). The ruler and the ruled are in different positions; they look at problems from different angles and their interests are not the same. The contradiction between the head of an enterprise and the workers is that they look at a problem differently. This is a non-antagonistic contradiction. But when it develops from quantitative change to qualitative change, it will erupt as an antagonistic one. A miniature Hungarian incident, the strike in Yumen, broke out in China [the reference is to a workers' strike at an important oil field in northwest Gansu Province]. It is necessary to see that this law is playing its part in real life and that the leadership has certain limitations. If these limitations are not overcome by subjective initiative, problems will develop. Men in different positions have different points of view. He who was previously ruled but has now climbed into the ruling position (from worker to head of a factory) speaks a different language; everything has changed.

To FEEL dissatisfied with reality is a good thing. People should be encouraged to feel this way. The philosophical foundation of being contented with reality is the soul of Hegel coming back to life. Hegel had absolute ideas. Now some of the Party leaders too have become Hegels.

Socialism is the best, highest, and most beautiful form of society. The word "most" is metaphysical. In the future, there will be a better form of society. If I were to live in "X" society five hundred years from now, I would be dissatisfied, for society is progressive. If we are satisfied with existing society, there will be no further development. Had the apes been content with reality, we would not be men today. Dissatisfaction with reality should be supported. But now some gentlemen chant cheap anthems, continually making comparisons with the Guomindang and capitalism, always looking back rather than ahead. When lecturing, teachers also make comparisons with the Guomindang and capitalism.

Some people say that dissatisfaction with reality will cause the people to lose their faith in socialism. I think this is incorrect. Of course, it is necessary today for us to sing songs of praise; genuine praise is good. But there should be neither rote praise nor bragging praise; this corrupts people's hearts and does great harm. It is necessary to tell the people the truth about all current problems.

IT IS necessary to tell the people about the true condition of things, to effect a thorough reform, and to mobilize the people in discussion. Socialism belongs to the people, not only to Party members. All the people should be allowed to air their views to their heart's content. The present "contending and blooming" is confined to the upper strata only. This won't do. The top layer is made up of old men who are not bold enough, who are too experienced in life, and dare not speak up. To consolidate their present positions, they dare not quarrel with the Communist Party. Let the broad masses discuss and air their opinions and then synthesize them. This is the ideal way.

THE problem is that the Party has taken the place of the government. The Communist Party is the party in power; its prestige is very great and it is the seat of all real power. The law is only a matter of formality. The Soviet Constitution is even more specious. Although judicial organs exist in the Soviet Union, Stalin could in fact completely destroy the judicial system. We have no judicial system; the judge's verdict is final. For instance, on the question of whether the suppression of counterrevolution has been enlarged, I think it has been; but the Chairman says no. I disagree. The destruction of the judicial system in the Soviet Union is shocking. The case in China, of course, is much better: 770,000 people have been executed. This is not a small figure, and 720,00 of them, equal to the population of a small nation, were condemned on false charges. The theoretical basis used to justify the suppression of counterrevolution is also incorrect; Luo Ruiqing's report on it was influenced by Stalin's erroneous theory that class contradictions will become more and more acute after socialism has been established.

DOCUMENT 11

On the New Development of "Class"

Taken from a wall poster, author unknown, Beijing University, May 28, 1957.

YOU may say, "Has not the life of the workers and peasants been improved?" Yes, I am aware of it, but to what extent? Just how much improvement has there actually been? The income of the workers and peasants in our country for several years now has not been raised much; it is just barely enough to keep them from starving to death. If some defend the inequality of distribution and politics nowadays, using the argument that formerly for six months out of the year they had only husks of grain to eat—well, are we looking ahead toward a slave society or toward a more rational one?

Capitalism is irrational and I am opposed to it. However, the present state of affairs also needs to be changed. True representatives of the laboring people and true leaders of the people should share their joys and sorrows. They should respect the great stature of the people. The people are the masters of history. Those leaders who are dishonest and hypocritical must step down.

DOCUMENT 12

Heaven, Water, Heart
Democracy? Party Rule?

Taken from a wall poster, Beijing Normal University, June 6, 1957.
"Heaven, Water, Heart" is the pseudonym of a student.

THE Constitution states that the people have the right to vote; however, the People's Deputies are selected by the Party. The people don't know who their Deputies are, and the Deputies don't represent the people.

The Constitution states that the people have freedom of speech, but the press, broadcasting networks, and radio stations are all monopolized by the Party. Those whose words differ from the Party line are invariably accused of being counterrevolutionaries.

The Constitution states that the people have freedom of assembly and freedom to form societies; however, all meetings and societies held or formed without permission from the Party or without accepting a leader appointed by the Party may be dubbed counterrevolutionary.

The Constitution states that the people have the right of personal freedom; however, the "suppression of counterrevolution" has made it clear that the responsible persons of Party organs at various levels have the power to restrict, in the name of the Party, the freedom of any upright citizen.

Chairman Mao has said that, at the present stage, the nature of the political setup in our country is that of a people's democratic dictatorship. However, the Party monopolizes, dictates, and decides everything. The democratic parties are mere puppets; there is people's democracy in name, but one-party dictatorship in fact.

The Party Central Committee is elected by the Party Congress, representing twelve million Party members; however, the Party Central Committee issues orders and instructions to the six hundred million people of our country and everyone has to obey.

The Constitution states that the government is responsible to the democratically constituted National People's Congress (NPC), but actually all governmental policies are decided by the Party. The government is responsible only to the Party. The People's Congress is nothing but an empty name.

We want Party leadership, but we are resolutely opposed to the Party alone making decisions and implementing them. We are not opposed to "Party rule" (because the Party also has its areas of authority), but we are opposed to replacing "democracy" with "Party rule." Give the people their democratic rights. Let the people enjoy their democratic rights under the full protection of the Constitution.

DOCUMENT 13

I Accuse, I Protest

Taken from a wall poster, author unknown, Qinghua University,
June 2, 1957.

I WAS born and raised in the liberated area. For twenty years I've seen through the imperialists. Facing the enemy, my eyes are red with anger and I would risk losing my head and shedding my blood; but facing the dictatorship of the Communist Party I am cowardly and powerless. How small and pitiful is one individual! We have given our blood, sweat, toil, and precious lives to defend not the people but the bureaucratic organs and bureaucrats who oppress the people and live off the fat of the land. They are a group of fascists who employ foul means, twist the truth, band together in evil adventure, and ignore the people's wish for peace both at home and abroad.

DURING the past few years the achievements in construction were used to deceive the people. What kind of construction? Both a luxurious super-structure divorced from the people and a national defense construction which is really an endless preparation for war. Various murderous acts against humanity are being carried out under cover of the word "peace" and given the beautified name of "Communist activities." Party, you are now betraying our nation and the innate goodness of our young people; you have smashed the peace. This is how I feel about you from the bottom of my heart.

What does it mean when the Communists say they suffer so that the people may not suffer and that they let the people enjoy things before they do the same? What do they mean when they speak of suffering now in order to have a happy life later? These are lies. We ask: Is Chairman Mao, who enjoys the best things of life and passes the summer at Jinwangdao and spends his vacations at Yuquanshan, having a hard time? Are the starving peasants, with only a cup of spring water, enjoying the good life? In Yan'an was Chairman Mao, who had two dishes plus soup for every meal, having a hard time? Were the peasants, who had nothing to eat but bitter vegetables, enjoying the good life? Everyone was told that Chairman Mao was leading a hard and simple life. That son of a bitch! A million shames on him! Scholars, try to find out the meaning of the words "good life" and "suffering." Never mind, you don't have any guts. Our pens can never defeat Mao Zedong's Party guards and his imperial army. When he wants to kill you, he doesn't have to do it himself. He can mobilize your wife and children to denounce you and then kill you with their own hands! Is this a rational society? This is class struggle, Mao Zedong style! This is the spiritual side of our age!

IN THE Soviet Union, there are still many grown-up orphans who never knew their fathers. Some of their fathers, of course, died on the battle-field—but how many of them were killed by their own men? They were buried alive! They were buried alive by men they relied upon and trusted. Alas, this is the meaning of "comrade"!

The Chinese people have been deceived. When they courageously drove out the imperialists and the Chiang Kai-shek gang, they put their trust in the wrong man. We used a robber's knife to drive out another robber.

LET THE Party send its special agents to arrest me! Let them expel me from the Party! But if I am killed, there are still thousands and tens of thousands of others who won't let the robber live in peace.

DOCUMENT 14

WANG FANXI
Seven Theses on Socialism and Democracy

In an article written in Macao in 1957 the Trotskyist Wang Fanxi (Wang Fan-hsi, born 1907) recalled positions that he had advanced between 1936 and 1940 in exchanges with Chen Duxiu, founder of the Chinese Communist Party and also of its Trotskyist offshoot. In the mid- to late 1930s the Moscow show-trials and Stalin's alliance with Hitler caused Chen to conclude that Lenin's denial of the value of democracy was in part responsible for Stalin's crimes and that dictator-ship of any sort, revolutionary or counterrevolutionary, is incompatible with de-mocracy. Whereas for Lenin proletarian dictatorship was simultaneously—at least for the workers—the most extensive form of democracy, Chen no longer bothered to distinguish the various democratic rights from democracy as the bourgeois governing form. Wang and other Trotskyists believed that democracy was not abstract but bounded by class and time, but for Chen after 1938 it was a transcendental concept embodied in universal institutions. Even so, Wang did not dismiss from hand Chen's formulations, but strove to develop along Marxist lines what he found in them to be perceptive and valuable. In the course of their ex-change, Chen and Wang raised—decades in advance of the mainstream of Com-munist dissent—issues that bear directly on the vexed relationship between social-ism and democratic freedoms. (For Wang Fanxi, see also Documents 20 and 58.)

1. Under present historical conditions if the proletariat through its po-litical party aims to overthrow the political and economic rule of the

bourgeoisie, it must carry out a violent revolution and set up a dictator-ship to expropriate the expropriators. So in nine cases out of ten it is bound to destroy the bourgeoisie's traditional means of rule—the parlia-mentary system. To complete such a transformation "peacefully," through parliament, is practically if not absolutely impossible.

2. A proletarian dictatorship set up in such a way neither must nor should destroy the various democratic rights—including habeus corpus; freedom of speech, the press, assembly, and association; the right to strike; etc.—already won by the people under the bourgeois democratic system.

3. The organs of the dictatorship elected by the entire toiling people should be under the thorough-going supervision of the electors and re-callable by them at all times; and the power of the dictatorship should not be concentrated in one body but should be spread across several struc-tures so that there is a system of checks and balances to prevent the emer-gence of an autocracy or monocracy.

4. Opposition parties should be allowed to exist under the dictatorship as long as they support the revolution. Whether or not they meet this condition should be decided by the workers and peasants in free ballot.

5. Opposition factions must be tolerated within the party of the prole-tariat. Under no circumstances must organizational sanctions, secret ser-vice measures, or incriminatory sanctions be used to deal with dissidents; under no circumstances must thought be made a crime.

6. Under no circumstances must proletarian dictatorship become the dictatorship of a single party. Workers' parties organized by part of the working class and the intelligentsia must under no circumstances replace the political power democratically elected by the toilers as a whole. There must be an end to the present system in the Communist countries, where government is a facade behind which secretaries of the Party branches assume direct command. The ruling party's strategic policies must first be discussed and approved by an empowered parliament (or soviet) that in-cludes opposition parties and factions, and only then should they be im-plemented by government; and their implementation must continue to be supervised by parliament.

7. Finally, . . . since political democracy is actually a reflection of eco-nomic democracy and no political democracy is possible under a system of absolutely centralized economic control, . . . to create the material base for socialist democracy a system of divided power and self-management within the overall planned economy is essential.

All these points are not in themselves enough to save a revolutionary power from bureaucratic degeneration; but since they are not plucked from the void but rooted in bloody experience, they should—if formulated with sufficient clarity—(*a*) help workers and peasants in countries that have had revolutions to win their antibureaucratic struggle when the conditions for the democratization of the dictatorial state have further ripened; and (*b*) enable new revolutionary states from the very outset to avoid bureaucratic poisoning.

CHAPTER THREE

CULTURAL REVOLUTION, 1966–1976

DOCUMENT 15

Nie Yuanzi
What Have Song Shuo, Lu Ping, and Peng Peiyun Done in the Cultural Revolution?

China under communist rule did not develop a tradition of *samizdat* literature comparable to that of the Soviet Union; in the Cultural Revolution, both opponents and supporters of orthodoxy generally used big-character posters to promulgate their views; after 1969 such posters were often used by dissidents. The following poster by a philosophy teacher at Beijing University was one of the most fateful in the history of contemporary China: it marked the start of the Cultural Revolution. After the disaster of the Great Leap Forward, Mao Zedong and cadres identified as his supporters tended to be sidelined from positions of power in ministries and other institutions. In Beijing University, Lu Ping was appointed president and secretary of the university Party committee in 1959. He concentrated on raising professional and academic standards, reduced the numbers of worker and peasant undergraduates in favor of a better-educated intake, and was generally identified with the "rightist" clique around Liu Shaoqi and Deng Xiaoping. Among staff severely criticized by Lu was a woman instructor in the Department of Philosophy, Nie Yuanzi, who was a "leftist." In May 1966, Nie learned that the group around Mao Zedong, Kang Sheng (the chief of the security services), and Jiang Qing (Mao's wife) had maneuvered themselves into a strong position in the Party power struggle. On May 25 Nie put up a wall poster denouncing the top leadership of the university. It is not known to what extent she did so on her own initiative, as an act of rebellion for a political cause she believed in, and to what extent she was a pawn in Mao's game. The initial reaction on campus to the poster was stupefaction and total silence. It was the biggest, perhaps the only, public challenge to senior Party bureaucrats since 1949 (Peng Peiyun and Song Shuo were also very important Party members and university administrators). It seemed impossible that Nie could survive, and for a week she was attacked by her colleagues. Suddenly, on June 1, 1966, Mao Zedong and

Kang Sheng personally intervened in the situation, insisting that the wall poster be broadcast and published. It appeared in the official organ *Renmin ribao* (People's Daily) on June 2. After students and staff sided with Nie, there were strong protests against Lu Ping, other university administrators, and their perceived backers in the bureaucracy. The movement at Beijing University spilled over into a movement to support Mao against his rivals, and the Cultural Revolution had begun. Nie soon became a vice chairperson of the Beijing Municipal Party Committee, and in 1969 an alternate member of the Central Committee of the CCP.[1]

AT PRESENT, the people of the whole nation, in a soaring revolutionary spirit which manifests their boundless love for the Party and Chairman Mao and their inveterate hatred for the sinister anti-Party, antisocialist gang, are making a vigorous and great cultural revolution; they are struggling to thoroughly smash the attacks of the reactionary sinister gang, in defense of the Party's Central Committee and Chairman Mao. But here in Beijing University the masses are being kept immobilized, the atmosphere is one of indifference and deadness, whereas the strong revolutionary desire of the vast number of the faculty members and students has been suppressed. What is the matter? What is the reason? There is something fishy going on. Let us take a look at what has happened very recently!

It took place after the publication on May 8 of the articles by He Ming and Gao Ju and the upsurge in the nationwide struggle to denounce the "Three-Family Village." On May 14, Lu Ping [President of Beijing University and Secretary of its Party Committee] hastily transmitted the "directive" issued by Song Shuo [deputy head of the department in charge of university affairs under the Beijing Municipal Party Committee] at an emergency meeting of the department. Song Shuo said that at present the movement

> badly needs a strengthened leadership and the Party organizations in the colleges are required to strengthen the leadership and stand fast at the posts. . . . When the masses arise they need to be led onto the correct path. . . . This ideological struggle is a serious class struggle, and the anti-Party antisocialist remarks have to be completely repudiated theoretically. Persist in reasoning, use whatever method which proves to be adaptable to repudiating them, and provide good leadership in the study of documents, the holding of small group meetings, and the writing of small-character posters and critical essays. In short, this serious struggle must be conducted in a very careful and penetrating manner. Big meetings can in no way serve to completely discredit the anti-Party, antisocialist remarks and theoretically repudiate them. . . . In case the angry masses demand that a

big meeting be held , do not suppress them but guide them to hold
small group meetings, study documents and write small-character
posters.

Lu Ping and Peng Peiyun [a cadre in the department in charge of university affairs under the Beijing Municipal Party Committee and Deputy
Secretary of the Beijing University Party Committee] conducted the movement in Beijing University entirely in the same vein. They said,

> The situation in the cultural revolution in our university is excellent,
> . . . . more than 100 articles had been written before May 8, the
> movement is healthy. . . . as the movement deepens, active guidance
> must be given. . . . Right now, leadership is urgently needed to guide
> the movement towards a correct orientation in its development. . . .
> Only by energetically strengthening the leadership can [the move-
> ment] be led to its normal development. . . . It is not suitable for
> Beijing University to stick up big-character posters. . . . Big-character
> posters must not be encouraged; if the masses want to post them,
> actively guide them away.

Is this the line for the cultural revolution laid down by the Party's Central
Committee and Chairman Mao? No, absolutely not! It is an out-and-out
revisionist line that runs counter to the Party's Central Committee and to
Mao Zedong's thought.

"This is an ideological struggle." "The anti-Party, antisocialist remarks have to be completely repudiated theoretically." "Persist in rea-
soning." This struggle "must be conducted in a very careful manner."
What does all this mean? Can it be considered a theoretical problem? Is
it all just remarks? Whither do you want to "guide" the life-and-death
political struggle we are waging to counterattack the sinister anti-Party,
antisocialist gang? Isn't it one of the main tactics of Deng Tuo and his
instigators in resisting the cultural revolution to divert this serious political struggle to "purely academic" discussions? Why are you still doing
things this way up to this moment? What kind of people are you actually?

"The masses, when they arise, need to be led onto the correct path."
"Guide the movement towards a correct orientation in its development."
"Only by energetically assuming the leadership can [the movement] be
led to its normal development." "What is meant by "correct path"? What
is meant by "correct orientation"? What is meant by "normal development"? You have "guided" the great political class struggle into a "purely
theoretical" and "purely academic" trap. Not long ago, was it not you
who personally "guided" the comrades of the law faculty to consult fifteen hundred volumes of books and material running to fourteen million

characters to study the question concerning the "reversal of wrong verdicts" by Hai Rui? Was it not you who have given great publicity to this
as "correct orientation and the right method," asking everybody to learn
from this "good experience"? In actual fact, this is "good experience"
which has all been created by you and Deng Tuo and his sinister gang:
and this is also the very essence of your talk that "the movement is
healthy." The Party's Central Committee and Chairman Mao have long
since shown us the correct path for the cultural revolution and its correct
orientation. You say nothing about them and work out your own so-
called "correct path" and "correct orientation" in the hope of drawing
the revolutionary mass movement into your revisionist orbit. Frankly
speaking, this is a vain hope!

"Big meetings can in no way serve to theoretically repudiate them." "It
is not suitable for Beida to stick up big-character posters," we "must
guide them to hold small group meetings and write small-character posters." Why are you so afraid of big-character posters and the holding of
big denunciation meetings? To counterattack the sinister gang which has
frantically attacked the Party, socialism, and Mao Zedong's thought is a
life-and-death class struggle. The revolutionary people must be fully
aroused to vigorously and angrily denounce them, and to hold big meetings and put up big-character posters, is one of the best ways for the
masses to do battle. By "guiding" the masses not to hold big meetings, not
to put up big-character posters, and by creating all kinds of taboos, aren't
you suppressing the masses' revolution, not allowing them to make revolution, and opposing their revolution? We will never permit you to do
this!

You shout about having to "strengthen the leadership and stand fast at
the posts." This only exposes who you really are. At a time when the
revolutionary masses are vigorously rising up, in response to the call of
the Party's Central Committee and Chairman Mao, to firmly counterattack the anti-Party, antisocialist sinister gang, you shout, "strengthen the
leadership and stand fast at the posts." Isn't it clear what "posts" you
want to hold fast, and for whom, and what kind of people you are and
what despicable tricks you are up to? Right up to today you are still
desperately resisting. You still want to "stand fast" at your "posts" so as
to sabotage the cultural revolution. We must tell you, a mantis cannot
stop the wheel of a cart and mayflies cannot topple a giant tree. You are
simply daydreaming!

All revolutionary intellectuals, now is the time to go into battle! Let us
unite, holding high the great red banner of Mao Zedong's thought, unite
round the Party's Central Committee and Chairman Mao and break
down all the various controls and plots of the revisionists; resolutely,

thoroughly, totally and completely wipe out all ghosts and monsters and all Khrushchevian counterrevolutionary revisionists, and carry the socialist revolution through to the end.

Defend the Party's Central Committee!
Defend Mao Zedong's thought!
Defend the dictatorship of the proletariat!

Beijing University, Department of Philosophy
Nie Yuanzi, Song Yixiu, Xia Jianzhi,
Yang Keming, Zhao Zhengyi,
Gao Yunpeng, Li Xingchen
May 25, 1966

DOCUMENT 16

Red Guard Statements, 1966–1967

Much of the politics of the Cultural Revolution can only be understood in terms of factional intrigue, behind-the-scenes manipulation, and personal vendettas. However, the chaos, and the statements by Mao himself that "to rebel is justified," allowed an unprecedented freedom of expression to groups of young people. Many of them were undoubtedly expressing heartfelt grievances and sincere appeals for political change rather than acting as mouthpieces for politicians. Some of their ideas may seem rather attractive: opposing corruption, special privileges, bureaucratic arbitrariness, and capitalism. They also demonstrate an appalling naiveté, xenophobia, and resentment: attacks on styles of haircuts, secondhand book stalls, street names, and so on. Many of the authors were in their teens or early twenties. "Declaring War on the Old World" and "A Big Disturbance Must be Made at Qinghua University" are among the earliest Red Guard statements from Beijing. Obviously to suit the interests of certain politicians, they were soon reprinted in *Renmin ribao* (People's Daily) on August 26, 1966. Only the next day a similar piece appeared in Guangzhou, in *Yangcheng wanbao* (Guangzhou Evening News).

"On Collective Boarding Schools for Children of Cadres" is taken from the Beijing Red Guard paper *Spring Thunder* of April 13, 1967. It is a vivid example of Red Guard journalism, somewhat more sophisticated than the earlier statements and with a specific target: the specially privileged schools that had been established for the children of the elite. The writers also name the three politicians—Liu Shaoqi, Deng Xiaoping, and Lu Dingyi—who were branded as the leading "capitalist-roaders" by Mao and his supporters. It is interesting that it was in fact the children of cadres, most of whom had been through the elite school system denounced here, who were major targets of the 1989 protests, hated for their unscrupulous abuse of power: as the document says, they became in effect a new lineage. All four documents provide fine examples of the revolutionary rhetoric of the time.

Declaring War on the Old World
Red Guards of Beijing No. 2 Middle School

WE ARE critics of the old world. We want to criticize and smash all old ideas, old culture, old customs, and old habits. We make no exception for any barber shops, dress shops, studios, old book stalls, etc. that serve the bourgeoisie. We want to rebel against the old world!

Seventeen years have lapsed since our country was liberated. But the old ideas, old culture, old customs, and old habits left behind by the old society still exist. The overthrown reactionary classes are not reconciled to their extinction. They always try stubbornly to show themselves and seize from us the ideological front, in an attempt to use old ideas, old culture, old customs, and old habits of the exploiting masses, conquer the people ideologically, and achieve the aim of reinstating themselves. Chairman Mao has said: "In order to overthrow a political power, it is always first necessary to form a public opinion and to carry out ideological work. The revolutionary class acts in this way, and so does the counterrevolutionary class." Facts prove that Chairman Mao's dictum is wise, great, and correct.

The bourgeois lords understand that, in order to reinstate themselves, they must make a breach in their everyday life and cause a deluge of capitalism. In order to please these bourgeois lords and satisfy their extravagant hopes, the employees of barbershops, dress shops, studios, and old book stalls, . . . some of those in power and the so-called technical authorities who take the capitalist road have been racking their brains to serve the bourgeois lords and give them every possible convenience. You have put money in command and in the topmost position! You are guilty before the people!

First, we want to lodge the strongest protest against you—barbershops, dress shops, studios, and old book stalls that serve the bourgeoisie . . . and those in power and the so-called technical authorities who want to take the capitalist road!

In order to stage a capitalist comeback, you have cut hair styles as "airplane style," "seamless style for youths," "spiral pagoda style," and "wavy style for youths." You have also sprayed perfume on their hair and dressed it with pomade, making the hooligans act frivolously and feel elated.

To restore capitalism, you have made a great number of Hong Kong–style clothes and skirts. Those "cowboy trousers" and "cowboy jackets," together with all sorts of nauseous Hong Kong–style clothes and skirts of different colors and fashions make the hooligans feel delirious and act ridiculously.

In order to restore capitalism, you have taken a great deal of vulgar photographs, exalting the young film stars of the bourgeoisie to the skies and making young people insane and infatuated. The photographs you have taken are disgusting, hateful, and annoying!

In order to restore capitalism, you have sold a great deal of vulgar, obscene adventure novels, with ancient and modern Chinese and foreign backgrounds so as to satisfy the scum of society. A large number of bourgeois spirits have been released from your place to poison the youths and teenagers and nourish the buds of their crimes.

There are also the shops. You stock them with great quantities of perfume, face cream, lipstick, necklaces, and other luxuries, together with Hong Kong–style clothes and dresses and rocket-style shoes. For whom have you got these things ready? Do the workers, peasants, and soldiers really need perfumes and pointed shoes?

You dislike from the depth of your hearts the innocent, honest, natural beauty of the broad masses of worker, peasants, and soldiers. The object of your service are the heavily made-up and gaudily dressed lords and ladies. Your souls are filthy and reactionary. You say superficially that you also serve the workers, peasants, and soldiers, but in fact you serve some other people. Now is the time for you to remold yourselves thoroughly!

Have you ever thought of this? If you go on acting in this way, in a few years or a few decades to come, capitalism will be restored in China and the whole of China will change color.

At present, the mighty torrents of the great cultural revolution are pounding all fronts occupied by the bourgeois lords. It is impossible to hold the hotbeds of the bourgeoisie any longer! In the past seventeen years after the liberation, the former Beijing Municipal Committee did not pay any attention to these matters. It heard and saw them, but ignored them. It indulged these hooligans and disregarded their styles and behavior. It embarked on the road of revisionism and capitalism. It traveled on a road different from ours. Now, we have stood up as masters of the house. With the Party Central Committee and Chairman Mao backing us up, we want to look into these matters and look into them thoroughly, though they were neglected before. We want to destroy the hotbeds and uproot the seedlings of revisionism and capitalism thoroughly and rebel against these old ideas, culture, customs, and habits.

Chairman Mao has said: "*In the last analysis, all the truths of Marxism can be summed up in one sentence: 'To rebel is justified.' It was always said in the past several thousand years: 'It is justified to suppress and to exploit, but unjustifiable to rebel.' Since the emergence of Marxism, the decision of this old case has been reversed—this is a big merit. This truth has been obtained by the proletariat through struggle and summed up by Marxism. According to this truth, we can give resistance, make struggle, and conduct socialism."* We want to rebel against the old world. It is justifiable for us to make rebellion!

Now we can no longer allow the existence of a situation in which "airline-style hair," "cowboy trousers," obscene photographs, and vulgar books rule our barbershops, dress shops, studios, and old book stalls. We have this proposal to make to the revolutionary employees in the haircutting, tailoring, and photographic trades: Do not dress hair in the Hong Kong style! Do not make any clothes and skirts of the Hong Kong style! Do not take any vulgar photographs! Do not sell any obscene books!

We want to get rid of the Hong Kong–style clothes and skirts, eliminate the peculiar hairstyles, and burn all obscene books and vulgar photographs in the shortest possible period of time. "Cowboy trousers" can be cut into shorts, and the leggings thus cut away can be used to mend worn-out clothes. "Rocket-shoes" can be converted into sandals. High-heel shoes can be changed into practical low-sole shoes. Bad books and photographs can be discarded as refuse.

We have this appeal to make to the Red Guards throughout Beijing and to all revolutionary comrades: *This struggle is a big development that affects the future of China and the World revolution. These problems must not be belittled. These places are exactly where doors are open to bourgeois restoration. Is not the Soviet Union an excellent example? Therefore, we must block all channels leading to capitalism, and unsparingly smash all hotbeds where revisionism is bred.*

We also have this appeal to make to the proletarian revolutionaries all over China:

Open fire on all remnant old ideas, culture, customs, and habits.
Long live the spirit of revolutionary rebellion!
Long live the great proletarian cultural revolution!
Long live the Chinese Communist Party!
Long live Chairman Mao! Long, long life to Chairman Mao!
Long live the great ever-victorious thought of Mao Zedong!

A Big Disturbance Must Be Made at Qinghua University
The Red Guards, Department of Automation, Qinghua University

"THERE is now too much disturbance at Qinghua University." No! We say that there is not enough "disturbance." Many old influences and old stereotypes have been preventing us from making disturbances. The emergence of the Red Guards has come under fierce attack; the holding of revolutionary meetings has been condemned; even some people who came out to fight the black gangs have been accused of creating splits. This is really absurd!

There are too many stereotypes at the old Qinghua University. They are disgusting! It is necessary to make a big disturbance in order to defeat the black gangs and rightist elements and to smash the old stereotypes, ideas, influences, and habits.

"You fear that there is no disturbance in this world!" Yes! We fear that there is no disturbance at the old Qinghua. Ruled for more than ten years by a black gang, the old Qinghua has been deeply poisoned and has suffered heavily. It is like a stagnant pool of water. How can it be stirred if no vigorous effort is exerted? How can a new Qinghua be created if a big disturbance is not made?"

Those people who fear disturbances and criticize new initiatives are representatives of the old habits and influences of the bourgeoisie. Wake up quickly! You must not unconsciously become royalists with old habits and influences again!

"We cannot tolerate anarchism if leadership is to be strengthened." Yes! We want to strengthen leadership. But, to do so, we are not going to reinforce the stereotypes or to tie the hands of the masses, but to encourage and call for the birth of new things in accordance with the greatest interests of the broad masses, to open a new road for these things, and defend the orientation of the great proletarian cultural revolution in accordance with the spirit of "struggle, criticism, and correction" of the Party Central Committee!

We are absolutely not anarchists. We only oppose the old order and want to build a new one. In this course of destroying the old and establishing the new, the state of "anarchy" will inevitably exist for a period of time.

"You are causing splits. You must pay attention to strengthening unity." If anybody who puts forth his political viewpoint is said to cause splits, then we certainly are splitters. We want to follow persistently the main orientation of "struggle, criticism, and correction" and oppose the delay in fighting the black gangs. We must study the "Sixteen Points" in the course of the struggle for adhering to the orientation of "struggle, criticism, and correction." We must uphold unity in the course of our common struggle against the enemies. This is a problem of principle, in which we must persist without fail.

We oppose unprincipled unity. Those people who only talk about unity but pay no attention to struggle and classes are either fools or cowards who fear disturbances and fear the mass movement.

"You only lead a small group of people to advance blindly. You are alienated from the masses." Formerly, Marx and Engels were alone and yet they dared put forth the *Manifesto of the Communist Party*. Did the revolutionary forerunners not make revolution by initiating it among a small number of people? Is it really a proper attitude toward new things to reproach without reason the small number of people who are willing to make revolution and who explain their viewpoints?

We must know that the truth may sometimes be in the hands of a small number of people. But, this minority will eventually become the majority. It is necessary to make a big disturbance at Qinghua University at present. In the midst of this disturbance, our comrades must keep their heads clear:

Never forget the class struggle. Never forget the dictatorship of the proletariat. Never forget to bring politics to the fore. Never forget to hold aloft the great red banner of the thought of Mao Zedong!

Vigorously and Speedily Eradicate Bizarre Bourgeois Hairstyles: Major proposals put forward by revolutionary workers of the hairdressing trade in Guangzhou

HOLDING high the great red banner of the thought of Mao Zedong and displaying vigorous revolutionary spirit, young revolutionary fighters in Guangzhou have been busy putting up revolutionary posters in big characters along the streets to attack the old ideas, culture, customs, and habits of all exploiting classes—in a determined effort to build Guangzhou into a city extraordinarily proletarian and extraordinarily revolutionary in character.

This revolutionary rebel spirit displayed by these young fighters is indeed splendid, for it has greatly boosted the morale of revolutionary people and provided us with profound inspiration and enlightenment. We want to learn from these young fighters and their revolutionary rebel spirit by launching a proletarian revolutionary rebellion in the hairdressing trade of the city. The following proposals are put forward by us before all revolutionary workers of the hairdressing trade in Guangzhou:

1. All revolutionary workers of the hairdressing trade should ardently and resolutely support the revolutionary actions of young revolutionary fighters and the revolutionary masses. We should warmly welcome their criticisms and ardently support big-character posters that speak out against us. We should provide young revolutionary fighters and the revolutionary masses beforehand with necessary facilities such as tables, benches, brush pens, ink, paper, and paste so they can write big-character posters and paste them up on the walls.

2. All revolutionary workers of the hairdressing trade should promptly take action and make revolution alongside young revolutionary fighters and the revolutionary masses in a highly militant

spirit. They should tidy things up and make corrections where necessary. They should demolish all old ideas, culture, customs, and habits and establish new ideas of culture and customs. But with respect to new proletarian hairdos, they should energetically and promptly promote them.

3. All revolutionary workers of the hairdressing trade should take prompt action by smashing all shop signs tinged with feudal, capitalist, and revisionist ideas. They should replace old signs with new ones fraught with revolutionary significance so our shops will forever shine with revolutionary brilliance!

4. All revolutionary workers of hairdressing salons should first and foremost make self-revolution in a determined manner, whether concerning what they have in mind, what they wear, and their own hairstyles. They should conform to Mao Zedong's ideas. They should forego the "cowboy" hairstyle and shed their "cowboy" outfit. They should uphold revolutionary ideas, go in for revolutionary hairstyles, and put on revolutionary clothes.

5. We refuse to serve those customers who insist on "cowboy" or "bun-like" hairstyles! We boycott all customers who are dressed like "cowboys" or "cowgirls"!

6. We welcome customers who want to change their bizarre hairdos. We may even attend to them on a priority basis so that their bizarre hairstyles and newfangled ideas may be changed as soon as possible!

7. We should give prominence to politics and put the thought of Mao Zedong in the lead. We should place the great red banner of the thought of Mao Zedong in the show windows of our shops, in this way turning them into a front for propagating Mao Zedong's ideas.

8. We should seriously and creatively learn and apply Chairman Mao's writings, remold our thought, and transform ourselves into both hairdressing personnel and propagandists for spreading Mao Zedong's ideas.

9. We should vehemently open fire on all outmoded practices of commercial enterprises and all things that do not conform to the superstructure of the socialist economic base.

10. We should seriously learn, master, and apply the 16 points (of the CCP Central Committee decision) and use these to unify our understanding and action—in this way carrying through the great proletarian cultural revolution to the end.

Cheng Yulian, barber, Nan Yi Hairdressing Salon,
Chen Shu, barber, Mu Fan Hairdressing Salon, and
Huang Songchun, barber, Guo Jian Hairdressing Salon

On Collective Boarding Schools for Children of Cadres

"The spring thunder resounds through the skies,—
the east wind sweeps across the great earth. . . ."

THE torrent of the Great Proletarian Cultural Revolution is attacking all the superstructures which are not adaptable to the foundation of our socialist economy.

All the old educational systems are in a state of great confusion and collapse.

Doomsday has come for the bourgeois educational line which is represented by Liu Shaoqi, Deng Xiaoping, and Lu Dingyi!

The war drum is beaten aloud for thoroughly liquidating and smashing to pieces the revisionist system of collective boarding schools for children of cadres!

The collective boarding schools for children of cadres were first introduced in the warring years before the Liberation. They had their glorious history in the past.

In those years of civil war, the broad masses of fighters and cadres were risking their lives to fight for the liberation of the whole nation all over the country. Furthermore, they were paid in kind. So that their children could be looked after and educated, it was necessary to establish a number of collective boarding schools for the children of cadres. At that time, these schools were situated in mountain villages and the students lived through hardships along with the broad masses of the local people. They had developed our glorious tradition of fighting amid great hardships and trained themselves to be successor to our revolutionary cause.

In the period immediately after the liberation of the whole country, the cadres were frequently transferred, and the system of paying cadres in kind was not entirely altered: it was permissible to continue for a certain period these collective boarding schools for the children of cadres. However, under the domination of a handful of persons in the Party in authority taking the capitalist road, the nature of these schools has gradually changed. Schools have undertaken large-scale construction projects, built splendid dormitories, and allowed the children of cadres to live a very comfortable life in their "paradise of another world." They have been cut off completely from their contact with the masses of workers and peasants. The glorious tradition of fighting among hardships has been given up. This handful of bad eggs has openly opposed the educational policy of Chairman Mao, energetically peddled the black goods of revisionist education, and led these collective boarding schools for children of cadres gradually onto the road of "schools for aristocratic children" of the British and Soviet types.

The CCP Central Committee and Chairman Mao very quickly realized the seriousness of the problem concerning the collective boarding schools for children of the cadres, and have issued many orders and instructions to prevent these schools from enjoying any special privileges. Furthermore, there is no need for these schools to continue to exist. Following the development of our economic and cultural construction, a huge network of schools which will meet the educational requirements of the children of cadres already covers the whole country. The cadres of all levels have also generally carried on their work steadily. Particularly since July 1955, they have all been paid wages. It is, therefore, unreasonable for the state to continue to appropriate large sums of money to run schools for children of the cadres.

Consequently, in 1955 the Party Central Committee issued instructions to abolish gradually the schools for children of cadres. However, under the domination of a handful of persons in the Party in authority taking the capitalist road, not only were the collective boarding schools for children of cadres not abolished, their number has rapidly increased. According to statistics, at present two-thirds of the thirty-odd collective boarding schools for children of cadres in Beijing were established after 1955.

In this way, schools which fostered revolutionary successors in former years have gradually transformed themselves into hotbeds for nurturing the seeds of revisionism. The big families of revolution which were full of revolutionary vitality in former years have gradually taken black positions against Mao Zedong's thought. Those collective boarding schools for children of cadres which were set up after 1955 have, from the first day of their founding, slid toward the abyss of "peaceful evolution."

MANY of our cadres are able to follow the teachings of Chairman Mao, make strict demands on themselves, and educate their own children with Mao Zedong's thought. Among them, some have already seen the dangers of the collective boarding schools for children of the cadres and have never allowed their children to enter these schools. Though a number of cadres wanted to educate their children, they did not see clearly the nature of these schools and blindly sent their children to them. Consequently, they have been greatly disappointed.

Besides, we also have to see that during the whole period of socialism, classes and class struggles will exist for a long time. The exploiting class will try by any and every means to spread through various channels of the society the poisons of capitalism, feudalism, and revisionism in order to corrode our revolutionary rank and file. Chairman Mao has said: "It is possible that there are a number of Communists who have never been conquered by enemies holding guns and are worthy of the name hero before these enemies. However, they cannot withstand the attacks of people using sugar-coated bullets. They will be defeated by the sugar-coated bullets." Truly, there are some cadres who have, for a long time and in peaceful circumstances, lived in special political and economic positions. They have relaxed their vigilance and allowed the bourgeois ideology and the force of habit in society to corrode their own souls in different degrees. They have not treated their own children and the children of the broad workers and peasants on an equal basis, but have considered that theirs should be higher than others and should enjoy special privileges. They refuse to allow their own children to develop the glorious tradition of the years of fighting in making contact with the masses and fighting amid hardships, and to take the road of becoming one with the workers and peasants. They hope that their children will grow up in comfortable circumstances and enjoy life in hothouses. Therefore, when the Party persons in authority taking the capitalist road raised the signboard of "looking after the welfare of the cadres" and started to set up collective boarding schools for the children of cadres so that these students would be entitled to special treatment in politics and living, they came forward quickly and sent their children to these schools.

The persons in the Party in authority taking the capitalist road have intentionally taken advantage of the bourgeois ideology in the minds of the cadres; however, the latter have never expected that behind the signboard of "looking after the welfare of the cadres," there are rolling dark clouds showing a big black flag of a scheme to transform the world!

In foreign countries, the imperialist prophets have, on the basis of changes taking place in the Soviet Union, also pinned their hopes for peaceful evolution on the third and fourth generations of the Party in China, and on such a revisionist educational system as ours, which fosters the privileged strata.

In short, the existence and development of the collective boarding schools for children of the cadres meets the requirements of the bourgeoisie in the country represented by Liu Shaoqi and Deng Xiaoping in carrying out the restoration of capitalism in China, and meets the requirements of the imperialists and revisionists in foreign countries to engineer a "peaceful evolution" in our country.

THE collective boarding schools for children of cadres have been deeply influenced by the old educational systems and have become a compound of feudal, bourgeois, and revisionist educational systems.

Through this educational system runs a black line which is a bourgeois educational line represented by Liu Shaoqi, Deng Xiaoping, and Lu Dingyi.

The key idea which this black line of education has spread among the collective boarding schools for children of cadres is special privileges, and more special privileges!

In other words, they are promoting special privileges and benefits, infusing into the students the thought of special privileges, and fostering privileged strata!

Just to promote special privileges and benefits in the work of recruiting students, these schools have openly opposed Chairman Mao's teachings to turn one's face toward the workers and peasants and "to give priority to the workers and peasants and their children in receiving education." They have introduced a strict system of preference so that not only have the children of the broad workers and peasants been refused admission, but the decision whether or not the children of cadres may enter these collective boarding schools for children of cadres is made on the basis of the official ranks of their parents.

Just to foster specially privileged strata the schools have openly opposed and revised Chairman Mao's educational policy by refusing to foster laboring people with socialist consciousness and culture. Instead, they have openly declared themselves for fostering spiritual aristocrats who are sitting tight over the laboring people and "keeping their four limbs idle and making no distinction among the five kinds of grain." They even told the students: "In future you should become generals, ministers, and prime ministers. You are the hard-core of the successors and should not go around selling soy and vinegar."

Just to infuse the thought of special privileges, in the area of political thought these schools have openly opposed Chairman Mao's theory on class and class struggle; instead of promoting the ideological revolutionization of the young people, they have spread the absurd idea of being "born Red," rejected the necessity of ideological reform among the children of the cadres, and infused into them the reactionary feudal "theory of lineage" by saying that "the children of the cadres are the successors by lineage to our proletarian revolutionary cause."

Just to ensure the birth of privileged strata, schools of this category have, in the field of education, openly opposed letting politics take command, refused to study Chairman Mao's works hard and, instead, given priority to intellectual education, let academic achievements take command, and frantically tried to increase the number of graduates who could pass the entrance examination to higher institutes of education with a view to enabling their students to climb up to the position of privileged strata through the channel of continuously attending schools of a higher grade. In the last ten years and more, only a very few graduates from schools of this category have gone to mountainous and rural areas to undertake common physical labor.

Just to promote special privileges and benefits, in the matter of living conditions these schools have openly opposed Chairman Mao's teachings on guarding against special privileges and running all enterprises with diligence and frugality. They have built gorgeous premises and made living very comfortable and plentiful. They have asked their teachers to act as the "mothers" of the students by busily engaging in looking after the students' personal clothing, food, and lodging. They have told the students to pay attention to their life by taking care "not to be drowned when swimming, not to be shot during target practice, not to crash to death when practicing gliding, and not to fall to death while mountain climbing."

From all the above-mentioned facts, we can see that the collective boarding schools for children of cadres are the compound of feudal, bourgeois, and revisionist educational systems, because of their special privileges, because they are the hotbed for breeding the seeds of revisionism and the tools of Party persons in authority taking the capitalist road represented by Liu Shaoqi and Deng Xiaoping, who are trying hopelessly to restore capitalism in China.

The moment has come to thoroughly liquidate and smash into pieces the collective boarding schools for children of cadres.

Chairman Mao has said: "To ensure that our Party and nation will not change their colors, we not only need our correct lines and policies but also have to foster and train thousands upon thousands of successors to our proletarian revolutionary cause." The collective boarding schools for children of cadres foster only privileged strata and are creating conditions for a "peaceful evolution" toward capitalism. To foster successors to our proletarian revolutionary cause, we must cherish the spirit of "seizing the day, seizing the hour" and topple to the ground this hotbed for breeding the seeds of revisionism! This has a bearing upon the destiny of Party and our nation, and upon the very important problem of the strategic significance of safeguarding our proletarian state by forever maintaining its colors.

The "16 Points" pointed out: "One of the exceedingly important tasks of the current proletarian Cultural Revolution is to reform the old educational system and reform the old policies and methods of teaching." The revisionist collective boarding schools for children of cadres constitute a stubborn bulwark of the worst crimes under the old educational system. We should take it as an opening for a breakthrough in our general offensive against the whole front of old education, concentrate our firing power, and open fire at the same time! Amid the rumbles of gunfire, the countless crimes of the old educational system will be exposed in the broad daylight! Amid the rumbles of gunfire, the poisons spread by the germs of the old educational system will be thoroughly washed away!

"With power and to spare we must pursue the tottering foe." Smashing into pieces the collective boarding schools for children of cadres is only the beginning of the struggle and not its end. We have to wipe out all the social bases and sources of thinking which generate revisionism by carrying out long-term hard struggles.

Comrades of the revolutionary teachers and students!

The moment for burying the bourgeois educational line represented by Liu Shaoqi, Deng Xiaoping, and Lu Dingyi has come!

Let us give play to our proletarian revolutionary rebel spirit and throw the hotbed breeding the seeds of revisionism into the garbage bin of history!

Let us dash out from the "paradise of another world," walk with chin up and with big strides onto the road of making an alliance with the workers and peasants, steel ourselves and grow up in the actual struggles of the three great revolutionary movements!

"People are talking about the violent changes in nature." Let us look forward to the future. Our educational position must be a new type, of the great school of Mao Zedong's thought, and a good classroom for training successors to our proletarian revolutionary cause.

Amid the clarion songs of triumph, the great red banner of Mao Zedong's thought will forever flutter high on the position of education!

The Jinggangshan Fighting Corps of Beijing
Normal University for Smashing the Collective
Boarding Schools for Children of Cadres, and
the Liaison Center for Smashing the Collective
Boarding Schools for Children of Cadres

DOCUMENT 17

"Revolutionary" Power-holders

One feature of the Cultural Revolution period was that everyone, from the top leadership to schoolchildren, adopted similar vocabulary, symbolism, and rhetoric in their writing and speeches. It is often almost impossible to distinguish between "rebels" of the left or ultra-left, idealist youngsters, careerist bureaucrats, and cynical manipulators at the top of the Party. The two items here were published in English in *Peking Review*, which suggests that they were perceived as promoting the interests of the dominant faction at the Party center. Mao's document is of historic significance: it launched the high-tide of the Cultural Revolution, which had been announced by his support for Nie Yuanzi's campaign in Beijing University. At first sight it represents a kind of dissent against the then Party leadership, because Mao seemed to have lost his power-base, and it set a rhetorical style that was universally adopted. But of course Mao did not make the slightest effort to implement democracy or even to eliminate corruption once he regained power. The document from Guizhou is apparently "revolutionary" but is most likely merely a smoke screen created by one clique of the bureaucracy for the purposes of factional intrigue.

BOMBARD THE HEADQUARTERS
My Big-Character Poster
August 5, 1966

MAO ZEDONG

China's first Marxist-Leninist big-character poster [a reference to the poster by Nie Yuanzi] and Commentator's article on it in *Renmin ribao* are indeed superbly written! Comrades, please read them again. But in the last fifty days or so some leading comrades from the central down to the local levels have acted in a diametrically opposite way. Adopting the reactionary stand of the bourgeoisie, they have enforced a bourgeois dictatorship and struck down the surging movement of the great cultural revolution of the proletariat. They have stood facts on their head and juggled black and white, encircled and suppressed revolutionaries, stifled opinions differing from their own, imposed a white terror, and felt very pleased with themselves. They have puffed up the arrogance of the bourgeoisie and deflated the morale of the proletariat. How poisonous! Viewed in connection with the Right deviation in 1962 and the wrong tendency of 1964 which was "Left" in form but Right in essence, shouldn't this make one wide awake?

Proclamation of the Guizhou Proletarian Revolutionary Rebel General Headquarters

ON THE evening of January 25, 1967, the great alliance of proletarian revolutionaries of Guizhou Province, under the guidance of the revolutionary line of Chairman Mao, successfully took over all the powers of leadership of the Provincial Committee of the Chinese Communist Party and of the Provincial People's Council, the Guiyang Municipal Committee of the Party, and the Municipal People's Council. The Guizhou Proletarian Revolutionary Rebel General Headquarters, which comprises forty revolutionary organizations, issued a proclamation on that same day. Excerpts follow. [Editor of *Peking Review*]

The Provincial Committee of the Communist Party of Guizhou, in which a handful of counterrevolutionary revisionists were entrenched, made great efforts to restore capitalism in the province over the past seventeen years, faithfully carrying out the will of their counterrevolutionary revisionist "supreme masters." This handful of people gathered together a group of counterrevolutionaries, renegades, and degenerate elements and turned the province into a revisionist "independent kingdom."

They worked hand in glove with landlords, rich peasants, counterrevolutionaries, bad elements, and Rightists in the area, to carry out a large-scale retaliatory counterrevolutionary counterattack and bring about a capitalist restoration; they energetically advocated "going-it-alone" [i.e., the restoration of individual economy]. As a result of all this, a foul atmosphere pervaded the province. They showed a total disregard for the people's livelihood and degenerated into bands who sucked the blood of the Guizhou people.

Where there is oppression there is resistance. Our great leader Chairman Mao personally kindled the raging fire of the great cultural revolution. The people of Guizhou Province rose in rebellion! This handful of blackguards in a fit of hysterics frantically suppressed the revolutionary masses. They stigmatized thousands of the revolutionary path-breakers as "counterrevolutionaries," "anti-Party elements," and "ghosts and monsters," and even set up their own jail where they illegally detained and tried to extort "concessions" from revolutionary rebels. In this way they exercised savage bourgeois dictatorship over the people. After the Eleventh Plenary Session of the Eighth Central Committee of the Chinese Communist Party this handful of blackguards still followed their revisionist ringleaders and opposed Chairman Mao's revolutionary line.

When all their schemes were smashed by the revolutionary rebels, they resorted to another even more treacherous device—economism. They squandered the money of the state and were careless of its property, squandered the people's sweat and blood, used money to corrupt our revolutionary rebels, bought over scabs and renegades and disrupted state finances, economy, and production so as to blacken the name of the great proletarian cultural revolution. This handful of persons lined themselves up completely with the Soviet revisionist clique and with U.S. imperialism.

These blackguards recently hatched another plot: they pulled strings behind the scenes in an attempt to paralyze the work of the whole province; they also tried in vain to sow discord between the peasants and workers and to sabotage agricultural production. The handful of counterrevolutionary revisionists in the Guizhou Provincial Party Committee have committed towering crimes against Chairman Mao, the Communist Party, and the people over the past seventeen years.

It is high time to settle the criminal accounts of this handful of blackguards! It is high time to smash this revisionist "independent kingdom!"

To ensure that the great cultural revolution in Guizhou Province will advance victoriously along Chairman Mao's revolutionary line, the Guizhou Proletarian Revolutionary Rebel General Headquarters solemnly declares that beginning January 25, 1967, it is taking over all the powers of leadership—Party, political, financial and leadership over the great cultural revolution—of the former Provincial Committee of the Party, the Provincial People's Council, the Guiyang Municipal Committee of the Party, and the Municipal People's Council.

We call on the people throughout the province to carry out the following tasks:

1. Put all power in the hands of the proletarian revolutionary rebels.

Everyone must be put to the test in the current great storm and be accepted or rejected. All revolutionaries should support this revolutionary action without reserve, and should support and obey the leadership of the Guizhou Proletarian Revolutionary Rebel General Headquarters. Anyone who dares to disrupt the seizure of power by the revolutionary rebels should be dealt with as attempting to undermine the great cultural revolution.

2. Take firm hold of the revolution and promote production.

All workers, peasants, cadres, and functionaries of enterprises should resolutely follow Chairman Mao's instruction to "take firm hold of the revolution and promote production," remain at their posts, and carry on production. Revolutionary rebels should not only be path-breakers in revolution but should also be exemplary in production. We call on all revolutionary people in the province to work hard and to be enthusiastic in production, to struggle for the fulfillment and overfulfillment of the Third Five-Year Plan and win honors for the great proletarian cultural revolution.

3. Resolutely oppose economism.

All persons must strictly carry out the directives to oppose economism issued by the revolutionary rebels in Shanghai and in the Guiyang area. Immediately resume production, restore communications, freeze all circulating funds, and prohibit speculation. The Guizhou Proletarian Revolutionary Rebel General Headquarters have full authority to deal with any deliberate violation of these directives.

4. Strengthen the proletarian dictatorship.

Anyone who opposes Chairman Mao, Vice-Chairman Lin Biao, or the Cultural Revolution Group under the Party's Central Committee should be dealt with as an active counterrevolutionary and immediately arrested. Anyone who sabotages production, instigates struggle by force, and undermines the great proletarian cultural revolution should be dealt with according to law by the public security organs. Anyone who directs the spearhead of his attack against the People's Liberation Army, uses weapons and ammunition, or steals or divulges state secrets, should be investigated and dealt with according to law.

5. All revolutionary organizations are called on to propagate and implement the above points. Any violation should be investigated and dealt with by the General Headquarters in collaboration with and under the supervision of the revolutionary masses and the appropriate bodies.

All revolutionary comrades unite, hold high the great red banner of Mao Zedong's thought, and carry the great proletarian cultural revolution through to the end!

DOCUMENT 18

SHENGWULIAN

Whither China?

This document is one of the most famous and influential produced by the "ultra-left" in China. In some provinces and cities, there developed a genuine power struggle during 1967 in which substantive issues were at stake. Mao Zedong had called for a popular rising, for the arming of the people against the bureaucracy, and for a new revolution. Even if this call was merely intended to enhance his own position, some groups took it seriously and actually threatened to overturn, or even did overthrow, the established power structures. In such cases Mao, backed by Zhou Enlai, called in the army to suppress the revolutionary movement that exceeded its permitted limits. One of the groups that demanded a new revolution was Shengwulian, the "Hunan Provincial Proletarian Revolutionary Great Alliance Committee." These extracts from the long document, "Whither China?" support the distribution of weapons among the workers, the overthrow of the bureaucracy, and the establishment of a Paris Commune type of government. Authors seemed to believe that Mao's retreat from these aims was only apparent, a necessary tactical maneuver, and they still regarded him as the "Great Helmsman" of the Revolution; they were also enthusiastic about Jiang Qing. The text appeared in January 1968, and refers to events in 1967.[2]

THE JANUARY REVOLUTIONARY STORM

Lenin made the celebrated statement: "Any revolution, as long as it is a true revolution, is, in the final analysis, a change of class. Therefore, the best means of heightening the awareness of the masses and exposing the deception of the masses with revolutionary vows, is to analyze the class changes that have taken place or are taking place in the revolution." Let us follow this teaching and make an analysis of the class changes which took place in the January Revolution, so we may expose how the masses were deceived by revolutionary promises.

As everybody knows, the greatest fact of the January Revolution was that 90 percent of the senior Party cadres were made to stand aside. In Hunan, Zhang Pinghua, Zhang Bosen, Hua Guofeng, and the like had their power reduced to zero. In Beijing, representatives of the Cultural Revolution seized power in the Ministry of Finance, the Radio Broadcasting Administration Bureau, and other departments; and the power of people like Li Xiannian, Chen Yi, Tan Zhenlin, as well as that of Zhou Enlai, who represented them, was greatly diminished. Into whose hands did the assets go at that time? They went into the hands of the people, who were full of boundless enthusiasm, and who were organized to take over the urban administration and the Party, government, financial and cultural powers in industry, commerce, communications, and so forth. What the editorial had called for was truly realized, namely, "that the masses should rise and take hold of the destiny of their socialist country and themselves administer the cities, industry, communications, and finance."

The storm of the January Revolution turned all this within a very short time from the hands of the bureaucrats into the hands of the enthusiastic working class. Society suddenly found, in the absence of bureaucrats, that it could not only survive, but could live better and develop quicker and with greater freedom. It was quite different from the threats of the bureaucrats who, before the revolution, had said: "Without us, production would collapse, and society would fall into a state of hopeless confusion."

As a matter of fact, without the bureaucrats and bureaucratic organs, productivity was greatly liberated. After the Ministry of the Coal Industry fell, production of coal went on unhindered. The Ministry of Railways fell, but transportation was unaffected. All departments of the provincial Party committees also fell, but the various branches of their work went on as usual. Moreover, the working class were greatly liberated in their enthusiasm and initiative for production. The management of industrial plants by the workers themselves after January was impressive. For the first time, the workers had the feeling that "it is not the state which manages us, but we who manage the state." For the first time, they felt that they were producing for themselves. Their enthusiasm had never been so high and their sense of responsibility as masters of the house had never been so strong. Changsha Weaving and Spinning Mill and other factories also created rebel working groups and countless other new things.

This was the true content of the class changes in the January revolution. As a matter of fact, in this short period some places realized, though not very thoroughly, the content of the "People's Commune of China." The Society found itself in a state of "mass dictatorship" similar to that of the Paris Commune. The January Storm told people that China would go toward a society which had no bureaucrats, and that 90 percent of the senior cadres had already formed a privileged class. The objective law of the development of class struggle caused the majority of them to stand aside in January. The fact that 90 percent of the senior cadres had to stand aside in the storm of the January Revolution was certainly not an error by the "masses." "The masses are the real heroes." Those who committed the most serious crimes were duly punished: "very few received undue punishment."

Facts as revealed by the masses, and the indignation which they brought forth, first told the people that this class of "Red" capitalists had entirely become a decaying class that hindered the progress of history. The relations between them and the people in general had changed from relations between leaders and the led, to those between rulers and the ruled and between exploiters and the exploited. From the relations between revolutionaries of equal standing, it had become a relationship between oppressors and the oppressed. The special privileges and high salaries of the class of "Red" capitalists were built upon a foundation of oppression and exploitation of the broad masses of the people. In order to realize the "People's Commune of China," it was necessary to overthrow this class.

The January Revolutionary Storm was a great attempt by the revolutionary people under the leadership of Chairman Mao, to topple the old world and build a new one. The program of the first great proletarian political [sic] revolution was formulated at that great moment. Chairman Mao stated: "This is one class overthrowing another. This is great revolution." This shows that the Cultural Revolution is not a revolution of dismissing officials or a movement of dragging out people, nor a purely cultural revolution, but is "a revolution in which one class overthrows another." With relation to the facts of the January Revolutionary Storm, the overthrown class is none other than the class of "bureaucratism" formed in China in the last seventeen years.

There is no place here for reformism—combining two into one—or peaceful transition. The old state machinery must be utterly smashed. "Completely smash the old exploitative system, the revisionist system, and the bureaucratic organs."

The policy issues raised in the January Revolution mainly concerned capitalist patterns of employment such as contracted labor and temporary labor, as well as the revisionist movement of going to the mountainous areas and the countryside. At present, the "Ultra-Left" must organize people to study and assess the multitude of things created by the January Revolutionary Storm. These new things are the embryonic form of a new society of the Paris Commune type.

THE FEBRUARY ADVERSE CURRENT

The force and intensity of the January Revolution caused the bureaucrats to hurriedly usurp power. Contrary to their usual attitude, they adopted the most urgent and savage means of suppression. This proves negatively the intensity of the "redistribution of property (of means of production) and power" resulting when 90 percent of the senior cadres stood aside in the January Revolution. The tragic consequences of the February Adverse Current also prove the correctness of Comrade Mao Zedong's prediction that "there can be no immediate victory."

The "Red" capitalist class gained an almost overwhelming ascendancy in February and March 1967. The property (of means of production) and power were wrested away from the hands of the revolutionary people and returned to the bureaucrats. In early spring, in February, Long Shujin, Liu Ziyun, Zhang Bosen, Hua Guofeng, and bureaucrats throughout the country and their agents at the Center, wielded unlimited power. It was their heyday, while the power of the revolutionary people evaporated. Moreover, large numbers of revolutionary people were thrown into prison by the state organs—public security, procuracy, and judicial organs—controlled by the capitalist class.

Intoxicated by his victory of February–March, Zhou Enlai—at present the chief representative of China's "Red" capitalist class—hurriedly tried to set up revolutionary committees in all parts of the country. If this bourgeois plan had been achieved, the proletariat would have retreated to its grave. Therefore, without waiting for the establishment of all the revolutionary committees, the Central Cultural Revolution Group [Jiang Qing and her clique] gave orders at the end of March to launch a counteroffensive. From then on, the great August Storm began to brew.

In the struggle to hit back at the February Adverse Current, the important sign that the revolution had entered into a higher stage was that the problem of the army really began to surface. During the January Revolution, the revolutionary people had very naive ideas on the problem of the army. They thought that as soon as the local capitalist-roaders were overthrown, the armed forces would unite with the revolutionary people in accordance with Chairman Mao's order for union from the upper to the lower levels. The bloody facts of the February Adverse Current made the people aware that orders from above could not by themselves bring about an implementation of Chairman Mao's intentions in the armed forces.

The common interests of capitalist-roaders in the armed forces and those of local capitalist-roaders would make it impossible for the army to carry out Chairman Mao's revolutionary line. It was necessary to carry out cultural revolution from the lower level upwards in the army, and to rely on the people's revolution—the locomotive of progress in history—in order to change the antagonism between the army and the people that was brought about by the bureaucrats' control of the army.

The struggle since February has placed the grave problem of the army before the broad masses (previously it had been discussed only between Chairman Mao and a few others). This is gradually providing the conditions for solution of the problem through the strength of the broad masses of the people. It has been scientifically foreseen that in the new society of the "commune," the military force will be very different from the present-day army. The struggle since February has enabled this idea of Chairman Mao gradually to take hold of the masses.

THE AUGUST LOCAL REVOLUTIONARY WAR

1. It is now clear that the present army is different from the people's army of before the Liberation. Before Liberation, the army and the people fought together to overthrow imperialism, bureaucratic capitalism, and feudalism. The relationship between army and people was like that of fish and water [Mao's favorite image for the ideal relationship between guerrillas and the masses]. After Liberation, the target of revolution changed from imperialist, bureaucratic capitalism and feudalism to capitalist-roaders, and these capitalist-roaders are power-holders in the army. For this reason, some of the armed forces have not only lost the intimate relationship with the masses that existed before Liberation, but have even become tools for suppressing the revolution. Therefore, if the first Great Proletarian Cultural Revolution is to succeed, it is necessary to bring about a basic change in the army.

2. It is now clear that a national revolutionary war is necessary before the revolutionary people can overcome the armed Red capitalist class. The large-scale armed struggle in August between the proletariat and the Red capitalist class, the local revolutionary war, proved this prediction. The great experience created by the local revolutionary wars in August is unparalleled in history. Contrary to expectations of the mass of mediocre people, history advanced in the direction predicted by the "heretics." Hitherto unimaginable, large-scale, gun-seizing incidents occurred regularly in accordance with the pace of historical development. Local wars of varying magnitude broke out in the country in which the armed forces were directly involved (in some places, including Jiangxi and Hangzhou,

the army fought directly). The creative spirit and revolutionary fervor displayed by the people in August were extremely impressive. Gun-seizing became a "movement." Its magnitude, and the power and heroism of the revolutionary war, were so great that in that moment people were deeply impressed that "the people, and the people alone, are the motive force of historical development."

For a short time, the cities were in a state of "armed mass dictatorship." The power in most of the industries, commerce, communications, and urban administration was again taken away from Zhang Bosen, Hua Guofeng, Long Shujin, Liu Ziyun, and their like and put into the hands of the revolutionary people. Never before had the revolutionary people appeared on the stage of history in the role of masters of world history as they did in August. Primary school children voluntarily worked in communications and security. Their brave gestures in directing traffic, and the pride with which other mass organizations directly exercised some of the financial-economic powers, left an unforgettable impression on the masses.

August was the time when the power of the revolutionary mass organizations rapidly grew, while that of the bureaucrats again withered. For the second time, a temporary and unstable redistribution of property and power took place. Once more, society tried to realize the great "People's Commune of China." Once more, people tried to solve the problem raised in the May 7 Directive, namely, that "the army should be a great school" and "workers, peasants, and students should all study military affairs." This attempt had not been made in the January Revolution. Before Liberation, the army actually was a great school which maintained excellent relations with the masses, and which combined the roles of soldiers, students, civilians, peasants, and workers. This was summed up by Chairman Mao just before the victory of the Democratic Revolution. Why then, more than ten years after Liberation, should the question again be raised of improving army-civilian relations, and transforming the army into a great school? As said above, it is because the army has undergone changes since Liberation and, to greater or lesser degree, has separated itself from the masses. As a result, the question is again on the agenda.

The great pioneering act of the August Storm was the emergence of an armed force organized by the revolutionary people themselves, which became the actual force of the proletarian dictatorship (or dictatorship over the capitalist-roaders). This force and the people are united, and fight together to overthrow the "Red" capitalist class. The people, instead of lamenting the fall of the Military Region command—a bureaucratic organ—rejoice at it; yet formerly they used to think they could not survive without it. This fact has enabled the proletariat to foresee more realistically where China's army is going, and to envisage the armed strength of the new society—the "People's Commune of China." It may be said with certainty that China will be a society in which the army is the people, the people are the army, the people and the army are united as one, and the army has shaken off the control of the bureaucrats.

The September Setback

To seize the fruits of victory won by the proletariat in August, and turn the mass dictatorship again into bureaucratic rule, the bourgeoisie in the revolutionary committees must first disarm the working class. The weapons in the hands of workers have infinitely strengthened the power of the working class. This fact is a mortal threat to the bourgeoisie, who fear workers holding guns. Out of spontaneous hatred for the bureaucrats who tried to snatch the fruit of victory, the revolutionary people shouted a resounding revolutionary slogan: "Giving up our guns amounts to suicide." Moreover, they formed a spontaneous, nationwide mass "arms concealment movement" for the armed overthrow of the new bureaucratic bourgeoisie.

The August gun-seizing movement was great. It was not only unprecedented in capitalist countries, but also, for the first time in a socialist country, it truly turned the whole nation into soldiers. Before the Cultural Revolution, the bureaucrats did not dare actually to hand over arms to the people. The militia is merely a facade behind which the bureaucrats control the armed strength of the people. It is certainly not an armed force of the working class, but rather a docile tool in the hands of the bureaucrats. In the gun-seizing movement, the masses, instead of receiving arms like favors from above, for the first time seized arms from the hands of the bureaucrats by relying on the violent force of the revolutionary people themselves. For the first time, the workers held their "own" arms. Chairman Mao's inspiring call, "Arm the Left"[3] was the intensive focus of the courage of the working class. But the September 5 Directive [to return the weapons to the Army] completely nullified this call. The working class was disarmed. The bureaucrats again came back to power.

When a truly stable victory gradually becomes possible, the following questions will become salient:

> 1. The unevenness of the revolution will assume prominence. The possibility of first winning true, thorough victory in one or several provinces, overthrowing the product of bourgeois reformism—the rule of revolutionary committees—and reestablishing political power of the Paris Commune type, will become a crucial problem if

the revolution is to be able to develop in depth with rapidity. This is unlike the previous period, which was a blind and spontaneous stage in which the unbalanced character of the revolution played a decisive role.

2. To truly overthrow the rule of the new aristocracy and completely smash the old state machinery, it will be necessary to thoroughly evaluate the past seventeen years. A major task is to fundamentally teach the people why it is necessary to carry out the Cultural Revolution, and what its final objective is.

3. To make the revolution really victorious, it will be necessary to settle the question: "Who are our enemies, who are our friends?" This "paramount question of the revolution" requires that we make a new analysis of China's society, where "a new situation has arisen as a result of great class changes," so as to revise the class hierarchy, rally our friends, and topple our enemies.

These new questions were raised by Comrade Jiang Qing in her speech on November 12, 1967. This speech announced the beginning of a new stage, unparalleled in history, into which the great Proletarian Cultural Revolution has entered. Though this important speech dealt only with the literary and art circles, "the revolution of literature and art is the vanguard of political revolution." The joyous reviving and burgeoning struggle among Chinese literary and art circles shows the direction which China's revolution will take.

The genesis and development of Hunan's Shengwulian reflects the growth in strength of the proletariat since September. Shengwulian was in fact born of the experience of the mass-line *Attack With Words, Defend With Arms Headquarters*—a form of dictatorship of the January Revolution. It is a powerful organ of mass dictatorship of a higher level than those of January and August. It may be compared to the soviets of the 1917 Russian Revolution when power was usurped by the bourgeoisie. The Provincial Revolutionary Committee Preparatory Group also is comparable to the bourgeois Provisional Government in Russia of that time. The contradiction between Shengwulian and the Preparatory Group is a new situation in which "power organs of two systems coexist" as the soviets and the Provisional Government coexisted in the Russia of 1917. However, the actual power is in the hands of the Provincial Revolutionary Committee Preparatory Group—the bourgeois Provisional Government.

Shengwulian is a newborn sprout comparable to the soviets of 1917. It is an embryo form of a more mature Commune. This correct newborn Red political power of Shengwulian will certainly mature and gather strength amid great storms.

Refute the Reactionary "Second Revolution Doctrine"

The bourgeoisie always describe the political form of their rule as most perfect and flawless in the service of the whole people. The new bureaucratic bourgeoisie, and the Rightist pig-dogs of the petty bourgeoisie who depend on them, are at present doing exactly that. They ignore the provisional character of the "Revolutionary Committee" while praising it nauseatingly. Marxist-Leninists must relentlessly expose the suppression of the revolutionary people by the Revolutionary Committee, must energetically declare that the People's Commune of China is the society which we proletarian and revolutionary people must bring about in the Cultural Revolution, and must energetically make known the inevitable doom of the Revolutionary Committee.

Some people criticize us for wanting to reach communism in one step by immediately eliminating classes. They say that a regime of the Paris Commune–type, as envisaged by Chairman Mao, is a dream; and that all this is unrealistic before the realization of communism. These people deliberately distort our views. We certainly do not wish to do away immediately with classes or with the legal rights of the [remaining] bourgeoisie. This is indeed impossible before realization of communism. They are taken only as our highest program, not our lowest. Our minimum program calls for the overthrow of the rule of the bureaucratic bourgeoisie. It is of course not yet possible to destroy the exploiting classes. After the victory of the first Great Proletarian Cultural Revolution, there will inevitably be new class changes. It is these new class changes that will again lead to new social reform, and so push history forward.

People who criticize us in this way actually are saying that all our efforts will be in vain, that society cannot take a new leap, and that property and power cannot be "redistributed" but can only be somewhat altered. Forgetful gentlemen! The January Revolution and the August Storm already did bring about (although only temporarily and locally) a redistribution of property and power, and a qualitative leap of the whole society. Has that not already shattered the gloomy liquidationist views you spread?

Cadres of the proletariat have not yet matured politically, and the revolutionary people have not yet produced cadres with true proletarian authority. Hence, we are almost unanimously condemned by people saying that we have no use for cadres and want to make them all stand aside. We really believe that 90 percent of the senior cadres should stand aside; and that at best they can only be reeducated. This is because they have already come to form a decaying class with its own particular interests. Their relation with the people has changed from that between leaders and the led to that between exploiters and the exploited, between oppressors and the oppressed. Most of them, consciously or unconsciously, yearn for the capitalist road, and cherish and nurture capitalist things. Rule by their class has completely blocked the development of history.

Is it possible, instead of overthrowing this class, that they can be persuaded to give up the vested interests derived from their bourgeois legal rights, such as high salaries, and follow the socialist instead of the capitalist road? The proletariat truly has made steady efforts in that direction. Chairman Mao's extensive concessions to the bourgeoisie are the pure expression of these efforts. However, the bureaucrats have once again launched a counterattack with increasing frenzy, pushing themselves closer and closer to the guillotine. All this proves that no decaying class has ever been willing voluntarily to exit from the stage of history.

In the new society of the Paris Commune–type, this class will be overthrown. This was demonstrated by the indisputable facts, so surprising to mediocre people, of the great changes in the January Revolution and the August Storm. Those who will rise and take their place will be cadres with true proletarian authority who will be produced naturally by the revolutionary people in the struggle to overthrow this decaying class [the Red bureaucrats]. These cadres will be members of the commune. They will have no special privileges. Economically, they will receive the same treatment as the masses in general. They may be dismissed or replaced at any time at the request of the masses. Such new cadres with true authority have not yet emerged. However, such cadres will be produced spontaneously as the political thinking of the revolutionary people grows in maturity. This is a natural result of the political and ideological maturity of the proletariat.

Refute the "Leftist" Doctrine of One Revolution

Some infantile revolutionaries of the revolutionary ranks suggest that there is no first or second Cultural Revolution, and that the revolution should proceed until communism is realized. This is the "Leftist" doctrine of one revolution. People who hold this idea are very few in number and they have a low political level. Chairman Mao's theory that the transitional period will be divided into different historical stages is the best enlightenment for them. The revolution must necessarily be in stages. We are for permanent revolution, and also for revolution by stages.

Where China goes determines where the world goes. China will inevitably go toward the new society of the "People's Commune of China." If dictatorship by the Revolutionary Committee is taken as the final goal of the first Great Cultural Revolution, then China will inevitably go the way already taken by the Soviet Union, and the people will again be returned to the bloody fascist rule of capitalism. The Revolutionary Committee's road of bourgeois reformism is a dead end.

This is because the present is the age of the great banner of Mao Zedong-ism; a great age in which imperialism is going downhill toward its debacle, while socialism goes uphill toward world victory. Today's world is one in which capitalism is definitely dying and socialism is definitely flourishing. In this great revolutionary period of unprecedented significance, in this era of rapid changes, "miracles—at present not yet thought of but completely conformable to the law of historical development—are bound to happen in the history of mankind" (Chen Boda, March 24).

Both the victory of the Chinese proletariat and the broad masses of revolutionary people, and the extermination of the new bureaucratic bourgeoisie, are likewise inevitable. The world-shaking great festival of the revolutionary people—the overthrow of the Revolutionary Committee and birth of the "People's Commune of China"—will surely come.

The commune of the "Ultra-Left faction" does not conceal its views and intentions. We publicly declare that our objective of establishing the "People's Commune of China" can only be achieved by forceful overthrow of the bourgeois dictatorship and the revisionist system of the revolutionary Committee. Let the new bureaucratic bourgeoisie tremble before the true socialist revolution that shakes the world! What the proletariat can lose in this revolution is only their chains, what they can gain will be the whole world! The China of tomorrow will be the world of the "Commune." Long live Mao Zedong-ism!

DOCUMENT 19

Li Yi Zhe
On Socialist Democracy and the Legal System

In 1973 and 1974, the first criticism of the policies of the Cultural Revolution period began to emerge, a forerunner of the events of April 1976 and the eventual restoration of Deng Xiaoping. A key document from the period is *On Socialist Democracy and the Legal System,* written by four activists in Guangzhou, Wang Xizhe, Li Zhengtian, Chen Yiyang, and Guo Hongzhi. (The name Li Yi Zhe is an abbreviated combination of three of the authors' names.) It was "published" as an immense wall poster on Beijing Road in Guangzhou: it contained twenty thousand characters and occupied sixty-seven sheets of newsprint paper. It was also distributed in stencil copies. Its authors were soon detained and subjected to harsh treatment.[4]

In late 1974 Wang, Li, and Chen were sent to work "under supervision" in the countryside, and were intensely criticized. It was not until March 1977, several months after the fall of the "Gang of Four," that they were formally tried and sent to labor camps. With supreme irony, they were charged with being followers of the "Gang," as well as with having links with Taiwan and with the Hong Kong Trotskyists. Under the "Gang" they had been labeled merely as "reactionaries"; now they were charged as "counterrevolutionaries." In 1978, China's unofficial press began a campaign for Li Yi Zhe's release and Amnesty International adopted them as Prisoners of Conscience, but it was not until 1979 that the three were finally freed and rehabilitated. For further writing by Wang Xizhe, see Document 21.

WHAT is the Lin Biao System? It is the set of policies implemented by Lin Biao in opposition to Chairman Mao which poisoned the whole Party and nation while Lin led the opportunist line within the Party. Let us remember the scenes when the Lin Biao System was at its height!

We have not forgotten the vaunting of (empty) politics which rewarded the lazy and punished the diligent, the "daily reading [of Mao's works and quotations]" which resembled the incantation of spells, the "discussion-application [of Mao's works and thoughts]" which became more and more hypocritical, the "revolution erupts from the depth of the soul" which became ever more absurd, the "manifestation of loyalty" which encouraged political opportunism, the grotesque "loyalty dance," and excruciatingly ridiculous rituals of displaying loyalty—morning prayers, evening penitences, rallies, falling-in, reporting for and quitting work and making duty shifts, buying and selling things, writing letters, making phone calls, even taking meals—which were invariably painted in violent religious colors and shrouded in a mystical atmosphere. In short, loyalty occupied 100 percent of the time and 100 percent of the space. The movements of this "good" and that "good" were, in fact, competitions of "left! left! and more left!" and contests for "the most . . . the most . . . and the most." The innumerable meetings of activists were in fact exhibitions of hypocritical, evil, and ugly behavior, and gambling dens which offered a huge payout for a small investment.

We also have not forgotten the "wind of public property" which jeopardized the basic interests of the worker and peasant masses, the style of Party management which meant that "when one man has understood the Way, chickens and dogs also go to heaven with him,"[5] the style of study which trumpeted "whatever is useful is truth" and "a pole casts a shadow as soon as it is set up,"[6] the "new stereotyped writing style" which encouraged lying, the theory of "small details [mistakes] do no harm" which promoted a corrupt and villainous style of work, and the widespread corruption.

Still more, we have not forgotten the formulaic "sermons" of class struggle, and the "scum hole" type of cow-pens [i.e., the detention camps] and the massacres that were no less inhuman than the historical incidents such as "March 18," "April 12," "May 30," and "June 23";[7] because in Guangdong Province alone nearly forty thousand revolutionaries and cadres were massacred and more than a million were imprisoned, put under control, and oppressed.

But there are some people who shut their eyes and do not admit that the Lin Biao system, which has been witnessed by 800 million people, was firmly established. They stubbornly say that Chairman Mao's revolutionary line has, "at all times and in all places," occupied the ruling position. Is this not to say that all these bloody butcheries and long-standing cases of injustice are based on decisions made by the "revolutionary line"?

The emergence of the Lin Biao System developed within the historical conditions of the Chinese society. Our China was transformed into a socialist society directly from a semifeudal, semicolonial society. The feudal rule which continued for more than two thousand years has left its ideology deeply rooted. It was not destroyed in the period of old democracy, nor in the period of new democracy. The bad habits of autocracy and despotism are deeply imbued in the minds of the masses, even in those of most Communist Party members. These are the conditions that permitted the Lin Biao System to flourish for a certain period, even to the degree of forcing Chairman Mao "to join the Liangshan rebels."[8] These are the factors that allowed Lin Biao's cohorts to gain complete victory in their spheres of influence by suppressing the people's democracy.

1. New Questions in the Socialist Revolution

There have been two great struggles since the advent of the Great Proletarian Cultural Revolution: one is the struggle waged by the proletariat and the revolutionary people against the Liu Shaoqi clique, and the other is the struggle against the Lin Biao clique.

The essence of these struggles is whether to take the capitalist road or the socialist road, whether to further the dictatorship of the bourgeoisie or the dictatorship of the proletariat. In the anti-rightist socialist education movements in the past, similar struggles were conducted, and these movements aimed to solve the same questions. Then, what is the new question? The new question is that what the Liu Shaoqi clique, and especially the Lin Biao clique, wanted to cook up was not an ordinary dictatorship of the bourgeoisie, but a feudal social-Fascist dictatorship.

The social base of the capitalist-roaders and careerists in the Party emerged from special privileges. Under the conditions of the present Chinese society, it is only possible for the newborn bourgeois class to set up a feudal social-Fascist dictatorship, while it is impossible for them to share their vested profits with the old landlords and old compradors who were overthrown. That the unhealthy flourishing counterrevolutionary changes made by the Khrushchev-Brezhnev clique did not restore the white Russians to their aristocratic heritage is the proof.

Already in the early 1960s, Chairman Mao warned the Party and the whole country of the danger of social-Fascism. He told us that if a restoration occurs in a country like ours, it will not be an ordinary dictatorship of the bourgeoisie, "but a reactionary, Fascist type of dictatorship." He has said: "This is a question which deserves vigilance, and I hope that the comrades will carefully think about it."

Ten years have passed, and the Chinese people have thought about it for these ten years. Was it not the disasters that the Lin Biao line brought on the people which helped them really begin to understand Chairman Mao's warnings?

The specific feature of the current socialist revolution is the attempt of the representatives of the bourgeoisie who have infiltrated the Party to establish a feudal social-Fascist dictatorship. What weapon should the revolutionary people take up to resist them?

2. Lessons from the Great Proletarian Cultural Revolution

In his profound study of the social, political, and economic relations in contemporary China, Chairman Mao has discovered the Great Proletarian Cultural Revolution. In form, the Great Proletarian Cultural Revolution is actually a great revolutionary democracy of the people on the most extensive scale; it is to "mobilize the broad masses from the grass roots, openly and comprehensively, to expose our dark sides"; and it is the weapon to prevent and oppose social-Fascism.

From the strategic point of view, the purpose of the Great Proletarian Cultural Revolution is to temper the masses with the revolutionary democratic spirit for self-liberation, rather than merely to expose and destroy Liu Shao-chi's capitalist headquarters. "The revolution is to liberate productivity"; and what could be a more appropriate symbol than the rigorous and enthusiastic discussion of important state affairs and the criticism of erroneous lines by the proletariat and broad masses of people?

The freedom of speech, the freedom of press, the freedom of association, which are stipulated in the Constitution, and the freedom of exchanging revolutionary experience, which is not stipulated in the Constitution, have all been truly practiced in the great revolution and granted with the support by the Party Central headed by Chair-

man Mao. This is something which the Chinese people had not pos-
sessed for several thousand years, something so active and lively; and
this is the extraordinary achievement of the revolution. But our
Great Proletarian Cultural Revolution has not accomplished its tasks
because it has not enabled the people to grasp the weapon of mass
democracy.

In the summer of 1968, the socialist legal system suddenly became
inoperative, while, on the other hand, "state power is the power to
suppress" became operative. All across the land, there were arrests
everywhere, suppressions everywhere, miscarriages of justice everywhere. What happened to the socialist legal system? Allegedly, it was
no longer of any use because it belonged to the Constitution established by the old People's Congress whereas the new People's Congress was not convened yet. There was no law and no heaven! This
was a rehearsal of social-Fascism in our country; and the com-
mander-in-chief of the rehearsal was Lin Biao. "Should the broad
masses of people be protected or suppressed?" Chairman Mao asked
indignantly.

To worship the Lin Biao System as orthodox Mao Zedong
Thought was an unavoidable historical mistake committed by the
Chinese people in the Great Proletarian Cultural Revolution. Lin
Biao and his cohorts exploited the people's revolutionary movement
as the "borrowed force" to usurp power and restore capitalism.
One's attitude toward "genius" became more important than
whether one took the capitalist road or the socialist road. The principles of "together [we] eradicate them," "together [we] punish them,"
and "whoever resists will be struck down" challenged the legal system; and they became a Magic Sword which protected the absolute
worship of the "genius." Once Lin Biao's position was established
and when the Party announced that the affirmation of his position
was the landmark of the "all-out victory" of the Great Proletarian
Cultural Revolution, he immediately wanted to establish the "new
order" and to "correct the terms." In this respect, he also had his
Dong Zhongshu![9]

What is the "new order"? It is the "theory of the final victory,"
"theory of the four-obsoletes,"[10] the "theory that state power is suppression," and the "theory of the military-Party." In short, it is the
theory of social-Fascism which intends to force our Party and our
army into a relationship of "ruler-vassal and father-son; no one is
allowed to challenge his superiors."

The Great Proletarian Cultural Revolution has taught us that the
people's Great Democracy cannot drift away from the correct line;
otherwise, not only the revolution will fail to accomplish its mission,

but it will also be exploited by the bourgeois careerists. The masses of people will gain nothing but new fetters. The reality in China since 1968 has thus grimly brought before the people this question: Is the Great Proletarian Cultural Revolution "dead"?

3. Expectations for the Fourth National People's Congress

Revolution is without doubt the most authoritative event in the world. The deep shock, and also the profound significance, that was given to Chinese society by the Great Proletarian Cultural Revolution, which once left the whole world wide-eyed and open-mouthed, will in the future influence the whole historical stage of our socialism.

How will the approaching Fourth National People's Congress reflect the Great Proletarian Cultural Revolution, which is known as China's "Second Revolution"? Law is the manifestation of the will of the ruling class. So how can the will of the Chinese proletariat and the broad masses of people who have experienced the Great Proletarian Cultural Revolution be manifested in the fundamental law of the state—the new Constitution—which the Congress will formulate? What are the masses thinking about right now? What do they demand? And what expectations do they have of the Congress of "the people of the whole state"?

(i) Legal system, not the "system of rites"!

The basic content of the Great Proletarian Cultural Revolution is, in fact, "to rebel against the capitalist-reactionary line" and "to seize power from the capitalist-roaders." But one may say that suppression (of the people's democracy) and resisting the suppression (by the capitalist-reactionary line) have been the main activities throughout the whole course of the Great Proletarian Cultural Revolution. Moreover, the numerous movements since 1968 were all designed to attack the people who rose in rebellion during the Great Proletarian Cultural Revolution, and the attacks continued until the rebels were beaten down into the depths of hell. When the mass movements in the Great Proletarian Cultural Revolution were suppressed, the Lin Biao System gained a secure power base, and Lin Biao and his cohorts were able to cram feudal and patriarchal terms into the draft Constitution of 1970. This crude fact illustrates that the feudal, social-Fascist dictatorship is the main danger to our dictatorship of the proletariat.

Our country has been transformed into socialism from a semifeudal, semicolonial society; thus, the tradition formed by the feudal autocracy over several millennia is stubbornly entrenched in all domains of the superstructure such as ideology, culture, education, law, etc. The strong elements of feudalism and patriarchy manifested in Liu Shaoqi, and especially in Lin Biao, are sufficient to prove that antifeudalism is still an important aspect of our continued revolution.

What could be a more sacred pillar to support the "rule by rites" of the Lin Biao System than the principle of "Whoever opposes Mao Zedong Thought will be struck down"? In name, this principle upholds Mao; in fact, it protects Lin and his clique. If Lin Biao had formally assumed power, then would it not be "whoever opposes Lin Biao will be struck down"? (In reality, that is precisely what did happen.) Furthermore, any one of the VIPs can become sacred as long as he claims to be the incarnation of Chairman Mao's revolutionary line, whereas "the handful" of revolutionary masses who dare to affront his dignity will never receive legal protection!

If we do not oppose this feudal principle of the "system of rites," can we really implement the rule by law of the dictatorship of the proletariat which emphasizes "suppressing the enemies; protecting the people"? This is a great contradiction. On the one hand, the Party's centralized leadership must never be shaken, while, on the other, "the emphasis of the movement is to rectify the capitalist-roaders in the Party." But these capitalist-roaders are precisely the embodiment of the centralized leadership in areas and departments which have been monopolized by them.

How should the rights of the masses of people to struggle, under the Party's centralized leadership, against the capitalist-roaders in the Party and their erroneous line, be protected? This is a great task confronting the Fourth National People's Congress. It is superfluous to say that the Party leadership should listen carefully to the opinions of the masses; it is equally superfluous to mention the rights of the masses of people to exercise revolutionary supervision over the Party leadership at various levels; and it is yet more superfluous to say that it is justified to rebel against the capitalist-roaders. Even if the opinions of the masses are erroneous and excessive, even if the masses, due to misunderstandings, are unhappy with certain aspects of the Party's policies, should they be suppressed when persuasion fails, and apprehended when suppression fails? Moreover, it is not always easy to distinguish between fragrant flowers and poisonous weeds, between the correct and the erroneous, and between the revolutionary and the counterrevolutionary. There must be a process; and the distinction must be tested by time. Therefore, we should not be afraid of upright and honest opponents as long as they restrain themselves by not making intrigues and conspiracies.

The Fourth National People's Congress should stipulate in black and white that all the democratic rights which the masses of people deserve should be upheld, and that dictatorship will only be exercised over the criminals who commit murder, arson, gangsterism, robbery, and theft, and the elements who incite armed struggle and organize conspiratorial cliques.

(ii) Restriction on special privileges

Do we recognize that there is emerging in China a privileged stratum (of which Liu Shaoqi, Lin Biao, etc. were the political agents only) similar to that in the Soviet Union? This is the fundamental theoretical question determining the nature of the Great Proletarian Cultural Revolution.

It must be pointed out immediately that most of our Party members are good or comparatively good. However, this privileged stratum is an objective fact that is generated out of our country's socioeconomic conditions and cannot be changed according to men's will.

Why is there such corruption in today's society? Why are resources squandered, why do some enjoy such shockingly high-class luxuries? Why do a considerable number of children of the high-ranking cadres routinely enjoy the right to own property and a disguised form of inheritance? What political measures initiate and protect this mode of ownership by a new bourgeois class? In literature and art, in education, in the cadre schools, in rustication and other political movements, in university admissions, in the grooming of successors, in short, in almost every sphere which is popularly called a "newborn thing," the privileged can assert their divine presence and demonstrate their miracles.

May we not say that the Soviet Union's change to revisionism began with the practice of a high salary system for its high-ranking cadres, which was intended to keep up with the payments to bourgeois experts? In China, the tradition permits the practice of giving preferential treatment to the veteran cadres who have allegedly shed much blood and sweat for the revolution, and the people do not object much. But can we belittle its corruptive effects on the regime, as well as its influence over the new social relations?

We are not Utopian socialists; therefore, we acknowledge

that there exist in our society at the present stage various kinds of differences which cannot be eliminated by a single law or decree. But, the law governing the development of the socialist revolutionary movement should eliminate rather than enhance the differences, and still more, should not allow these differences to be expanded into economic and political privileges. Special privileges are fundamentally opposed to the interests of the people. Why should we be so shy about criticism of special privileges? Why should the rights and wrongs of this crucial issue be stealthily replaced by the so-called question of "good people" and "bad people"?

The Fourth National People's Congress should write in black and white a clause to restrict special privileges. The Fourth National People's Congress should answer these questions.

(iii) Consolidating the dictatorship of the proletariat and sanctions against reactionaries

Are the people's democratic rights not written in our Constitution and Party Constitution and Central documents? Yes, they have been written down. Not only that, but there also are the stipulations for "protecting the people's democracy," "not allowing malicious attack and revenge," and "forbidding extracting a confession by torture and interrogation." But these protections have never been implemented, while, on the contrary, Fascist dictatorship over the revolutionary cadres and masses has been allowed—some of them were imprisoned, some executed, and some framed in fabricated cases; even the unlimited practice of savage corporal punishments cannot be "strictly forbidden."

The basic task of the Chinese people in the entire historical stage of socialism is to consolidate the dictatorship of the proletariat, under the guidance of the correct political line. However, this revolutionary program, when placed in the hands of the reactionaries, becomes a mockery of the revolutionary aspirations of the masses; it even becomes the most ferocious, murderous weapon in the hands of our irreconcilable enemies.

If we do not punish the Jiang [Nationalist] gang who have aroused great popular hatred by insisting on the counterrevolutionary line, by turning the proletarian dictatorship into a Fascist dictatorship, and by bloody suppression and massacre of the people, then a socialist democracy and legal system will not be established and the proletarian dictatorship cannot be consolidated. Those who suppress the people must themselves be

suppressed. The Fourth National People's Congress should stipulate in black and white the regulations for punishing the "ministers" who have committed the heinous crimes of deliberately
transgressing the law, violating the law while enforcing it, creating fabricated cases, using official positions to avenge personal
grudges, establishing special cases without authorization, setting up private prisons, using unchecked corporal punishment,
and committing wanton murders.

4. From Each According to His Ability, to Each According to
His Work
Since the summer of 1968, and owing to suppression of democratic rights in the political sphere, especially by Lin Biao's Fascist
organizational line and its nepotist system of personnel appointments, as well as punitive transfers and reshuffles of the disobedient,
the principles of "from each according to his ability" and "employ
only the competent" have been sabotaged and the people's socialist
initiative trampled underfoot.

At the same time as special privileges are expanding, we also see
clearly that the worker and peasant laboring masses are deprived of
many of their reasonable economic benefits under slogans of "public
property-ism." For many years, the workers have not had their
wages raised, but had the reasonable bonuses, which were part of
their wages, abolished. The peasants suffered even greater losses as
a result of the uncompensated donations known as "loyalty grains,"
high quotas of requisitioned grain, and the campaigns for "cutting
off the tail of private ownership." Now, the dangers of Lin Biao's
"ultra-leftist" line become increasingly evident.

Did Lenin not laud "communist voluntary service on Saturday"
as a "great pioneering undertaking"? Have there not been innumerable self-sacrificing and selfless revolutionary heroes who emerged
from the Chinese working people in the period of revolutionary war,
in the high tide of socialist construction, and in the Great Proletarian
Cultural Revolution, characterized by rigor and vitality? This is precisely the invaluable historical initiative of the masses of people. But,
can it really be thus absolutized? Can spirit can substitute for everything, even the principle of "from each according to his ability, to
each according to his work" in this historical stage of socialism? Obviously, it is absurd. It is bound to be punished by the law of history;
it already has been.

In the Great Proletarian Cultural Revolution, we have opposed
high wages, high bonuses, and high payments; but should we abso-

lutely negate the role of monetary rewards? Why could a worker who is more enthusiastic, more conscientious and responsible, and has overfulfilled the set production quota, or invented or created something, not get more appropriate rewards than his colleagues? Why could a worker, a peasant, a revolutionary intellectual who has engaged in creative writing in addition to his assigned works, or made new discoveries or new inventions, not get appropriate material incentives? The principle of empty politics is to reward the lazy and to punish the diligent. The principle of "from each according to his ability, to each according to his work," with proletarian politics in command, is to stimulate and protect the socialist initiative of the masses; moreover, conscientious practice of this principle is also the most effective measure to restrict special privileges! The Fourth National People's Congress should stipulate in black and white a clause to ensure "from each according to his ability, to each according to his work."

We harbor great expectations of the Fourth National People's Congress. We hope that it can be a congress of unity, a congress of victory, and a congress that reflects the united will and wishes of the broad masses of people who have gone through the Great Proletarian Cultural Revolution. But the tragic and heroic *Internationale,* which was sung aloud by Chairman Mao when he was waging violent battles against the Lin Biao anti-Party clique, has deeply shocked and moved the broad masses of people. They know that the stipulations in the new Constitution would once again give us a weapon. To really implement them will depend on the struggle waged by the broad masses of people themselves.

Did not the Constitution of 1954 also stipulate the people's democratic rights? Has Chairman Mao not said many times that "without extensive people's democracy, the dictatorship of the proletariat cannot be consolidated"? But, partly because there exists the antidemocratic force which was represented by Lin Biao, and partly because the masses of people have seldom made use of these democratic rights (owing to the deeply entrenched feudal tradition in China and a lack of democratic spirit resulting from our country's comparatively backward production and the limited cultural level of the people), the objective of "creating a lively and vigorous political situation" proposed by Chairman Mao many years ago is far, far away from being achieved.

Just like a traveler from the fertile south who treasures water only when he comes to the desert, the masses of people appreciate more the value of the democratic rights when they were deprived of them during the Great Proletarian Cultural Revolution. Although the broad masses of people were cruelly suppressed in 1968, "in the world-wide tides today, the anti-democratic, reactionary faction is only a counter-current." A mass movement to thoroughly destroy the Lin Biao System will come in the not too remote future, it will restore and develop all the spirit of the Great Proletarian Cultural Revolution.

First draft: September 19, 1973
Second draft: December 12, 1973
Finalized draft: November 7, 1974

Postscript

IN RESPONSE to the suggestions proffered by a few comrades, we intend to mimeograph this article so that many more people can study, criticize, and comment on the viewpoints presented in this poster. Due to the shortage of paper, we sincerely request that the broad masses of revolutionary comrades provide us with as much paper as possible, for instance, ten, one hundred, a thousand, or ten thousand sheets of paper, no matter how few or many they are.

Those who are willing to help should keep in touch with Li Zhengtian whose address is Xinkang Road, Guangdong People's Arts College (originally Canton Fine Arts College), Guangzhou. And to those we render our

Sublime Revolutionary Salute!   Li Yi Zhe November 11, 1974

DOCUMENT 20

WANG FANXI
On the "Great Proletarian Cultural Revolution"

In 1967, Wang Fanxi published a long pamphlet in Hong Kong presenting his analysis of the Cultural Revolution. At the time the world was utterly confused by the Red Guards and Maoist ideology. European Maoists and even some Christian groups saw the Cultural Revolution as an expression of the possibility of the transformation of human nature. Western politicians saw it as a call for world revolution, and Soviet leaders too felt threatened. Wang's essay reveals a perceptive and prescient analysis, which gradually became shared in its essentials by many commentators: that the Cultural Revolution was both a power struggle between leadership factions, and an outburst of popular discontent. His prediction of a rapprochement with the United States was also fulfilled after the Nixon visit to Beijing in 1972. Unlike academic commentators, however, Wang believed that the Cultural Revolution could be deepened and transformed, and might become the starting point for a genuine revolution in China: a dream that failed to materialize.

RED GUARDS AND THE GENERATION OF YOUTH

The question of "Red Guards" is the most perplexing of the many perplexing phenomena arising out of the "Great Proletarian Cultural Revolution." Obviously, among all the leaders of the Communist Party at present, Mao is still the most powerful. The control he holds on the Party, the administrative apparatus, the Army, and the Police (open or secret) might not be greater than that held by Stalin in the thirties (I believe it is greater); it would certainly not be less. But then Stalin harnessed his secret police to eliminate his opposition in the Party, the army, and the administrative apparatus. Why then does the more respected, more powerful Mao Zedong who is also in a firmer position not use similar, simpler methods like organized techniques, administrative orders, or the secret police to deal with Liu-Deng (i.e., Liu Shaoqi and Deng Xiaoping) and their followers? Why must he mobilize the masses of young people and authorize them to rebel, resulting in upheaval everywhere in the whole country?

This is the question that has puzzled so-called "China-experts" who call the Red Guards' movement the enigma wrapped in the mystery of the Cultural Revolution. People are unable to solve this mystery and they say that Mao is very sick and has lost the power to make judgments because of brain damage; some say that he is dead and that the person appearing at the Gate of Heavenly Peace is a fake, with all ideas originating from Jiang Qing and Lin Biao; some say that he has gone nuts and is having epileptic fits and would not trust anyone but the "Queen," close courtiers, and the faithful head of the army. The assumptions of these "clever people" are all wrong. No matter how strange this phenomenon of the Red Guards is, it can be adequately explained, and it is quite in accordance with Mao's thoughts.

For the Red Guards Movement to be possible, there is an exceedingly important objective foundation which must have been built, namely, the spiritual life of the generation of youth under communist rule. This life is "frustrating, hopeless, earthy, and empty." It is of course an inevitable result of the bureaucratic rule of the Chinese communists. It is also a passive protest and a manifestation of extreme discontent with this rule and its absurd youth policy.

Mao Zedong established himself through leading student movements, and he has a thorough understanding of the feelings and characteristics of youths. He is also a superb tactician and is quite good at manipulating various contradictory forces without regard to principles. When he discovered that the Party and administrative apparatus had been, to a large degree, usurped by his opponents, he would have no hesitation in utilizing the young people. He utilizes their deeply felt but passive discontent; mobilizes them; supports them; and turns their passive discontent into aggressive actions directed against his opponents—the "capitalist-road-ers in the Party." In Mao's estimation, when such action is taken, several birds are killed with one stone. First, the anger of the young people which would originally have been directed toward him would now be redi-rected, purifying his black spots, alleviating him of responsibilities; he became the "Great Helmsman" in an effort to combat bureaucratism, corruption, and capitalist degeneration. Second, Mao is able to fight against the Liu-Deng clique and totally destroy his opposition while, in the process, he actually strengthens his own absolute rule. Third, in the form of a mass movement, "making revolution" on one hand while "edu-cating" on the other, Mao hopes to train a massive number of new cadres who will be absolutely faithful to the Thoughts of Mao and who will be able to replace those bad, old, corrupt, cadres and thus prevent the next generation from entering the road to "revisionism."

With these aims in mind, Mao uses every means to mobilize the young people. The most important is the announcement he made that the old idea "heroic fathers bear heroic sons and reactionary fathers sire lay-abouts" is a "reactionary theory of lineage"; he announced that this class line which had been used to suppress young people is "thoroughgoing historical idealism." ("Carry the Great Proletarian Cultural Revolution Through to the End"—editorial, *People's Daily*, January 1, 1967.)

We may divide youth in China into the following three categories: (*a*) offspring of workers and peasants, the majority; (*b*) offspring of "bad families," a smaller number; and (*c*) offspring of "heroes and great men," the smallest group. Among these three categories of people, the most un-happy and the most discontented would be the second. They would be the most willing to see disturbances because they have everything to gain and nothing to lose. In the past they felt frustrated and hopeless because they only saw the absolute control of the Communist Party with few indica-tions of change. Now it is different—Chairman Mao turns out to be on the side of justice, redressing their unjust repression and explaining that their mistreatment is entirely due to the power holders in the Party and the apparatus men. Mao calls them to rise up and "rebel," to "seize power," and to get rid of "the handful." What an awakening spring thun-der and what a gigantic impulse! It is no wonder that the youthful gener-ation appeared frantic, their "enthusiasm reaching the sky." They pledged to "defend Chairman Mao to their deaths" and swore to "over-throw those power holders who have taken the capitalist road."

Of course very few of those who have had the opportunity to enter school and to become Red Guards belong to the second category. Among the students and the Red Guards, the majority are not offspring of "he-roes and great men" either. (This third category is, in fact, discriminated against by the Cultural Revolution Group of the Central Committee.

They have been specifically advised not to become the leaders of Red Guard organizations.) The majority of the Red Guards belong to the first category—the offspring of workers and peasants and the ordinary dwellers in the cities. They are unhappy with the status quo; they are antibureaucratic and their dissatisfaction is partly caused by their own experience and partly a reflection of the discontent of their parents. Therefore they can also be inflamed and agitated by the tricky "anti-power holder" slogans of Mao Zedong.

With Mao Zedong's Red Guards, many people are reminded of Hitler's "Youth Corps." Of course there are many fundamental differences between the two. If we equate the two without taking into account major differences, the analogy will be absurd. There is, however, at least one point on which the two are similar, that is, a section of "power holders" in both cases have harnessed the discontent of the masses of young people to attack the ruling class and the system. They both raise high the specter of revolution and preach high-sounding slogans; they mobilize the youth, organize them, and attack the opposition within the ruling class as well as the genuine revolutionary elements. Hitler utilized the discontent of the young people caused by the degeneration of capitalism to "make revolution" in order to defend capitalism. Similarly, Mao Zedong utilized the discontent among the young people caused by the bureaucratic rule of the Communist Party and called on them to "make revolution" in order to protect this bureaucratic rule.

The class nature of Hitler's "revolution" and Mao Zedong's "revolution" are different, but they are similar to the extent that the causes and the circumstances under which the masses of the young people are used are very similar. The intense contradictions between the ruling class and the people, especially the masses of young people, are very much the same.

In the "normal" capitalist countries, if crisis develops in the existing ruling system, the problem is solved through parliamentary struggle. But when capitalism develops into an "abnormal" stage, when there exists an "abnormal" crisis in the country, democratic parliamentary struggle becomes useless and so the result is fascism, nazism, or some similar "revolutionary" method of dealing with the crisis and thus preserving the capitalist system. Similarly, within the communist parties themselves and in countries ruled by communist parties, when conditions are normal and healthy, all kinds of problems (large and small contradictions) should be solved by methods of democratic centralism. It should be so with the Party; it should be so with the government (the soviets). During Lenin's time, there arose continuously contradictions and crises which were overcome by using this method. But when the conditions of the Party and the country became more and more abnormal, that is, more and more degenerated, the traditional means of resolving contradictions become inappropriate and other "emergency actions" are used. History has shown us two different kinds of emergency actions: one is Stalinist—the use of secret police and judicial frame-ups to carry out large-scale murders and massacres: the other is that if Mao Zedong—the mobilization of the masses supplemented by the Stalinist method. The Mao method is a conspiracy of the few which seeks the approval and participation of the masses, but seeks the same goals as the Stalinist one.

That Stalin and Mao should use different methods in attempts to resolve their contradiction is, of course, partly due to their differences in personalities, but more important, the difference arises from the fact that the two are in different positions. Mao has not followed Stalin in this respect, which may be attributed to the fact that Mao is confident (maybe even overconfident) of his authority and prestige. With such confidence, Mao seems to believe that it would be inadequate, incomplete, insufficient, and furthermore non-educational to use "organizational tactics" or other conspiratorial means to eliminate his enemies (who occupy many positions in the Party, the administrative apparatus, and elsewhere). So he decided to mobilize thousands and millions, to practice "great democracy," to "struggle, criticize, and transform," in order to thoroughly crush the opponents he dislikes and to train a large number of new cadres who are inoculated against "revisionism." He realized that to do what he is doing would lead to large-scale opposition and disturbances, but he believes that every development will follow the line that has been laid down and will not go astray.

Will Mao Zedong's Aims Be Realized?

Mao's first aim is to redirect popular discontent. Can the Red Guard Movement relieve the discontent of the masses, especially that of the sensitive young students, accumulated over the years against Mao and the Communist Party? Can they then attack the "handful of power holders who have taken the capitalist road" and at the same time support the prestige of Mao?

This is unlikely. Even if it appeared to be so, it was inevitably a fleeting phenomenon that has now passed. Of course, Mao has made use of his advantage in this respect. That is, he has always been the accuser and never the accused. If he also defeated his opponents, he would have placed all sorts of accusations and responsibilities onto them, and used the vanquished as scapegoat to be sacrificed to God. But as the Chinese Communists have always said: "the people's eyes are bright and clear," meaning that no great dictator can manage to deceive all the eyes and ears under the sun! Victory itself of course implies tremendous persuasive powers, but the more important questions are how these victories have been achieved and what kind of victories they are. But if what has brought victories to Mao is blatant suppression by force, shameless lies and unprincipled tactics, and if Mao, in order to secure victory, uses the same methods to treat his enemies and supporters, and furthermore, if the victory that he has won is not commendable but corrupt, then Mao Zedong, following a victory of this kind, would be unable to find his scapegoat to sacrifice to the "God of the People."

Right now, Mao is using exactly these means to secure his victories. As a result, Mao's victory will only bring dissatisfaction to the Great Helmsman. The victory only brings the focus of the dissatisfaction, especially those of the disillusioned youths, onto Mao himself.

Let us have a look at the other aims that Mao has in mind. First, Mao wants to organize this mass movement to defeat all of his opponents in the Party and in the country so that ideologically the Party and the country would be united by the "Thoughts of Mao Zedong" and, organizationally, the Party and the country would be controlled by Mao. Second, Mao wants to train a large group of new cadres who would be immune from "revisionism" and "bureaucratism."

Can these ends be achieved? To answer the first point, we have to make clear as to the degree of "unity" and the degree of "control." Up to a certain degree, the ideology of the Chinese Communist Party during the past twenty years has always been unified under the thoughts of Mao Zedong, and likewise organizationally Mao has always been in control. However, Mao was not happy with the extent of unity and the extent of control, especially during the last few years. This "unity" and this "control" have been seriously challenged. Dissatisfied, Mao wanted to strengthen them. Yet how absolute do "unity" and "control" have to become before Mao is satisfied? Obviously he wants them to be more so than Stalinist Russia, even than Hitler's Germany! He wants to become the most absolute Pope during the Medieval dark ages; he wants to become the supreme head of a religion like Mohammed. He wants to cause every single word or phrase of his to become "the highest instruction," "the absolute truth"; he wants his Selected Works to be the Bible and his quotations to be some sort of "magical incantations." He wants this Bible and the "magic incantations" to substitute for the sum total of human knowledge, present and past; to be the encyclopedia of "proletarian culture." In order to fulfill his objective, he calls all other works "feudal" and "capitalist" and burns them. And by calling them "evil dirt," he persecuted all those intellectuals who have attained a certain degree of achievement in literature, history, philosophy, or art.

Mao Zedong's policies in this respect are totally and ridiculously reactionary and are contrary to Marxism-Leninism. However, this will be discussed elsewhere. All that needs to be said is whether it is possible to establish this kind of unity and this kind of absolute control.

Impossible!

It is impossible regardless of what angle we examine it from. Starting from the general pattern of human thought, submission to authority and resistance to it always coexist; considering the present stage of progress in human thought, the new collectivism cannot but include individualism; considering the development of China's culture, it has reached such a level that the masses have been more or less enlightened and the intellectuals have been baptized by science and democracy; and considering the development of culture on a worldwide scale, no matter how strong the adverse current, socialism will inevitably replace capitalism and democratic communism will supplant police-controlled communism.

Therefore Mao's ambition in this respect, which surpasses that of Shi Huangdi and Stalin, will be proven by history to be a sheer illusion and a ridiculous instance of anachronism. Granted that Mao succeeds in achieving the absolute unity and control in appearance for a short period of time, this would only mean that history will be punishing him and the system he tries to establish with extra strength at a much higher speed.

Concerning the other question as to whether or not through the Red Guards movement Mao would be able to train a whole generation of new cadres who would be immune to "revisionism" and "bureaucratism," we would answer this way. The new cadres are being trained and eventually they will become fully fledged cadres, but the cadres thus trained would not be immune to degeneration into "revisionism" and "bureaucratism."

Why? We have explained elsewhere and we shall not discuss it in great detail again. All in all, if we don't follow the policies of permanent revolution, if we don't thoroughly give up the reactionary policy of "socialism in one country"; if we don't regard the success of the Chinese revolution as the spark for socialist revolutions in other parts of the world (including the underdeveloped part and the highly developed capitalist countries) and regard it as a self-sufficient base for "the construction of the prosperous and strong socialist fatherland"; if we don't hold up the preliminary socialist construction as an example of the superiority of socialism (even in poor countries) over capitalism in order to attract the working class and the poor of the old capitalist countries to the side of socialism so that they carry out socialist revolutions in their own countries; then in a "poor and empty" country, the leaders of the victorious socialist revolution will find no effective ways to oppose or prevent "revisionism" and "bureaucratism."

Under Mao's policy of the Stalinist "communism in one country," the great number of cadres to be selected from the Red Guards of today will degenerate into bureaucrats easier and faster than the old cadres (who presently are having their heads bashed, but who once went through a long period of real struggle) because they seized power through a revolutionary dress rehearsal. They completed their "long march" with free train tickets, and they are immature successors who have been artificially raised in the greenhouse of Mao Zedong's "Cultural Revolution."

WHAT CLASS INTERESTS DOES THE CULTURAL REVOLUTION SERVE?

What has been discussed above concerns mainly the political and factual aspects of the "Great Cultural Revolution." We would like to discuss a deeper theoretical question, namely, what class interest does Mao Zedong's "Great Cultural Revolution" serve?

The case with Stalin was crystal-clear—he represented the interests of conservative bureaucrats of the USSR and the position of the "centralists" of the bureaucrat caste in particular. He engaged in every kind of maneuver, now attacking the left, now the right, savagely and stubbornly, protecting the interests of the bureaucrats and at the same time the social foundations on which the bureaucrats depend for their survival—the system of nationalized and state-owned property.

What about Mao Zedong? Of course, he also represents the interests of the bureaucrats. However, his stands are somewhat different from Stalin's. It appears that Mao directly represents the left of the ruling class and the "Great Cultural Revolution" is directed at what was vaguely equivalent to the right in the Communist Party of the Soviet Union in those days. Is this indeed the case? No. Since the time around 1930 when the Chinese Communist Party made a decisive break with the left opposition, it does not have any more genuine left wing among its ranks (at least not among its leadership). Since then, all internal struggles which have ever happened inside the Chinese Communist Party, be it between Mao Zedong and Wang Ming, between Mao Zedong and Zhang Guotao, or between Mao Zedong and Liu Shaoqi, were all caused by tactical differences or even by personal interests. Seldom have they been due to differences in revolutionary principles. If ever the question involves ideologies, at the most, they are differences within the Stalinist School: Stalinist Right and Stalinist Left. Both of them, right and left, if measured by the rule of Marxism-Leninism, are Centrists. It was the case with Stalin himself—during the over twenty years of his absolute rule, he sometimes jumped to the left and sometimes to the right, but at the same time, he remained a Centrist.

The Chinese Communist Party, which has long been dominated by Stalinism, was naturally affected by this "jumping back and forth." Every jump would correspond with an internal change in the Chinese Communist Party and to complete this change would often imply some kind of struggle, large or small—a struggle between those supporting the new stand and those supporting the old one. In these struggles, Mao has not always been on the left, although generally speaking he was with the left; he would not retreat on the question of seizure of political power by force, and would not bind himself to keep any promise on the question of uniting with the bourgeoisie.

Therefore, generally speaking, Mao Zedong should be considered as a successor to the Stalinist left wing. He particularly accepted Stalinism of the later thirties, namely, the political and economic adventurism, narrow-minded political sectarianism (clothed in ultra-leftist clichés), personal authoritarian bureaucratism, and the Bonapartism that manipulates class contradictions.

The left wing of the Stalinists is, of course, not equivalent to the left wing of Marxist-Leninists. It is the left in the Centrists. It is called the "left" only in comparison with the right in the same group. The Stalinists have only had two kinds of attitudes toward capitalism and capitalists: one is submission, compromising at the expense of principles or even surrendering shamelessly; the other is opposition by adventurous, thoughtless, savage, and criminal sectarianism and bureaucratism. The former is "right" and the latter is "left." Its "right" is, of course, a betrayal of Marxism-Leninism but this kind of "left" has nothing in common with Marxism-Leninism either. Whether "left" or "right," whether it embraces or attacks the capitalist class, it does nothing beneficial for the proletariat or socialist revolution, and in some cases does more harm than good. Therefore we must not confuse the left and right of Stalinism and the left and right of Marxism-Leninism. It is because the essence of the two belongs to different categories and if we equate the two or take the face value of the radicalism of the Stalinist left turn, we would have deceived ourselves.

We can find examples in the internal struggles of the Soviet Communist Party when Trotsky represented the left. On many occasions, for example, on the slogan of constituent assembly for China after 1928; on the question of collectivization in the Russian countryside in 1930; and on the question of forming a united front in Germany with the Social Democratic Party, Stalin appeared to be on the "left" but in reality he was very "right," because his policies delayed the revolution, or cost a great deal to the progress of the revolution. All of these objectively rendered immense service to the bourgeoisie and therefore in essence were "right" or even "ultra-right."

The alleged "left" nature of Mao Zedong and his clique should be viewed similarly. Among those who oppose Mao from the "right," there are, of course, some genuine right-wingers (especially among those leaders who have consistently backed the Stalinist position) who support a line of prolonged cooperation with the capitalists. However, there is another group, a very large group, the masses (including some in the higher level of the hierarchy) who have not been tied down by Stalinism and who may not really be "right." Most likely they just appear to be "right" but, in fact, are "left." In other words, what they support may well be more in the interests of the proletarian revolution of China and the world. Mao's position would be "left" in relation to the first category of anti-Maoists, but would be "right" in relation to the second category. Like Stalin in his day, Mao's position is that of the "Centrist bureaucrats." Mao's "Great Proletarian Cultural Revolution" is similar to Stalin's "antirightist" struggle in the sense that although it has some "anticapitalist" connotations, it does not serve the interests of the proletariat. Oscillating and jumping back and forth, it invariably serves the interests of the most privileged and the most powerful bureaucrats.

"But isn't Mao Zedong's Great Cultural Revolution mobilizing thousands and millions of the non-bureaucratic masses to seize power from the bureaucrats and to rebel? Isn't this solidly attacking or even defeating the bureaucrats?"

True enough. This we have discussed before, and this is what makes things different from Stalin. However, we have also explained that this difference is not fundamental. The forms are different but, in essence, both are for the protection of the interests of the bureaucracy, only it was more obvious with Stalin. With Mao there were some phony phenomena confusing the perspective.

Yet there seems to be a little bit of real difference which arises from the different tendency and nature of the bureaucracy which each of them represents. Stalin represented the more conservative part of the bureaucracy. These bureaucrats had incessantly yielded to the pressure of the capitalist elements in internal affairs, and only when they found their position in serious danger did they begin to wage the counterattack in a panic. Externally, they always submitted to the pressure of the imperialists and so finally abandoned the task of world revolution. The bureaucrats that Mao Zedong represents, however, seem to be more radical. Their internal or external policies appear to be extremely left and uncompromising. Under hostile pressures from within and outside the country, Mao has not shown indications of backing down. On the contrary, his fighting spirit has been heightened. Does this difference in performance mean that the Maoists at least represent the revolutionary section of the ruling caste of the CCP?

I don't think this can be considered true. Any Centrist can oscillate to the right and from right to left. Let's take the case of Stalin. From the late 1920s until his death, his whole tendency was "right" indeed: compromising with international imperialists and betraying the world revolution. Nevertheless, there were cases when Stalin turned "left." The most famous of them was the period known as the "Third Period" (from 1929 to 1933) during which Stalin used ruthless and terrorist methods to eliminate the rich peasants internally, while externally he resolved to fight alone, blindly, against imperialism. It was this "Leftist" policy of Stalin's, as we all know, that created the opportunity for Hitler's victory in Germany and a reactionary situation throughout the world, which in its turn forced him to jump drastically to the right, adopting the policy of the "people's front."

Mao Zedong's present policy, internal and external, is roughly speaking somewhat equivalent to Stalin's "Third Period." It is the antithesis of the reactionary policy of "people's democracy." It will receive new, heavier blows, and when its head bumps against the wall, it will probably turn to the right again, to a new submission to the international imperialists, especially American imperialism. The ultra-left policy of today is the result of the ultra-right policy of yesterday, and it can become the cause of a new ultra-right line tomorrow.

How can we break this "Centrist" chain of causes and results? There is only one way, and that is to make use of the opportunity created by today's ultra-left policy to deepen the pseudo-revolution, turning it into a genuine revolution so that proletarian democracy will prevail in China.

NOTES TO CHAPTER THREE

1. For further details, see Victor Nee, *The Cultural Revolution at Peking University* (New York: Monthly Review Press, 1969).
2. For further discussion of Shengwulian, see Livio Maitan, *Party, Army and Masses in China*, translated by Gregor Benton and Marie Collitti (London: NLB, 1976), pp. 234–39.
3. We have been unable to locate any specific statement by Mao to this effect.
4. A full translation of the text and analysis of its context may be found in Anita Chan, Stanley Rosen, and Jonathan Unger, eds., *On Socialist Democracy and the Chinese Legal System: The Li Yizhe Debates* (Armonk, N.Y.: M. E. Sharpe, 1985).
5. A popular saying, meaning that hangers-on obtain sinecures from successful politicians.
6. In other words, immediate results are all that matter.
7. These incidents were massacres, usually of demonstrators, in the 1920s.
8. This idiom means to be forced to engage in unlawful activities despite one's wishes. It suggests that Mao Zedong did not participate voluntarily in the excesses of the personality cult.
9. Dong Zhongshu was an ancient philosopher who asserted that dynastic changes should be accompanied by elaborate rituals and the creation of new orders among the nobility. The authors are referring sarcastically to the personality cults surrounding Mao and Lin.
10. Refers to the abolition of various freedoms mentioned above—such as freedom of speech—that were declared obsolete by Lin Biao.

CHAPTER FOUR

CHINA SPRING, 1979–1981

DOCUMENT 21

WANG XIZHE
Mao Zedong and the Cultural Revolution

Wang Xizhe was a student in Guangzhou City when the Cultural Revolution began in 1966. Like millions of other Chinese youth, he joined in denouncing the authorities and "making revolution." In 1968, the Maoist leaders decided to put an end to the Cultural Revolution, which was by then getting out of hand. Wang, along with many other of Mao's "little generals," was arrested in late 1968. A year later he was freed and sent to work in the countryside, but was allowed back to the city when his parents pointed out that he was their only son. Through his parents, he found a factory job. In 1973–74, Wang and three others wrote the well-known wall poster *On Socialist Democracy and the Legal System*, for which they were imprisoned (see Document 19).

After Wang's release from prison, he joined the newly born democracy movement. In April 1979, he wrote a manifesto titled "The Struggle for the Class Dictatorship of the Proletariat" in the Guangzhou unofficial journal *Renminzhi sheng* (Voice of the People), which he described as a refinement of the 1974 Li Yi Zhe poster.[1] This manifesto is a sustained and theoretically original critique of post-capitalist society. It argues that when the proletariat takes power in a backward country, it can either close its doors to the outside world and retreat into a regime of "feudal socialism" or enter the world system and become a "big cooperative factory"—"a bourgeois state without a bourgeoisie"—producing for the capitalist world market. But because the workers are uneducated, not they but the vanguard—the Communists—will administer this cooperative. In future, either the workers' cultural level will rise so that they can take over administrative tasks, or the vanguard will become "alienated into something opposed to the proletariat," that is, a dictatorship of "Communist bureaucrats." The social basis for such a dictatorship still exists in China: the "Gang" was not the cause but the symptom of social conditions.

The essay translated here analyzes Mao's role in the Chinese Revolution. Wang's view—expressed at a time when it was still dangerous to say anything critical about Mao—is that Mao was not a Marxist revolutionary but a peasant leader, and that this was both his strength and his weakness. Like peasant leaders throughout Chinese history, Mao's aim was to become emperor. Although he boldly incited movements against the bureaucracy, his real aim was to remove his rivals and become sole ruler. On many points Wang's positions coincide with those of party reformers like Deng Xiaoping, and this has led some observers to suggest that he was not really a dissident at all. But this is to misunderstand Wang's tactic. His support for Deng was never uncritical, and the extended logic of his position was not Deng's. His criticisms of the system go much further than Deng's, and his aim is clearly to push reforms to the limit. Wang's article throws important light on the way in which the Cultural Revolution influenced Chinese youth. China's present rulers, and many foreign observers too, now argue that the Cultural Revolution was irredeemably bad. But Wang's article suggests that it taught some youth to think independently, and thus paved the way for the democratic opposition.

In May 1980, when the dissident Liu Qing was arrested, Wang published an open letter in which he said: "A precise legal system and trials that conform rigorously to the law: that is the best lesson China could learn from the last thirty years. . . . The people expect no miracles. They expect no one to produce democracy and a legal system out of a hat. They are content to advance one step at a time, but they will tolerate no turning back."

Wang Xizhe was rearrested in 1981, and sentenced (together with Xu Wenli, see Document 24) in June 1982 to a fourteen-year sentence for "counterrevolutionary propaganda," sedition, forming a "counterrevolutionary group," and inciting the masses to defy the state. From 1988 to 1991, Wang was held in punitive solitary confinement in a special compound for political prisoners. He was released on parole in 1993, when he defended his political beliefs and reaffirmed that what he had done was "worthwhile." He continued to speak to foreign journalists and publish in the Hong Kong press despite warnings from the authorities.

The text published here has been greatly abridged, and deletions have not been indicated.

THE STRUGGLE FOR AND AGAINST REFORM IN CHINA

My friend Jin Jun of the Democratic Youth group wrote me a letter saying: "Mao's greatness lies in the fact that he spared nothing in criticizing the state he had set up. He disrupted order in a society in which he, as Chairman, was supposed to maintain it. He disrupted the party that called him Chairman."

But why did Mao disrupt the state and the Party? Was he dissatisfied with their growing Stalinization? Not at all. He was suspicious of the forces for change that were springing up irrepressibly in them, and thought that they were not autocratic and authoritarian enough. He wanted to set up a new state and Party that would be a Mao dynasty disguised as a dictatorship of the proletariat.

After the victory of the revolution in 1949, the Party set up a new democratic order that was to be long-lasting and stable. Since China was economically and culturally backward, socialism could not yet be brought in. Instead, production would be organized through state capitalism, within which were the germs of socialism. Individual and corporate capital and the communal economy of the villages were to be preserved and developed, for economic laws are natural laws, not to be circumvented.

Mao Zedong, however, disagreed. He would be even greater than the legendary three kings and five emperors. He would make miracles to prove that Marx's view of development through stages was that of a mere academic. And so he began to issue commands to the country's economy.

Mao Zedong, this peasant from Hunan, declared his great principles of agro-socialism. He said that despite primitive tools and peasant ignorance, socialism could still be built by mobilizing human labor and changing the forms of ownership. He believed that the poor peasants, because of their misery, are a vast reservoir of resources with which to build socialism. Marx and Lenin thought differently. For Lenin, even workers in big industry would never come to socialism without an outside agency. But Mao said that poor peasants are instinctively socialist, and that the Party's task is simply to mobilize them and nothing more. Now if the peasants are instinctively enthusiastic about socialism, then anyone who is not so is probably a reactionary. And if the Party's task is to mobilize existing potential, then any Party member who does not do so can only be a right-opportunist and a capitalist-roader. Furthermore, since agro-socialism develops not naturally but through human agency, the power of decision must be concentrated in the Party, and more specifically in the Great Leader, Mao. And so the theory of agro-socialism turns out in practice to be the theory of Maoist authoritarianism.

From the very start leaders like Liu Shaoqi opposed the authoritarian trend, and called for the democratization of Chinese politics. Their struggle more or less coincided with Khrushchev's denunciation of Stalin and his calls for Party democracy and a collective leadership. This was good news for Liu Shaoqi's group, which in September 1956 succeeded in getting the references to Mao Zedong Thought deleted from the Party rules, and in winning other reforms that marked the first stage in the Party's democratization.

The Twentieth Congress of the Soviet Communist Party created waves of anti-Stalinism throughout Eastern Europe, and in Hungary Soviet tanks, with Mao's strong support, quelled a people's uprising. The events in Hungary caused a great ferment in China, where students and intellectuals began to call for democratic reform. Faced with pressure from both inside and outside the Party, Mao decided to hit back. His strategy was to lure his "rightist" opponents into the open by telling them to speak freely, and then to destroy them.

Who were these so-called rightists? True, some were reactionaries, but most were simply people who were unhappy with the bureaucratization of the Party, the collusion of state and Party, Party control of appointments, and the bureaucratic ways of petty officials. They were opposed to Russia's chauvinist foreign policy. They wanted more freedom in think-

ing, academic study, and politics. For Mao, all these demands were subversive, although as a revolutionary he had fought for the same demands
ever since graduating from Hunan Normal School.

The purge of the "rightists" outside the Party was at the same time a
warning to the "rightists" inside it. From now on these "rightists" would
be wise not to oppose Mao's speeding up of the revolution. Having acqui-
esced in the concentration of Power in Mao's hands, they could hardly
oppose the Great Leap Forward. Soon the personality cult was revived,
and Mao started out on his agro-socialist experiment.

Irrigation is central to the Asiatic mode of production. In China, Mao
hoped to abolish droughts and floods overnight as proof of the miracu-
lous power of agro-socialism. He wanted to mobilize the bare hands of
millions of peasants through a huge administrative network, and to na-
tionalize without compensation the innumerable stocks of capital scattered throughout China's countless villages. Mao's administrative "new
creation" was the People's Commune. Marx and Engels could never quite
bring themselves to construct for posterity a model of how communism
would be, but Mao not only projected such a utopia but even put it into
action. In the commune political and social life were to become fused, as
were industry, agriculture, commerce, education, and defense. Mao even
told the peasants (and announced through a resolution of the Central
Committee) that China would finish building Communism in eight to ten
years, and catch up to Britain in steel production in one to two years by
mobilizing 90 million peasants to run small village furnaces.

Mao Zedong obviously believed that the national economy could be
directed in the same way as an army. But putting the economy under
military rule requires a commander. The obvious choice for such a commander was Mao, who now began his assault on the idea of collective
leadership. He said:

> It is interesting that some people are opposed to the cult of the
> individual. Well, there are two forms. One is correct, such as that of
> Marx, Engels, Lenin, and Stalin. These we must forever and ever
> revere. We can't do otherwise; the truth is in their hands. . . . A
> squad should revere its squad leader. The question at issue is not
> whether there should be glorification of the individual, but whether
> what is being upheld is the truth. If it is, then the individual should
> be revered. If it is not, then even collective leadership will not help.
> Better that I become a dictator than let you become one.[2]

The ground won by the Party democrats in the fight for collective leadership was soon lost. This was not so much because of Mao's influence as
because Mao's agro-socialism is a product of the Chinese Communist
Party's basic constituency: the peasants. China's peasants have never even
seen modern industry, let alone worked in it. Scientific socialism therefore

means nothing to them. For them, Communism is a heavenly kingdom of peace where all are equal. If Mao can bring such a kingdom into being, then Mao shall reign over it. But the Party democrats did not simply sneak from the battlefield. Mao's Great Leap Forward led to widespread famine and chaos, and as a result Mao was severely challenged in the leadership by Peng Dehuai and Zhang Wentian. Peng courageously argued that "it is abnormal and dangerous to build up personal rather than collective authority." At this Mao, who could tolerate anything but a challenge to his own authority, flew into a rage against Peng, venting all the anger and frustration he felt as a result of the failure of the Great Leap Forward. He declared Peng an opportunist and a reactionary, stripped him of the right to speak, and subjected him to hysterical and unscrupulous criticism. At the same time, he had Peng replaced as head of the armed forces by the Maoist Lin Biao.

Nevertheless, the economic collapse in 1960–61 forced him to retreat from his Great Leap Forward and to grudgingly agree to new economic policies. Liu Shaoqi described the crisis of 1960–61 as "due 30 percent to natural disasters and 70 percent to human error." These mistakes, he said, were caused by the pride and conceit of some comrades and by the weakening of democratic centralism. Thus Liu aligned with Peng and Zhang Wentian. For the time being, Mao had no choice but to accept the situation, and he even made a now famous speech praising democratic centralism and admitting that his own authority was limited by the Central Committee and the Politburo. But he was put under scarcely any pressure. The Chinese, unlike the French or the British, are traditionally forbearing with their rulers.

Before long Mao was back on the attack. After the crisis of 1959–61 consumer goods were scarce, especially in the villages. Some officials were taking advantage of their office to embezzle collective property, and while Liu Shaoqi's new liberal agricultural policy did revive the village economy somewhat, it also led to hoarding and other illegal activities. With time these problems, which can be explained as the lingering after-effects of Mao's leftism, could have been resolved, but Mao was determined to exploit them to show that his opponents in power were on the capitalist road, and that he was the one who had always followed socialism.

His strategy was to begin by attacking Khrushchevism. In Chinese eyes Khrushchev's policy toward China was unpardonable. But if Khrushchev was wrong and bad, then so must be de-Stalinization and democratic reform, and anyone who favored these must be a Chinese Khrushchev. The obvious candidate for this label was, of course, Liu Shaoqi, who had reformed the village economy, carried out Libermanist experiments, loosened the controls imposed in 1957 on intellectuals, and even tried to rehabilitate Peng Dehuai just as Khrushchev had tried to rehabilitate Bukharin.

Mao began his counterattack with plots and intrigues. By 1963 no one trusted him any longer, so he introduced his wife Jiang Qing into literary circles, and in less than two years she had gathered around her a large coterie of writers ready to support Mao. In September 1965 Mao tried to get the Party's backing for a criticism of two plays by Wu Han that he saw as veiled defenses of his disgraced critic Peng Dehuai. But Peng Zhen, representing the Central Committee, courageously resisted Mao's demand, so Mao had no choice but to move to Shanghai, where Jiang Qing and Yao Wenyuan drafted their own pro-Mao critique of Wu Han's work. Soon Peng Zhen was brought down, and the way was opened for a general assault on the reform group in the Party.

So to answer my friend Jin Jun, the reason Mao "spared nothing in criticizing the state he himself had set up" was not because he was great, but because he was reactionary. He wanted a more autocratic and centralized party-state, but the democratic reformers thwarted him. He could no longer ride the Party like a horse. That is why he set out to destroy it and to found a Mao Zedong fascist party.

THE CULTURAL REVOLUTION AND MAO'S VICTORY

People throughout China rejoiced at the fall of the Gang of Four in October 1976, but some young democrats both at home and abroad said that this was a defeat for the left and a victory for the bureaucrats. They believed that Mao, who never knew when to put a stop to the revolution, had come in his old age to the same conclusions as Trotsky and Tito: that China was bureaucratic not just in parts, but to the core; and that society must be mobilized to crush the bureaucratic institutions, even though it was against Mao's personal interests to do so. But, they conclude, Mao failed because he depended on the wrong people and because the bureaucratic institutions were too strong.

However, this view is wrong. Mao may now and then have said things against bureaucracy, but he saw nothing wrong in principle with a system whereby several hundred thousand ruled several hundred million. All he wanted was that the cadres should be disciplined to prevent them from oppressing the people.

Of course, there's nothing new here. Throughout history rulers of bureaucratic systems have always tried to discipline their middle and lower ranks. Otherwise they would risk a complete breakdown of the whole system.

Marx wanted the workers to crush bureaucracy and replace it by democracy, and the Bolsheviks followed him in this. But Stalin and Mao simply replaced the old bureaucratic system with a new one—the Communist bureaucratic system. True, this new system was the inevitable product of the turmoil of the October Revolution. But whereas for Lenin it was a bitter fruit, for Stalin and Mao it was sweet.

Why, then, did Mao repeatedly summon the Red Guards to disrupt what he called the bureaucratic stratum, and why did he declare the Paris Commune to be a model? The answer is, because he wanted to be in sole control of the Party. He knew that conflict between local officials and the people was inevitable, especially after his own extremist policies had plunged the country into poverty and chaos. His aim was to wipe out his opponents in the Party. But to do that, he needed support. How could he get such support? By painting his opponents as the scoundrels and bureaucrats who were responsible for all the suffering, and by calling on the people to overthrow them and to put Mao Zedong, the true Marxist, in power forever. By late 1966, he had succeeded in his main aim: amid the bluster and confusion, it really did seem as if Mao was on the side of the people against the bureaucrats.

But in a deserted back-street of Beijing a bespectacled young man of slight build was coolly jotting down his thoughts:

3 August 1966. Took part in purge session against Song Yuxi organized by a factory unit. Song stayed rather cool. During the session, it rained. Most people managed to find umbrellas or some other shelter. Song had to stand there in the rain. If I had had an umbrella, I would have let him share it. . . . Did I sympathize with him? Not at all. He had been living well enough, and he was always good at finding fault with others. All these years he had served only himself, and for that I hated him. But I could never endorse the stupid charges the crowd made against him: "Why did you censor the eight principles?" "Why didn't you let us study Mao's works?" "Why didn't you let Mao's works be printed?" This was ridiculous. It was as if being against Mao was a heinous crime.

The man who made these notes was Yu Luoke, who was executed as a "poisonous weed" in March 1970 at the age of twenty-seven. Yu's comments mirror three kinds of conflict: that between cadres and the people; that between cadres and Mao Zedong; and that between the people and Mao Zedong. The people purged the cadres as bureaucrats. But bureaucratization was the fault not of individual cadres but of Mao's autocratic system, which did not allow people to control their own fate. This the people could not see; they criticized the cadres because the cadres opposed Mao. In the second half of 1966, therefore, the people's instinctive struggle against bureaucracy became a weapon in Mao's fight for even greater autocracy. The people threw up the spears when the battle cry rang out, but were pierced by them as they fell back to the ground.

Now things were going well for Mao; he called a plenum of the Central

Committee where he vanquished Liu Shaoqi and Deng Xiaoping and appointed Lin Biao as his successor, under the watchful eye of Maoist "teachers and students of the revolution" and backed by the 38th Army, which was stationed outside the city. But Mao won by only one vote, so the crisis was not yet over. In order to wipe out the opposition from top to bottom, the people would have to be mobilized. Accordingly, Mao dressed up in a soldier's uniform and went to Tian'anmen Square, where he summoned millions of Red Guards to "rebel" against all those who opposed him or who were suspected of opposing him.

At first Mao encouraged people to believe that the aim of the Cultural Revolution was to destroy bureaucracy and replace it with a democratic system based on the Paris Commune. But when the Shanghai "rebels" set up the Shanghai Commune on 23 February 1967, Zhang Chunqiao told them on Mao's behalf

> If everything were changed into a commune what would happen to the Party? Where would we put the Party? On the commune committee are both Party members and non-party members. What would we do with the Party Committee? To change the system throughout the country would require a change in the political system and in the country's name. Some people might not recognize it, and that would cause a lot of trouble. In any case, such a change would be of no practical significance.[3]

A few months later, talking with foreign visitors about the Cultural Revolution, Mao was quoted as saying:

> Some people say elections are very good and democratic. To me, the word "election" is quite civilized, but I don't think there can be real elections. I was elected as a people's representative for the Beijing area, but who in Beijing really understands me? Zhou Enlai became premier because he was appointed by the Central Committee.

For Mao, democracy was just a means to an end. As soon as he alone represented the people, his democracy would become theirs, and his wishes would become theirs. If you were against him, you were against the people. This is the sum total of his political philosophy.

THE CULTURAL REVOLUTION AND MAO'S DEFEAT

On 13 September 1971 Lin Biao, Mao's "close comrade-in-arms" and heir apparent, died in a plane crash over Mongolia after a failed coup attempt. This event rocked China. No one could imagine Lin Biao without Mao's Little Red Book gripped firmly in his hands. What in heaven's name was going on?

For many years Lin Biao had fitted nicely into Mao's political scheme. Mao wanted to turn China into a military camp in which industry, farming, trade, schooling, and the army would be merged. Moreover, it was very important during the chaos of the Cultural Revolution that there should be a strong army in the background. And so Lin Biao's power grew formidably in those years.

When an impostor finally wins out, his first big problem is how to remove his cronies from the scene. After Mao's victory in the Cultural Revolution and at the 1969 Ninth Congress, the question of what to do with Lin Biao became pressing. But once Mao's interests clashed with those of Lin and the rising class of military bureaucrats, Lin's worship of Mao stopped, and the battle started.

But unlike Mao's struggle with Peng Dehuai in 1959, this was a battle not between good and evil, but between rival intriguers, without any obvious principles at stake. As a result, people's eyes were opened, and all kinds of repressed social currents flooded to the surface.

To boost his flagging credibility, Mao published a letter of July 1966 to Jiang Qing in which he had expressed some doubts about Lin Biao, but it had little impact. Some suspected it was forged. Others wondered why Mao had chosen Lin as his successor if he had doubts about him. But Mao's letter heartened those cadres purged during the Cultural Revolution, who now reasoned that since Mao had taken so long to discover that Lin Biao was a scoundrel, he might also eventually come to see that they were not scoundrels, and rehabilitate them.

By 1972 the campaign to criticize the extreme "left" had become so strong that it turned into a spontaneous mass movement. The implications of this movement were all too clear. It expressed the forces of reform that were resurfacing within the Party, as well as the Chinese people's new awareness of their interests and their willingness to defend them. Mao would never again be able to deceive millions of people into joining a crusade against his political opponents.

Toward the end of 1972, Mao's counterattack against this movement started. A series of articles in the official press insisted that Lin Biao was not a leftist but a rightist, and that to criticize him as a leftist was a veiled way of criticizing the Cultural Revolution. Why did Mao organize this hasty counterattack? The answer may be found in the new relationship between the classes in China after the Lin Biao affair. Lin's downfall had not only raised the question of how to evaluate the Cultural Revolution, but had also left behind a power vacuum.

Who would fill this vacuum? The only survivors of the victorious Maoist bloc were the Cultural Revolution Group of Jiang Qing and her associates. These people had made their fortunes instantaneously. They were ambitious and greedy for more power. They wanted to perpetuate the social as well as the political relations consolidated at the Ninth Congress in 1969.

The other main contenders were the group defeated in the Cultural Revolution, including both the democratic reformers and those opportunist bureaucrats who were brought down in the general turmoil. These people were able to breathe more easily now that the pressure was lifted somewhat. With Liu Shaoqi dead, they now looked to Zhou Enlai as the only person capable of uniting the Party and saving them from oblivion. Within a short time a large number of veteran leaders, including Deng Xiaoping, were rehabilitated under Zhou Enlai's auspices. Thus a new power center gradually formed around Zhou, even though he may not have wanted this to happen.

As for the people, they had long had enough of Maoist oppression and deceit and looked back wistfully to the early sixties, when the new economic policies were in force. They were angered by an education system that produced only "ignorant fools." Among them support for the veteran cadres grew ever stronger, and Zhou Enlai became the symbolic focus of this support.

With endless patience Zhou Enlai tolerated a series of veiled insults and challenges from the Cultural Revolution Group, who were determined to bring him down. In 1974, the Movement to Criticize Lin Biao and Confucius got underway. There is no evidence that the criticism of Confucius was originally meant to topple Zhou Enlai, even though it was clearly aimed at stemming the anti-leftist tide in China. Although Mao's old rivals were gathered around Zhou, Mao knew Zhou as a man without personal ambition, and needed him as a symbol of justice in the regime. It is the same with autocratic regimes everywhere: if the emperor himself is not a symbol of justice, then some good minister must be one, so that the oppressed people have somewhere to look in their suffering; otherwise, there is bound to be trouble.

But the Cultural Revolution Group were determined to turn the movement into a new Cultural Revolution. Unfortunately for them, however, the world had changed since 1966, and the people turned a deaf ear to their calls to overthrow Zhou Enlai. Moreover, a famous wall poster went up on the streets of Guangzhou titled *On Socialist Democracy and the Legal System*. This poster symbolized the rejection of Mao Zedong by those who had grown up in the Cultural Revolution. It argued that to criticize Lin Biao was not enough, and predicted a mass movement that would overthrow the entire system of which Lin Biao was a mere symptom.

It was at about this time that Deng Xiaoping, a resolute opponent of the Cultural Revolution Group, returned to political office. In January 1975 Zhou Enlai proposed launching the Four Modernizations. This proposal was widely supported in China. Millions of former students were without work and wages had been frozen for many years, so that social tensions were rising. Moreover, rapid economic development in other countries was putting pressure on China to accelerate the rate of growth of her own economy.

As chief executive of the modernization plan, Deng Xiaoping began to propose measures for its implementation. But shortly after Zhou Enlai's death in January 1976, Deng suddenly disappeared from the political scene again, not to reappear until after Mao's death several months later. After 1949 most Chinese had boundless confidence in Mao. They believed he could make the sun shine and the rain fall. Even his failures they were prepared to blame on his opponents. But the Lin Biao affair changed all this. When Mao tried to dismiss Deng Xiaoping after more than ten years of "antirevisionist" struggle, the people turned in a trice to the "revisionists," and took to the streets to demonstrate against Mao.

The Tian'anmen Square incident of April 1976, one of the greatest revolutionary mass movements in Chinese history, was a plebiscite in which the people, in the absence of proper democratic procedures, cast their votes in the form of wreaths, poems, and speeches. But Mao Zedong was always contemptuous of elections, so he was determined to suppress the movement. His clubs and bayonets easily scattered the tens of thousands of unarmed demonstrators. But his victory was short-lived. He died on the day of the Mid-Autumn Festival, when Chinese are traditionally reunited with their families. Some people say that this symbolizes the fact that Mao will never be reunited with the Chinese people.

MAO'S MERITS AND DEMERITS

Mao himself said that during his life he had accomplished two things of note: driving out Chiang Kai-shek, and launching the Cultural Revolution. We have already looked at the Cultural Revolution; and everyone agrees that Mao chased out Chiang Kai-shek. So does that mean that Mao's achievement was 50 percent good and 50 percent bad? No, that is too simplistic a view. Let us recall some of the milestones in Mao's struggle against Chiang.

In the autumn of 1927 the first Chinese revolution was in tatters as a result of Stalin's defeatist line. All Stalin could think of was to put the blame on Chen Duxiu. As for Trotsky, he came up with the impractical call for a Constituent Assembly. This was out of the question in a country where the landlord class had just put down a revolution of the workers and peasants. Besides, the people would never have welcomed it. Obviously Trotsky's strategy was modeled on the experience of the 1905 Revolution in Russia. Luckily the Chinese revolution did not adopt this strategy of retreat, or it would have plunged into a disaster from which it would never have recovered even to this day.

Mao Zedong was the only one to come up with the right strategy. He showed great courage in those difficult times. He called on Communists still wanting to continue the struggle to go out into the villages. He formulated a strategy that combined land reform with the use of revolutionary war to generate a revolutionary crisis. And so he saved the revolution from disaster. During the war against Japan and the ensuing civil war against Chiang Kai-shek, Mao once again resisted Stalin's orders and went ahead with strengthening and expanding the revolutionary army, right up to final victory.

Without doubt, Mao was a national hero. His outstanding achievement was that he firmly resisted Stalin's attempts to tailor the Chinese revolution to suit Soviet foreign policy. But one must not forget that the revolution he led was a peasant uprising. True, Mao overthrew a landlord regime, but this was something peasants too can do. Zhu Yuanzhang overthrew the Yuan dynasty and founded the Ming. Li Zicheng led a huge uprising against the Ming. And the Taipings almost overthrew the Qing. As for Mao's Jinggangshan stronghold, it had many predecessors in the history of Chinese banditry, of which the most notorious was the Liangshanbo. Mao Zedong, as someone who got his learning in China, stood head and shoulders above most Communist dogmatists in that he was more interested in the road to Liangshanbo than the road to St. Petersburg.

As a peasant leader Mao was unsurpassed, and it is not surprising, considering his peasant outlook, that he later became an emperor. But as a Marxist and a workers' leader he had few achievements. Marxists must search for ways of freeing the proletariat, of realizing popular democracy, and of making the people prosperous. But Mao achieved none of these—on the contrary, he raised obstacles in the way of achieving them.

The launching of a mass movement to purge the democratic reformers from the Party in 1966 had two main outcomes. On the one, it led to Mao's personal dictatorship. On the other it taught masses of young people to see themselves as equal rather than inferior to government officials. It taught them self-confidence through confrontation. And this is precisely the first step to democratic reform. Some even learned to analyze discrete problems of Chinese society in terms of the system as a whole. It was as if the Cultural Revolution had succeeded in molding a new generation that dared to think independently about questions of national import and to shoulder the responsibility for bettering society.

Some young comrades of the democratic group see this as a positive outcome of the Cultural Revolution, and treasure it. But they are wrong. Mao's aim was to found a dynasty, and he had no wish for a "thinking generation." The aim of his Cultural Revolution was to destroy several hundred million brains. When he had routed his opponents in the Party and installed new loyalists in their place, did he let the Red Guards say what they thought about the new regime or express their doubts and criticisms? Ask the young democrats in Shanghai! They can vividly recall how the Shanghai Red Revolutionary Association was immediately suppressed when it criticized the Maoist Zhang Chunqiao. Need I remind you that those who were suppressed in Tian'anmen Square in April 1976 were precisely the "thinking generation"?

The emergence of a "thinking generation" in China was merely a by-product of the Cultural Revolution. But all reactions have revolutionary by-products, just as all revolutions have reactionary ones. Of all the European nations, the Italians are the most politicized and have the biggest political parties. Scholars say that this is because the mass movements launched by the fascists got people used to political participation. Should we thank Mussolini for that?

Carry Socialist Democratic Reforms through to a Conclusion!

The victory of October 1976 was won by a united front of all those forces opposed to the Gang of Four. But after the victory splits were inevitable. The first split came over the question of reform: here the group around Wang Dongxing, which was opposed to the Gang of Four but not to Mao, came out against Deng Xiaoping and the reformers. The second split, which has not yet happened, will be over how far reform should go.

Right now Deng Xiaoping is in the same position as was Khrushchev in 1965. Unless he exonerates the millions of Chinese who suffered under Mao, social tensions will persist. Unless he breaks completely with the Stalin-Mao economic system, opens wide to the outside world and carries out reforms, the national economy will stagnate. Unless he stresses socialist legality and civil rights, intellectuals and young people in particular will trust socialism even less. Unless he improves the relations with sister parties that were strained by Mao's dogmatism, China will lack access to the theory and experience she needs to guide and defend her reforms.

But none of these things can happen unless thinking is liberated, and thinking can only be liberated if we drop the Mao cult and point out that Mao was fallible. This the dogmatists around Wang Dongxing were not willing to accept, so battle was joined between them and the Party pragmatists.

At the same time the dogmatists were being criticized even more severely from outside the Party. The extra-party democratic movement of 1978-1979 was in every way a continuation of the Tian'anmen movement of April 1976; many of its leaders had actively participated in the Tian'anmen demonstrations. The democratic movement developed in the struggle to reverse the verdict on the Tian'anmen incident (which the Maoists had labeled counterrevolutionary). Their chief opponents in the Party were precisely the dogmatists around Wang Dongxing, who supported the suppression of the Tian'anmen movement because Mao had ordered that suppression. Not surprisingly, these dogmatists were scathingly criticized by the young people of Beijing, and under blows from both within and outside the Party they were soon defeated.

The criticisms of the Party reformers and of the extra-party democratic movement were so well coordinated that both the dogmatists and many Western observers believed (groundlessly, as it happens) that this was a Maoist-style operation launched simultaneously from within and outside the Party. But whatever the similarities, the young people's struggle could no longer be directed by the Central Committee, unlike in 1966. Since April 1976, young people have learned to work for policy changes that are in line with their own interests.

Deng Xiaoping welcomed the democratic movement and even told Western reporters that "the Chinese people need freedom, freedom!" and that "we do not have the right to stop people putting up wall posters."

But some members of the democratic movement soon extended their criticism of the Party dogmatists to the bureaucratic system as a whole, which is the ultimate source of dogmatism and Maoist autocracy. In the nineteenth century there were no professional revolutionaries in Communist movements, and revolutionaries earned their living like everyone else. This was in line with the Social Democratic policy of carrying on struggles within the confines of the law. At the beginning of this century Lenin, as part of his preparation for armed struggle, set up a vanguard party staffed by full-time revolutionaries. And he was right to do so, since the revolution could never succeed without people who were prepared to devote their whole time and energy to it. But every thesis has its antithesis. After the victory of the revolution, the question arose of what to do with the professional revolutionaries. Lenin died before he could answer this question adequately. But it is well known that Lenin wanted elections along the lines of the Paris Commune, so that no one would be allowed to occupy a post permanently, however great his or her contribution to the revolution. If this principle is not followed, there is nothing to distinguish a Communist revolution from a peasant one. Unfortunately, under Stalin's influence the group of professional revolutionaries became lifelong bureaucrats, first in Russia and then in China, thus ensuring the reproduction of a new generation of bureaucrats.

However, two kinds of Communists must be distinguished. First, there are those who dislike bureaucracy and who dislike belonging to the bureaucratic system. They see bureaucracy as something contrary to the socialist convictions to which they commit their lives. They fight ceaselessly against the growth of bureaucracy and autocracy in the Party. These are the Party's democratic reformers. Then there are those who, having tasted victory and won high office, gradually began to search for ways of securing the system from which they benefit. To be fair, most of them started out as sincere revolutionaries. But now the general welfare of the people is secondary to them, and they lack firm principles. In the Party struggle, they bend before the strongest wind. These are the opportunist bureaucrats.

The opportunist bureaucrats were purged along with the democratic reformers during the upheavals of the Cultural Revolution. They had not much liking for Mao and the Red Guards, and they were jealous of upstarts like Jiang Qing. When they regained their former positions after the fall of the Gang of Four, they were in a hurry to make up for their losses over the previous ten years. So when they saw the young people of the extra-party democratic movement daring to criticize the bureaucracy, they became angry and worried, and wanted to close the movement down.

In the democratic movement too there were some disturbing developments. Some young people misunderstood the reasons for the disasters of recent years, and put the blame on Marxism. Moved by the misery around them, they demanded that the Party immediately realize their wishes, or they would overthrow it. The many social problems inherited from the Mao era are fertile soil for adventurism. The democratic youth movement that had spread throughout China was in danger of being closed down as a result of a few subversive incidents to which the people were opposed.

In these circumstances, Deng Xiaoping decided to put out a warning. He ordered a severe sentence on the dissident leader Wei Jingsheng. Some people criticize Deng for sentencing Wei Jingsheng simply for having spoken up. I disagree. Deng's main problem was how to keep the situation under control after a long period of repression. Both history and common sense show that social upheavals that are too radical often alienate the people.

But in another sense Deng Xiaoping was undoubtedly in the wrong. With undisguised contempt, he refused to distinguish between the different sorts of democratic activists. He forgot that in the darkest night most of them had openly come out in his support and had even shed their blood for him. In banning wall posters he said that "the Four Freedoms never did any good." This remark broke many hearts. Will today's youth, remembering the Four Freedoms that Mao gave them, support a revival of the Gang of Four? Perhaps Deng Xiaoping did not give sufficient thought to whether or not he had the support of the "thinking generation." Some day, when he sees his reforms jeopardized by the opportunist bureaucrats in the Party, he may have reason to regret that.

If the aim of the dogmatists is to "protect the Cultural Revolution," then the aim of the opportunist bureaucrats is to go back to the days before the Cultural Revolution. They don't want reforms, they only want safe jobs. Before the Cultural Revolution they had just that, and were under no threat whatsoever.

But China can no longer afford a policy of stagnation and seclusion. China must throw open its doors to the outside world if it is to become developed. If China is still propelled by the engine of bureaucracy, it is bound to capsize in the waves of world competition. The bureaucratic machine is in disrepair. It is wasteful and inefficient, and the officials who run it are alarmingly ignorant and incapable of coping with the immensely expensive foreign technology that they have been importing over the last three years. The national economy is in grave crisis. Khrushchev's political career was cut short by the wheels of the bureaucratic machine. Khrushchev did try to change things here and there, but he never touched the basic machinery of the bureaucracy. It seems as if all reforms in Eastern countries are doomed to fall at this second hurdle.

Should we retreat to a policy of isolation? The opportunist bureaucrats would like to do precisely that. But the people want to go forward, to dissolve the bureaucratic system completely and to achieve the Four Modernizations. Retreat would mean the failure of modernization and the defeat of the Party reformers; which is precisely what the dogmatists want.

The Central Committee, now led by the reformers, has already taken the first step toward overhauling the bureaucratic system. It has scrapped jobs-for-life, and it has permitted elections and workers' councils. It has investigated the Baoshan Iron and Steel Works [which was assigned a construction site in the middle of quicksands] and even put those responsible for the Bohai II disaster [a notorious accident where seventy-two people died] up before the courts. All these measures have unsettled the opportunist bureaucrats, who are preparing for the worst and grabbing what they can while they can. Their active interference in the elections is further proof of their hatred for democracy. But by doing these things they are simply stoking up even more resentment among the people, and thus hastening their own downfall.

But the opportunists are bound to unite in defense of their power. When the pragmatists defeated the dogmatists, the opportunists stood by with folded arms, since that struggle did not touch their vital interests. Even if ninety-nine of Mao's hundred principles were discarded it would matter to them not one jot. But now that their privileges are threatened, they too rally to the great banner of Mao Zedong.

The Party reformers should understand that if they duck an open and scientific discussion of events and experience since the Communist Party of the Soviet Union's Twentieth Congress, especially the failure of Khrushchev's reforms, then some day they will be attacked as Chinese Khrushchevs by the joint armies of dogmatism and opportunism. This struggle has not yet come, but it will. "The wind will not subside just because the tree is tired." Human will cannot avert class struggle. But when the struggle comes, the Party reformers, the young democrats, and the Chinese people will once again join hands.

Postscript

Dear Comrade Jin Jun,

A year ago I received your letter headed "The Precious Thoughts of the Older Mao Zedong." This essay is a belated reply to it. I first thought of writing such an essay in 1969, when the Cultural Revolution was being wound up and peace was returning. So many of my comrades had died that I felt I owed it to them to elucidate the causes and consequences of the Cultural Revolution. Surely they could not have died for nothing? With this essay I repay my debt to them.

The writings of Yang Xiguang, leader of Hunan's Shengwulian group in the Cultural Revolution, gave me valuable insights. Yang was the precursor of the "thinking generation." But I never quite agreed with his social and political analysis. He thought that Zhou Enlai represented the conservative bureaucrats and that Mao and Lin Biao were radical revolutionaries. But if so, then why did people hate Lin Biao and look back fondly to when the "capitalist-roaders" were in power? I asked this very question in discussions with friends, and for doing so I was subsequently charged and persecuted.

I was accused among other things of "opposing Mao Zedong Thought," like everyone else who fell foul of the political authorities in those days. But actually I was then quite loyal to Mao and always tried to see him in the best light. In 1973, when I wrote *On Socialist Democracy and the Legal System,* my attitude to Mao was like yours is now. But events revealed Mao's true nature. In the face of mounting evidence, I resolved to thoroughly reassess my past positions.

My present views on Mao are shared by only a minority of people, even in unofficial circles. Perhaps I will be severely criticized or even suffer another disaster as a result, but that is a risk I am prepared to take. Deliberate vagueness would be the more discreet course, but it is not the style of a Marxist.

Some people may say that I am too optimistic about the Party reformers, and that Deng Xiaoping, Mao, and the Gang of Four are all equally bureaucrats and therefore equally incapable of initiating a thorough reform. But my optimism stems from my belief that the CCP is not just a petty-bourgeois or a peasant party, but that it is imbued with a revolutionary ideology, Marxism. We have already seen what an enormous influence ideology or tradition can have on a society, a nation, or a political community. Even though being determines consciousness, being can never be reduced to mere economics.

The Party reformers know that China's present economic system is irrational and inefficient, and that it is bound to disintegrate under the impact of international capital. Moreover, the reformers have been oppressed for twenty years. They have lived close to the people, and know their sufferings. Therefore they are more determined than Communist reformers in other countries to make a thorough reform, and have an exceptionally wide basis of support. In today's China, is there any organized political force outside the Communist Party that could carry out thorough reform? I don't think so.

I am criticized for viewing the Cultural Revolution through the eyes of a sentimental petty bourgeois, and for not understanding that it was the product of acute social contradictions. But today millions of former Red Guards are convinced that the Cultural Revolution was a fraud perpetrated by Mao rather than a genuine rising against oppression. Was beating up school teachers "the product of acute social contradictions"? Is that why students criticized officials for not letting them read Mao, or for protecting intellectuals? Was it because of "acute social contradictions" that fanatical Red Guards burned books (but not Mao's, of course) and destroyed historical relics? Wherever the student movement won control strict censorship was enforced, on the pretext that the press was "spreading rumors" and "not propagating Mao Thought." But whenever the workers organized, they turned out to be "die-hard conservatives" in opposition to the students, and refused stubbornly to respond to the manipulations of a handful of malicious bureaucrats.

If the Cultural Revolution really was the product of acute social contradictions and if Mao really was on the side of those oppressed by the bureaucrats, then why did Mao's support not grow as the movement quickened? In 1966 the Red Guards and some workers supported Mao. In 1974, at the time of the Movement to Criticize Lin Biao and Confucius, the former Red Guards and the workers were indifferent to Mao's appeal. When they finally did rebel, in 1976, it was against Mao, not for him.

In fact there were two Cultural Revolutions: Mao's, and the people's; and only the people's Cultural Revolution can be rightfully described as the product of acute social contradictions. The people's Cultural Revolution had its roots in the early sixties, when the Party reformers began to relax the controls introduced by Mao's extremist regime in the late fifties, and when there was what people today describe as a golden age. This liberal interlude greatly hampered Mao's efforts to Stalinize the bureaucracy. The people's Cultural Revolution finally erupted in April 1976. It is continuing even today, and no one person could declare an end to it.

Nowadays many young theoreticians are writing letter after letter to convince me that Mao was a great Marxist. They claim that it is precisely because Mao saw so much wrong with Stalin that he began the Cultural Revolution. Clearly their minds are full of cobwebs. They should gather facts dispassionately and talk less carelessly.

With best wishes,
Xizhe

DOCUMENT 22

Yi Ming
China: A History That Must Be Told

Yi Ming's article is interesting for its analysis of the roots of the Party's degeneration and the causes of its gradual alienation from the Chinese people. Like Wang Xizhe, Yi Ming thinks that it is wrong to reduce the Cultural Revolution to a political ploy by the Mao group, and that in some ways the Cultural Revolution was a genuine mass movement. He also makes the important point that there was as much continuity as there was change between Mao's regime and that of the "revisionist" Liu Shaoqi, who is today revered as all-wise but who was a hate-figure for the Red Guards of the Cultural Revolution. It is not known who Yi Ming is, or what has been his fate.

THE Cultural Revolution is dead, but it has left a deep mark on our people. Millions of China's sons and daughters died during that immense mobilization and we must analyze its causes and look for its deeper source rather than content ourselves with blaming individuals.

During the war years enemy pressure forced us to correct mistakes quickly and to replace the leaders responsible for them. But after 1949 there was no longer anyone to pressure us, so that over the years a left opportunist line developed and spread. More than once it damaged the Party's gains, and finally it led to the catastrophe of the Cultural Revolution. . . . Immediately after liberation there were two different points of view in the Party. One current, represented by Liu Shaoqi and Bo Yibo, favored the consolidation of new democracy and based itself on Lenin's theory of state capitalism. . . . Its supporters thought that in an economically backward country like China the proletariat in power could and should let capitalism develop within the limits of law in order to gradually build up the bases for socialism. The other current, which was utopian socialist, advocated peasant egalitarianism. Its supporters saw that the economy was being progressively rehabilitated and that a section of the peasantry was beginning to enrich itself and regain prewar living standards. They argued that the classes were polarizing, the workers and peasants' alliance was in danger, and the rich peasant line was winning out.

The struggle between these two groups ended in compromise. The Party decided that there would be a fifteen-year period of transition during which China would be industrialized and there would be a socialist transformation of capitalist agriculture, handicrafts, and trade. But this line was quickly pushed aside by the ultra-leftists. . . . In 1955, 500 million peasants were collectivized. Ration coupons were introduced, and the number of coupons required grew daily. . . . Before the lower-stage agricultural cooperatives had had time to stabilize, they were transformed into higher-stage ones: by 1957 tasks that were supposed to take fifteen years to accomplish were done in less than four. . . . Although class struggle largely died out after the main socialist transformations and collectivization had been carried out, the left opportunists began for their own purposes to falsify the doctrine of "class struggle." They made no effort to use democratic methods in the ideological field, and refused to use discussion as a means of advancing Marxism and overcoming differences. Instead, they . . . resorted to repression, pinning the "rightist" label on oppositionists and sending them off for labor reform. Thus they not only struck at the elite (millions of intellectuals) but helped create a favorable climate for the Great Leap Forward. After this, no one dared speak the truth within or outside the Party.

After liberation we threw away the chance to establish relations with the Western countries, and leaned toward the Soviet Union instead. This was not intelligent, but at least with Soviet aid we achieved the economic goals set by the first Five-Year Plan. Under Zhou Enlai and Chen Yun the economy grew at an annual rate of 10. 9 percent (18 percent in industry, 4.5 percent in agriculture) between 1953 and 1957. But then came the Soviet condemnation of Stalin's mistakes, and our confidence in "big brother" disappeared. The traditional idea of "greater China" began to flower again.

As a result, strictly Chinese inventions like the Great Leap Forward and the People's Communes began to mushroom on all sides, and Party journals began to fantasize about one *mu* of land producing ten thousand *jin* of rice, or about reaching Communism after one year's hard struggle. . . . Of course, not everyone had gone mad; some simply kept quiet because they were interested in saving their skins. Only Peng Dehuai dared speak the truth, but he was purged.

As a result of the left line, food output fell from 250 million tons in 1958 to 150 million in 1959. In 1960 it fell by another 12.6 percent and by 1962 it dropped a further 2.4 percent. In 1961 industrial production fell by 38 percent and in 1962 by a further 16.6 percent. Twenty million workers lost their jobs and were sent back to the villages. More than one hundred million people suffered from malnutrition.

Faced with this crisis, the ultra-leftists were forced for a time to withdraw. For a few months, it seemed that democracy was reestablished and that cultural life was freer. Under "rightist" direction the economy began to revive. . . . But in the second half of 1962 the leftists returned to the attack . . . and at the Ninth Congress in 1969 they got their political program accepted. They had finally established their feudal overlordship. They had reached the pinnacle of their power, and were thus in position for their downfall.

Reading Comrade Mao's letter to Jiang Qing (criticizing Lin Biao) and his conversation with Edgar Snow, it is easy to see that he disliked the cult of the personality. He knew that it was not materialist and that it was against Party principles. But he still considered it an effective weapon in the factional struggle. History has shown that Lin Biao and the Gang of Four took advantage of this to pursue their own ends.

It is not possible to advance history by relying on people's superstitions and backwardness. Nor is it possible to consolidate the Party's gains if you damage democracy within it. Our Party is made up mainly of peasants and petty bourgeois. It lacks the democratic life (from the bottom to the top) of the Bolsheviks, and its regime is even further removed from that of the original Marxist organizations in the West. To lead the revolution it had to fuse Marxism with traditional Chinese culture. But since feudal society has no democratic or humanist traditions, this aspect of Marxism was neglected.

The democracy of the Yan'an period is a model in our Party's history, but even it was not entirely healthy [cf. Documents 1–4]. Some educated youth with more definite ideas about democracy were shocked and discouraged when they went to Yan'an from the White areas and found veteran cadres enjoying the pleasures of the dance floor and chasing the women students. When they voiced their discontent they were denounced as spies and counterrevolutionaries. These people were the forerunners of millions of others since denounced on the same charges.

It was the rule in old China that "the winner is king and the loser is a bandit." This attitude stayed deeply rooted in the Party. After some of

Mao's views were proved to be correct, he was widely flattered as the people's "savior." Even Comrade Liu Shaoqi flattered him. When he drew up the Constitution and the Party statutes, he included references to named leaders.

Khrushchev's revelation of Stalin's mistakes deeply shocked our Party. Shortly after it Comrade Deng Xiaoping made a report in the leadership's name in which he stressed the need to combat the personality cult, and at the Eighth Congress individual leaders' name were removed from the Party statutes. But after the Sino-Soviet split these changes were reversed, on the principle that "what our enemy defends, we must denounce." Narrow nationalism distorted the thinking of some comrades, and the anti-Marxists took advantage of this. After 1960 Lin Biao wore the title of Chairman Mao's "star pupil" on his chest in order to peddle his voluntarist schemes and promote the idea of "absolute authority." According to the information available, there was very little resistance before the Cultural Revolution to the excesses of "Lin Biao thought," except for some disapproving comments by Deng Xiaoping, Lu Dingyi, and Luo Ruiqing.

For a long time, many older comrades did not understand the need for democracy in the Party. They made no effort or sacrifice to achieve it (except for Peng Dehuai, who was farsighted). They thought that the personality cult could protect the Party, and thus they helped prepare public opinion for Lin Biao's counterrevolution. They woke up when disaster struck, but by then it was too late.

Today there is a tendency to make a sharp distinction between eleven years after liberation (i.e., the end of the Great Leap Forward) and seventeen years after (when the Cultural Revolution began). According to this view, seventeen years after was heaven, and eleven years after was hell. But this view is ahistorical, and deliberately tries to cover up the link between the two periods.

No one could create the Cultural Revolution on their own, and that goes both for the glorious Mao Zedong and for the Gang of Four. History is always written by the people, whether it is the April Fifth Movement of 1976 or the Cultural Revolution. Clearly, without the support or passive acquiescence of the majority of youth and citizens, the Gang of Four and Lin Biao would never have been able to take on the Party as a whole.

In the twenty-eight years between [the CCP's foundation in] 1921 and [its taking power in] 1949, the Chinese people got to know it as a firm, honest, and courageous fighting force that represented hope for the future. . . . They therefore willingly gave it their support. These qualities of the Party were forged in prisons and on the battlefield. After 1949 the Party became a fount of honors and social rank, and some members became degenerate as a result of flattery. But the Three Anti's campaign of

1951–52 rooted out much of this corruption, and saved the Party's honor.

By 1957 the Party had been in power for eight years and it was becoming increasingly difficult to combat bureaucracy and corruption simply through ideological reeducation. So the Party appealed to the people to rectify it from the outside. This measure was very popular, but it was soon rescinded. Those who had responded to the Party's appeal for criticism were labeled "rightists" and sent for labor reform. So the cadres, far from improving their behavior, grew even more arrogant. Now they could say: "Anyone who dares touch me is against the Party."

The main targets of the "anti-rightist" campaign were the intellectuals and most workers and peasants were not yet affected, but nevertheless the tie between the Party and the people disappeared, and people deliberately avoided the Party. Between 1958 and 1962 the Party's honor was fatally damaged as cadres became more and more corrupt, violent, dishonest, and deceitful. Now it was the workers and peasants' turn to suffer. . . . They continued to support the Party, even though their confidence in it was shaken. . . . But the leadership took no measures to resolve these problems, and instead simply tried to pin the blame on the rank and file. Successive political mobilizations only widened the gap between the cadres and the people, and between the Party and the people.

At the same time the Party launched the anti-revisionist movement internationally, even though the people were not familiar with the situation in the Soviet Union.

In China the cadres, worn out by the "two-line struggle," felt their revolutionary determination faltering. They were getting older, and were concerned with their own privileges, rather than with the interests of the people.

The younger generation, which was not fully informed, was blaming the bureaucrats for the disasters of the previous few years. Young people put all their hope in "absolute authorities". . . . They wanted to destroy the bureaucratic caste so that they could develop their knowledge and intelligence. So they tried to carry the fight against "revisionism" from the international to the domestic sphere.

In 1966 people felt a certain distaste, even contempt, for the "seventeen years," especially the last nine of them. The people dreamed of something better, although they did not yet know what. And so Lin Biao, Chen Boda, Kang Sheng, and Jiang Qing, taking advantage of the prestige of the Great Helmsman, could offer the Cultural Revolution as a panacea. History knows many similar episodes. The French king linked with the citizens in order to weaken the aristocrats who were threatening his throne. The Cultural Revolution Group relied on the Red Guards to destroy the structures of the Party.

During the Cultural Revolution the people educated themselves. They learned through experience that the new authorities were a hundred times harsher than the old, that "eleven years are not as good as seventeen," and that the revival of feudalism is a much more real danger in China than the rebirth of capitalism.

Combating corrupt officials will not solve society's problems. Superstition and anarchy are no match for the bureaucracy and the privileged class. Only democracy and a socialist legal system can bring the Four Modernizations to China and ensure it a brilliant future. We must draw deep inspiration from the experience of the last thirty years, firmly follow the path of Marxism, and advance boldly under the correct leadership of the Chinese Communist Party.

DOCUMENT 23

WEI JINGSHENG
Democracy or a New Dictatorship?

Wei Jingsheng, who is in his early forties, worked as an electrician at Beijing Zoo while continuing his studies at Beijing University. He was born in Anhui Province in Central China. He was editor of *Tansuo* (Explorations) and author of a famous article titled "Democracy, the Fifth Modernization." As a result of his writings, and the persecution they brought him, he became China's best-known dissident both at home and abroad. But he was hardly typical of the democratic movement. He was the most right-wing of its better-known activists, and few other dissidents shared his view that the main source of socialist totalitarianism and of China's "poisoning" is the philosophy of Marx.

In mid-March 1979 the Chinese authorities began criticizing people who were advocating an "individualistic" philosophy and announced restrictions on the democratic movement. In Beijing the municipal authorities decided to ban posters and publications "opposed to socialism and to Party leadership." Wei Jingsheng was arrested on 29 March, a day before these restrictions were announced. Six months later he was tried and sentenced to fifteen years' imprisonment after a show trial from which his friends and family were excluded. Wei's publishing activities were described as "counterrevolutionary." He was also charged with giving "military secrets" to a foreigner, but the information he was said to have given was common knowledge at the time, according to foreign sources.

Wei was frequently held in solitary confinement and beaten, lost most of his teeth, and suffered from heart and lung ailments. According to Asia Watch, Wei was guarded by a special team of security officers. "No single official was allowed to be alone with him. His condition was reported directly to Deng Xiaoping's office. Deng decided personally on everything related to Wei."[4] His release in 1993 was ordered to enhance the Chinese bid to host the Olympic Games in 2000.

In 1994, it was reported that Wei might soon be sentenced to a further five to fifteen years' imprisonment.

This article was first published in a special issue of *Explorations* in March 1979. The text was cited by the prosecution at Wei's trial as an "incitement to overthrow the dictatorship of the proletariat" and as an example of "counter-revolutionary agitation and propaganda."

EVERYONE in China knows that the Chinese social system is not democratic and that this lack of democracy has severely stunted every aspect of the country's social development over the past thirty years. In the face of this hard fact there are two choices before the Chinese people. Either to reform the social system if they want to develop their society and seek a swift increase in prosperity and economic resources; or, if they are content with a continuation of the Mao Zedong brand of proletarian dictatorship, then they cannot even talk of democracy, nor will they be able to realize the modernization of their lives and resources.

Where is China heading and in what sort of society do the people hope to live and work?

The answer can be seen in the mood of the majority. It is this mood that brought about the present democratic movement. With the denial of Mao Zedong's style of dictatorship as its very prerequisite, the aim of this movement is to reform the social system and thereby enable the Chinese people to increase production and develop their lives to the full in a democratic social environment. This aim is not just the aim of a few isolated individuals but represents a whole trend in the development of Chinese society. Those who doubt this need only recall the April Fifth Movement in 1976, for those who were judged by the court in the minds of the people then, even when they were some of the most powerful in the country, have not escaped its ultimate verdict.

But are there people who remain unafraid of such a judgment? Of course there are—and more than a few of them. Several of those at the top who are drunk with wielding power often forget such niceties as the people's judgment, and others out of personal ambition and despotic inclinations abuse people's credulity. For example, the speech that Vice-Premier Deng Xiaoping made to leading cadres of the Central Committee on 16 March 1979 was an attempt to take advantage of the people's past confidence in him to oppose the democratic movement itself. He leveled all sorts of charges at the democratic movement and tried to lay on it the blame for the failure of China's production and economy when it was Hua and Deng's political system that was at fault. Thus the people are made scapegoats for the failure of their leaders' policies. Does Deng Xiaoping really deserve the people's trust? No political leaders have a right to expect the people's unconditional trust. If they carry out policies beneficial to the people along the road to peace and prosperity, then we should trust them. Our trust in them is for their policies and the means to apply these policies. Should they carry out policies harmful to the people's interests, the path they are treading is a dictator's path and should be opposed. The people are as much opposed to this path as they are to measures harmful to their interests and to policies undermining their legitimate rights. According to the principles of democracy, any authority must give way to opposition from the people.

But Deng Xiaoping does not give way. When the people are demanding a widespread inquiry into the reasons for China's backwardness over the last thirty years and into Mao Zedong's crimes, Deng is the first to declare: "With no Mao Zedong there would be no New China." In his speech he even flattered Mao Zedong's ghost when he called him "the banner of the Chinese people" and claimed that Mao's weaknesses and mistakes were so insignificant as to be unworthy of mention.

Is he afraid that an investigation into Mao's mistakes would lead to an investigation into Mao's collaborators? Or is Deng simply preparing to continue the Mao Zedong brand of dictatorial socialist government? If the former, then Deng has nothing to fear, since the tolerance of the Chinese people is great enough to forgive him his past mistakes provided that he now leads the country toward democracy and prosperity. But if the latter, we will never forgive him, even if recently he has been the best of the leaders. If his aim is to continue the Mao Zedong style of dictatorship, his course of action can only lead to economic ruin and the abuse of the people's interests. Anyone forgiving such a criminal would be indirectly guilty of crimes against the people.

Does Deng Xiaoping want democracy? No, he does not. He is unwilling to comprehend the misery of the common people. He is unwilling to allow the people to regain those powers usurped by ambitious careerists. He describes the struggle for democratic rights—a movement launched spontaneously by the people—as the actions of troublemakers who must be repressed. To resort to such measures to deal with people who criticize mistaken policies and demand social development shows that the government is very afraid of this popular movement.

We cannot help asking Mr. Deng what his idea of democracy is. If the people have no right to express their opinions and criticisms, then how can one talk of democracy? If his idea of democracy is one that does not allow others to criticize those in power, then how is such a democracy different from Mao Zedong's tyranny concealed behind the slogan "The Democracy of the Dictatorship of the Proletariat"?

The people want to appeal against injustice, want to vent their grievances, and want democracy, so they hold meetings. The people oppose famine and dictatorship, so they demonstrate. This shows that without democracy their very livelihood lacks any safeguard. Is it possible, when the people are so much at the mercy of others, that such a situation can be called "normal public order"? If "normal public order" gives dictators the right to wreak havoc with the people's interests, then does it benefit the careerists or the people to safeguard such an order? Is the answer not painfully obvious? We consider that normal public order is not total uniformity; particularly in politics, where there must be a great diversity of opinion. When there are no divergent opinions, no discussion, and no publications, then it is clear that there is a dictatorship. Total uniformity must surely be called "abnormal order." When social phenomena are interpreted as the occasion for criminal elements to make trouble and are used as an excuse to do away with the people's right to express their opinions, this is the time-honored practice of fascist dictators both new and old. Remember the Tian'anmen Square incident, when the Gang of Four used the fact that certain people had burned cars as an excuse to crush the popular revolutionary movement. Above all, the people should be forever wary of placing unqualified trust in any one ruler.

The people should ensure that Deng Xiaoping does not degenerate into a dictator. After he was reinstated in 1975, it seemed he was unwilling to follow Mao Zedong's dictatorial system and would instead care for the interests of the people. So the people eagerly looked up to him in the hope that he would realize their aspirations. They were even ready to shed their blood for him—as the Tian'anmen Square incident showed. But was such support vested in his person alone? Certainly not. If he now wants to discard his mask and take steps to suppress the democratic movement then he certainly does not merit the people's trust and support. From his behavior it is clear that he is neither concerned with democracy nor does he any longer protect the people's interests. By deceiving the people to win their confidence he is following the path to dictatorship.

It has been demonstrated countless times throughout China's history that once the confidence of the people has been gained by deception, the dictators work without restraint—for as the ancients said: "He who can win the people's minds, can win the empire." Once masters of the nation, their private interests inevitably conflict with those of the people, and they must use repression against those who are struggling for the interests of the people themselves. So the crux of the matter is not who becomes master of the nation, but rather that the people must maintain firm control over their own nation, for this is the very essence of democracy. People entrusted with government positions must be controlled by and responsible to the people. According to the Constitution, organizations and individuals in the administration must be elected by the people, empowered and controlled by an elected government under the supervision of the people, and responsible to the people: only then is there a legality for executive powers.

We would like to ask the high officials who instigate the arrest of individuals—is the power you exercise legal? We would like to ask Chairman Hua and Vice-Chairman Deng—is your occupation of the highest offices of state legal? We would like to know why it is the Vice-Chairman and the Vice-Premier and not the courts or organizations representing the people who announce who is to be arrested. Is this legal? According to Chinese law, is a "bad element" a criminal per se? And on whose judgment is such a criterion made? If these simple questions are not clearly answered there is no point in talking about rule by law in China.

History shows that there must be a limit to the amount of trust conferred upon any individual. Anyone seeking the unconditional trust of the people is a person of unbridled ambition. The important problem is to select the right sort of person to put one's trust in, and even more important is how such a person is to be supervised in carrying out the will of the majority. We can only trust those representatives who are supervised by us and responsible to us. Such representatives should be chosen by us and not thrust upon us.

Only a genuine general election can create a government and leaders ready to serve the interests of the electorate. If the government and its leaders are truly subject to the people's mandate and supervision those two afflictions that leadership is prone to—personal ambition and megalomania—can be avoided. No one should blame leaders for being prone to power fever. Nor should we blame the people for not daring to strike a blow in their own interests. This may happen because we are without a social system in which a wise people supervises and counterbalances equally wise and worthy officials.

Furthering reforms within the social system and moving Chinese politics toward democracy are prerequisites for solving the social and economic problems that confront China today. Only through elections can the leadership gain the people's voluntary cooperation and bring their initiative into play. Only when the people enjoy complete freedom and expression can they help their leaders to analyze and solve problems. Cooperation, together with policies formulated and carried out by the people, are necessary for the highest degree of working efficiency and the achievement of ideal results.

This is the only road along which China can make progress. Under present-day conditions, it is an extremely difficult path.

DOCUMENT 24

Interview with Xu Wenli

Xu Wenli, the son of a doctor, was born around 1945. After leaving the army in 1963, he became a maintenance electrician in a Beijing factory. In 1979 he and Liu Qing founded *Siwu luntan* (April Fifth Forum), whose title commemorates the demonstrations of April 5, 1976 in Beijing's Tian'anmen Square. *April Fifth Forum* became the most influential and widely published unofficial journal in north China. In November 1979, Liu Qing was arrested (see Documents 38–40), but Xu continued to publish the journal until the spring of 1980, despite the government ban. He was arrested in 1981 and sentenced in 1982 to fifteen years' imprisonment. He spent eleven years in almost complete solitary confinement in horrendous conditions. He lost most of his teeth, his hair turned white, and he was malnourished and possibly tubercular. He was released on parole in May 1993. He maintained he had committed no crime "because what I did was for my country and my people."

XU WENLI lives with his family in two small rooms, where he received us. Visitors of all ages knocked at the door during the interview, some asking for the latest issue of the journal and others to take part in the conversation or listen to it.

Xu Wenli vigorously rejects the charges leveled at the democratic movement because of its contacts with foreigners. "We are all patriots," he said. "Many had the chance to emigrate but didn't, because they want to devote themselves to building the country." Xu Wenli is shocked at the suggestion of "manipulation by foreign agents," which he regards as a sign of Soviet-type thinking. He said: "There are elements close to the Soviet Union within the CCP. They disapprove of Soviet foreign policy but think that Soviet domestic policy is just and socialist. We do not deny that from Stalin to Khrushchev and Brezhnev the Soviets have made economic progress, and that some reforms might be seen as constructive. But these reforms have not changed relations between the bureaucracy and the masses. Domestically there are no forces capable of opposing the Soviet bureaucracy's expansionist foreign policy. Oppression by the bureaucrats and the technocrats is preventing the Soviet masses from expressing their views on this question. Naturally, no one in China supports Soviet foreign policy. But since our whole system stems from the Soviet Union, the same system is still in force here. So who can guarantee that China will not one day become hegemonistic too? We should oppose not only Soviet overseas aggression, but also the Soviet system's internal antidemocratic practices."

After this statement, Xu Wenli answered our questions. He is thirty-six-years old, married, with a seven-year-old daughter, and an electrician—"not a technician or engineer," he specified. He was born in Anhui Province, son of a doctor and great-grandson of an official in the old regime. After finishing his secondary education he joined the army and was therefore not a Red Guard during the Cultural Revolution. He said he could have gone to a university but preferred to pursue his own studies. I asked him the following more general questions.

Q: What is the present state of the democratic movement?

A: Since the suppression of Democracy Wall and the sentencing of Wei Jingsheng the movement has been curbed. Many young people were deeply wounded by what happened, and their enthusiasm has been crushed. Publications are becoming rare, but at the same time some new publications are appearing in the provinces (in Anyang, Baoding, and Shanghai). Although people don't dare express their views freely, they don't believe that the movement can be completely suppressed. After developing in the open, it has gone underground.

Q: You deny that you are dissidents like in the Soviet Union. How do you define your relationship to the regime and to the CCP?

A: In China most young people in the democratic movement have a basically Marxist viewpoint. We want to make China a democratic and socialist country. From a theoretical standpoint, our aims are the same as the CCP's. The democratic movement is formed by young workers and intellectuals, while in the Soviet Union the dissidents are famous intellectuals. Nonetheless the aim of the young people in the democratic movement is humanitarian socialism, and so they have some points in common with certain movements in the Soviet Union and with the Eurocommunists. But I don't like the word "dissident," which means "enemy" in Chinese.

Q: You have pictures of Zhou Enlai and Mao Zedong in your room. What is your assessment of Mao?

A: Opinions in our movement differ on this question. Personally, I think Mao was a great man but that he made serious mistakes. These mistakes result in large part from the fact that he was born among peasants. This tendency is not exclusive to Mao, it's found throughout the Party. I agree with the view that Mao's policy was correct up to the Eighth Congress of 1956. But a large part of his later work was already foreshadowed in his thinking even then.

Q: What are the main obstacles to democracy in China?

A: The main obstacles are economic. Political democracy presupposes economic competition. For example, if you don't like your newspaper, you can buy another one. Not in China. Here, individual autonomy is very limited. The people have to eat and cannot rock the boat too much.

However, competition here would not necessarily be the same as in the capitalist countries. In the Chinese society of the future it will be limited by the state plan.

Q: Is the low level of education of China's 800 million peasants not also an obstacle to democracy?

A: Yes, but the peasants have a spontaneous leaning toward democracy. For the past twenty years they have opposed several centralizing stages in agricultural policy. The leaders are aware of that, and that is why they are now agreeing to extend the peasants' autonomy.

Q: What are the similarities between the Chinese and Soviet systems?

A: This is a heavy burden for the democratic movement. It will take several generations to achieve scientific and democratic socialism. At present we are paving the way for the future. This is necessary in all spheres. It is vital to prepare the ground.

Q: What are the most serious violations of human rights in China today?

A: China is very sensitive about this question at the moment. Deng Xiaoping refused to discuss it when he was in the United States. The situation now has nothing in common with the one under the Gang of Four. However, I prefer to talk of "civil rights," since if you say "human rights" you are regarded as an agent of (Jimmy) Carter. Some people say that the main thing now is to work to modernize China, and that there will be time to discuss civil rights after that. For the time being we should not bother about affairs of state. But in that case, how could the people express their power? Is the aim to turn the Chinese into conveyor-belt workers like in Chaplin's *Modern Times?* What then would be the point of human intelligence? Ever since there has been a more open policy toward the outside world, Chinese intellectuals have been able to go abroad. Many have not come back. That is a very clear sign. A person who cannot think freely feels wounded. Only a minority are allowed to express their views. It is impossible to modernize the country unless you let the intelligence of a thousand million individuals unfold. So the problem of freedom of thought is more serious than that of physical attacks on people, although it is true that such attacks are very widespread in the countryside. . . . Carter is not going to solve this problem. We must rely on the Chinese people themselves to do it.

Q: Much is said about cadres' privileges. Is this an important problem? Can it be solved by the present campaign?

A: The problem of privileges is a major obstacle to the country's modernization and to the movement for democracy. The leaders are aware of that. But this problem cannot be solved by directives. For instance, a recent ruling says that those who use official cars for private purposes must pay. But what driver would dare to ask his boss for money? This is a typically stupid decision.

It is wrong to say that all society's faults are due to the Gang of Four. It's like the mother of an extremely ugly child denying she gave birth to it. . . . What produced the problem of privileges? Partly it's a carryover from the old society, but above all it's due to the present system. If our cadres are dismissed, they have no redress. So they take care to protect their personal power in order to safeguard their private interests. . . . Cadres must be replaced and monitored by the people, And if they are sacked they must be able to find another job. Like teachers, for instance, or like Mr. Kissinger. But if privileges grow, there is a risk of a serious popular backlash. Take housing, for instance; a department chief with a small family has an apartment of seventy to eighty square meters. But workers sometimes live, boys and girls together, as many as ten to a room no bigger than that.

Q: Several newspapers have mentioned a "crisis of conviction" and a "crisis of confidence" among the people. Why is this?

A: There is such a crisis, and it affects not only young people. I don't think this crisis is such a bad thing, since it is bringing about a reappraisal. The main reason for it is that in the past many projects were not carried out. This is not only true of China. Other socialist countries have also met enormous problems in building up their societies. Things have been drifting since the fall of the Gang of Four. People are better informed about the outside world and are inevitably asking questions. It is repeatedly said that Marxism-Leninism-Mao Zedong Thought set out the most correct path, but how can people help doubting this? It is vital to examine the faults of the system, even those of Marxism-Leninism. The Eurocommunists have encountered this problem in seeking solutions appropriate to conditions in their own countries. If the Italian Communists had not made these changes, they would never have got so much influence.

Q: Does this crisis not also have a moral aspect?

A: Some moral crises are necessary. It is useful to make people understand that practices like "getting in by the back door" must be eliminated, since otherwise cadres who resort to them will no longer inspire confidence. Privileges are the cause of the moral crisis. If it were not for these privileges, people would be less inclined to seek influential friends. However, the circle of privileged people has grown quantitatively since the fall of the Gang of Four.

DOCUMENT 25

Xu Wenli
A Reform Program for the Eighties

Xu Wenli drew up this program in the autumn of 1980. It brings together in one place a whole series of reform proposals raised at different times and in different places by supporters of the democratic movement. Wojtek Zafanolli, writing in *Esprit*, where this text was first made available outside China, drew a telling parallel between Xu and the Qing dynasty reformer Kang Youwei. Just as Kang tried to save the declining imperial system by urging it to modernize and democratize its institutions, so Xu urges the Party to renew its mandate by carrying out fundamental political and economic reforms. Certain of Xu's proposals are even directly inspired by Kang's program.

CHINESE society has reached a critical point in its history, and further progress is only possible at the price of a thoroughgoing political reform.

The democratic socialist movement that grew up in late 1978 across China and whose main components are the young workers, the democratic ferment at the Third Plenum of the Fifth NPC and the Fifth CPPCC, and the movement now developing around the student elections shows that the desire of the younger generation for national renewal is irrepressible.

There can be no doubt that China must change. Head-in-the-sand conservatism will not resolve our problems, and nor will tinkering with the system.

The issue boils down to this. What road should the reform movement take? Should it be from above, from below, or both?

At present reform from below must be ruled out, since the Chinese people will tolerate no more public disorder. On the other hand, history shows that the bureaucratic resistance of the old structures will prove too strong for a movement that relies entirely on forces for change at the top. So only a combination of reforms from above and from below can be really effective.

The management of our affairs can no longer be left to a tiny minority. Government must hand power back to the people. The reform process must become an occasion for uniting and strengthening the nation.

Therefore, despite their rough and ready nature, I am presenting these few proposals on reform for the consideration of the Central Committee, the NPC, the CPPCC, the State Council, and the Chinese people as a whole.

1. The general elections now taking place at *xian* and *qu* level are un-democratic and should be annulled. The Twelfth Congress of the CCP as well as the Sixth NPC and the Sixth CPPCC should be adjourned.

The point of democratic consultation is that the power to select candidates should lie with the electors. But in the present elections this right has been withdrawn. Our electoral law is unscientific. Our society has no tradition of democracy. We lack experience of democratic consultation. Above all, antidemocratic forces have interfered with and sabotaged the elections. The result is that in most places the electors have not even had a chance to meet the official candidates, let alone to ask them questions or give their own opinions. So these candidates can in no sense be said to have received a mandate, since they have not even bothered to explain their political program (which they could easily have done during their free time). In fact the campaign was carried out not by the candidates but by officials of the electoral commissions.

Moreover, in many places normal electoral competition was suppressed. This is not true democracy. The right to vote is a right, not a favor, and it must be exercised without constraints. Otherwise we have only a parody of elections, amounting to authoritarian rule under another guise.

We must use democratic electoral campaigning as a scientific method for promoting social progress. We must abolish the pyramidal structures we inherited from feudalism, by which officials are responsible to their superiors but never to the people. These structures mean that political rights are stratified according to social group. We must progressively ensure that the people's representatives are responsible to the electors and can be dismissed by them. We must realize a new democratic socialist system in which the people are the country's true masters, through a new anti-pyramidal structure in which the NPC, the organ of supreme authority, will supervise the administration at all levels.

2. A consultative committee for the reform should be immediately set up, drawn from the Central Secretariat of the CCP, the Standing Committee of the NPC, the State Council, and the Chinese Guomindang, as well as political parties, groups, and experts from all sectors. This committee should be invested with independent authority.

Under its direction a six-month discussion should be opened in the press so that the opinions of the masses on the reform can be concentrated. A reform project should then be drawn up based on the views of the majority. After genuine elections, it should be presented to the Sixth NPC and the Sixth CPPCC for implementation.

In drafting the reform plan we must draw the lessons of the constant left-right zigzags that have plagued us since the crushing of the Gang of Four. We should publish plans for raising the standard of living of citizens. These plans should be realistically attainable year by year, so that our policies are both credible and corruption-free.

3. Before the reform is carried out the old legislation and the old rules must be followed to the letter.

4. We should stop venerating only Marxism-Leninism and Mao Zedong Thought and practice freedom of belief. We should consider the progressive thought of all human civilization as our heritage, and rescue Marxism from deductive scholasticism by letting a hundred flowers bloom and a hundred schools of thought contend. Marxism is a science, but science must be continually developed and does not fear the open competition of conflicting theories. That the CCP holds to Marxism as its guiding ideology should in no way debar other parties and groups from holding their own beliefs and points of view. In pursuit of truth we should adopt the democratic principle that while the minority must submit to the majority, the majority has no right to suppress it.

5. Replace the "Four Modernizations" slogan with that of integrated modernization.

6. The CCP should reregister its members, but without turning this into a political campaign. The Party's main source of finance should be its members. This will reduce the burden on the exchequer and on the people. After the reform is implemented the CCP, along with all other parties, should get a state subsidy proportionate to its membership.

The CCP has glorious traditions. It is without doubt the only party in China capable of carrying through the reform program. Its political qualities will decide the success or failure of the reform. The proposal to reregister its members should open up new perspectives for it.

7. Leave historical balance sheets to the historians, including the balance sheet of the conflict between the CCP and the Guomindang.

8. The four powers should be separated in the Chinese political system. The structure should be restored whereby the President presides over the State Council and commands the armed forces. Appointments for life should be abolished and no individual should hold the same office for more than two successive terms.

"Separation of the four powers" means that the CCP is the guiding power, the NPC and the CPPCC are the legislative power, the state organs are the administrative power, and the courts have judicial independence.

9. The present system, in which power is concentrated at the center, should be progressively replaced by a federal one that combines central direction with local, regional, and city autonomy. Taiwan should be treated as a special area in order to arrive at a peaceful solution of the Taiwan problem.

10. The Chinese armed forces are the defenders of the state and the

people. They should stay out of politics, and if they don't, they should be severely punished. No soldier should serve in a government post. The minister of defense should be chosen from the civilian personnel. This measure is necessary for society's stability and the people's security. It permits military professionals to concentrate on developing military science and modern strategy and tactics.

11. The present conscription system should be progressively changed so that compulsory military service is replaced by a combination of volunteers and career soldiers. The system of people's militia should be extended. The research and teaching of modern military science should be strengthened. The quality of the troops should be improved and their numbers reduced.

12. We should continue to restrain military expenditure while increasing investment in qualified personnel. Part of the funds released from military spending should be used to raise the standard of living of the lower and middle ranks or allocated to the parents of military personnel from the countryside.

13. The Sixth NPC and the Sixth CPPCC should be convoked to revise the present Constitution and draw up a new one based on popular sovereignty. The law should be revised in line with a modernized form of government so that citizens have the right to publish, associate, form political parties, strike, and demonstrate.

14. All prisoners of conscience like Wei Jingsheng, Ren Wanding, and Liu Qing should be immediately set free. People imprisoned in the past for political offenses should be given retrials. The vague and ambiguous articles of the penal code dealing with counterrevolutionary activities should be amended. The administrative ordinances that permit the Public Security Bureau to exercise judicial powers should be abolished. The freedoms to speak, assemble, associate, publish, march, demonstrate, and strike, which citizens have on paper, should be guaranteed in practice.

The focal point of all reforms should be human liberation, and the respect for human value and human rights. The free development of each individual is the basis for all social progress. Military-style authoritarianism must be replaced by government by moral persuasion; all government must act strictly within the law. Administrative units should no longer have control of dossiers on individuals. Instead, there should be a system of passports, and the state should set up archive bureaus from which individuals can get their identity papers. Employment agencies should be set up, and staff should be engaged on the basis not of unified appointment but of job advertisements, exams, and proper selection methods, with the signing of short- or long-term contracts. Provision should be made for job allocation in case of unemployment. Restrictions on residence permits should be progressively relaxed so as to eventually guarantee freedom of resettlement.

15. In all enterprises apart from state organs directly dependent on the center, it should be the administrative committee nominated by the assembly of representatives of the workforce that exercises administrative power, takes care of its own accounting, and takes responsibility for profits and losses, taxes, and free competition. Cultural and educational bodies should be grant-aided and should gradually carry into effect a system of free universal education. After fulfilling its quota as set out in the Plan, each unit and enterprise should have the right to decide its own provisioning, production, and marketing. As long as no employee earns less than the national minimum set by the state, each unit should have the right to fix its own wages, bonuses, and social security provisions.

Income tax should be introduced after salaries have been increased on a broad scale. Invisible deductions from salaries should be explained. Those who work harder should get higher wages and those who are more able should make a greater contribution, so that each citizen recognizes his or her own worth and cherishes his or her democratic rights.

The workforce and property of firms bankrupt as a result of lack of competitiveness should be put at the disposal of the people's government at the relevant level which will, acting in accordance with the relevant legislation and in consultation with employees' representatives, take the necessary measures.

16. The problem of the countryside is essentially that of the land. A new agrarian law should be drawn up to put an end to the present chaos. Popular assemblies should be set up in each village and each *xiang* and these should become organs of supreme power. They should be made up of people from all backgrounds (families with much labor power, families with little labor power, intellectuals, parents of martyrs and soldiers, families benefiting from the five guarantees, pensioners, etc.) and should create permanent bodies to exercise administrative power in the villages and the *xiang*.

17. In accordance with the various periods into which the history of modern China is divided, cadres who were dismissed or retired early, military personnel who were honorably discharged, and other deserving people should get certificates of merit and material benefits according to a system centrally administered by the state.

18. As an experiment, a four-hour working day should be introduced for married women so that they can cope with their household tasks and with bringing up the younger generation.

19. Education is the foundation stone of modern society. We should progressively establish free and universal education, encourage higher education on a half-work, half-study basis and introduce a trial system of grants. Adult education, professional education, cultural education of a social nature, recreation centers, and sports facilities should figure in the

administrative programs of the various units and of the people's governments at each level.

20. Reduce the number of deputies elected to the various levels of the
NPC and the CPPCC. Deputies at all levels should be released from production so that they can devote themselves to serving society. At every
level of the NPC and the CPPCC permanent bodies and specialized commissions should be established to listen to citizens' opinions and maintain
organic links with the people.

The state belongs to everyone, and democracy is everyone's business.
If everyone thinks that nothing can be done, then our nation will accomplish nothing. But if everyone believes that something can be done, then
we will accomplish great things. As long as the youth and the people as a
whole retain the will to work hard toward the goal of national prosperity,
there will be great hope for China.

DOCUMENT 26

EDITORIAL BOARD, *RENMINZHI LU*

A Statement of Clarification

Guangzhou, the capital of Guangdong Province in South China, was a stronghold
of the democratic movement and the home city of Wang Xizhe, one of its most
persuasive and brilliant writers. Students from the two universities in the nearby
British colony of Hong Kong often visited Guangzhou to meet Wang and his
comrades, and to exchange views and opinions with them. Back in Hong Kong
these students organized an energetic campaign to publicize the views of the democratic movement, and to defend it when it came under attack. Although there
was nothing unconstitutional about these links, the Guangdong provincial government accused the democratic movement of illegally liaising with foreigners.
The "four principles" mentioned in the provincial government's warning were
announced in Beijing in March 1979. They required adherence to the socialist
road, the dictatorship of the proletariat, Communist Party leadership, and Marxism-Leninism-Mao Zedong Thought. Most unofficial journals paid lip service to
these four principles, but in reality the logic of their campaign was fundamentally
at odds with this strongly Stalinist conception of socialism. The provincial authorities also accused the unofficial journals of violating the ordinances on publications. This issue is discussed in greater depth in the text "Democracy and Legality Are Safeguards of Stability and Unity" (see Document 27).

THE democratic movement and the unofficial journals, born in late 1978,
are now both more than a year old. Although still infants, they have come
under intense pressure, yet they persevere. Young people in China have
come to recognize their duties to nation and people, and strive for democracy and reform. But the struggle spares none, and permits no illusions.

Now our movement is being suppressed throughout the whole country, including here in Guangdong. On 4 April 1980, *Nanfang ribao* (Southern Daily) published a warning by Comrade Xi Zhongxun, Governor of Guangdong Province, in which he told the democratic movement:

Anarchism and extreme individualism are masquerading under the banners of democracy and human rights. In the past, these people were keen on writing wall posters and publishing magazines. Now, they even secretly liaise with foreigners. They are violating the ordinances on publications, and continue to publish wrong and even counterrevolutionary articles. It is clear that they have deviated from the Four Principles, damaged stability, harmed the Four Modernizations, and virtually placed themselves on the opposite side to the Party and the people.

Readers in Guangzhou will know that after the suspension *of Renminzhi sheng* (Voice of the People), there only remain *Renminzhi lu* (People's Road), *Shenghuo* (Life), and *Hongdou* (Red Bean) (this latter published by students of Zhongshan University). We believe that it is our duty to clarify our position on the points raised in Xi Zhongxun's statement:

1. Ever since we split from *Voice of the People* in September 1979, we have been publishing bimonthly. We have published four issues in all, and we have sent each issue to the Publications Bureau and other relevant government departments. On 18 December 1979, the Provincial Committee told us via the Communist Youth League that we should no longer sell our journal publicly, and so we stopped. But at the same time we affirmed that we would continue to publish, and we stressed that the 1952 regulations on the registration of publications, which require guarantees from two private shops, are clearly outdated, since shops are now publicly owned. These regulations do not conform with present social conditions and they contradict the Constitution, which guarantees freedom of the press. But the authorities replied that it was not possible to change the law. This means unofficial journals cannot be registered.

2. It is only natural that young people who are concerned about their nation and committed to the democratic movement should liaise with and support one another. It is entirely legal to do so, and it is wrong to call such liaison "secret coordination." The freedom of correspondence stipulated in the Constitution gives individuals the right to keep certain things secret. Our correspondence is legal and aboveboard, although our letters are frequently opened and inspected. We deeply regret the charge of "secret coordination," a term inherited from the period of the Gang of Four's reign of terror.

3. Since its emergence in 1979, the democratic movement has had much impact in Hong Kong and Macao, particularly among patriotic

students disillusioned by the downfall of the Gang of Four and the collapse of the Maoist faction in the student movement. These people feel that their liberation from colonial rule—Hong Kong is a British colony—is intimately bound up with China's progress. They see hope in the democratic movement.

In August 1979, students at Hong Kong University organized a "discussion camp" in Guangzhou so that they could contact people here and see what changes are taking place. Since then Hong Kong students have frequently visited us to discuss politics and the democratic movement. Through them we have deepened our knowledge of world affairs, of the international Communist movement, and of new developments in Marxism in the various countries. Young workers and teachers as well as students have contacted us. We feel encouraged by these gestures of solidarity. Needless to say, we cannot investigate the background of every person we meet, and it is possible that we may have come into contact with people of a political background. But we insist on restricting our communication with such people to the democratic movement, and we will never agree to take instructions from others or to accept aid to which conditions are attached.

We affirm the Four Principles and Marxist teachings. We welcome criticism so long as it is directed at specific points raised in our magazine. We believe that dialogue is useful both to us and to our readers. Finally, we believe that socialist democracy and the legal system will develop under Party leadership. The road is hard, but the new generation, baptized by the Cultural Revolution and led by the Party, will bravely follow it.

DOCUMENT 27

COMMENTATOR, ZEREN
Democracy and Legality Are Safeguards
of Stability and Unity

Zeren (Duty) is the name of the journal published by the National Federation of Unofficial Journals, set up in the autumn of 1980. The following article by "Commentator" was published on January 16, 1981, shortly before the government's final crackdown on the democratic movement in April. It is a brave and forceful protest against the quickening turn toward repression. Despite the crackdown, several further issues of Duty appeared, published from bases within the underground.

IS OUR country stable and unified today, four years after the fall of the Gang of Four? Most people think that things have improved, since at least they no longer need worry that they will be suddenly searched, arrested, put before a criticism meeting, or sent to jail merely for voicing an opinion. Most people think that the situation has stabilized, and that the country has become more unified. These changes are the result of a long, hard struggle, and people cherish them. Now that people are awakened, they will never agree to a revival of the sort of social fascism that plunged China into turbulence and disaster, and that brought them great suffering and despair.

But some officials feel uneasy when they see our freedoms even slightly widened. In their view ordinary people should be voiceless, like beasts or machines. In their dictionary, democracy means they speak, we listen.

What a masterpiece is Commentator's article in *Jiefang ribao* (Liberation Daily) of January 10, 1981! It lays bare the contradictions in the thinking of some people at the top. We would like to ask the author of this explosively charged article a question. Mr. Commentator, you talk much about "illegal organizations" and "illegal publications," as if you yourself were some heroic defender of the law. But this law that you worship, is it royal law or constitutional law?

The Constitution says that citizens have the freedom to meet and associate. Any organization of citizens is therefore constitutionally legal. Specific provisions on how to organize should have been clearly set out in a Law of Association and Organization, so that citizens can act according to them. But even though China has had the name of "People's Republic" for the past thirty years, no such law has ever been enacted. Similarly, the Constitution says that citizens have the freedom of speech and publication. Constitutionally, any publication that citizens produce is therefore legal. But unfortunately no Law of Publication has ever been decreed.

It seems that Commentator is only concerned with royal law, the law that might is right. So he denounces as illegal any organization that, although constitutional, has not yet won the approval of the authorities; and he refers to publications started by the people as illegal, even though they have tried repeatedly to apply for official registration.

Commentator's authority is apparently even above that of the NPC. One word from him and many organizations and dozens of unofficial publications are trapped in the law's net. But a closer look shows that this net is woven by royal law. When royal law rules supreme, the royal labels factory will have no lack of markets: old labels like "counterrevolutionary" will be joined by 1980 and 1981 models like "extreme individualism," "the Democracy Wall Gang," "turbulent agitator," "dissident," and "hostile element." If this goes on much longer, Commentator will begin to match the Gang of Four, and could even leave them in the shade!

Commentator also takes a swipe at grassroots elections, which he calls "so-called elections" and views as a mere pretext for reactionary speeches. If Commentator had a longer memory, he would recall that *Liberation Daily* itself carried many reports on elections and election campaigns, and made a great fuss about the need to strengthen people's awareness and sense of initiative through them. How can he deny it? If this goes on much longer, *Liberation Daily* will become like newspapers were during the last years of the Gang of Four—fit only for wrapping paper.

Without election campaigns there can be no real elections. And what if a counterrevolutionary does run for election? As long as the people themselves are not counterrevolutionary, such a person will simply be exposed and isolated. Only those without guts and who are opposed to the people fear election campaigns. Commentator is very hostile to elections. Doesn't that say something about his politics?

Commentator muddles together publishing and speaking with crimes like robbery and causing explosions. His method is all too familiar. Our country is now on the point of perfecting its legal system. Criminals who cause explosions or commit other crimes will be dealt with by law. Ordinary Chinese, unlike our anxious Commentator, are confident that the legal system will safeguard social order. But what does Commentator have in mind when he puts publishing and speaking on a par with criminal acts? Can we expect a new round of "literary hell" and of manufactured public opinion? We hope not. We would prefer to view Commentator as a second-rate scribbler and self-advertiser than as the harbinger of a new wave of repression.

Commentator is deeply worried about our national economy. Of course, we share his worry. But we are diametrically opposed to him on how to change things. He says that in times of difficulty we need stability and unity. What he really means is that ordinary people should be gagged. Why doesn't he just say outright, "We cadres botched things, but we forbid you to grumble about it! Keep your mouths shut! We big shots will put things right. You must believe that the future is infinitely bright and beautiful!"

But unfortunately for him, the people are no longer wrapped in ignorance. Without their active participation the national economy will never prosper. So much money has been squandered—money earned by the hard toil of the people. Why should they not complain? If we rely only on some savior and make no effort to win the enthusiasm of ordinary Chinese, we are on the road to disaster. Is that so difficult to grasp? If ordinary people are not allowed to discuss things, and if everything is left to people like the Oil Minister (who wasted huge sums of money and was responsible through his incompetence for workers' deaths), then it will be truly difficult to maintain "unity and stability."

Our position is: practice democracy, win people's enthusiasm, pool all talents, share out responsibility—and then there will be no difficulty that we cannot overcome. Every citizen should be encouraged to speak out boldly and often. The people are the masters of the state. Only when they give of their best will China prosper and stability and unity be strengthened.

We think that particular attention should be paid to election campaigns. Only through such campaigns can citizens become aware of the value of their own existence and work hard for the country. Only then will they ditch the time-servers and chair-warmers so that skilled and talented newcomers can take up public posts. Only then will people's potential be fully tapped. As for Commentator, he will be able to exchange his blunt pen for another job more suited to his talents. Otherwise, a few more lousy articles like that and the world will be in a right mess.

We have repeatedly asked the authorities to draw up and promulgate laws of speech, association, and election, so that citizens have something to which they can refer. Otherwise, people with ulterior motives will exploit the confusion. Commentator's article in *Liberation Daily* is a good example of this.

We should also recognize that China's unofficial publications, which have been appearing for two years now, have achieved much and are on exactly the right course. Again and again ideas and proposals that first appeared in unofficial publications have ended up part of official government policy. Of course, there are people who would like to deny our contribution, but history will sneer at their efforts.

As an unofficial publication we risk much by speaking out like this. We are not like Commentator, who presents himself as always reasonable, and stable as Mount Tai. We refuse to earn our living by bending before every wind; our own security means nothing to us. We long ago weighed the value of our lives: if we can help China overcome poverty and backwardness and achieve civilization and progress, and if we can help to win lasting happiness and true stability and unity for our beloved people, then our consciences will be clear and even if we die, we will die content.

DOCUMENT 28

GE TIAN

A Guangdong Youth Forum on Wall Posters

During the Hundred Flowers campaign of 1957, the Cultural Revolution, and the winter of 1978–79, critics of the regime or of factions in it could express their opinions through wall posters. The government, particularly its radical element, used such posters to give the appearance of spontaneity to its campaigns, but courageous individuals could use them to publicize dissident views, although many were persecuted for doing so. Wall posters became particularly associated with the Maoist faction in the Party, and the Four Greats—speaking out freely, airing views fully, holding great debates, and writing wall posters—were seen as Mao's policy. The Deng government's decision in February 1980 to erase the Four Greats from the Constitution (where Mao had put them) dismayed the democratic movement, which saw it as a betrayal. The government argued that wall posters, being anonymous, could be used to spread slander, and that in any case they were no longer necessary now that China was restoring democracy and opening the official media to public opinion. But this argument did not convince oppositionist youth, who rightly reckoned that views like theirs would never be officially published. It is interesting that the forum described below was organized by the Communist Youth League. The democratic movement had friends in the Party throughout China, and would otherwise never have come so prominently into the public eye.

On 4 April 1980, the Guangdong Provincial Committee of the Communist Youth League held a forum on the Communiqué of the Fifth Plenum of the CCP Central Committee. Those invited included Li Zhengtian, Chen Yiyang, and Wang Xizhe, authors of the famous Li Yi Zhe wall poster; student representatives; members of the editorial boards of the four non-governmental journals *Renminzhi sheng* (Voice of the People), *Shenghuo* (Life), *Langhua* (Spray), and *Renminzhi lu* (People's Road); cadres of the Ocean Shipping Bureau; and reporters of the official journal *Zhongguo qingnian bao* (China Youth).

A teacher named Xu from Zhongshan University said: "Most students cannot see why the Four Greats should be abolished. They think that if the Four Greats are abolished, it will be impossible to make proposals. Are the central authorities scared of criticism? Can't they tolerate a few suggestions?"

Liu Guokai (of *Voice of the People*) said: "Most of our workers feel that if the Four Greats are abolished, there will be no way left to supervise the bureaucrats. They dare not post their joint letter exposing the serious problems of bureaucratism in their factory because none of them believes that such a letter will have any effect."

Student Cai X from the Chinese Department of Zhongshan University said: "Some people say that those comrades on the Central Committee who supported abolishing the Four Greats are probably those who were lashed by wall posters in the past. If the meeting had been attended by ordinary people, there would have been no mention of this issue. No one at our student meeting supported abolishing the Four Greats. After all, there are laws, so everyone who uses wall posters to spread slanders can be punished."

A representative of Huanan engineering students said: "Our students' faith in the Party vacillated recently. Some demanded a rational explanation of the rehabilitation of Liu Shaoqi. Some said that all these things were the result of a power struggle. They said that they do not understand the handling of the four people [Wang Dongxing, Ji Dengkui, Wu De, and Chen Xitian, the Maoist old guard that was dismissed from the leadership once Deng Xiaoping had tightened his grip on it]. In the past, we said that Wang Dongxing contributed to the struggle against the Gang of Four. Now we say that he made mistakes in opposing the Gang of Four. How can we account for this sudden switch? Some students do not understand why Liu Shaoqi was rehabilitated. They say that to remove Liu Shaoqi from power was the main aim of Chairman Mao's Cultural Revolution. But now the Party claims that Liu's rehabilitation is aimed at restoring the true features of Mao Zedong Thought."

Most students disagree with abolishing the Four Greats. They think that with democracy weak in China, the Four Greats have an important role to play. Why aren't we allowed to use the Four Greats as weapons against bureaucratism? The demonstrations of 5 April 1976 (against the Gang of Four) also made use of the Four Greats. But now it's alleged that the Four Greats never played a positive role.

Students from Shaoguan, Zhanjiang, and Meixian reported that there was a serious trend toward dividing up the fields among the peasants. They said that the central authorities should spend more time studying social problems, for if such trends spread unchecked, problems will emerge, and the images of Chairman Mao and premier Zhou Enlai will be besmirched.

A representative of the students of Huanan Teachers' College said: "None of us sees why the Four Greats should be abolished. Without wall posters, what other means are there for us to show what we think? In the past, students could use wall posters to reflect problems. Now they no longer dare to write them. We think that the Party should guide us in the right way to use wall posters rather than just abolish them."

The secretary of the Communist Youth League at the Ocean Shipping Bureau said: "Since we Communists are fearless and dauntless, what reason is there to be afraid of wall posters? As for the four dismissed leaders, I also fail to understand their treatment. Why weren't their mistakes made public? Did Wang Dongxing not render outstanding services? Why treat him badly now? If he made mistakes, then his mistakes should be made known to the public. Some young people believe that the Party always follows this rule: Whoever wields power dominates everything."

Li Min of *Spray* said: "Many articles eulogizing Liu Shaoqi have appeared in the press. It seems as if this is another movement to create a god.

All this publicity implies that Chairman Mao's Cultural Revolution was aimed merely at overthrowing Liu, and that it was just power play. But I believe that things were not that simple. As for the Four Greats, I have neither a bad nor a good opinion of them. However, I am sure that people in our socialist society would still find them useful."

Wang Xizhe said: "[Wang Dongxing and his supporters] should not have been removed from power. They should be allowed to make statements and speeches. Why aren't they allowed to explain their position and talk about their problems? As for the Four Greats, I think that Deng Xiaoping is not respecting the Constitution. In 1978 he told some foreign visitors that the people have the constitutional right to put up wall posters, and that no one has the right to stop them. But now he says that the Four Greats have never played a positive role. Although wall posters have been abolished, the people still do not know how to apply democracy. So the people now have even fewer democratic rights. Nongovernmental journals should be allowed to exist."

Li Zhengtian said: "Before the National Peoples' Congress discusses abolishing the Four Greats, our leaders should try to get it to discuss a new publications law. Every society needs some way of reflecting public opinion. To embody democracy in our society, we need a publications law."

DOCUMENT 29

GONG BO
The Wind Rises from among the Duckweed:
Elections at Beijing University

Normally elections in the People's Republic are strictly controlled by the Party, which permits only officially approved candidates to win. The elections of 1980 were different in that in some places unofficial candidates insisted on running against the official ones. Where the authorities did not intervene, electors could therefore choose for the first time ever between genuinely different points of view. One place where the authorities were particularly tolerant during the elections was Beijing University. Candidates and voters played their parts with great gusto, and the history of the campaign was recorded with loving care by a commission specially set up for the purpose. But the Central Committee of the Communist Party was not happy about this, and forbade the publication of the writings of Hu Ping, the successful candidate, on the grounds that he had "resorted to a Cultural Revolution-style movement" (*Zhengming* [Contention], 1 May 1981). This account of the elections was first published in the Beijing University students' journal *Sixu* (Train of Thought), no. 1.

THE ELECTION: AN OVERALL SKETCH

The election campaign lasted for six weeks. There were 6,084 electors and 29 candidates. Most of the candidates organized teams of canvassers, although the way in which they did so varied. People like Xia Shen and Wang Juntao set up election committees before announcing their candidacies, while Hu Ping formed his team only later. Other candidates like Zhang Manling did not set up any stable support group, although they never lacked people ready to work for them. In some groups people already knew each other from school or university; in others, they were drawn together for the first time by their commitment to the election.

Each team explained its goals and viewpoints on hoardings set up at points specified by the university. Candidates also organized open forums in the canteen, the hall, and the lecture rooms, where they answered voters' questions. There were altogether eighteen such forums during the six weeks of campaigning, attended by twenty thousand people. Some committees held regular consulting sessions where they received voters or comrades from other units who came with questions. Many candidates visited student voters in their hostels and discussed with them formally and informally. During the campaign, many voters volunteered to help candidates copy and put up wall posters, and to publish and distribute information. As a result, some ten publications were produced, with names like "Election Affairs," "Election Short-Wave," and "Reporter Station." These publications were nonaligned and carried general campaign reports. Together with some of the election committees they conducted a dozen or so opinion polls and general investigations. Students from the Department of History and the Department of Chinese volunteered to set up a Board to Edit and Collect Election Information in order to preserve documents and recordings of the campaign. During those six weeks the whole campus was in a lively ferment. Even unenfranchised students expressed their views and preferences. Everywhere there were wall posters, leaflets, opinion polls, investigations, advertisements for forums, and candidates' opinion boxes. Everywhere people were arguing, discussing, asking naive questions, and making stirring speeches.

On 1 December 1980, the first round in the election resulted in the elimination of all but three candidates. On 11 December the first round of the main election was held, resulting in the election of Hu Ping. The turnout was 5,509, or 90.55 percent. The voting was 3,457 (57 percent) for Hu Ping, 2,964 (48.72 percent) for Wang Juntao, and 2,052 (33.77 percent) for Zhang Wei. The second round of voting was on 18 December. Since 198 electors were out of the district at the time, the number of

potential voters fell to 5,976. Of these 4,778, or 81.63 percent, voted.
Wang Juntao got 2,934 votes (49.1 percent) and Zhang Wei got 1,456
(34.36 percent); neither was elected.

HOW THE ELECTORS VIEWED THE ELECTION

An opinion poll conducted early on in the campaign revealed that 8.6
percent of the electors thought that the election was an empty formality,
52.6 percent saw it as a first step toward socialist democracy, and 37.9
percent thought that it might have some positive effect, although not a
lasting one. Voters were also asked what their attitude was toward political life in our country: 5.6 percent neither cared about it nor participated
in it; 46.2 percent cared little and did not participate much; 48.2 percent
cared much and participated actively.

The apathy revealed by these statistics can be partly explained by the
powerlessness of people's congresses at all levels, particularly at county
level. But most electors expected something of the elections, and this
roused them to action. They hoped that the people's congresses would
acquire some real power so that they could represent at least some of the
people's interests; that it would be an election, not an "appointment";
and that members of the people's congress at county level could also become representatives at a higher level. What particularly heartened them
were the frank discussions. Discussions of this sort were a novelty, and
threw new light on a number of theoretical, social, and political issues.

THE CANDIDATES' VIEWS

(1) Wang Juntao alone among the candidates made a critical assessment of the last thirty years of Chinese history. He believed that
    (i) If Liu Shaoqi's line of "consolidating New Democracy"
had been followed in the early years of the People's Republic,
the economy would have developed more quickly, society
would have developed more healthily, and the subsequent
switch to socialist construction might have had some real meaning. But as it turned out, socialist construction simply meant
superimposing advanced forms of ownership on underdeveloped productive forces.
    (ii) Agriculture was collectivized too quickly and without re-
gard to what was objectively possible, thus slowing down agricultural growth. The same is true of handicrafts. Producers' interests were neglected and city dwellers suffered great hardship.
However, the reform of capitalist industry and commerce was
more successful.

(iii) The "anti-rightist struggle" of 1957 was based on a mistaken view of the state and class struggle, and should not have happened.

(iv) The Great Leap Forward was a leftist initiative. For reasons of vanity some Party leaders wanted China to be the first country to reach Communism, and they manipulated the masses accordingly. The result was disaster.

(v) The 1959 Lushan Plenum led to the frame-up of Peng Dehuai. We should criticize Mao's wrong treatment of dissenters.

(vi) The anti-revisionist campaign correctly opposed the idea of a "father-party" and Soviet great-power chauvinism, but irreparably weakened its whole case by promoting Stalinism as the alternative to Khrushchev.

(vii) The "general-line" led to a new and more dangerous phase of leftism. The theory of uninterrupted revolution under the proletarian dictatorship was anti-Marxist.

(viii) Corruption was a product of Mao's wrong line and of the irrational cadre system. But the Four Clean-ups Campaign tried to deal with it simply by purging lower officials.

(2) On the Great Proletarian Cultural Revolution, Wang Juntao believed that it was a mass movement directed by Mao's wrong line, but he also thought that it had produced some valuable new ideas. Fang Zhiyuan thought that the Cultural Revolution was an unsuccessful antibureaucratic revolution, but that reactionary forces like Lin Biao and the Gang of Four had tried to exploit it in their own interests. Most candidates had rather simple ideas about the Cultural Revolution. The majority thought that it was reactionary. A large minority saw it as a complex affair that required further analysis. A few saw it as a failed revolution. But so far there has been no deep or detailed discussion of it.

(3) On 29 November Wang Juntao and nine others held a discussion on whether or not Mao was a Marxist. Wang pointed out that the core of Marxism is historical materialism, and that Marxism starts by analyzing the productive forces and only then analyzes productive relations, the productive mode, and the mode of social development. But all along Mao based his analysis of Chinese society on class relations, and consistently ignored the determining role of productive forces. Second, Wang pointed out that Marxism stresses the role of the masses in history and opposes historical idealism, whereas Mao ran a sort of oligarchy both inside and outside the Party and was a historical idealist who refused to learn from the experience of advanced democracies. Third, Wang pointed out that Marxists have

always emphasized that people should critically accept and preserve their cultural heritage, but Mao denounced a large part of that heritage as bourgeois and feudal, and so did great harm to Chinese culture. Wang concluded from his analysis that Mao was not a Marxist. In three subsequent essays he elaborated these views. Among other things he said that if Mao was not a Marxist, then perhaps other leaders like Liu Shaoqi and Zhou Enlai were also not Marxists. He criticized Mao's view, formed in his old age, that a new class of bourgeoisie had grown up inside the Party. But not all candidates agreed with Wang's assessment of Mao.

(4) Most candidates, in discussing the nature of Chinese society, used terms like "socialism in the broad sense," "semisocialism," and "near socialism." Xia Shen said that society's intangible interests had superseded the practical needs of individuals. Abstract ideas of the collective had come to dominate over personal values. The high degree of centralization in politics, economics, and ideology had become a serious obstacle to social progress. Fang Zhiyuan pointed out that collective ownership of the means of production does not equal socialism, and that socialism must also embrace democracy. Democracy is both a means and an end. Without democracy, collective ownership is illusory. Wang Juntao pointed out that after the crushing of the Gang of Four, at first only the most extreme manifestations of Mao's wrong line were discarded. Since then there have been some good developments and some bad. The people and some leaders have come to realize that bureaucratism is a problem of the system, and that it would be sensible to adopt certain aspects of the political system of capitalist societies. But at the same time Democracy Wall, which mapped out China's path for the eighties, has been closed down. Yang Peikuai said that intellectuals are the most progressive force in society. Wang Juntao said that intellectuals, supported by youth and students, provide the main impetus for reform. The peasants enthusiastically support reform, while the workers are already its main beneficiaries. The main obstacle to it comes from sections of the cadres. Tian Cheli said that the middle cadres were the main obstacle, and that they should be pushed into action from two sides (the Central Committee, and the rank and file).

(5) There were various views on how reforms should be carried out. These views can be summarized as follows:

(i) Xia Shen and others said that China's shortcomings originate in the extreme centralization of political, economic, and ideological control, and that this centralization must be destroyed. The achievement of a modern economy and modern thinking are intimately connected to the achievement of political democracy. Chinese society will be reformed throughout or not at all.

(ii) Fang Zhiyuan and others said that the further liberation of thought is the main precondition for successful reform in any sphere.

(iii) Hu Ping and others said that democracy and the legal system must be strengthened. Democracy means not only that the majority should rule, but also that the rights of minorities are properly protected and that the powers of the leaders are checked. Genuine democracy is therefore impossible without the separation of powers and free public opinion. Other candidates said that the main task now was to interpret and elaborate the law, so that it becomes clear.

(iv) Yang Peikuai and others said that the economy is the basis of society, and that without economic development there could be no political democracy. Economic reform should come first, since without it no other reform was possible.

(v) Wang Juntao proposed four goals of political reform: inner-party democracy, separation of Party and government, a system of checks and balances, and supervision of government by society.

(6) The question of freedom of speech was widely discussed. Hu Ping said that free speech was beneficial both to the ruling class and to the ruled. The reason it was suppressed was the low level of awareness of the masses. Others replied that free speech must be class-specific, and that counterrevolutionaries should not have it. But most candidates believed that the problem was not whether counterrevolutionaries should have free speech, but whether the rulers alone should have the right to decide who is revolutionary and who not. Some candidates said that in the absence of freedom of the press, Democracy Wall and the Four Great Freedoms were the only outlets for free speech, and with their abolition even the most minimal free speech was wiped out.

(7) The case of Wei Jingsheng also became an issue in the election. Some said Wei's entire prosecution was wrong. Some said that the sentence was too harsh. Some said the trial was improperly conducted. Some said they were ignorant of the background and circumstances of the case. An opinion poll of eighteen candidates found none who thought the trial was completely correct.

(8) All candidates called for the reform of tertiary education. It was generally thought that tertiary education should aim to give students an all-round education and develop their abilities to the full,

rather than turn them into instruments or machines. Many candidates favored the credit system and open-book examinations. Some said that the administration and process of learning should be democratized and that students, teachers, and other staff should form a representative council to which the Chancellor and other administrators would be directly accountable. Graduates should be assigned to jobs on the basis of a combination of their own personal wishes and the country's needs. Many candidates said that the main problems facing youth in China were the crisis of faith, unemployment, and the difficulty of getting an education. But many thought that present-day youth have many good attributes, including skepticism, independent thinking, enthusiasm for new things, a zeal for reform, a commitment to democracy, a strong desire for learning, and an awareness of their own interests. They are a thinking and exploring generation.

(9) A main point in Xia Shen's manifesto was the need to respect human individuality, and to allow it to develop freely and to the full. The female candidate Zhang Ailing raised the same question from another angle. She called for women's liberation and said that the beauty of eastern femininity must be restored and issues concerning Chinese women should be further studied. Toward the end of the campaign she set up the Chinese Women's Study Association. (For further information, see Document 41.)

Voters' Political Views and Tendencies

Asked what sort of candidates they would like to see elected, voters replied as follows:

Radical social reformers	36.6%
Moderate social reformers	19.5%
Gradualists	18.8%
Nonpolitical candidates	10.2%
Others	14.9%

Most favored moderate reform, although some wanted "major surgery." As to who should have responsibility for carrying out reform, many felt that they themselves were impotent, and looked for reforms initiated from above. Other felt that the leadership and the rank and file should act in concert, with the latter exerting pressure on the former, and that reforms would only be effective if the masses (especially their advanced sections) had a stake in them. Many voters voiced varying degrees of opposition to the closing down of Democracy Wall, the abolition of the Four Great Freedoms, and the sentencing of Wei Jingsheng. Some students from the faculties of economics, law, and politics drafted an Ordinance on Publication, Printing, and Distribution which is now being circulated for signatures and will be submitted to the law commission of the NPC. Those elected to represent the constituency would be asked to bring the matter to the regional people's congress and ultimately to the national one.

"PARTICULARITIES" VERSUS "GENERALITIES"

Candidates tended to concentrate on local issues or "particularities," whereas from the very beginning of the campaign voters showed an interest in overall political, theoretical, and social issues—the so-called "generalities." The wider the campaign ranged, the more these "generalities" come to the fore. This is partly because the electors were in this case students, who are more interested than most people in ideas, politics, and broader culture. But there are more general reasons too. First, county-level congresses have little power and what power they do have is ill defined, so that they rarely take up local issues.

Second, people tend to judge candidates by their general political stand and theoretical competence, for if these are lacking, then what chance have they of fulfilling their "particularistic" promises? Third, successful candidates at the county level stand the chance of being elected upward into congresses at higher levels, in which case what were previously "generalities" would become "particularities." Fourth, China has too little experience of democracy, and in the past people have had little chance of voicing their opinions on important social issues. It is therefore only natural that with the deepening of the reform movement some people should seize the chance to make their general needs known, and that candidates should tend to discuss these broader issues. The Party and government leaders should pay attention to this trend. Finally, it should be noted that student voters also voiced concern over various "particular issues such as the shortage of shops and services in the area, the inadequate cultural facilities, the traffic congestion, and the noise pollution on the roads around the campus.

GUIDING THE ELECTION

Before the election the university administration indicated that it would not interfere in the proceedings. The local electoral authority abided by the electoral laws and provided various facilities to ensure the smooth running of the election, including places to put up posters, paper, and halls and lecture rooms. Campaigning was organized by the students themselves. But a free election was not what some Party and government leaders wanted. Some top leaders outside the university accused various candidates of being "dissidents." The wall posters were torn down immediately after the first round of voting, even though the results had not yet been announced and there was still another round to come.

THE CAMPAIGN WAS TOO
NARROWLY CONDUCTED

Various important questions were raised during the election campaign, but they were not discussed in enough depth. For example, the assessment of the Cultural Revolution was too simplistic, and there was no real discussion of the causes of the absence of free expression in China. There are five main reasons for this. First, some voters were simply not interested in broader issues, and especially had no time for radical views. This reflects China's political and theoretical tiredness. Second, some voters are still bound by the orthodox ideology that had dominated them for all these years, and counter original opinions simply by parroting the official textbooks. Third, some of those who were interested in discussing broader and more important issues did not research them deeply enough. Fourth, an election campaign is not the most appropriate forum for a serious and detailed discussion of sensitive issues. Fifth, the election was conducted in too gentlemanly a way. Candidates rarely confronted one another's views, although when they did so, the exchanges were serious and substantial.

THE IMPLICATIONS OF THE ELECTION

This and other elections showed that the Chinese people have a certain basic grasp of politics and are no longer satisfied with letting Party officials speak in their name. These elections also showed that the people want to make the congress at various levels the sole legislators and the sole source of the executive, and to place them under popular supervision.

DOCUMENT 30

HE NONG
Election Scandal in a Rural Commune

The democratic movement was mainly confined to the cities, but here and there it made headway into the vast countryside. This complicated account of shenanigans in a Shanxi commune shows some of the problems of introducing democracy to the Chinese villages. The story is further confused by the fact that the four men named in it have only two family names between them: Meng and Liu. This suggests that lineage ties still cut across political divisions in the brigade.

UP TO 1974 Comrade Liu Xijian was secretary of the Party branch of Xiangshanzhuang brigade in Xi County, Shanxi Province. While he was secretary members of the brigade got lots of food and a good income, and the three fixed quotas (for production, purchase, and marketing of grain) were fulfilled for twelve years running. In 1974 Liu was promoted to commune level, and Meng was appointed brigade secretary in his place. Under Meng the brigade's performance worsened and individual income dropped catastrophically to 0.5 yuan a day and 200 catties of food a year. Naturally brigade members were dissatisfied, and during the democratic election of cadres at the beginning of this year they urged Liu to run as candidate for the brigade leadership. Liu felt that he could work better in the brigade than in the commune, and agreed to run. The commune secretary, also named Liu, was away at a meeting in Taiyuan at the time, but Liu Xijian first discussed his decision with other commune leaders. Officers of the commune disciplinary board and the commune military board also ran as candidates in the brigade election. The result was that Liu Xijian was elected brigade secretary in Meng's place, a youth was elected brigade officer, and Meng was elected as brigade vice-secretary. On his return from Taiyuan the commune secretary said: "Liu has returned to the brigade and pushed out the incumbent secretary. He did not give others a chance, so he won't be given a chance either. All he's done is to create trouble in the brigade." In the brigade study-group that the commune had organized the commune secretary, far from promoting unity, deliberately set about creating splits. The ten cadres in the study-group lined up for and against their new brigade secretary, and were so deeply split on this issue that they even refused to eat together. Brigade secretary Liu was under intense pressure and could only remain at his post because of the support he got from brigade members and from a section of the cadres. After his election he worked closely with the brigade members, stood firmly on the Party line, and applied it with the necessary flexibility. The result was that despite a summer drought the harvest was good, and the three fixed quotas were once again fulfilled. By the end of the year average pay was expected to rise to between 1.3 and 1.5 yuan a day. The county radio even did a report on the brigade's achievements. This greatly annoyed the commune secretary, who could only swear and deny the facts.

The commune secretary's meddling was not without effect. Of the brigade's five teams, from now on only three could be counted on to attend brigade discussions. The other two teams, which were led by brigade vice-secretary Meng, did not dare attend for fear of offending him. If he wanted to he could easily make difficulties for them. For example, the former officer of the brigade women's federation was beaten and cursed as a traitor simply because she had voted for Liu Xijian in the election. During the summer drought the brigade organized the repairing of wells, but Meng's two teams refused to send anyone to help. Nonetheless they jumped the queue for water after the repairs were done. To avoid conflict, the other three teams gave way.

There was another Meng in the brigade whose father had some historical problems (previous clashes with the authorities) and who was treated as a "bad element." He had several times requested the commune to remove this label in line with the new Party policy. The commune's organization board asked the brigade for a report and then passed on an announcement that Meng's label should be removed. Since Meng was in a team led by brigade vice-secretary Meng, this announcement could not be made at a meeting of the brigade, for both "bad element" Meng and vice-secretary Meng were boycotting these meetings. Therefore the brigade officer, who had been asked by the commune to relay the announcement as soon as possible, broadcast it over the radio. Vice-secretary Meng's mother and wife then took to the streets reviling "bad element" Meng and proclaiming that their family had been ruined by the brigade officer. When the brigade officer's wife went to work that day, she was surrounded in the brigade square by six members of the vice-secretary's family, who cursed her and severely beat her. Since things were getting out of hand, the brigade officer asked for a meeting with the commune secretary. The commune secretary said: "I refuse to take any further action. You were wrong to make the announcement about Meng's label. You should apologize to the brigade vice-secretary. That man Meng has been labeled a bad element for more than twenty years now, and your broadcast was very damaging to the vice secretary. If I were him I would have beaten you even worse. You've never had any respect for me. If you had, there wouldn't be so many conflicts in your village. This would never have happened if you had not been brigade officer." The brigade officer replied: "I'm not brigade officer just because I want to be, I was elected to the post." The commune secretary said: "You could still have refused. If you'd refused, then Meng could have been elected." The brigade officer replied: "Well, you can always sack me and appoint him." The commune secretary did not appear at all worried and still refused to act on the matter of the beating. Later the brigade officer appealed to the county disciplinary board and the consultation board, but they did not dare take action because the commune secretary was a member of the county standing committee and vice-officer of the revolutionary committee. Later the brigade officer took his wife to the home of the commune secretary, who grudgingly promised to ask his assistant to deal with the problem. This assistant sent for brigade vice-secretary Meng five times but each time Meng failed to show up, so the assistant had no choice but to transfer it to the county court. The court in its turn transferred it to the Public Security Bureau. But despite all this transferring, the case was not resolved. In the brigade work came to a standstill. The brigade members were very angry, and said: "The policies of our elected representatives can never be carried out as long as we only have the right to elect lower cadres. If the leading cadres don't control the elections, those who are elected cannot work."

DOCUMENT 31

ZHENG XING
The Election Movement Is in the Ascendant

Where the democratic movement was represented in the factories, its supporters tried with varying degrees of success to run in factory elections in 1980. Little is known of these campaigns, except that where dissidents were not prevented from running, they got big votes. But many obstacles were placed in the way of their campaigns by factory managers and Party bureaucrats.

IN 1980 the word "election" officially entered China's political vocabulary. This was an event of great consequence, joyously welcomed by many. Only a handful cut off from the people by an abyss fear this change, and are seeking ways to reverse it. But they will never succeed; however much they may resent and resist the progress of history, elections are spreading everywhere across this vast, ossified land.

After the elections in several of Shanghai's major universities, there was a spectacular chain reaction in universities throughout China, particularly in Beijing. Even more spectacularly, workers all over the country have followed the example of workers at Shanghai Motor Factory, who set a precedent by holding their own elections.

On 17 November 1980, He Defu, a young worker at the Organic Chemical Factory who was also an editor of *Beijing qingnian* (Beijing Youth), and Gong Ping, a worker at an oxygen factory, ran for election as people's representatives in Chaoyang district. They wrote a joint manifesto: "The Chinese people suffered for ten long years from the ravages of the Cultural Revolution. This was clear proof that because the people did not rule the country or control their own destinies, power fell into the hands of a small minority whose mistakes have cost us dear.

"We view this election as a test of how far democracy can be implemented, and we view the electoral process as a struggle for democratic rights. At the same time, this election is a test of how far popular awareness has grown. Habit and tradition suggest that elections are a mere formality and that the representatives will have been secretly chosen in advance. We believe that this was true of previous elections. But now we must resolve that from now on things will be different. We have the protection of the law (although it is still far from perfect). We have support from inside and outside the country. And most important of all, the people are more aware. As long as we dare to struggle and know how to struggle, we can win recognition for the people's democratic rights. Voters should be confident and determined.

"At present the positions of master and servant are reversed in China. But the people strongly want those that they elect to truly represent them. The role of people's representatives is to defend and fight for the people's basic interests, to ensure that government works in the interests of the people, and to supervise the policies and measures of the ruling party. A people's representative must understand the people's wishes, dare to express them, fight to realize them, and firmly resist policies and measures that contradict them. We view this as our duty and obligation, whatever the consequences for us personally; which is why we want to be elected. If voters support us, we will fight to the end for their basic interests.

"The long-term aims of our struggle are as follows: a rise in the people's living standards must be a first priority, and should be written as such into the Constitution; we must realize socialist modernization in all spheres, including in democracy, ideology, consciousness, and people's livelihood; all these are interrelated aims, and none can be omitted. We view this election as a test of the ruling party. Does it believe in the people and stand together with the people? Or does it stand against the people?"

In the first round of "discussion and negotiation" He Defu got 202 votes; in the second round he got 451 votes, and finished third in the election. In the oxygen factory Gong Ping came fourth; but in his case leading cadres held "individual discussions" and "greetings sessions" with each voter, so there were many abstentions.

Early this month, there were also elections for people's representatives in Qingyuan, Hebei Province. After the officially approved nominations had gone through, Wang Yifeng, a young worker in the sales department of a hardware factory, courageously rose to his feet to announce his candidacy. He distributed and posted up an election manifesto headed "Citizens, you must control your own fate." In it he wrote: "People's representatives, as the name shows, should represent the people's wishes and interests. To be a people's representative is not to wear hero's laurels, nor to carry official rank, nor to be in a position to pursue fame or to repress the people. People's representatives should be militants and servants of the people. They should dare to fight bureaucracy, to speak up for the people, and to work for the people. They should be neither selfish nor self-effacing.

"Citizens! The nomination of candidates is now closed, but what do you know of those who have been nominated? Are they prepared to accept your mandate? Do they stand for reform of the state, and are they capable of carrying it out? Obviously you do not know, since the candidates have not explained their views and aspirations to you. But experience shows that without campaigns there can be no elections, especially not elections for people's representatives. What is a campaign? It is a competition among those up for election. It is the process whereby candidates (nominated or self-nominated) try to get elected by making the best speech or writing the best manifesto, and by demonstrating their ideological level and their aspirations.

"I was born on 4 October 1954 into a peasant family in Qingyuan County. My family was poor. After a serious illness I became poverty-stricken and had to beg for my living. The endless bleakness stimulated my young ambition, and I studied hard to change the world. I had no money to enter school, but I managed with the support of others to study for five years, although it was not easy. That was during the Cultural Revolution. At the age of sixteen, I went to work in commerce. At eighteen, I joined the army. This experience tempered my ambition and character. It also taught me that poverty is general, and that it is caused by the underdevelopment of the social system of production. And so it became my burning ambition to help liberate the people of the whole world and build a world of peace and happiness. From then on I began to pay attention to social issues, to study history, politics, and philosophy, and to look for ways of changing the world. By the age of twenty, I had learned that the science of Marxism is the ideological weapon with which to transform oneself and society. Since then I have always used Marxist theories as my guide, transformed myself through practice, and learned from others in order to improve my knowledge and skills. I devote my spare time to the theoretical study of Chinese society and of the world. In April 1976 I was discharged from the army and worked for a while in a native products factory. In 1978 I was transferred to the sales department of a hardware company. Since the Party's Third Plenum issued the call for the liberation of thought, I have put all my energy into researching theoretical questions of the Chinese Revolution. In October 1980 I submitted my article 'Socialist Revolution: A Special Transitional Period' to the state theoretical institute.

"Although the electoral law has been drawn up and general elections have begun, some bureaucrats have tried to control the elections, and have failed to explain their true meaning and procedure. The result is that when it comes to voting, many people are still in the dark. Even worse, the candidates are chosen by the leaders. I believe that this is wrong, that it breaches electoral law, and that it defiles public opinion. I hope voters will fully understand the meaning of their vote. If we all vote for someone who genuinely represents our views, such lawless acts will lose their point: for what is small will become big, and few will become many. All power will return to the hands of the people. As a start, here are three proposals that will benefit the people of our area: (1) A procedure must be worked out, and immediately implemented, for electing and dismissing leaders of the administrative units. (2) Units must be autonomous, accounting must be done at unit level, and workers must get a share in profits. (3) A procedure must be drawn up at once to shorten the working hours of women and to protect their health. Electors, please vote for me. I will speak and work for you."

Wang Yifeng put up his manifesto on the north wall of the County Committee building on the night of 6 January, but by the next morning it had been torn down. The same day Wang protested that the election was being "barbarously and illegally sabotaged."

Mr. Guo of the County Committee phoned the head of the hardware company on the 6th to inform Wang Yifeng that his manifesto had been torn down in line with the recent constitutional ban on wall posters. On 7 January Wang replied in an open letter:

1. The Four Great Freedoms, which include the freedom to write wall posters, were struck out of the Constitution on the grounds that Article 45 already guarantees the freedom of speech, to which category wall posters belong. So striking out the Four Great Freedoms does not make wall posters a crime.

2. It is not against the law for people to write wall posters. If it is, then please tell me what law, since I know nothing of it. If wall posters were illegal, then so would be all propaganda put up on walls. Are notices put up by the Judicial Department wall posters? Are commercial adverts wall posters? Are the black-on-yellow notices outside the County Committee wall posters? If so, why are they not banned?

On 9 January Wang Yifeng wrote out a "Proposal for disallowing official candidates who have been illegally nominated." In it he pointed out that in his electoral constituency "nine candidates had been reduced to three; there was no proper discussion—voters were simply instructed to raise their hand in support of the three people decided on by the Commercial Bureau. No particulars of the other six nominees were presented for discussion, and I, as a self-nominated candidate, was completely ignored. This is not election but a disguised form of appointment, and as such a serious offense against the law." Wang ended his proposal as follows: "I shall wait three days for an answer to these points. If I do not get one, I shall join with other voters to complain directly to the Legal Committee of the People's Congress, and I shall call on all voters to rise up and struggle against this lawless bureaucracy, and to fight for the rights of which they have been deprived." Needless to say, no answer came, so after three days Wang Yifeng lodged a complaint with the Central Committee.

DOCUMENT 32

The Student Movement in Hunan

In the early spring of 1927 "an unknown young man called Mao Zedong" (as Victor Serge described him at the time) wrote a report on the Peasant Movement in Hunan that was destined to become a classic of the Chinese Revolution. Perhaps the author of "The Student Movement in Hunan" had Mao's report in mind when he wrote this interesting account of events in Changsha in the early winter of 1980. The account shows that it was still possible even after the first crackdowns of 1979–80 to persuade the national leadership in Beijing to intercede on the democratic movement's behalf against conservative provincial leader Tao Sen, the leader of the Changsha students, who was later arrested and imprisoned as a dissident.

This article, here abridged, first appeared in *Renminzhi sheng* (Voice of the People), no. 6.

ON 9 October 1980 two thousand students of the Hunan Teachers' Training College marched to the office of the provincial Party committee. They were protesting against the college administration, which had broken the Election Law. They organized mass meetings, processions, petitions, and a hunger strike. This finally led to victory. Students from other colleges supported them, and strikes were organized in colleges and factories. There follows a report of this struggle.

On the evening of 20 September Liang Heng, a student at the Hunan Teachers' Training College, announced that he would run for election to the local government. He said: "I do not believe in Marxism-Leninism. I favor democratic socialism. I want to reform the university's distribution system." The students Liu Zhongyang and Tao Sen also announced their candidacy. All three organized forums and put up posters. But the college's vice-president, Su Ming, said that this was bourgeois electioneering, and that since the Four Greats (including wall posters) had been banned by the national leadership, the posters were illegal. Tao Sen protested to the provincial Party that these activities were in no way "bourgeois."

Between 22 September and 6 October three primary elections were held to determine who would go forward into the final round. But the college authorities were unhappy with the outcome, and organized a fifth and even a sixth primary. The electors boycotted the fifth round. On 6 October the authorities nominated their own candidate for the final round of voting. On 8 October the fourth round ended and the college administration said that the names of the six official candidates would be announced the next day.

Next evening the college radio said that the election committee, in line with majority feeling, had chosen seven official candidates (including Tao Sen and Liang Heng). This attempt by the election committee to impose its will on the voters angered the students, thousands of whom marched spontaneously to the College office singing the *Internationale* and other songs. Three representatives demanded to meet Su Ming, and asked for an explanation. Su Ming responded rudely and refused to give an explanation. He accused the students of acting like in the Cultural Revolution, of disturbing social order, and of behaving illegally. Saying that he was going to sleep, he returned to his office.

The students were furious at his bureaucratic attitude. Two thousand of them marched to the office of the Hunan Party provincial committee. They called on Tao Sen to come out and lead them, which he did, his eyes filled with tears.

The marchers shouted "Down with bureaucratism!," "Down with feudalism!," "Let the people be the masters!," "We want democracy!," and "No to autocracy!" They arrived at the provincial office at midnight. They elected sixteen representatives (including Tao Sen), three secretaries, and two special secretaries. These people marched into the office. At 2:25 A.M. local Party leaders negotiated with them. Reporters from *Guangming ribao* (Guangming Daily) and two provincial papers were present. Two hours later the provincial Party committee conceded that the students' petition was legal and promised to send a work team to investigate.

At 4:30 A.M. the negotiators left the office. Tao Sen shouted: "We've won!" The two thousand waiting students cheered and lifted the representatives onto their shoulders. After Tao Sen had reported on the discussions, the students marched back to the college. It was by now six o'clock in the morning.

Early on 10 October the students' union executive held an emergency meeting. In the afternoon the Party and youth cadre of every department also met. At the same time, the students were celebrating their victory. At the Party meetings, members were told to trust in Marxism-Leninism and the Party leaders, and to stand firm and not join in illegal activities. One

Party leader in the Chemistry Department said he would find out the names of the students who had signed the petition, and that he would educate these people and help them.

That afternoon the provincial Party work team arrived. They met with the student representatives, but concluded that the college election committee had acted legally in adding one more name to the list of six final candidates. This only encouraged the college administration. On 11 October Tao Sen sent the following telegram to Party General Secretary Hu Yaobang, and to Peng Zhen, Wang Zhen, and Yuan Renyuan:

> Some leading cadres have suppressed the democratic election at our college. Two thousand students protested spontaneously. Their protest was well organized and disciplined. As a citizen, a candidate, and a students' representative, I ask you to send a work team to Changsha. Please reply at once.

On 12 October Tao Sen, Liang Heng, and another announced their temporary withdrawal from the election in protest against the college's action. They demanded that the election be postponed, but the voting went ahead on 14 October. Again the students petitioned the provincial Party office. This time there were three thousand of them. They arrived at 11 P.M. Two hours later the provincial Party turned down their demands.

At 2:40 A.M. eighty-seven students, including Tao Sen and Liang Heng, went on a hunger strike. While expressing their determination, they began to weep. The other students wept too. Their tears were a protest against bureaucratism.

The next morning Tao Sen telegrammed Hu Yaobang and the Premier, Zhao Ziyang, asking them to intervene. Four out of five of the college students came to the provincial Party office to show their support for the hunger strikers. As a result, the election planned for 14 October could not go through.

The same day eight hundred students of the Hunan Medical School marched through Changsha in support of the Teachers' Training College students, and three thousand marched that afternoon. On 15 October the students went on a general strike. The famous writer Ou Yangshan went to visit the hunger strikers. He gave them his support, and said he would go on a hunger strike too if necessary. Thousands of students at other Changsha colleges also went on strike. In the meantime Wang Zhen, of the central Party leadership in Beijing, telephoned Tao Sen twice, but his calls were intercepted by a local Party leader. Finally Wang Zhen got through to Tao Sen. Wang told Tao that the central authorities (in Beijing) had already sent an investigating team to the college, and told him to end the hunger strike. Tao Sen refused to do so until the students' demands were met. By 7 P.M. twenty-one hunger strikers had fainted.

Students from all over Changsha and ordinary citizens gathered to show their support, and even representatives of Beijing University flew into the city. Later that evening students' and workers' representatives decided to organize a citywide general strike and march.

But then disaster struck. Tao Sen described what happened:

Some bourgeois rightists and splitters emerged from the ranks. Together with the college and provincial authorities and gangsters, they undermined the struggle. On 16 October the hunger strike collapsed. I was the last to leave, in the cold wind. Tears flowed down my face as I looked at the workers, students, and newspaper reporters who had come to show their support. The flame of socialist democratic reform was out. Intellectuals are so weak!

The next day the investigating team sent by the NPC arrived in Changsha and met with Tao Sen, and on 19 October the Party General Secretary Hu Yaobang arrived in the city. However, by deception the provincial officials prevented him and other central government officials from meeting the students' representatives.

When negotiations with the investigating team produced no results, the students decided to send representatives to Beijing to report on what had happened. The Provincial Party Secretary, Mao Zhiyong, warned them not to go to Beijing, and said that if they did, they would be arrested by the security police. But at 9:50 the next morning the twenty-one students got on the train bound north. En route they were feted by student union officials and representatives.

On 27 October the Hubei provincial Party committee sent some officials on board the train to listen to Tao Sen's story. Their leader said:

If the Hunan committee can solve your problem, they should do so quickly. Otherwise, it's quite legal for you to petition the Beijing authorities. That means that you trust the Party center. We did not know that you were coming, so we were unable to prepare lodgings and meals for you. We must apologize. But we will take you by car to the Hubei Provincial Lodging-House no. 2. We will help you with daily necessities. If you have any request, let us know. You are our country's hope and future. We must take good care of you.

The Hubei committee sent cars as promised but the students decided to continue the trip to Beijing, so they turned down the offer. The Hubei students said they hoped a students' federation would be set up on a national level to truly represent students' interests. They said they wanted to maintain contact with us.

Back on the train, the students explained to the head conductor what had happened. He was very concerned, and reported to the Railway Department. The Railway Department told the head conductor and all stations along the line that they had known that Tao Sen was traveling north and that he and the other representatives had difficulty in paying their fare. The Railway Department told all stations that they should be allowed to pass.

The petitioners arrived in Beijing early on 29 October. They were received by the Central Committee and the State Council, and welcomed by democratic militants and by college students in the capital. They sent the following telegram to their college: "The situation is fine. The Central Committee leaders are very concerned. Unite against the bureaucrat, resolutely carry out reforms, learn the lessons and continue the struggle."

In Beijing the petitioners were received several times by Central Committee officials. The government finally decided that Su Ming had to make a self-criticism and permit a new election. The team returned to Hunan on 11 November.

DOCUMENT 33

CHEN DING
Youth Disturbances in China's Far West

Cities in most developing countries have grown at an alarming speed in recent years as birthrates soar and peasants leave the villages in search of a better life. But the urban economy is unable to absorb all comers, so that many stay unemployed or semi-employed. City-born educated young people also find it hard to get jobs in societies where the education system and the labor market are often badly matched. As a result urban society becomes tense, violent, and unstable.

For many years China was considered the exception to this pattern. Between 1968 and 1975 China's urban authorities sent twelve million former students "up to the mountains and down to the villages," and at the same time stopped peasants from resettling in the towns. For most of these urban youth the transfer to the villages was meant to be lifelong. The aim of this program was to control the growth of the towns, help develop the villages, and reduce the "three great differences"—between town and country, worker and peasant, and mental and manual labor.

These transplanted youth often organized to protest their exclusion from the cities. During the Cultural Revolution groups of them called for the system of permanent resettlement to be turned into a system of rotation, and some even wanted to abolish it altogether. Others called for an end to abuses in the implementation of the program. Many believed that the procedure by which they were chosen for rustication was arbitrary or discriminative, that it was used to punish rebels, and that young people with good family connections could usually manage to stay in the towns.

The word "youth" is quite elastic in People's China. Officially it refers to those between the ages of fifteen and twenty-four, if you take eligibility for membership in the Communist Youth League as your criterion, but there are often difficulties in getting over-age members of the League to retire from it. Some of the people called "youth" in Chen Ding's article are in their thirties, but this is because they are still officially seen as belonging to the category of "sent-down youth."

After the fall of the Gang of Four, the government recognized that the rustication program had largely failed. Living conditions for sent-down youth were hard, and it was clear that most would never accept the idea of a lifetime among the peasants. Because they were in the villages by compulsion and not by choice, their morale was low and they contributed little to village society, so that most peasants saw them as a burden rather than as a vital part of the community.

The government therefore took steps to improve the conditions of sent-down youth and allowed many to return home—some four hundred thousand in Shanghai's case. But many were still denied permission to leave the villages. According to an official of Shanghai's labor bureau, more than half a million young Shanghainese sent to the countryside had not returned, and there were no plans to let them return (*The Guardian* [London], September 29, 1981).

IN LATE 1980 disturbances broke out in Xinjiang, involving as many as seventy thousand people. When the incident reached its climax, some government offices were taken over. Finally, the local authorities got the situation under control, but they had to make concessions. The incident touched off a general shock whose repercussions have not yet completely died down even today.

Nine out of ten of those who took part in the disturbances were young men and women from Shanghai or local people married to them. A handful of local ruffians joined the crowd and tried to take advantage of the crises, but they were few in number. Nonetheless, they caused some trouble, thus giving the authorities the excuse to use force.

This incident happened in the city of Aksu, in western Xinjiang. Disturbances continued for more than a month. It was one of the most serious outbursts in Xinjiang since the founding of the present regime. This protracted and widespread commotion may be compared with the uprising in the early 1960s when the Soviet Union incited minority nationalities on the frontier to flee in large numbers. The bloody conflict in the last stage of the disturbance was not entirely unavoidable. Unfortunately the young people were too stubborn and went to extremes, and local authorities mishandled the situation.

As early as last autumn, youth on farms near Aksu began to discuss returning to Shanghai with the local authorities. They established ties among themselves, formed an alliance, and elected scores of representatives to conduct negotiations.

At these talks, the Party committees said that they had no authority to make a decision on this important issue, but must first ask the Aksu Prefecture Administrative Office for instructions.

The instructions read: "It is difficult to accept the demands of the Shanghai youth. It is up to the grass-roots units to enlighten these young people." But the Party committees on the farms knew well that as long as the basic problems of the Shanghai youth remained, it would be difficult to persuade them ideologically. They therefore tried to shift the responsibility back to the higher level. They told the representatives that they had done their best to present the case to the higher level and that if the Prefecture would accept the delegates' demands, they would create no obstacles. This was a hint to the representatives to go to the Prefecture for a solution.

The representatives took the hint, and decided after consulting the masses to approach the Aksu Prefecture Administrative Office. When they arrived for negotiations, the office made an emergency call to the Xinjiang Autonomous Region Party Committee in Urumqi, which telegraphed back that the problem should be dealt with on the spot. The Prefecture Party committee knew that the Shanghai youth would make trouble if they were not allowed to return to Shanghai, but they had no choice other than to try to negotiate.

During the negotiations the representatives found that the two sides held incompatible views and that talks would not resolve the matter, so they decided to force concessions. Instead of marching to far-away Urumqi to present their case, they decided to create disturbances in Aksu, where all the Shanghai young people gathered.

During the negotiations, the authorities stressed that Shanghai youth who had immigrated to Xinjiang before the "Cultural Revolution" were not included among those who were allowed by the central government to return to the big cities. They explained that if the government made an exception of the Shanghai youth, then people who had been sent to the villages would strive for the same thing everywhere. They warned that Xinjiang stood on the front line in the struggle against the Soviet Union, and that any reckless action would harm China and its people. They therefore asked the delegates to refrain from any rash move. At the same time, they recognized that the Shanghai youth had a real problem and promised that the government would gradually resolve it.

But the representatives held radically different views and said that the official position merely repeated the clichés of the past twenty years, and did nothing to improve their conditions. They had waited patiently for twenty years; would they now have to wait another twenty? They alleged that many young people with good connections managed to get their residence registration transferred to big cities. This was a major complaint of the Shanghai youth.

Moreover, a small handful of people hated the socialist system and poured oil on the fire, so that negotiations broke down. By mid-November, the two sides were like fire and water. After mid-November Shanghai young people began to leave their farms and go to Aksu city to support their representatives; meanwhile, representatives returned to the farms to consult with other young people. The Party committees could do nothing to stop them leaving. Most young people were determined to stage a mass demonstration in Aksu, and vowed not to give up until they got satisfaction.

By late November, about ten thousand Shanghai young people had gathered in Aksu, and their numbers grew daily. The representatives were ready to take extreme action.

They organized a protest rally and a hunger strike in front of the Prefecture Office. As the young people were leaving their farms, they heard rumors that the authorities had allowed the ringleaders to transfer their residence back to Shanghai, so they sold their belongings and hurried with their wives and children to march on Aksu.

The news spread quickly, and they grew to as many as seventy thousand. The situation soon got out of control.

These young people, having sold all they had and cut off all means of retreat, were strong in fighting spirit. They were a pitiful sight. They thought that the time had come to burn their boats and fight with their backs to the river.

Of the tens of thousands of people who took part in the hunger strike, about a hundred, including women and children, died of exhaustion. During the demonstration the Aksu authorities did much ideological work and several times sent delicious food, hoping to persuade the demonstrators to end their fast. But the demonstrators were determined to fight to the bitter end, and the organizers called on the young people not to take food offered by the authorities. When some died, tension mounted and disturbances broke out. The demonstrators held the authorities responsible for the deaths, and pointed the spearhead of their struggle at the local government offices.

They elected a leading group and set up a command of seven members. Under the slogan "Die at Aksu or return to Shanghai alive!" they took military-style action against government offices in Aksu. The authorities sent forces to suppress the attackers, but neither the troops nor the security personnel opened fire. The confrontation was limited to hand-to-hand fighting and scuffles.

The riot leaders decided to risk everything in the hope of gaining the attention of the Xinjiang Regional Party Committee and even of Beijing. They organized a "dare-to-die corps," a "pickets team," and a "dog-beating team," and tried for an all-out attack on the government offices.

The "dare-to-die corps" were dauntless and quick in action. Whenever the security forces slackened their vigilance, the corps would lead a large group of followers to charge forward and take over a building. The "pickets" were to maintain order and prevent people from creating anarchy. The "dog-beating team" was a unique invention. The riot leaders knew that when the struggle escalated many would try to back out even though they had sworn that it was "better to die in glory than live in dishonor." To enforce internal discipline, prevent defections, and deal with outside opponents, a special gang was therefore organized. The "dog-beating team" was cruel and very unpopular.

According to an old Chinese saying, "An army burning with righteous indignation is bound to win." The demonstrators with their superior numbers and organization were in a good position. The members of the "dare-to-die corps," the "pickets," and the "dog-beating team" were determined fighters who acted swiftly and effectively. Even more important, the local authorities and the military had shown extreme self-restraint and never once opened fire. The demonstrators soon occupied all important government offices in Aksu.

Between late November and early December, all government offices, including the Administrative Office, the Bureau of Agriculture and Reclamation, and the Bureau of Public Security, were seized by rioters. The government leaders slipped away in an effort to avoid further conflict. Even the security personnel went into hiding. All political functions were paralyzed, and the entire city seemed in the hands of the demonstrators.

But most demonstrators were not against the socialist system, and had started the riot mainly as a way of getting back to Shanghai. They committed no outrages and maintained fairly good discipline. Some lawbreakers wanted to stir up trouble, but they were too few to have any effect. The demonstrators made no move and waited for the local authorities to come to the conference table.

The prefecture Party committee understood the intentions of the demonstrators, and agreed to send them back to Shanghai by rail. They even announced that those who were determined to return home could have their residence registration transferred back to Shanghai. This removed the cause of grievance, and pacified the demonstrators.

As a result, the young people withdrew from the government offices, and made preparations to depart. They were sent back to Shanghai in groups. But on arriving in Shanghai, they were not welcomed, not even by their own parents. This was not really surprising. After more than twenty years, family members had become estranged. In Shanghai living quarters are very restricted, and could hardly accommodate the returned young people with their wives and children. Worse still, even though the Xinjiang authorities had sent their residence registration back to Shanghai, the Shanghai authorities refused to accept it. This was an especially hard blow.

The returnees refused to accept their fate and tried to repeat what they had done in Aksu. Once again they held street demonstrations. But this time they met with failure. They did not have the support of local people, and even their families wanted them to return to Xinjiang. Their parents and brothers gave them some money to buy articles for daily use back in Xinjiang. When things reached this stage, only a few young people from rich families could stay in Shanghai; all the rest knew that they had played a losing game. They realized that they should not have sold their belongings on leaving Xinjiang, since now they had to return there. Had they known beforehand what they now knew, they would never have gone to Shanghai.

Meanwhile, on instruction from the central government, the Xinjiang authorities made preparations for resettling the Shanghai youth. They repeatedly announced that those who had taken part in the disturbances would be treated no differently from the others. But for the seven ringleaders and those who had committed crimes, the outcome was not so fortunate. Early in December 1980, when all the demonstrators had left Aksu and were preparing to depart, the local authorities arrested these people.

By then, the disturbances in Xinjiang were over. On January 23, 1981, New China News Agency published the following report: "Recently Wang Zhen, member of the CCP Central Committee's Political Bureau, paid a visit to Xinjiang and urged cadres and young people of all nationalities to carry forward the glorious tradition, continue their hard struggle, step up the frontier construction, and bring benefit to future generations." According to reliable sources, the Party Secretariat and the State Council held a joint conference to discuss ways of dealing with the consequences of the policy of sending young people to the countryside. The conference held that the past policy of persuading young city people to settle down for good in frontier regions is harmful to China, the peasants, and the young people, and could lead to social unrest. Undoubtedly, the Xinjiang incident proved this point.

The conference recognized that China will have to continue sending large numbers of people to remote frontier areas, but they agreed that there must be changes in the way in which this policy is implemented. Experience shows that the young city people cannot be the main force for this policy. They find it hard to settle down, and each year the central government has to spend big sums of money on their resettlement. Economically, the loss outweighs the gain.

Finally the conference decided to mobilize peasant families in densely populated provinces such as Shandong, Henan, and Hebei to migrate to remote frontier areas. But this migration should be voluntary, and proper material incentive should be given, for example, each peasant family should get 500 yuan rehabilitation expenses. On arrival at their destination they should be given large private plots of land, and no grain tax should be levied on newly reclaimed wasteland for five years. Peasants in Shandong and Hebei Provinces can now move of their own accord to Heilongjiang Province, and peasants in Henan can move to Xinjiang. Since Heilongjiang and Xinjiang are on China's border and both have large areas of virgin land, resettling people there is strategically advantageous. Moreover, peasants in densely populated provinces lead hard lives and gladly move to these regions. According to reports, the CCP Central Committee considers this project both practical and effective, and is planning to send one hundred thousand peasant families to Heilongjiang and to Xinjiang over the next year or so.

DOCUMENT 34

Advertisement: Modern Clothes

In the heady days of 1978, all sorts of "petty-bourgeois" taboos were suddenly broken. People began to tint their hair and wear "outrageous" clothing. In October 1978 the Communist Youth League said yes to this new personal freedom, and many youngsters began to sew their own "trumpet pants," that is, bell-bottomed or flared trousers. In Shanghai, at the new fashion's cutting edge, factories even began to make such trousers. This so annoyed the Party that Deng Xiaoping apparently even mentioned trumpet pants in his speech of March 1979, when he made his first serious attack on the democracy movement. This caused much merriment along Democracy Wall, where the following "advertisement" went up. Thanks to Flemming Christiansen, who alerted us to this piece.

IN accordance with a directive from the leadership, in line with the propaganda in our press organs, and in order to uphold the boycott on trumpet pants coming in from abroad, our firm has solicited the opinions of all social groups and has newly created a pair of trousers in true Chinese style. We have decided to call them "crutch-covers" or anti-trumpet trousers.

Our product has the following advantages. The model does not differ in any way whatsoever for men or women, for fat people or thin. It can be worn either back to front or front to back. It is suitable for people of all ages and of all body shapes. The color is dark, solemn, tasteful, and dirt-resistant. The model can be worn at all times of the year and by all members of the family.

The cut is practical, the manner of production is simple, and no individual measurements need to be taken, so our crutch-covers are cheap and correspond to the modern system of low wages.

Please buy! A thousand thanks to our leaders, who have forbidden the sale of trumpet pants and thus freed the way for our new product.

> Folk-Costumes Shop,
> 79 Clean Country Alley,
> Nostalgia Street,
> Resurrection Gate,
> Beijing.

DOCUMENT 35

FENGFAN
The Reawakening of the Chinese Working Class

The democratic movement tried hard to widen its social base by organizing, publicizing, and defending struggles for higher wages and better conditions in the factories. One particularly disadvantaged group are the single workers: workers who, although married, live apart from their families. Their conditions are described in this article. In February 1981 Reuters and AFP reported that according to the *Taiyuan ribao* (Taiyuan Daily) steel workers in Taiyuan, Shanxi Province, launched a struggle against the "privileged bureaucratic class" and called for a "struggle for democracy and freedom." They demanded an end to the dictatorship, and the power to determine their own future. The newspaper announced that the authorities had smashed a "counterrevolutionary clique" of political dissidents, and would put them on trial. It is likely that those arrested included the author of this article, which appeared in December 1980 in the inaugural issue of the unofficial Taiyuan journal *Fengfan* (Boat's Sail).

RECENTLY the single workers at the Taiyuan steel works spontaneously demonstrated for improved conditions and in defense of their rightful interests. The single workers in our country are the worst treated of any category of workers. They earn very little and enjoy few social benefits. They eat every day in the staff canteens, which are invariably badly managed. In theory they are entitled to fixed food rations, but in practice they never get more than 80 percent of their rations. They pay twice as much in the canteen as workers living with their families, and for worse food. They spend their lives in cramped single quarters that are seldom properly looked after. Some of these quarters are falling apart through neglect or are poorly lit and dirty, just like the capitalist slums they show us in the films. These single workers are separated from their families for years on end, and only have twelve days' leave a year in which to visit them. Although they are married, they live like widows or widowers. They too create social wealth, just like the worker cadres. But their families get no medical care insurance. Other workers whose families are here in Taiyuan get coal allowances, but not so the single workers. Female single workers are often reduced to tears because their husbands are not there to help them with their problems. The single workers at the Taiyuan steel works are right to put forward their ten demands.

The leading cadres at the steel works should canvas opinions and devise long-term solutions to the problems of these single workers, so that they can forget their worries and commit themselves wholeheartedly to the Four Modernizations. But instead, some of these leaders range themselves against the people's interests, denouncing legal meetings as "Black Gatherings" and criticizing people even for visiting one another.

The actions of these single workers are proof that the working class of our country has reawakened. On the surface it would seem that they are merely out to protect their own legal rights. But in reality they have voted for democracy, whether they are aware of it or not. They know that if they want change, they must rely on their own power of organization and on their own elected representatives, for no messiah will achieve change for them. And if those they elect no longer represent them, then the election must be reheld. The demands of broad sectors of the people are the social base upon which democratic change in our country will be founded.

DOCUMENT 36
<hr>

FU SHENQI

In Memory of Wang Shenyou,
Pioneer of the Democratic Movement,
Teacher, Comrade

Fu Shenqi was born in 1954 in a worker's family in Shanghai, and on leaving middle school went to work in a Shanghai generator factory. In 1977 he entered Shanghai Number Four Normal College, and returned to his factory the following year. He was a member of the Communist Youth League. In 1979 he joined with others to found Shanghai's unofficial journal *Voice of Democracy*. When *Voice of Democracy* declared its support for the "strikes of Polish workers fighting for democracy and against bureaucratic tyranny," the authorities branded it as "anti-party and antisocialist." When the National Federation of Unofficial Journals was formed in the autumn of 1980, it started its own journal, *Zeren* (Duty). From issue no. 3, Fu Shenqi became its chief editor. In October Fu ran for election in a factory in south Shanghai. Factory officials threatened that people who voted for

Fu would not get a wage increase and the Communist Party branch flouted the regulations to stop his election. Still he got 43 percent of the vote. In April 1981 Fu went to Beijing to petition the authorities for the right to publish freely, but he was arrested and received a seven-year sentence for "counterrevolutionary offenses." He served most of the term in solitary confinement. He was detained between May 1991 and February 1993 for publishing underground pro-democracy material, and arrested yet again in June 1993 for allegedly "inciting trouble" and speaking to foreign reporters. He was sentenced to three years in a labor camp.

Fu's article on Wang Shenyou, an early martyr of the democratic movement, shows that even after the fall of the Gang of Four the regime continued to repress and even execute dissidents. Because Wang Shenyou was a critic of the Maoists and an admirer of Deng Xiaoping, Fu hoped that his work would be made public and his name rehabilitated; but it is unlikely that this ever happened.

TODAY (28 April 1980) is the third anniversary of the death of Wang Shenyou, whom I mourn deeply. Although I have no time to write more than a brief recollection of him, having spent the day giving out leaflets at my factory and campaigning in the election, I am convinced that he would approve of my priorities. I dedicate my commitment to his memory.

I first met Wang in May 1976, shortly after the suppression of the demonstrations in Tian'anmen Square against the Gang of Four. China was then under a dark cloud, and menaced by "Red Terror." In the thick fog, people were numbed, depressed, and frustrated. But underground the fire was still burning, and people were seeking their way out of the darkness. Foremost among them was Wang Shenyou.

Wang grew up in a working-class family. His father was a cadre in the Jiabei district committee, and many of his relatives and friends were also officials or Party members. Wang was intelligent and thirsted for knowledge. While still in his first year at Huadong College of Education, at the age of eighteen, he had already begun to formulate his independent standpoint. At college he excelled in all subjects.

Besides studying, he kept his "never-ending" diaries. In these diaries he discussed current affairs and recorded his views on social injustices and on China's domestic and foreign policies. These writings revealed his youthful talent. Although not yet familiar with Marxism, he was a revolutionary by instinct, who criticized the present and looked forward to the future.

When the Socialist Education Campaign began in the early sixties, Wang's diary writing attracted the attention of the "professional organizers of class struggle." Wang was summoned to talk with cadres of the Communist Youth League, who said he should apply to become a League member; but while he was with them his room was searched and his diary was photographed. Secretly, the authorities began to concoct evidence of his "crimes."

Not long after this the Cultural Revolution broke out, and the attack on Wang Shenyou was temporarily postponed. At first Wang took no active part in the Cultural Revolution, but later he wrote some outstanding articles. It was during this time that he discovered Marxism, particularly the classical Marxist writings on the Paris Commune. He accepted Mao's later ideas, and saw the Cultural Revolution as an attempt to realize the Paris Commune. In his writings he defended the Cultural Revolution. One of his best works was *Follow Chairman Mao and Move Forward Bravely Amid the Great Wind and Waves*. Many university libraries probably still have copies of this tract.

But history is pitiless. Once Lin Biao, Jiang Qing, and Kang Sheng took the reins of power, strict discipline was imposed, and the Red Guards, once the fearless defenders of the revolution, were ruthlessly crushed, and tossed aside like broken tools. Wang Shenyou also came under fire. He was labeled a counterrevolutionary and evidence collected during the Socialist Education Campaign was used against him. The authorities staged a display of his diaries and organized a criticism forum against him on the local radio. But they did not succeed in convicting him.

For a time, he was sent to labor camps. Later he was detained by the Public Security Bureau for interrogation. Finally, he was sent off for reeducation. During all this time he was kept jobless. And yet he never once gave up. He kept physically fit, learned foreign languages, and studied Marxism, equipping himself as an outstanding Marxist and revolutionary. He made constant notes on his reading—his notes on *Capital* alone amounted to a million words. It was during this time that I got to know him. It was the evening of 6 May. I went to the Huangpu public library, with a book by Engels under my arm. I sat down to read. Wang Shenyou was sitting opposite me. His keen, deep eyes studied my young, naive face. He seemed to be interested in me. He smiled at me, and said something. I moved my seat nearer to his and we began to talk in whispers. In a short while we became close friends.

From then on we met and read together almost every day. We went for walks together, and discussed all sorts of problems. We were surprised to find that we shared similar views on many subjects. But his ideas were invariably more systematic, more profound, and better grounded than mine. We spent numerous evenings together in the People's Square, the People's Park, and the Shanghai Municipal Library.

For him Marxism, though not a perfect or absolute truth, was a systematic and well-rounded scientific theory, and there was no alternative theory that could transcend it. He particularly praised Marx's theory of historical materialism, and used it to analyze present-day society. He criticized the theory of social leaps, and believed that Marx's successors had corrupted the revolutionary essence of Marxism and turned it into a rigid dogma. He felt that the dogmas that Mao proposed in his old age were simply a cover for feudalism. Since China lacked a mature working class, the Communist Party developed as a peasant party led by revolutionary intellectuals, and the revolution it carried out was not proletarian-socialist but peasant, with a strong feudal tinge. After the revolution Chinese society therefore gradually evolved into a new form of oriental despotism. Once Wang said, "Mao is just a peasant with a military cap." Wang even challenged Mao's claim to be a Marxist. He advocated a new approach to Marxism and the need for a critical review of so-called Mao Zedong Thought. He founded a Marxist study group, and was determined to revitalize the revolutionary spirit of Marxism. He felt that ever since the Stalin era there had been a confrontation between feudal and scientific socialism in the world Communist movement, and that Mao and Stalin were both typical representatives of feudal socialism. At the time he believed that the reforms following de-Stalinization in the Soviet Union were a sign that scientific socialism was gaining ground. He therefore approved of comrade Deng Xiaoping's ideas and policies although they were not yet fully formed, and considered Deng a representative of scientific socialism. Even though the Cultural Revolution Group (the Gang of Four) was still at the height of its power, Wang confidently predicted that it would fall, and that it would be succeeded by an era of scientific socialism represented by Deng. Then China would be able to assimilate Soviet experience and work out its own plans for reform. Wang particularly valued the April Fifth Movement that ultimately brought down the Gang of Four. He anticipated that this new political development would differentiate China from the Soviet Union, and equip it with its own unique identity.

I have none of Wang's theoretical works to hand, and what I have written is based simply on my recollections of our conversations. But fortunately Wang put his views on paper shortly before he died, and if I am not mistaken they will soon become available to the public, which can then judge for itself the accuracy of my summary. Wang set out his ideas in a long letter to his girlfriend, and it was mainly on the basis of this letter that he would later be sentenced to death.

Wang had had more than one girlfriend, but for various reasons, mainly political, his relationships never lasted long. In July 1976 he was introduced to his last girlfriend. She was no ordinary woman, and had strong ideas of her own. After a few meetings they fell in love. Later, because she was somewhat pessimistic about the future, Wang wrote her his long letter, to lighten her spirits.

On 2 September 1976 I met Wang outside the Municipal Library. At the time he was busy writing articles. Before we parted, I held his hand and warned him to be on his guard. I had a feeling that he was in for trouble. We arranged to meet again on 10 September at the South Library, but this rendezvous never took place, since the library was unexpectedly closed that day due to Mao's death. Three days later, I went to his house. His mother told me that he had left home, and was unlikely to return. I realized that something must have happened. I guessed that with Mao's death, anyone with a background like Wang's would be put under surveillance. It turned out that his letter to his girlfriend had fallen into the hands of the authorities, and that he had been arrested. But at the time, I was convinced that he would be set free.

Very soon, the Gang of Four fell from power. I was delighted at this historic change, and hoped I would soon meet my teacher and comrade again. I joined in the criticism of feudal socialism, and in November 1976 I sent an article to *Hongqi* (Red Flag) entitled "The Deceptions of Left Opportunism as Revealed in the Essay 'On the Absolute Dictatorship of the Bourgeoisie.'" But feudal socialism did not easily quit the stage of history. Its supporters still wielded great influence, and used it to oppress the people.

In the municipal Party committee there were various views about Wang Shenyou, but at the time some big shots wrote that "it would be disloyal to Chairman Mao not to kill this person," and with those few words his death warrant was signed.

On 21 April 1977, six months after the fall of the Gang of Four, the verdict on Wang was announced: "Guilty of an extremely evil crime. If he is not killed, the people's anger cannot be assuaged." I held the verdict with shaking hands. I was in an agony of grief and rage. Just a few words from these people could send a man to his death! There was nothing I could do to avert this tragedy, but I was deeply convinced that things could not go on like this, and that change was bound to come.

Today, it is possible that the municipal Party committee will review the case of Wang Shenyou. Some people may continue to revile him, but most will see that he was a young man of great talent once they have read his last essay, and they will recognize him as a committed revolutionary, an outstanding Marxist theoretician, and an eminent fighter for democracy. Even if the power elite refuse to admit this, history will prove that they are wrong.

If Wang Shenyou were alive today, I do not believe that his ideas would remain unchanged. If he had lived, he would have produced even greater ideas. But that was not to be. As for me, what is important is to look to the future and to realize my plans and dreams, and to do what is necessary. The road to democracy is long and winding. Perhaps new blood must be shed, in which case I offer my own for the shedding.

On 28 April 1977, Wang Shenyou sacrificed his young life for the truth of Marxism, social progress, and the people's happiness. He was only thirty-two years old. He never flinched from the truth, and he never bowed his head even in the face of death. He lived his life with his eyes turned toward the democratic future. His body is destroyed, but his spirit lives on, in me and in every other young Marxist. Over these past three years Wang's smiling image has constantly appeared before me. It is as if every day he studies, discusses, and struggles with me. His kind and tender manner, his industriousness, his sincere and realistic way of working, and his devotion to truth will always be fixed in my memory, and will be reflected in my work.

DOCUMENT 37

Interview with Yang Jing

Yang Jing, born in Jiangling, Hubei Province, and now in his late forties, was a worker in the Beijing Steel Rolling Plant before his arrest in April 1981. Yang Jing became editor of *Siwu luntan* (April Fifth Forum) after it began publishing for the second time in November 1980. Yang served an eight-year sentence after his arrest. Ignoring advice, he made speeches in Tian'anmen Square immediately after his release, and is thought to have been rearrested in June 1989. Requests by the U.S. government for information about Yang met with no response from Chinese officials; his current circumstances are unknown.

This interview, conducted in March 1981, appeared in Hong Kong's *Guanchajia* (Observer); it is among the most important and informative documents to survive the democracy movement. It shows Yang Jing to be on the left of the movement and without illusions in the Party leaders.

Q: Why did April Fifth Forum *stop publishing in March 1980, and begin publishing again in November of the same year?*

A: Producing *April Fifth Forum* is a service to society, it is a service to the cause of true proletarian democracy. We stopped publishing in March 1981 for external and internal reasons. It is not necessary to explain the external reasons; you can draw your own conclusions from what you know about the political situation at that time. Nor do I want to dwell too much on the internal problems. To use a Chinese saying, "One should not publicize family disputes." During the period when we stopped producing, we had some wrong ideas internally that we believed would be resolved. Throughout that time, we received many letters of support, urging us to carry on and to reissue the journal. We strongly agreed with this, because *April Fifth Forum* is the social product of specific historical factors, and fulfills certain needs in society. None of our readers suggested that we should stop publishing. They even exaggerated the worth of *April Fifth Forum* saying that it is the angel of Marxism, and the sacred word of the suffering people of China. This made us rethink our hurried decision to cease publication, and encouraged us to overcome some internal problems that we had not thoroughly worked out. And so the journal eventually reappeared.

Q: *How does its reappearance relate to the development of the democratic movement nationally?*

A: Today the trend throughout society is toward progress and democracy, so the more people involved in the struggle the better. The reappearance of *April Fifth Forum* will naturally make some contribution to the movement, and consolidate the forces seeking democracy. Reissuing the journal will help us clarify some confusions, get us away from unhealthy influences, and widen our support, so that we can make a better contribution to the development of the democratic movement.

Q: *What was the situation before and after the reappearance of* April Fifth Forum?

A: Around the time it reappeared, most unofficial journals in other parts of China were still publishing. Unfortunately, due to internal and external problems, we did not take part in that movement. We must take responsibility for that. We can only hope that we will work harder in the future, and make further progress.

Q: *In September 1980, in Guangzhou, a meeting was called of representatives of unofficial journals from all over China, and subsequently a National Federation of Unofficial Journals was set up. What was the effect of this development on the democratic movement nationally?*

A: This meeting took place thanks to the comrades in the South, who took great risks and developed the democratic movement, which was at first quite primitive, to a higher level. I personally believe that this was a historic event. The setting up of the Federation was a historic contribution to the democratic movement. So our position is quite clear—even though we could not take part in it for various reasons, we support the Federation, we completely agree that we should work together to increase the internal solidarity of the democratic movement and to fight as a united body for democracy in China.

Q: *It is now more than four months since* April Fifth Forum *reappeared. How have the unofficial journals developed in other parts of China?*

A: You can sum the situation up in one sentence. It has only just begun. The democratic movement represents the general demands of society, and arose out of the internal demands of society, so it is as wide and deep as society itself. In spite of barriers and pressures, and differences between one place and another or one journal and another, in the long run these are problems that can be resolved. The democratic movement has not only influenced all social layers, but has even had some response from within the Party. There can be no doubt that it has support among all layers of society.

Q: *Some friends think differently—they say that the unofficial journals have big problems of distribution, and only produce between one and two thousand copies, and sometimes just a few hundred. In that case how can the democratic movement be said to influence all levels of society?*

A: There are two aspects here. First, external pressure. Because of the restrictions on democracy, the dialogue between us and the masses came up against big obstacles. Earlier, when Democracy Wall was still tolerated, we could sell thousands of copies in five minutes. Now things have changed. But we are still workers living at the bottom of society, so even if we had no publications, our aspirations would still be the same as those of the masses. If our social existence is the same then so will be our social consciousness. But we must still introduce ideas to our readers. They are precious comrades. By contacting us they run great risk of persecution. They do not just read our publications, they pass them around and exchange ideas with other people. Some of them cannot work with us because their ideological or theoretical level is low, but we believe that their thinking and their ability to draw conclusions will improve through propaganda and through our publications, and they will eventually work together with us.

Q: *Can you say something about the struggle of the democratic movement for a Publications Law?*

A: We believe that all civilized countries should have a Publications Law, but up to now our country does not have one. This means that democratic publications have no law to follow. This is a tragedy. So by fighting for a Publications Law we hope to change things, so that democratic rights can be realized in the Constitution. But the government has responded equivocally, even though some enlightened people in the Party feel, like the democratic movement, that there is a need for such a law. For example, in October 1980 the State Publications Bureau said that unofficial journals objectively existed, and that they should be authorized, but this was opposed by the State Council.

Q: *What about Liu Qing?*

A: The Liu Qing affair has been at the center of attention of unofficial journals throughout China. Even Hong Kong Chinese and Overseas Chinese are demanding that the government release him. However, the government's position is again unclear. It is still using the same old methods.

We believe that the Liu Qing affair will only change if the social environment changes. If the social environment remains backward, the lot of individuals is not likely to improve much. So we see saving Liu Qing as the collective responsibility of the democratic movement.

Q: *We heard that democratic movement activists ran for election to the People's Congress in Beijing, Shanghai, and Shaoguan. What were the results?*

A: To run for election is a constitutional right. But today a bureaucratic layer has already formed or is forming everywhere, and ordinary citizens who run for election will inevitably clash with the interests of this privileged stratum. The results therefore depend on the level of awareness and determination of the citizens. In areas where awareness is high, quite good results were achieved in the elections, for example, at Beijing University, Fudan University, and other places. But in places where people's consciousness is not high enough, and where bureaucracy is strong, all sorts of obstacles were put in the way of candidates, and in some cases even the right to run was taken away. At Beijing University Hu Ping was successful. He was the editor of an unofficial journal called *Wotu* (Fertile Soil). He emphasized freedom of speech especially. He is famous for saying that to have freedom of speech is not to have everything, but to lose freedom of speech is to lose everything; and that to recognize freedom of speech is not necessarily Marxist, but to deny freedom of speech is not even half Marxist.

Q: *It now seems that the authorities want further restrictions, and even want to eradicate unofficial journals altogether. What is your feeling?*

A: It is obvious that we are about to go through a difficult time. Ever since we started the movement, we knew there would be many difficulties, so today's tensions are not unexpected. If there were not factors in society to create this pressure, what would be the point in our movement? Are we to take up a Taoist position, and simply let things run their own course? I don't think so. China has aspirations, and so does the democratic movement. No matter whether there are difficulties or not, we still have to continue the struggle for a brilliant future.

Q: *Recently, the CCP proposed a rectification of Party work-style. Do you think that this could bring any change for the better?*

A: To know the root of the problem and to remove it are two different things. They might just as well be 108,000 li apart. [This was the distance that Monkey could leap in Wu Cheng'en's Buddhist classic *Xiyouji* (Pilgrimage to the West); it is a great distance!] Some people in the Party can see the root of the problem, and know how serious the problem is. Of course, all citizens welcome this. But we believe the leading layer lacks the will. They try to deal with the social evils produced by the old system with methods preserved from the old system. This is a dead end. Of course, it would be even worse if they went backward.

Q: Does the Polish workers' struggle encourage the Chinese democratic movement and Chinese workers? In the past, many people felt that in "socialist countries" workers don't even have the right to open their mouths, let alone set up independent trade unions.

A: We feel close to the Polish workers. The conditions we live under and our personal feelings are quite similar. This is because we are all workers, and we all live in a so-called socialist country. The struggle of the Polish workers is an encouragement and a model for us and for workers in similar countries. There can be no doubt about the historical and international meaning of the Polish workers' struggle.

Q: We see from some unofficial journals that some democratic movement activists admire Yugoslavia. But Yugoslavia represses its dissenters.

A: We are living in a closed society, we know little about what happens abroad. It may be that we have illusions because our understanding is deficient. In any case, our position is that if there is a movement in Yugoslavia that seeks socialist democracy, then we support that movement with all our strength and without hesitation. What workers most admire in Yugoslavia is workers' self-management. No matter how limited, that self-management is progressive. But nowadays most workers are more inclined toward the Polish struggles, since in those struggles workers' power and authority are affirmed by facts.

Q: What is your view on the government's policy of "economic readjustment"?

A: Premier Zhao Ziyang says that thirty years after the establishment of the People's Republic we have finally drummed a little sense into the economy. For people like us at the bottom of society, all we can say is, thank god, you finally realized. With or without "readjustment," ordinary Chinese never had any power, and they were never able to take part in this process. The system in China today is that politics and the economy are organically merged and highly centralized, so that economic policy is decided by the political power. The workers have no say in planning, so they have no chance to become expert or to work out better policies for the country and the people. So now that past mistakes are being recognized, our first reaction is of course, thank god. But we must go further than that. If the workers can't participate in economic policy and decision making and can't become masters of production, work enthusiasm will not improve. For them to become the masters would imply a radical innovation in politics. But without such an innovation any economic readjustment can have only limited results. Without radical changes in the political system, it is impossible to ask the masses to commit themselves to economic readjustment.

Q: *Since late 1980 a pro-Soviet group calling itself* Beijing qingnian *(Beijing Youth) has been active in the Beijing democratic movement. What is the weight of this group and what is its influence? What is the attitude of the democratic movement toward it?*

A: The pro-Soviet current is a small minority in the democratic movement. Of the dozens of unofficial journals only *Beijing Youth* is pro-Russian although they do have another theoretical journal called *Zhexue* (Philosophy). Their numbers are very small, and their influence is very limited. We do not agree with their position on Russia, but this reflects a problem, that is, the authorities have blacked out information, so that it's difficult to know the facts. Even though we don't share some of the views of *Beijing Youth*, we obviously agree with their support for the Polish workers' struggle. But if they are suppressed for publishing their views, then it's our duty to defend them, because we shall stand or fall together. Where it's a question of views or standpoints, we can only raise consciousness, clarify differences, and resolve problems through public debate.

Q: *What is your view of the future of the democratic movement?*

A: In a word, I'm optimistic. There may be difficulties, perhaps even big ones, and the cost may be high. But even though individuals may be silenced, views that represent a historical tide desired by the whole of society can't be stifled. That's why we're so confident.

DOCUMENT 38

XIAO RUI
Eyewitness Account of the Arrest of Liu Qing

Liu Qing, a machine technician in his late thirties, was an editor and cofounder, with Xu Wenli, of *Siwu luntan* (April Fifth Forum), and one of the first and most influential members of China's democratic movement. Like many other high school graduates, he was sent to work in the countryside in 1965. He probably returned to Beijing when the Cultural Revolution began in 1966. From 1973 to 1977 he was a student at Nanjing University, and was then sent to work in a factory in the region. Later he moved back to Beijing.

The following three documents describe Liu Qing's arrest and imprisonment after publishing a transcript of the trial of Wei Jingsheng in November 1979. In

October 1980, a "National Committee to Save Liu Qing" was set up by sixteen unofficial journals from different provinces in China. Many of those who joined in this appeal were arrested in April 1981. Liu himself was imprisoned until December 1989. Throughout his imprisonment, he was beaten, starved, and frequently placed in solitary confinement. He was detained for a further six months in 1990, and finally allowed to move to the USA in July 1992, after considerable pressure from the U.S. government.

Liu Qing managed to smuggle out from a labor camp a 196-page account of his detention. He attached three covering letters, dated January 1981, in which he appealed to his fellow citizens, to the Chinese press, and to leading public figures for justice. The prison testimony and the letters are said to have been written on paper provided by the prison authorities for the purpose of writing self-criticism.

Liu Qing calls on the press to have the courage to "protect the truth and uphold justice." He calls on Deng Xiaoping and other leaders to be faithful to the trust the public has in them. He reminds his fellow citizens of the Dreyfus case and tells them: "Our democratic system cannot develop from the benevolence of an emperor but depends on the efforts of society itself."

In this testimony Liu Qing reports instances in which he and other prisoners were maltreated. Torture and mistreatment of prisoners was common during the Cultural Revolution, but reports of it now are rare. However, Liu Qing himself was badly beaten, and he describes how Zhang Wenhe, a member of the Human Rights League, had his hands cuffed behind his back for several months, and how Wei Jingsheng was held in solitary confinement.

Since Mao's death and the fall of the Gang of Four, the Deng government has promised to guarantee citizens' rights and to safeguard these rights by appropriate judicial procedures, but arrests on political grounds are still happening despite the Constitution. According to the Constitution, offenders who go through a complete judicial process, from arrest to trial, should pass through the hands of the Public Security (police), the Procurates (who review cases), and the courts. Parallel to this system are organizations like the Party and the army that have their own internal control organs. Penalties for political offenders can be either informal (i.e., "persuasive") or formal. For serious offenses there are two sorts of penalties, "administrative" and "criminal." "Administrative" penalties can be inflicted by police order or by one's neighborhood, work, or Party unit; offenders so punished may still be sent to labor camp.

For a thorough analysis of the law, the judicial process, penal theory, and prison conditions as they affected political prisoners in China in the late 1970s, see *Political Imprisonment in the Peoples' Republic of China*, an Amnesty International Report (London 1978).

ON November 11, 1979, I arrived in Xidan's Democracy Wall at 2:30 P.M. to buy a copy of the pamphlet *On the Course and Outcome of the Trial of Wei Jingsheng*. As it turned out, I wasn't able to buy the pamphlet; but I saw some amazing scenes.

There was a big crowd of people waiting to buy the pamphlet, but everything was quite orderly: the crowd had organized itself and was waiting in a line. A few minutes later, a squad of police arrived; they pushed people around, shoved aside the onlookers, and carried out a brutal charge against those selling the pamphlets. The next minute there was chaos. Several people started shouting: "It's forbidden to arrest people like that!," "The police are picking people up!," "They're taking our comrades away!" Many young people threw themselves at the police, shouting. But they could not hold their own against highly trained policemen: the people buying pamphlets and the crowds surrounding them were drowned in an ocean of blue uniforms and visored helmets. Then the scuffles began. One policeman punched a foreign journalist, who was adjusting his lens to take a photo. Another foreign journalist, a woman, very tall, was struggling with policemen who were trying to tear from her the pamphlet she had just bought. Yet another foreigner who had climbed on top of something to get a better photograph was sent sprawling after a cop had knocked away the object he was perching on.

Afterward, the police left quickly, and a few fainthearted individuals in the crowd also went away. Those who stayed began to discuss what had happened. Everyone was seething with indignation. Then several people wanted to go to the Security Bureau to get news of those arrested. Along with Liu Qing (who had published the pamphlet), we went to the Xicheng office. The officer on duty claimed that they knew nothing of what had happened, so we went to the police station in Xi Chang'an Street. First of all the police there refused to see us, claiming that they too knew nothing of the matter. But then we recognized one of the policemen who had taken part in the arrests, so they had no choice but to let us in.

A policeman: "What's your name?"

"Zhao XX."

"Where do you work? Are you a worker or a cadre?"

"A worker."

The policeman turned to someone else:

"And you, what's your name?"

"Yang XX."

"Where do you work? Where do you live?"

"I was in the crowd and I am a witness to what happened. I refuse to say where I live or where I work. If you think you have no business with us, we will leave. If you need us as witnesses you only have to ask Liu Qing to come and fetch us."

"Hm."

The policeman turned to Liu Qing:

"Your name?"

"Liu Qing."

"What is your work unit?"

"The third unit at the Ministry of Industry."

"Are you a worker or a cadre?"

"A cadre." (The policeman was taking notes.) "This afternoon you arrested some of our people. I'd like to know what they were doing that was illegal. If you can't show that they broke the law, you must release them and give them back the things you confiscated."

The policeman, after a moment's hesitation:

"We do what we're told; I'm going to speak to my superiors." He went out.

A moment later, he came back with a "veteran policeman" whom he introduced to us as the commissioner. This commissioner noticed Liu Qing and hurried over to him.

"Ah!" he said warmly, "Liu Jianwei! Is it you? When did you change your name?"

"More than a year ago. Liu Qing is my pen name."

"How are you? Where are you living now?"

"In Dongcheng."

"Is your mother well?"

"Let's not talk about that for the moment, please. We'll have time later to discuss my family."

"But what do you expect, it's so long since we saw each other, we can chat a little, can't we?"

"For the moment I'm very worried, we should talk about what brought me here."

The commissioner took Liu Qing and comrade Zhao to one side so that they could discuss together, and the rest of us were made to go into another office with other policemen. They avoided giving us information. They only wanted to know our names, addresses, and work units. We refused to give them.

The conversation did not last long, and was a pure waste of time. They could tell us neither why they had arrested people nor what they had done with those arrested. They simply repeated that they had acted on orders from above, but they refused to say where these orders came from. We then went to the door of the floor above, which housed the municipal Security Bureau.

We announced the reason for our visit to the man on duty at the reception desk. He handed us a form. Liu Qing filled in his name, work unit, address, age, sex, purpose of visit, etc. The man on duty then asked us to wait while he went to get information from his superiors. A moment later he came back with another man (like him, in plain clothes) and the two began to question us. The man on duty asked Liu Qing:

"Are you responsible for this pamphlet?"

"Yes. I'm responsible for publishing it and for selling it."

"Your journal is *April Fifth Forum*?

"That's right."

"How many of you are there?"

Liu Qing acted as if he hadn't heard. The policeman went on: "Is this pamphlet published by *April Fifth Forum*?"

"It has nothing to do with *April Fifth Forum*. I published it myself, with the help of friends."

"What is the pamphlet based on?"

"I had a tape recording of Wei Jingsheng's trial."

"When did you finish printing it?"

"Several days ago."

"Have you sold it everywhere?"

"Of course. We have subscribers all over the country."

"Foreigners too?"

"Yes. In the whole world people will know."

One of us:

"A while ago, there were a lot of people in Xidan, including foreign journalists. They all bought the pamphlet, how could they not know about it? I was just passing by and saw police arresting people, just like that, for no reason! Those arrests were arbitrary. There are laws, aren't there?"

"Do you not know that you must distinguish between China and abroad?"

"Wei's trial was a public trial, the *People's Daily* talked about it to the whole world. What are the differences between China and abroad? What divine law are we breaking? What is there about it that's illegal?"

"What is there about it that's illegal? We arrest who we want to, that's what."

When he said this everyone shouted: "Ah, you arrest who you want to! What sort of world are we in?" "What about the law, who is the law for?" "You've really shown your true colors!" Just then four people arrived and took two of our comrades away with them. Liu Qing and I waited. It was already past eight o'clock in the evening.

They interrogated us separately, but they replied to none of Liu Qing's questions. When it was past nine o'clock, Liu Qing became impatient: "Why won't you discuss? I am the person responsible for this business. Won't you listen to me? Fine, I'm off then." The policeman on duty said hastily: "Wait! Wait a bit!" He then went back to reading his newspaper. Liu Qing again: "If you won't answer, I'm off. Tomorrow I'll tell people what happened." The policeman stood up. "You wait here," he said, and disappeared. At once new people began arriving, and asked Liu Qing to go into another office. The rest of us waited outside. We could hear snatches of conversation between Liu Qing and the police, but we could not make out what they were saying. We could only guess from the tone of their voices that they were arguing. Then the policeman on duty said to us: "Off you go, you've no further business here." But we insisted on waiting for Liu Qing.

Soon it was ten o'clock. They had already changed the men on duty twice, but Liu Qing was still inside.

At eleven o'clock we went to ask them to finish their interrogation as quickly as possible, since there would soon be no more buses. They did not answer. Then one of us said: "The rest of you go home. I'll stay here and wait for Liu Qing." At first we refused, but after he had repeated his proposal several times, we left, in spite of our misgivings. The next day, still worried about Liu Qing, I went looking for news, and I finally learned that he had been arrested.

DOCUMENT 39

THE FAMILY OF LIU QING
Liu Qing Is Innocent!

THE PUBLIC SECURITY BUREAU IS BREAKING THE LAW!

The Beijing Municipal Public Security Bureau acted rashly and recklessly in detaining, trying, sentencing, and disposing of Liu Qing. The legal procedure they followed was chaotic, and had no firm basis in law. On the principle that laws must be observed and wrongs must be righted, we demand that the Beijing Public Security Bureau annul its verdict.

On the afternoon of November 11, 1979, members of *April Fifth Forum* were selling transcripts of Wei Jingsheng's trial at Xidan Democracy Wall. The Public Security Bureau intervened to stop the sale and made arrests. Liu Qing, although present, was not arrested. After the incident, at about five o'clock on the same afternoon, Liu Qing and several others went to the Public Security Bureau to ask on what legal grounds their colleagues had been arrested. They stayed there until eleven o'clock, arguing with the officials who received them. Then the Public Security Bureau suddenly announced that "Liu Qing cannot return, he is detained."

Clearly the decision to arrest Liu Qing was taken on the spur of the moment, and had no basis in law. Law does not permit muddling, yet comrades in the Public Security Bureau acted quite arbitrarily. At the time, they did not explain to anyone the legal grounds for Liu Qing's arrest. Two days later they told Lin's family that he had breached the

State Council's Law on the Dissemination of Information, and that he was being "administratively detained." First the arrest, then the fishing around for charges—this makes a mockery of the legal system.

Liu Qing made no secret of editing and publishing the transcript of Wei Jingsheng's trial. He had put up posters announcing its sale several days in advance. If the Public Security Bureau considered this unlawful, it had time enough to warn him. In fact it was its duty to do so. Sadly, it neglected to carry out its duty.

The State Council has issued many regulations, but the Security Bureau has carried them out only selectively. Liu Qing was detained according to the Law on the Dissemination of Information, but the State Council has also stipulated that "administrative detention must not exceed fifteen days." The Bureau, however, violated this regulation. Which regulations the Bureau enforces and which it does not clearly varies from person to person and from case to case. "Regulations" are merely pretexts behind which lurks the real reason: Liu Qing was editor of *April Fifth Forum*.

Before the verdict, that is, during the nine months of so-called administrative detention, the Bureau refused all along to say where Liu was being held or to allow his family to visit him. This is inhumane. Even after the verdict the family was not informed of Liu Qing's whereabouts, and he was secretly led away without meeting any of his close relatives. This is a violation of basic civil rights. Why this secrecy? Has Liu Qing met with some mishap? Has he been tortured?

After the marathon trial the Security Bureau finally came up with three legal "grounds" for Liu Qing's arrest. In August 1980 they informed his family by word of mouth (not, as they are legally obliged to do, in writing) *(a)* that Liu had taken part in the petition, sit-in, demonstration, and rally initiated by the jailed woman activist Fu Yuehua, and that he was one of Fu Yuehua's chief collaborators; *(b)* that he had publicly sold the transcript of Wei Jingsheng's trial, contrary to the Law on the Dissemination of Information temporarily enacted by the State Council in 1950; and *(c)* that over a long period he had improperly obtained sick notes. As a result, Liu was sentenced to three years' reeducation through labor.

Liu Qing actively supports the spirit of the Party's Third Plenum. He hopes that the motherland will thrive and prosper, and realize the Four Modernizations before the century is out. But he believes that without true democracy and a healthy legal system such goals can never be achieved. Therefore, despite his ill health, he has risked his whole future by plunging into the movement spontaneously initiated by the people for democracy and a legal system. He long ago foresaw the consequences of his actions, but he has not retreated one step from his aims. He even foresaw the verdict against him. Is that not ironic, when democracy and legality are so vigorously advocated?

Article 45 of the Constitution unequivocally specifies that each citizen has the freedom of speech, publication, association, demonstration, and strike. This is the most basic of all civil rights, and guarantees the character, dignity, and personality of each citizen. It also guarantees the right of every citizen to supervise and address inquiries to the state, the government, and officials at all levels. If this right is upheld, we have democracy; if not, we have autocracy. Nothing Liu Qing did went beyond the limits set by the Constitution. He merely exercised his constitutional right to propagate the need for democracy and legality. Law should not be an empty word or mere window dressing. It should be the very pillar of society. It should place the same constraints on heads of state as on ordinary citizens. What, then, does Liu Qing's imprisonment show? It shows that we are being stripped of what we treasure. Do you want to express your views without constraint? To uplift your spiritual life? To openly criticize the bureaucracy when it violates your civil rights? If so, Article 45 is your guarantee of freedom from retaliation, persecution, and imprisonment. We are pained to see this freedom violated. We are told that all are equal before the law. If so, this violation means that no one can be sure that he or she will not be jailed for acting within the Constitution.

By collaborating with Fu Yuehua and publishing the transcript of Wei Jingsheng's trial, Liu Qing did not violate Article 45 of the Constitution. The Security Bureau based its case on regulations issued by the State Council thirty years ago, at the founding of the People's Republic. Even if we discount the fact that these regulations are thirty years old, that they were never published in official documents or circulars, that the Bureau did not cite them at the time of Liu Qing's arrest, and that they were clearly a temporary enactment, it still remains that they contradict the Constitution, and as such cannot be used to prove Liu Qing's guilt.

As for the third charge, Liu Qing's work unit and hospital can prove that he has been ill. First he was hospitalized in Guiyang and Shaanxi. Then he came to Beijing for treatment, with the approval of his work unit. At the time it was very difficult for people living outside Beijing to get treatment in the capital. Liu Qing's sick notes can be verified by his factory; in any case, this is outside the jurisdiction of the Security Bureau. Shortly before he was arrested he had agreed with his work unit that he would return to Shaanxi for treatment, and was preparing for the journey. How could he know that at the same time the Security Bureau was preparing to arrest him?

DOCUMENT 40

Liu Qing

Sad Memories and Prospects: My Appeal to
the Tribunal of the People

On the Tape Recording of
Wei Jingsheng's Trial

On 14 October 1979, I heard that the public trial of Wei Jingsheng was
to begin the following morning. I passed the news to some journals and
groups in the Beijing democratic movement, and we arranged to meet at
seven o'clock the next day outside the courthouse at No. 1 Zhengyi Street
and to try to attend the trial. When I got there, there were already a few
foreign journalists and people from the democratic movement shivering
in the fresh morning wind. A notice had been pasted up on the fence in
front of the court building: "Wei Jingsheng's trial has been postponed."
When we asked at the reception how long the trial would be postponed,
we were told that it was not yet known. We assumed from previous experience that it would be postponed indefinitely. But to our surprise we
learned the same evening that the trial would begin at eight o'clock the
following day (the 16th). At the same time we heard that only a hand-
picked audience would be allowed to attend the trial. Why so much secrecy surrounding a public trial?

The whole country was closely following what would happen to Ren
Wanding (of the Human Rights League), Wei Jingsheng, Fu Yuehua,
Chen Lü, Zhang Wenhe, and others arrested in March 1979. Even the
world press was interested, and it seems that the United Nations and Amnesty International corresponded with the Chinese Government about
them. Why this concern about the fate of a few ordinary Chinese? It was
because the arrests had created a cold March wind that was blowing
across the Chinese political horizon. It was not only a question of these
few individuals. Even more important was what the arrests implied for
the political situation as a whole in China.

Now the authorities had filled all the seats in the public auditorium
where the trial was to be held (why was that necessary?), we had to work
out another strategy. That same evening I visited an acquaintance who
was among those officially invited. I gave him a tape recorder to record
the trial.

On the evening of the 16th I got my tape recorder back and together
with a few friends spent four or five hours listening to the recording. We
all thought that Wei Jingsheng had been sentenced for leaking secrets, but

it turned out that the court had found him guilty of two serious crimes and had sentenced him to fifteen years in jail and three years' deprivation of political rights. We were not going to take that lying down. It was an attack on democracy and in open contempt of the principles of legality that were just beginning to win ground in China. This sentence shows that in China it is still not possible to speak one's mind. Genuine freedom of conscience and expression remains something for the future. Progress in this direction will depend on the efforts of individuals who have the courage to challenge injustice. If everyone averts their eyes and pretends that nothing is happening, there can be no progress. A people that acquiesces in injustice will be destroyed, and deserves to be. But the Chinese people have thrown up individuals who even in periods of darkest dictatorship speak the truth fearlessly.

As a result of the wide interest in the case and the obvious irregularities in the judgment, Wei Jingsheng's trial became a main topic of conversation. All the democratic journals in Beijing shared the view that it was our job to publicize the truth and get more people interested in the affair. We hoped in this way to exercise some influence on those national leaders who were serious about wanting to reform the Chinese system. Duplicating the entire recording turned out to be less work than we expected, so that it was not necessary to call on the assistance of people from the various Beijing democratic journals. Moreover, it was rather dangerous to expose the authorities in this way. Later we discovered that our premonitions were justified. It was essential to involve as few people as possible in this work. I therefore took responsibility myself, and used the help of a few good friends.

My Differences with Wei Jingsheng

From the very first time *Siwu luntan* (April Fifth Forum) hit the streets we have always openly stated our political views, and these differed in significant ways from the views expressed in Wei Jingsheng's *Tansuo* (Explorations). As editor of *April Fifth Forum*, I repeatedly debated Wei Jingsheng. When *Explorations* published Wei Jingsheng's "Democracy or a New Dictatorship" I answered with a critical article.

Although the authorities were very irritated by Wei Jingsheng's articles, to my knowledge they never once seriously countered them. At Democracy Wall some people honored Wei Jingsheng as a hero, while others cursed him. I am probably the only one who, however clumsily, actually criticized his arguments in an article. And I was not thanked for doing so. One friend told me to my face: "I'd like to tear that damned article of yours off the Wall." So some people see me as an enemy of Wei Jingsheng, and at the very least I cannot be considered his cothinker. Even my worst enemy would find it hard to put me in the same camp as Wei Jingsheng, so I was naive enough to think that I could go ahead and plead his case. The unofficial journals and groups in Beijing had set up a "joint conference" at the beginning of 1979. In it all currents were represented, and they signed a four-point agreement the most important point of which was that in the case of individual or collective arrests on the grounds of opinions or beliefs the surviving groups would come to the aid of those arrested. They would then have the duty to mobilize public opinion, to console the relatives of those arrested and to support them financially as far as possible, and to approach the authorities with requests to visit those held prisoner. The participating groups named me as contact person. The job was actually too much for me, but when Ren Wanding, Wei Jingsheng, and the others were arrested I had no choice but to carry out the four-point agreement. Although the "joint conference" no longer existed, it was up to me, the contact person, to do what had been promised.

WEI JINGSHENG ASKS ME TO DEFEND HIM

In June 1979 I heard from a court official, Luo Kejun, that Wei Jingsheng had asked whether I would defend him or find another lawyer to do so. I talked over his request with people in the law department of the University and with some other experts. At the time the penal code had not yet been promulgated, so I finally had to tell Luo Kejun:

> Since there is no penal code, there is no basis for a defense. That means that I cannot agree to Wei Jingsheng's request. But I am prepared to defend him if the court cooperates by announcing what legal provisions will be followed in this case. We request the court for permission to visit Wei Jingsheng and discuss the entire case with him, so that he can really defend himself during his trial. Finally I request the court in the name of all the democratic magazines and a great many individuals to conduct the trial in public.

Later the penal code was published, and with a few others we decided to set up a defense committee for Wei Jingsheng, Ren Wanding, and the others. Unfortunately the sentence was already passed before we had the chance to tell the court that we now agreed to Wei Jingsheng's request. Our national sickness—the inability to make decisions—had struck once again; we had acted too late. Although the trial's outcome was obvious even in advance, it was my moral duty to stand by Wei Jingsheng and not to dishonor the trust that had been placed in me. In early November, with the help of friends, I transcribed the entire trial proceedings. We carefully checked the transcript against the original, and the result can be considered a complete and literal rendering of what was said during the trial. The only exceptions are a few unintelligible words and short gaps while the tape was being changed. At first we intended to put the text up on Democracy Wall in the form of a wall poster, but later we decided to make stencils of it, and to duplicate between one and two thousand copies.

ARRESTS DURING THE SALE OF THE TRIAL REPORT

In early November we put up a notice on Democracy Wall that the transcript of Wei Jingsheng's trial would go on sale on the 11th. That day several thousand people had gathered by the early afternoon. At the request of many of those present we began selling earlier than planned. We tried to keep order with the help of some twenty people, but things still became rather chaotic. Potential buyers saw that the edition was limited and everyone began to press forward to make sure of getting a copy. While I was busy trying to restore order a friend tugged at my sleeve and told me that he had some important news for me. I followed him to a quieter place and then he told me that the security police were on their way and would arrive within half an hour. I hurried back but it was already too late. The crowd had grown so thick that I could no longer reach the sales point.

Someone told me that there had been arrests and that the .publication had been confiscated. This person took me to one side and I saw a lorry packed with people and a sort of ambulance which began to drive off with its siren on.

Later I heard what had happened after my departure. Suddenly the police had appeared on the scene. Some said that there were between seventy and eighty, others spoke of a hundred. The street in front of Democracy Wall was sealed off and some of the agents forced their way into the crowd, seized the transcripts, and arrested one seller, who was taken off in handcuffs. A few bystanders who protested at these arrests were also shackled hand and foot and put into a police vehicle. Altogether some four or five people were said to have been arrested. [Later Liu Qing was himself arrested when he tried to get these people released from custody.]

EXPERIENCE IN PRISON

Once you are in the hands of the security police you have no chance of struggling against their illegal behavior. You'll always end up the loser, all the more so since you can count on no support from the outside world. My present situation is proof of this. I am not protected by any law. My voice cannot reach the outside world. I shall lose out every time, since they can do whatever they want with me and they're planning to give me a hard time. But I'll resist to the end and use every opportunity to show how they trample on the law.

FRIENDS IN NEED

After three days I was transferred from the special observation cell to a bigger cell full of other prisoners. I realized that this was a move for the better. Up to then I hadn't been allowed to speak to the jailers. Now I was suddenly in a cell with more than ten people. The prison chiefs had realized that neither the soft nor the hard treatment would work on me, so they had obviously decided to try another ploy. I discussed my situation with a former Red Guard, and he thought that maybe I would now be officially arrested. That would be an enormous improvement, because it would give me the chance to plead my case in a court of law. Of course it was possible that this transfer was a trick, but if the cops thought they were going to defeat me that way, they were mistaken. Anyway, I decided to continue asking the prison authorities to request clarification from their superiors about my illegal imprisonment. I demanded correct treatment, and told my story to my fellow prisoners, so that as many people as possible would know what had happened to me. My account was so effective that the prisoners became restless. Some even asked the jailers why I was being held prisoner. Needless to say, the jailers went purple with rage, but there was little they could say to justify what had happened. They either said the case had not yet been clarified, or they argued that there will always be some cases that fall outside the rules.

But I was lacking in experience and knew too little of the tricks that the security police were capable of. They don't need the law; they can twist it just as they please. My companions in the new cell had the experience that I lacked, and they had rather a good insight into the workings of the security police. Yue Zhengping from Fangshan, who was serving five years for false accusation; Mai Mao, who had problems with rehabilitation and so was still in jail; Li Anjiang, sentenced to six years for working on the black market—they and others told me what was what under the prison regime. Yue Zhengping said:

> You haven't done anything? Fine. You haven't broken a single law? Even better. Then we won't sentence you; we'll just send you to a camp for reform through labor. If we think someone needs reforming, we send them to a camp. It's for your own good. Even if you haven't done anything wrong, you're capable of it, because you're the type that easily turns to crime. By sending you to a camp we're preventing you from making a serious mistake.

He held up his hand in admonition and ended his little speech on an unctuous note: "Please believe me, this is for your own safety and your own good. That's why I'm swallowing you up. You won't feel better until you're in my stomach, because there nothing can happen to you."

And they were right. These friends in need meant a lot to me. Some had something on their conscience, while others were innocent, but that made little difference in the long run. Packed together in a small room, we all depended on one another. Their help came just at the right time. They prepared me for all the possible tricks of which the security police were capable, so that when I was confronted with them I knew what to expect. I kept my cool.

I'm also very grateful to my friends for their practical help. I'm very unpractical myself, and I didn't even know how to keep my things in order. Every now and then my cellmates helped me tidy things up. They did my washing for me and even darned my socks; in fact they did so much for me that I was embarrassed by their concern. Thanks to them I even managed to get a bath every now and then. When you've had a good wash and your clothes are clean, you feel less vulnerable.

The most important way in which they helped me was by supporting me when I refused to live according to the humiliating regulations set by the guards. Suddenly, for no obvious reason, prisoners were ordered to fold their hands in front of their stomachs while they were out exercising, and at some points we were even expected to slow down and bow our heads. I refused to comply, and for two reasons: first, I had not been sentenced, but was being illegally held, so that guards' regulations were not binding on me; and second, even people serving official sentences should not be degraded, and the law says as much.

My cellmates decided unanimously to join me in my protest. Naturally, under pressure from the guards they were forced to bow their heads, but when they saw that I was punished for my disobedience they unanimously protested. Some said to the guards: "How dare you torture someone who is being held illegally?"

Yue Zhengping was so angry that he asked for writing paper and planned to accuse the Beijing Security Bureau of kidnapping and maltreatment. The authorities found it advisable to transfer me out of this cell to a smaller room. But when my former cellmates were let out to go to the toilet and passed my cell door, they would bang on it or shout out to show that they had not forgotten me.

At the time that I was transferred I was beaten black and blue, and I had a gag on so that I could scarcely breathe and handcuffs that cut deep into my flesh. I was not alone. There were two other prisoners in my new cell. One was named Luo Xinguo, a shoplifter who had moved illegally to Beijing from Shaanxi; and the other was named Wei Rongling. He claimed he was a deputy section-chief in the army's political bureau. He had worked for a long time as bodyguard for Zhang Chunqiao and Jiang Qing, and I already knew him from the previous cell. He knew a lot about the prisoners awaiting death sentences for he had worked with them (in cell 23) the previous year. When he learned who I was he told me a few things about Wei Jingsheng and Fu Yuehua. According to him, Wei Jingsheng had not been sent to the unit where he was supposed to serve his sentence, but had been locked up by himself in a condemned cell. He said he had got a letter from Wei Jingsheng, who had asked him to pass it on to Lu Lin after his release. But the message was confiscated and he got a beating for it. I didn't give much credence to this story. Wei Jingsheng had been sentenced seven or eight months earlier, and normally he would long ago have been sent off to the camp. But the dictatorship of the proletariat is capricious and full of surprises, for I later learned that Wei Rongling was telling the truth. When I got back from exercising on 1 July 1980 I suddenly came across Wei Jingsheng, who was looking very pale and thin. He saw me too, and I could see from his face that he was uncertain about what to do. He was led past me by two guards.

Another activist I came across in prison was Zhang Wenhe of the Human Rights League. He was as militant as ever. He protested at everything and gave the guards hell, however much he suffered as a result. At one point he was so heavily shackled that he even found it difficult to do things like eat, sleep, and go to the toilet. He was forced to wear a balaclava helmet and a gag, and he was repeatedly beaten. He was kept like this for months on end. For a while his cell was near mine. We were often let out of our cells at about the same time, and by deliberately slowing down our pace we occasionally got the chance to swap a few words and squeeze each other's hands.

MY STATE OF HEALTH

The period of my solitary confinement was not long and it has not affected me very seriously. But changes are already noticeable. One day I noticed a lot of loose hair on my bedsheet. When I looked at myself in the small mirror on the cell door, I discovered that part of my head is already bald. The dampness and coldness in the cell, plus my habit of curling up in a corner for long periods, must have been the cause of my swollen left foot, which still gives me great pain. My nearsightedness has got much worse. I started to talk to myself, sometimes loudly, debated with an imaginary opponent. I also tried to recall some mathematical or physical problems or did exercises against the wall. Please don't laugh at me. I think a lot about my mother, worrying about the anxiety I have brought her in her old age. This makes me very sorrowful. I looked through a broken window in the toilet and saw a small patch of grass near the foot of a high wall. The green blades seem to have just emerged from the dark, muddy soil. I was suddenly overcome by a strong desire: I wanted to get out there and be closer to the grass!

Lotus Temple Camp

On 21 July two policemen came to tell me to gather up my things, and that they were going to take me to a work unit in Shaanxi. Instead they took me to the Lotus Temple labor camp, in Hua district, Shaanxi. Only there did I learn that I had been sentenced to three years' reeducation through labor. Having reached this final stage, the Public Security Bureau was forced to make up lies to justify its actions. No doubt the Public Security Bureau people are pragmatists for whom the end justifies the means, but in my view it is not so easy to separate the state of a person's soul from the means that he or she uses.

The Lotus Temple was originally a prison reserved for people sentenced to "reform through labor," but nowadays all sorts get locked up there, and there are five main categories of prisoners: those sentenced to reform through labor (*laogai*); those sentenced to forced labor (*juyi*); those sentenced to rehabilitation through labor *(laojiao)*; those detained for less than two months and required to work (*qianglao*); and finally the "professionals" (*jiuye*), convicts who, having served their sentences, ask to be allowed to stay on in the camps as "free" workers. The camp is surrounded by a gray wall, fifteen feet high, with an electrified fence running along the top. At the four corners stand lookouts or soldiers, guns at the ready. When you enter the camp you go through four successive doors, all heavily barred, which slice up the prison compound like the squares of a chessboard. Each contains one category of prisoners—only the "professionals" have no special area reserved for them. The work is very hard. It consists of carrying heavy stones about. Common criminals sentenced by a court do labor of a technical sort, in effect a sinecure. The worst jobs are given to those in the "forced labor" category or those undergoing reform through labor, that is, people who have not been convicted by a court. The organization of the work teams is usually entrusted to prisoners who have been sentenced by a court. The warders trust these prisoners more than they trust the others. This is not only because they are especially obedient or because they have been given long sentences, but because they and the warders are engaged in all sorts of trafficking and swindling. And yet these are people who have gone before a judge for breaking the law, and have lost their rights as citizens. So what is the difference between them and those who have simply "committed errors" judged insufficient to merit a legal conviction and who have kept their rights as citizens (even though they may have been sent for forced labor or reeducation through labor)? As far as I can see, the difference is minimal and purely terminological. Those who are sentenced to reform through labor are told to "recognize their crimes and submit to the law"; and those sent for reeducation through labor are told to "recognize their errors and submit to reeducation." I think that even the administration would find it hard to explain the difference between reform through labor, reeducation through labor, and forced labor, since when it comes down to it they are all the same thing.

According to the Constitution there are two sorts of people in society: those who have their rights as citizens; and criminals, who do not. But in reality a third category of people has emerged—citizens who have full rights on paper, but no rights in fact. These are the people who are sent for forced labor or reeducation through labor. It is no use looking up this third category in the Constitution. In law it is only the courts that, with the help of an official document from the State Council, can take away someone's civil rights, that is, turn a citizen into a criminal. But the Public Security Bureau, if it so wishes, also has the power to frame anyone as a criminal and treat him or her as such. In effect this is tantamount to installing a second type of court in our society: a court that dispenses of the usual paperwork and simply ships off those it doesn't like to the camps, where they are turned officially into criminals and "reeducated through labor." It's all very easy. No public proceedings, no trial, no right of appeal, and absolutely no delay—the decision is immediately put into effect. In fact genuine criminals are treated far better than these people. Criminals are dealt with by the Bureau of Detention. Only then can they be put on trial. Before the trial they can find out what the charges are, clarify points about their case, and assert their right to a defense. They can also appeal against the verdict. But those sent for reeducation through labor have no chance to defend or even to explain themselves.

One category you find in the reeducation camps are those who have made the mistake of getting on the wrong side of the Public Security Bureau, or who have annoyed their bosses in some way, and were sent for reeducation as a result. Take for example the case of Shi Jinsheng, an apprentice at the Hong'an works in Shaanxi province, who gate-crashed an evening of entertainment organized by his work unit. A trivial incident, you might think. But Shi Jinsheng was caught, badly beaten up, and dragged before the Public Security Bureau, who took him back to the factory for a "criticism and struggle session." The worker Yu Zhonghai, seeing what was happening to his apprentice, got angry and insulted the chief foreman and the people from the works security section. The result: apprentice and apprentice-master both got two years in a reeducation camp. Even if we concede that Shi Jinsheng disturbed the public order, at most he deserved to be arrested and cautioned. But two years of reeducation! As for the way his master was treated, it is hard to imagine anything more childish. Even the camp guards were shocked when they heard about it.

A second category of prisoners are those who have broken the law badly enough to get a really heavy sentence from the courts, but who have influential family connections and are sent for reeducation through labor instead. These people have quite some clout. Inside the camp they do what they like. Often they are excused for "medical treatment" and return home to work under another name. Or they get their sentences reduced. At the Lotus Temple there was a whole gang of these people who had carried out more than ten burglaries and stolen over half a ton of copper ingots from a factory. Not only did they get a mere two years' reeducation, but they were freed well before the end of their sentence.

A third category are people who have committed "crimes or grave errors" but who have been held so long in pretrial detention that they are considered eligible for release, thus saving the expenses of a formal trial. But a year later their situation changes once again and they find themselves back in camp with "an old bill to pay." Take the case of Zhou Donglin, who was detained about a theft. Zhou spent a long time in the camp and was eventually freed without a trial. After his release he was filled with remorse and decided to go straight, even to the point of studying Lei Feng [a model soldier who sacrificed himself for the revolution and whose conduct ordinary citizens are urged to emulate]. But a year later he was rearrested without the slightest justification and dragged off to the camp. The reason? The same theft for which he had been arrested a year earlier. "Debts paid recently do not cancel old ones," he was told. As far as I can see this is a debt that he will never finish paying, at a usurious rate.

A fourth category are people who have committed grave errors or even crimes but whom the Public Security Bureau could not catch in the act. They are simply suspects; nothing has been proved against them. And in the absence of definite proof or a confession, there is no way in which they can be put before the courts. So the paper sending them for reeducation talks of "inner conviction"—backed up by suspicious circumstances—that they are guilty. This category includes some real criminals, but also some victims of judicial error. It is not good to treat suspects in this way. First, it makes the Public Security Bureau look incompetent, since they can't find solid proof and are forced to rely on presumptions. Next, it encourages the Public Security Bureau to be lazy, to neglect procedures, and to use bureaucratic maneuvers. Last, if one lacks the means to convict, this creates a psychology of revenge and recalcitrance in the criminal, which is bad for society. Today life is insecure. Many grave crimes are committed by people who have been released from reeducation. One reason for this is the irrational and illegal nature of reeducation through labor, and the bad way in which the Public Security Bureau treats its prisoners.

Today, when the accent is on legality and when we have realized, thanks to the blood that has washed the dirt from our eyes, the importance of laws and institutions, it is still very easy to manipulate policing and the law so that people understand nothing of them. So, do the authorities sincerely want to clean up the legal institutions and strengthen them, or do they prefer to look upon them as amusing decorations (thereby deceiving both the people and themselves)?

DOCUMENT 41

Women Are Human Beings Too

The author of this article set up a Chinese Women's Study Association at Beijing University and presented it to the public in December 1980. She also ran as one of the eighteen candidates for the university's two seats on the people's congress of Haidian district (where the University is). Her campaign slogan was "Oriental Beauty," meant to express Chinese women's need to define a role and an identity for themselves in society. Her election posters were repeatedly torn down and she received only seven hundred of the six thousand or so votes cast, but she persevered, and after the election she set up an organization (the subsequent fate of which is unknown) to "improve Chinese women's awareness of themselves and women's personal self-development, to put an end to women's self-censorship, and to call on society as a whole to alter the context of women's lives." Anita Rind first brought this campaign to light in the West.

YET another poster! My thinking is like the sections of a sliced snake that one wants to piece together again. I have difficulty in structuring it. Gaiety and life have abandoned me. My tears flow without end. I want to shout very loudly: women are human beings too!

From the platform in this big hall, it was not the people who were booing me that I saw, but sincere human beings. My nerves were very on edge, but I did my best to reply. At the end of the meeting, people approached me and surrounded me—people who were full of compassion.

I hate my own feelings of weakness, and the fact that I am not brilliant. I hate being a woman. It seems that everywhere being a woman generates impurity.

A woman? Women too are human beings. Women too are citizens. I am one of those young people who has suffered from the inequalities of this society. Like my male student comrades, I lived a carefree childhood and an ardent and blind youth, during which I scorned hardship and overflowed with courage. Like the whole nation, I suffered ten years of difficulties (during the Cultural Revolution). Like the rest of the youth of the seventies, I had to interrupt my studies and to waste eight years of my life in the countryside.

Along with others, I too went to honor the memory of Prime Minister Zhou Enlai and was treated as a counterrevolutionary as a result. The evil forces in China did not forgive me for my youth. They treated me violently because I am a woman.

Perhaps it is only today that I truly understand the objective causes of these difficulties and this violence, or at least some of them: I am a woman. You should not reject my energies and my struggle solely because I am a woman! Why can't women too carry within them thoughts and passions, just like other human beings?

Are courage and the spirit of self-sacrifice the prerogative of the male sex? Why can't I, in these democratic elections, stand up and bring you my tears?

Women are human beings too. Why should their specific attributes, their interests, their development as a sex, and many other aspects of their womanhood not be important questions? Don't the interests of women mingle with the ocean of the interests of the people? Should not women's rights form part of democratic rights? Why do people only find fault with me when the question of women is raised? Some people can't stand reading my posters. In that case, in the name of the honor of Beijing University, and in the name of democracy, perhaps I should not have the right to express myself?

But that would mean that we can discuss in complete equality great affairs of state, but we cannot approach the woman in question in scientific fashion.

The male candidates are not particularly good-looking. Why should you demand that women candidates are? Why do people always immediately associate the woman question with the idea of sex? As part of the right of human beings to fulfill themselves, women too should be allowed to freely develop their own personalities.

Women are not machines for making children. They are human beings, and as such they must fight for their rights, their interests, and their fulfillment. Why can people not accept this idea? Cannot women's points of view widen and reinforce the overall understanding of things?

Women too are human beings. Why should I be weaker than men? And even if I am, I want to be responsible for it, to be responsible for myself. I hope that women citizens, future women candidates, are more fortunate, stronger, and more perfect than I am. I hope that through struggle we women acquire the right to be human beings and the right to take up responsibilities and the honors that flow from them.

Or perhaps the problem of women is really of no importance? It is to you, as human beings, that I put this question.

DOCUMENT 42

China and Solidarnosc

Since 1949 radical Chinese have followed new movements in Eastern Europe as closely as available sources of information permit. Titoism and the Hungarian revolution of 1956 inspired dissident currents in the Hundred Flowers campaign, and in the late 1970s there was a lively interest in Solidarnosc, especially in the democratic movement. The first text here was published in the editorial column of *Lilun qi* (Banner of Theory), a dissident magazine published in the northern Chinese port of Qingdao in February 1981, just before the final crushing of the democracy movement launched in Beijing in 1978. The article is a good example of the thinking of the radical socialist wing of the democracy movement, which in the West is far less known than the movement's pro-western, pro-capitalist wing. The letters were written by editors of the influential dissident journal *Siwu luntan* (April Fifth Forum).

THE DEATH KNELL OF THE RULE OF THE PRIVILEGED CLASS OF BUREAUCRATS

Following the uprisings of 1948 in Berlin and 1956 in Hungary, the Prague Spring of 1968, and Czechoslovakia's 1977 Charter Movement, in 1980 Poland's independent trade union movement erupted onto the scene. The difference between it and its predecessors is that all the other incidents were suppressed by the class of privileged bureaucrats in collusion with Soviet social-imperialism, while Poland's independent trade union has not up to now been suppressed and has even been granted legal recognition. Is this because the bureaucrats have "laid down the butcher's knife and taken a benevolent stance"? Or is there perhaps another reason?

Clearly the bureaucrats have not, and probably cannot, become benevolent. On the contrary, they have shown themselves in their true colors, killing people and lying. As they absorb the reactionary poison of past generations of exploiters, they only hasten their own decay. The modern-day bureaucrats have gone one step beyond past exploiting classes by deceitfully pretending that they serve the people and that they are fighting for the people's gain, while actually they are colluding at the people's cost. But deception cannot be kept up forever. Over the past thirty years blood and tears have congealed into hard fact, revealing the bureaucracy to all people of sincere intent as wolves in sheep's clothing. "Workers now realize that these jackals earn at least thirty times as much as they do. They see exclusive cars take luxury items to these bigwigs' residences." "We common people always end up dying in the corridor, while the bureaucrats have private wards, private rooms, and first-class doctors to treat them. The bigwigs also have special shops and sanatoria." Among Poland's three million or more Party members, one in six enjoys special privileges. "The manager of a tiny import-export company not only grossed more than one million dollars in bribes from the company's Western trading partner but also managed to get his hands on 473,370 Deutschmarks and a further $300,000. In London he has a deposit account and an apartment with a live-in lover. He built a luxury villa, disguised as a construction industry training center, for a construction chief." It's interesting to note that "the Vice-President, while representing the government in negotiating in Gdansk, hemmed and hawed in utter embarrassment when the strikers asked him how many country villas he owned." Equally fatuous are those bureaucratic cliques in China, on the brink of economic collapse after the downfall of the Gang of Four, who astonishingly built villas for themselves as the order of the day. While the peasants starved and the people rotted in grossly inadequate housing, they shamelessly built mansions for high officials, for generals, and even for the officials' sons and daughters. People not only want to know where these notables, themselves incapable of creating wealth, have acquired the means to build luxury villas and buy luxury limousines. They also want to know whether this is an example of the socialist principle of distribution, that is, "from each according to his ability, to each according to his work." Can these "Red bigwigs" who squander our wealth, engage in rampant corruption, and view privilege as their daily diet while talking of the "superiority of socialism" do these things in broad daylight? Can the people, who have had the blood sucked from them, struggle to protect their right to exist? The main reason Solidarity won is the accelerated degeneration of the bureaucracy and the universal awakening of people's unity.

Moscow's tanks once rumbled through Berlin, Budapest, and Prague. But not long after that, the Soviet Union was unable to send its army—in the meantime even stronger than before—into Warsaw, the birthplace of its military alliance. This was not only because the Soviet military had been sucked down into the Afghan morass and felt bitter about the military entanglements of its younger brothers in countries like Vietnam. Even more important, it had lost its morale, for in today's world who does not look with angry eyes at the source of the violation of human rights, the Soviet Union? The Soviet Union is on the strategic offensive in the international struggle for markets and resources. Its imperialist adversaries are overbearing, but the system of Soviet socialist imperialism and the class represented by it are mercilessly spurned. The privileged bureaucracy has already lost the hearts of the people, and the spiritual supports of its rule are collapsing, consumed by raging flames.

The problem is, how to replace the rule of the bureaucracy? Shall we replace it by restoring the economic basis of the system of bourgeois private property and the ideology of Catholicism? Under no circumstances! Just as we should not replace bourgeois rule by bureaucratic rule, so too we should not replace bureaucratic rule with bourgeois rule (even though nowadays the capitalists are softer on the people than the bureaucrats). The only way forward is to set up a system of proletarian democracy appropriate to this specific period of transition, and organically to link a system of public ownership worthy of the name with a system of democracy, so that the two mutually reinforce one another, serve as guarantees for one another's continued existence, and proceed along the road to true socialism.

In today's world none of the so-called socialist countries can any longer ignore the existence of Poland's Solidarity. So the bureaucrats feel shaken and the people feel inspired. How should we evaluate and treat this fact of history, which has already become a litmus test of the political attitude of each social group? We have already seen that the Chinese Party can still report accurately on events in Poland. That is wise and sensible. Of course the criterion for true wisdom lies not in reducing bureaucratic corruption but in standing on the side of the people, and bringing about basic reforms in the political and economic system of so-called socialism. We must carry out a revolution against the system of feudal bureaucracy that has ruled China for the last two thousand years and is substantially unreformable. When it comes to the freeing of He Qiu and others connected with unofficial publishing enterprises after their illegal detention, the way in which the Changsha student movement was dealt with, the free elections now being vigorously pursued in some People's Congresses in the schools and colleges, and the general attitude of politeness and noninterference, we do not completely despair of the ruling party. China can avoid going down the same road as Poland, China can thoroughly reform itself. But it might also store up tensions that will soon result in a big explosion: so that China achieves thoroughgoing reforms only at the cost of even greater chaos than Poland. This depends on which methods those in power opt to employ. It is wrong to use just any old method. People who have enjoyed decades of luxury and abundance will not return to old paths unless they are compelled to do so. I hope the Party will not again disappoint the expectations of the people, that it will swim with the flowing tide, that it will promote social progress, and that it will carry through to the end this proletarian-democratic revolution heralded by the reforms!

The death knell of the class of bureaucratic privilege has already sounded! Let us unite under the banner of proletarian democracy, so as to put an end to all class rule, all class exploitation, and all class oppression, and to promote the all-round modernization of our country! "Water can hold up boats, but it can also sink them." Long live the people!

OPEN LETTER TO LECH WALESA

Dear Chairman Lech Walesa, and members of the National Consultative Commission of the independent and autonomous trade union Solidarity.

My friends and I learned with great joy that your independent and autonomous trade union Solidarity has successfully accomplished the legal formalities for registration. Thanks to your courage, your intelligence, and your perspicacity, there is now a shining model for working classes in socialist countries the world over. This opens a new era in the world socialist workers' movement.

We congratulate you from the bottom of our hearts, and we wish you even greater victories! Poland belongs to the Polish people! Long live the Polish people! Long live the friendship between the peoples and the working classes of China and Poland!

With the respectful compliments of Xu Wenli, veteran founder of the alternative Beijing journal April Fifth Forum, *electrician on the Beijing railways.*

MESSAGE OF GREETINGS TO THE POLISH WORKERS

Dear brother workers of Poland, your strikes have won a great victory which has impressed people throughout the world. It shows the tremendous power and new class consciousness generated by working-class solidarity. It shows clearly that the revisionist bureaucratic privileged class and expansionism are mere paper tigers in the face of the people's revolutionary power. It shows that proletarian democratic revolution is an inevitable trend in history. It breaks through national boundaries and achieves a wide international significance. We, the young generation of the Chinese working class, congratulate and salute you! We hope you will continue to progress in the direction of democratic socialism! Workers of all countries, unite!

April Fifth Forum *editorial board*
Beijing, China, September 1980

NOTES TO CHAPTER FOUR

1. For translations of Wang's article, see New Left Review, no. 121, June–July 1980; and Anita Chan, Stanley Rosen, and Jonathan Unger, eds. *On Socialist Democracy and the Chinese Legal System: The Li Yizhe Debates* (Armonk, N.Y.: M. E. Sharpe, 1985), pp. 133–56.
2. "Zai Chengdu huiyishangde jianghua" (Talks at the Chengdu Conference), in *Mao Zedong sixiang wansui*, (Long live the thought of Mao Zedong), (Beijing: n.p., 1969), pp. 159–80. English translation in Stuart R. Schram, ed., *Mao Tse-tung Unrehearsed, Talks and Letters, 1956–71* (Harmondsworth: Penguin, 1974). (There are important and rather misleading omissions in Wang's quotation of Mao's remarks.)
3. Wang is quoting from "Dui Shanghai wenhua da gemingde zhishi" (Direction on the Great Cultural Revolution in Shanghai), *Mao Zedong sixiang wansui*, pp. 667–72.
4. Asia Watch, *Detained in China and Tibet* (New York: Human Rights Watch, 1994), p. 509.

❦

CHAPTER FIVE

PRAIRIE FIRE, 1989

DOCUMENT 43

Proposal to Resign from the Party and Prepare an "Association to Promote China's Democracy Movement"

To all China's patriotic intellectuals,

The Chinese Communist Party big shots now in power are corrupt, incompetent, treat the people like dirt, consider democracy a heresy, close their ears to the reasonable demands of our patriotic youth, and have a manipulative and hostile attitude toward intellectuals. We therefore propose that the broad mass of intellectuals unite and resign collectively in stages from the Chinese Communist Party to which we have all along given our lives, and that we organize afresh an "Association to Promote China's Democracy Movement" (for short, APD) that represents the people's interests.

1. The Necessity of Resigning

(i) The Chinese Communist Party was a progressive force when it overthrew the old government, but it gradually degenerated and mutated as a result of the conservatism, narrow-mindedness, and backwardness that characterize the small peasantry.

(ii) Before gaining power the Communist Party considered the intellectuals as its allies, but afterward it went on its guard against them and treated them as targets for dictatorship. The repeated anti-rightist campaigns were mainly aimed at suppressing the intellectuals. Even in periods when they were respected they were used rather than put in important positions.

(iii) Despite the present calls for a rise in teachers' salaries and more expenditure on education, the Communist Party leaders do not sincerely intend to take such measures. One reason is because valuing the contribution made by education has few if any uses in the contest for power.

(iv) Intellectuals can no longer defend the people's and their own interests through the Chinese Communist Party. The Chinese Communist Party has already lost its reputation at home and abroad, and intellectuals who remain in it will harm their own glorious image.

2. Method and Procedure for Leaving the Party

First several dozen or several hundred celebrities from the realms of education, theory, and the arts should take the lead. After applying to resign in accordance with Party statutes, they should choose a day to hold a press conference in Beijing and explain openly why they are resigning.

Next, groups of intellectuals should take turns to make public statements resigning from the Party. If the celebrities find it inconvenient to resign collectively, the initiative can be taken by several hundred ardent middle-aged and young teachers and researchers from Beijing University, People's University, Qinghua University, Beijing Normal University, the Academy of Social Sciences, and the Academy of Sciences.

3. Setting up APDs

The Communist Party cannot represent the people's interests, and the democratic parties are its mere appendages. Intellectuals have no choice but to start again by setting up a party or organization of their own that represents the people's interests. Let it be called the "Association to Promote China's Democracy Movement" or APD. Initially it can simplify procedures and recruit broadly, including politically aware members of other parties. Its aim will be to promote democracy, realize freedom of the press and independence of the judiciary, punish corrupt officials, and pay serious attention to education and other issues.

4. Winning Legal Status for the APD

The Communist Party will not at present agree to the plans to set up an APD. So intellectuals must join the APD in their tens of thousands to create a fait accompli. Then it can fight like Solidarity in Poland for legal status. The history of China's modern democracy movement proves that the Chinese people and students need the organization and support of a political party—otherwise they are like a plate of scattered sand and will end up being suppressed by the authorities. So Chinese intellectuals must urgently set up a party organization that can stand up to the Chinese Communist Party. This is what the people want. This is the only hope for democracy. Let's start acting!

Some Communist Party teachers at People's University
mid-April 1989

DOCUMENT 44

Letter of Petition

1. Reevaluate Comrade Hu Yaobang's merits and demerits and affirm his ideas about "democracy, freedom, relaxation, and harmony."

2. Punish thugs who beat students and the people, and make those responsible apologize.

3. Promulgate as soon as possible a new media law that guarantees freedom of the press and permits ordinary people to publish newspapers.

4. Let leading state cadres make public their and their families' assets and income. Investigate speculation and profiteering by officials and publish the details.

5. Let the relevant state leaders make a self-criticism to the country for mistakes in educational policy and let them seek out those who are to blame. Let there be a big rise in educational spending and better treatment of intellectuals.

6. Reevaluate the "movement against bourgeois liberalization" and rehabilitate completely all those citizens who have been wronged.

7. We strongly demand that the media report fairly, accurately, and punctually on this democratic and patriotic movement.

Preparatory Committee of Beijing University Students
April 21, 1989

DOCUMENT 45

Ren Wanding
Speech in Tian'anmen Square

Ren Wanding, an accountant in his mid-forties, was a founding member of the Human Rights Alliance in 1979, when he was arrested and imprisoned for four years. In late 1988, sometime after his release, he issued a statement calling for the freeing of all political prisoners in China. During the 1989 people's movement, he continued to call for human rights, free speech, and the rule of law. He was one of few intellectuals to see the importance of building an independent workers' movement. He was rearrested on June 9, 1989. According to New China News Agency reports, Ren was "found guilty of grave crimes and showed no repentance" at his trial in 1991, and was sentenced to seven years' imprisonment. In 1994, he was reported to be suffering from serious medical problems, including cataracts and severe myopia, for which he was receiving inadequate treatment.

Before the crackdown, he is reported as saying: "I am no longer afraid. I've already died once in prison. Once you have been there, you are never really afraid again." Just before his arrest he is reported as saying: "I must speak, it is my fate to do these things."

This speech was given on April 21, 1989. It is here condensed.

STARTING on April 18, Beijing has seen a new eruption of a massive protest movement for democracy. The same numbers are taking part as in the April Fifth Incident of 1976.

Actually the death of an ex-General Secretary of the Chinese Communist Party (i.e., Hu Yaobang) does not warrant such excessive mourning. In the April Fifth revolution thirteen years ago people used the commemoration of the death of Zhou Enlai to launch an antiauthoritarian, antifeudal socialist people's movement. During the Democracy Wall movement of 1979 Hu Yaobang twice personally advised that "people should not be readily arrested," but in the end the main leaders of the movement were all seized and prosecuted. In the present movement people's emotions and ideas have again been channeled toward the shortcomings of the whole structure of China's social and political system. "I love my teacher, but I love truth even more."

The chants of "Long live democracy," "Long live human rights," and "Long live freedom" echo around Tian'anmen Square and constitute the main theme of today's movement. The *Internationale* is being sung here, with a wholly new meaning and purpose.

No fair, objective witness would attribute what is happening to a disruptive handful of provocateurs with ulterior motives. We do not need to answer such charges from those who are protecting their privileges. If the Party continues to mishandle this mass movement and tries to limit the commemorative activities, it will soon disappear from history. The workers' consciousness will be aroused, and students and workers will link hands.

Ten years ago, reforming our country's social system was the highest ideal and program of the Democracy Wall movement, and the same goes for present and future mass movements.

Fellow students, if the monolithic, imperialist structure is not radically reformed, how can education save China? How can science bring progress? Which is more important—the state and the Chinese nation, or the blooming of humanity, the liberation of human rights, and the struggle for civil rights? In other words, does the cohesion of the nation depend on external pressure by a political party or on the natural association of each member of the nation whose human rights have been allowed to flourish?

The efforts of the May Fourth movement (of 1919) to "save the nation from subjugation" were a historical necessity of that period. But the Democracy Wall movement had already gone beyond the illusion of the so-called state and nation, which it rightly interpreted as the interests of the rulers. It followed the tide of history and represented the people with its call for human rights and democracy. These demands were very different in meaning and consequences from similar demands in other periods, for example May Fourth. This is because they came after the Communist Party's assumption of power in 1949.

Human rights and democracy are the perennial themes of the people's movement. Even on the hundredth anniversary of the May Fourth movement, they will still be the Chinese people's political ideal and standard. Only people's democracy can claim the legacy of May Fourth.

The activists of Democracy Wall were exercising their civil rights in order to defend the people's democracy. But they were brutally suppressed and imprisoned, and some of them remain so. Those who have been released are repressed and discriminated against. The present reforms are in a seriously contradictory position, for they are in conflict with the monopoly position and secret privileges of the Party. There is greed and corruption everywhere. The law is abused and politics is bankrupt. Party regulations are flouted. Inflation is rampant. Theft and robbery are on the rise. The people are suffering and angry. Order is breaking down. The reforms are in danger.

China's contemporary democracy movement has taken various forms: the attempts in the 1950s by the democratic parties to exercise political power, and popular resistance movements like the Cultural Revolution, the April Fifth revolution, the Democracy Wall movement, the student movements of 1985 and 1986, the 1989 petitions, and the present movement. Time and again mass protests have forced the Communists in power to correct their mistakes and to avert national crises.

People's movements over the last few decades on both sides of the Taiwan Straits show that beyond the Communist Party, the Guomindang, the eight democratic parties, and the democratic Progressive Party there exists the everlasting force of people's democracy. Today no party, whether in government or in opposition, can represent this force.

The Democracy Wall movement produced a simple program, "The Chinese Declaration of Human Rights," and a loose political association known as the Human Rights League. The shortcomings of the 1986 students' movement included the vagueness of its slogans ("Democracy," "Human rights," "Freedom") and its lack of a concrete action program and of long-term political goals. It failed to oppose inflation on behalf of the people, or to call for higher wages. So it forfeited support.

Workers in this country should fight for the independence of their trade unions from the leadership of the Party. If this is impossible, they should form their own unions.

In the Democracy Wall movement and the 1986 student movement, workers were arrested and jailed. The lesson is that our organizations were loose and small. Students should help the workers.

Only when the several tens of millions of industrial workers realize that their democratic rights will not be given to them as handouts but need to be fought for, only when they take command of the country, will production in China truly race ahead and the tasks of democracy be quickly realized.

We must win the release of the imprisoned activists of Democracy Wall and of the 1986 students' movement, and have the verdicts on them reversed. This should be a main item on the agenda of our talks with the government.

We must also fight for higher wages and oppose price inflation.

Fight for basic housing and oppose the sale of houses at high prices.

Fight for democracy in the universities; oppose any intervention by the university authorities.

Fight for the freedom to publish newspapers; eliminate the concept of "counterrevolution" from the penal code.

Fellow worker brothers! Organize your own organizations legally! Long live the coalition of students and workers!

DOCUMENT 46

A Worker's Letter to the Students

Comrades:

You have kept going for several days and you will certainly want to gain the support of the broad mass of workers, peasants, soldiers, and private traders. How to do so? First, don't only stress the treatment of intellectuals and the need to increase educational expenditure and don't shout empty slogans about democracy, for that might affect relations between the students and the workers and peasants and thus harm unity.

Toward workers, peasants, and soldiers you should propagate the idea that "public ownership" has in reality become ownership by a minority of aristocratic bureaucrats. Wealth created by the workers and peasants is consumed by the minority of aristocratic bureaucrats. They call us "masters of the state" but we live crowded together in intolerable conditions while they, the so-called "public servants," build themselves villas everywhere. The "masters" crowd into buses to get to work while the "servants" have high-grade limousines and police cars to clear the road ahead of them with their sirens. Compatriots, under the banner of stability and unity they bar our way. But what causes instability and disunity? Should we close our eyes and ears to their theft of public vehicles? Where did they get this money from? Isn't it the product of our sweat and blood? They pay no attention to the country's interests. They just sit in their limousines and go off to spend hundreds of yuan on a game of golf. You may well ask what they earn, and what their expenses are. It's not surprising people say that "their wages are the gross national product." You may well ask what the difference is between them and feudal lords!

We should not place our hopes in one or two sagacious lords. We must set up a flawless democratic system in which the press is free, the courts are independent, and the people's representatives are elected by the people. A minority control the media to cheat the people and make fools of them. Unless they are exposed, the will of the people will never find expression.

If the representatives of the people are designated by a minority of aristocratic bureaucrats, how can they represent the people? How can they reflect the heart of the people?

Dear compatriots, I remember two years ago when the students were in turmoil that a minority of people used the media to cheat the whole of China and sow discord between the students and the workers and peasants. They said: "To produce one student the country spends more than ten thousand yuan, produced by more than one hundred workers and peasants. But the students don't value it." Whereas in reality the wealth created by the sweat and blood of hundreds of millions of compatriots is squandered by the bureaucrats, China's biggest capitalists. And they shift the responsibility for the country's calamities onto the shoulders of the people, for example by inflation. The students' movement and the interests of the workers and peasants are one and the same, we support you!

Beijing Normal University, April 28, 1989

DOCUMENT 47

A Choice Made on the Basis of Conscience
and Party Spirit: An Open Letter to
All Party Members

This wall poster went up at People's University on April 28, 1989.

Comrade Party Members:
According to the analysis of *People's Daily*'s commentator and to the general position of the Central Committee as transmitted by a meeting of Party members, the Central Committee has already adopted a tough position: "Only sixty thousand of Beijing's students are boycotting classes while a hundred thousand have not acted. We have three million troops.

What do we have to be afraid of?" (Deng Xiaoping said this.) This shows that it is highly likely that the government will use armed force to suppress the democracy movement. Tomorrow's demonstration may well be the occasion of another bloody massacre!

We have only two choices: to be a Chinese with conscience, a Party member with conscience, and to fight to make China democratic, prosperous, and strong; or to act as a qualified "Party member" and actively respond to the Central Committee's call in order to stay in the Party and assure one's future. Which should we choose?

I remember Comrade Zhou Enlai once said in reply to a foreign friend, "I am first a Chinese and only then a Party member." Some people are even prepared to shed their blood for democracy, freedom, and the promotion of reforms. For what is Party membership and one's future compared with these things? Actually, this decision by the Central Committee cannot represent the true feelings of Party members. We must cry out in the true voice of a Communist with conscience!

Just consider! Three student representatives kneel under China's solemn national emblem on the steps of the Great Hall of the People with a letter of petition, but no one pays the slightest attention to them. Where is the Party spirit of the leaders of the Central Committee? Does the Party speak for the people? Who is destroying the Party?

The government wants to use the three-million-strong armed forces—those protectors of the people—against the students and their campaign for democracy and freedom. Is this not a case of dictatorship against the people? As a Party member, I no longer want to shed tears on account of the corruption of the state and the apathy of the people. All I want is to be a true Communist, and to fight and shed blood for democracy and freedom!

History will prove me right! History will remember us as fighters for democracy: true Communists who fight for the prosperity and strength of the nation!

A Student Party Member of People's University

DOCUMENT 48

Hoist High the Flag of Reason

1. History's Strange Circle:
The tragedy of Hu Yaobang was the tragedy of a Chinese. Such tragedies permeate the entire history of the Chinese nation.

Looking back, I am astounded and heartbroken. I have given up all hope. The moment that Qin Shi Huangdi began his dictatorship, an autocratic kingdom was established. China's later history is merely a logical extension of this: successive peasant wars overthrew one corrupt dynasty after another, only to bring about a new period of autocratic rule. The Chinese nation has got caught up in a vicious circle of periodic shake-ups, and so our great motherland has been plagued by periodic disaster and the social forces of production have suffered periodic damage and destruction.

At a time when a number of Western countries were setting out on the capitalist road, ancient China was still treading the feudal dynastic cycle. While China was intoxicated with the power and prestige of the "supreme nation under heaven," Western cannon were blasting open China's gateway. But some progressive Chinese awoke and recognized that they could no longer content themselves with a cycle of dynastic rise and fall, so bourgeois revolutionaries represented by Sun Yat-sen staged the 1911 Revolution and overthrew the decadent Qing Dynasty.

But due to the strength of feudal influences the bourgeois were too weak to break the vicious circle and Yuan Shikai's attempt to restore the monarchy sounded the death knell for their republic, after which the tradition of warlord politics reasserted itself throughout China. Chiang Kai-shek got rid of the warlords and established a superficial unity, but it was clear to everyone that far from establishing a bourgeois republic, he had founded a semicolonial autocracy.

Is the socialist system set up by the Chinese Communists' revolution just another dynasty, a personal autocracy? In our country the Party leads everything, everything serves politics, the chairman and secretary of the Party lead everything, and the People's Congress is an ornament, a vase, a rubber stamp, a fig leaf. Under this autocracy, which decks itself out as socialist and Marxist-Leninist, the state chairman and other outstanding leaders have fallen foul of persecution and murder. Superstition and the personality cult have spread like the plague, the Constitution has been trampled underfoot. Only when one or two exceptional individuals air their political views does it have legal effect.

So what was the outcome of the Eleventh Plenary Session of the Third National People's Congress (NPC)? Deng Xiaoping raised slogans calling for the reform of the political system, but he lacked the wisdom and courage of Washington, who in order to establish a tradition of democracy refused to serve consecutive terms. The political system is the same as ever: the Chairman of the Military Commission has become a behind-the-scenes manipulator and Deng Xiaoping appears to be ruling from behind a silk screen, rather like the Empress Dowager Ci Xi. Lovers of democracy, when with tears in my eyes I examine the history of our nation, I find that *autocratic government* is the greatest obstacle on the road to reform.

2. My Grief and Indignation:

Let us break from our narrow and closed way of looking at the world and its history. The great flag of reason hoisted by fighters for democracy in the Renaissance opened a fresh page in the history of civilization. What is reason? Reason is the fusion of impulse, passion, and knowledge. Bacon said, "Knowledge is might." The knowledge and passion that I wish to fuse in reason possess an even more immeasurable might.

Over the past few days I have observed how the students of the Normal University were passionate and impulsive but lacking in knowledge, that is, knowledge about democracy. But with too little knowledge, how can there be self-confidence? And without self-confidence, how can there be courage? With the result that it becomes difficult to get organized.

We need knowledge of democracy, for without it we will slip into a state of blindness. Democracy means first and foremost democracy in government, that is, a rational mechanism for the exercise of authority and a highly effective mechanism for mutual restraint and mutual supervision.

Among the seven demands raised by Beijing University was one for "freedom of the press," but they forgot that a prerequisite for that is the *abolition of autocracy.* Why do American reporters dare to expose the unlawful behavior of the President and his officials? If *the legislature could not restrain the President, if the opposition could not supervise the government,* would the press still dare to report such things?

China's Constitution has an article on press freedom *but lacks corresponding guarantees regarding the system of government. The NPC is a rubber stamp, and the other parties dare not speak out.*

The movement for democracy must have proper goals: our slogans must have real substance and address and grasp the basic issues. To this end I propose these slogans.

a. Revise the Constitution and abolish one-party dictatorship!
b. Let all parties compete fairly in elections!
c. Implement a parliamentary system, abolish autocracy!
d. Freedom and legislation for the press!
e. Separate government from enterprise, abolish privileges!

A Professional Revolutionary at Beijing Normal University
April 30, 1989

DOCUMENT 49

Where I Stand

This wall poster went up at Beijing's Normal University on April 30, 1989.

I AM a member of the Communist Party. I joined the Party a few years ago, out of boundless admiration for it. I joined because the Party's aim was to represent the people's interests and promote its welfare. During the war years, the policies and behavior of the [old Guomindang] leaders lacked integrity. Water can hold up boats, but it can also sink them. Only a government that truly represents the interests of the people will gain their backing. The Communist Party and the motherland are not one concept. The people ardently love the Communist Party, but they love their motherland more. The Party has no other purpose than to represent the people of the country and to promote its welfare. During the war years and in the 1950s and the 1960s, the people supported, trusted, and loved the Communist Party. And today? If we are honest, how much trust do people now have in it? As a Communist, I am bitterly disappointed by what I know to be true. Nowadays the Party's Central Committee has lost the confidence of the people, so as a result the student movement has started up. It's not that the Communist Party is no longer great. It's because today, in governing the motherland, the Communist Party can only gain the people's confidence if it stands up for the country's interests. Nor are the Central Committee and the Communist Party a single concept. If the people criticize the Central Committee that does not mean that they no longer love the Communist Party. It is simply that they want to urge the Party on to do an even better job of reform. A high-handed policy and a policy of deceiving the people lacks righteousness.

The students are acting justly! I too am among their ranks. Communists of conscience, boldly speak out what you know to be the truth, say where you stand.

We will support whoever truly represents the interests of the people!

A Member of the Communist Party

DOCUMENT 50
_____

YANG XX
The Socialist Multiparty System and China

This wall poster went up at People's University on May 19, 1989.

THE author of this article is a student of the Chinese Department who thinks actively but lacks a high theoretical level. In this article he discusses the socialist multiparty system and presents his findings, in the hope of soliciting others' valuable opinions. I hope the mass of students and theoretical researchers will begin to argue about and discuss this issue.

The patent on the multiparty system would appear to be held by capitalist society, while with socialism it has had no such luck. This is a long-held theoretical prejudice; though there are democratic socialist countries like Sweden, we have never admitted that they practice socialism. But given that socialism with Chinese characteristics is possible, why can't there be socialism with Swedish characteristics? Now Hungary is discussing the question of a multiparty system, and Poland too is starting out on the path of political pluralization, yet GDR (East German) newspapers call this "revisionism." Meanwhile, other Communist countries (including the Soviet Union and China) still refuse to admit that a multiparty system is reasonable.

The reason Chinese leaders refuse to adopt a multiparty system is because it does not conform to national conditions. In China, only the Communist Party can direct the state. I don't deny that in China now the Communist Party is firmly in power, but I am puzzled why it bans other political parties (real independent political parties, not the [tame, government-controlled] democratic parties and groups of today). Here I will look briefly at the question of a socialist multiparty system.

Since a capitalist multiparty system is possible, can there be a socialist multiparty system? Can a socialist country put a multiparty system into practice? My answer is, yes it can. Political parties are a universal political form of modern civilized society: as long as different interest groups exist in society, there must be political parties to represent them. Since the interests of people in society differ, there should not be just one political party. This is the basis of the multiparty system.

The Communist Party has long regarded the people's interests under the socialist system as undifferentiated and monolithic. This is because it is seeking to justify its one-party dictatorship. In actual fact, however, the interests of the people of socialist countries vary, and there are different strata of interest. In China there are at least four strata: workers, peasants, merchants, and intellectuals. This is the "class" basis of the multiparty system. Although the Communist Party says it represents the interests of the whole people, it does not. It cannot truly represent the people. It is a party that has become divorced from the people, controlled from on high by bureaucrats. China still has no political organization that truly represents the interests of its own people.

The Communist Party is at present China's only political party (not including Taiwan; the democratic parties are merely a sort of branch of the Communist Party), so naturally it is the only party in power. It also has no opposition with which to compete, so its rule is not threatened, and it can do as it pleases, to the extent that corruption has become commonplace. As a party with private interests, it can afford to ignore the interests of the nation's people. Precisely because the Communist Party enjoys supreme privileges, it is above all frightened of losing those privileges. But under a multiparty system, the threat of losing power is ever present, so the Communist Party will not allow such a system. This is how the Communist Party really thinks. The argument that China is not suitable for a multiparty system is nothing but a subterfuge.

However, history invariably moves forward, and any foolish attempt to swim against its tide must eventually fail. In China, more than one political party must emerge to represent the interests of each stratum. China must move forward within a democratic and multiparty system.

Some people worry that if a multiparty system were implemented in socialist countries, socialism might change its nature. There are no grounds for such concern. In capitalist countries more than one political party exists, including socialist and communist parties. So why has the nature of these countries not changed? The reason is simple: people whose immediate interests are different can have similar ideological beliefs. In capitalist countries, the immediate interests of each party are different, but in regard to the development of capitalism, they are unanimous. Why can't socialism be like that?

Socialism is an ideology, not an interest. Under socialism the immediate interests of the people are not identical. Since more than one party can exist under capitalism, why can't different parties exist under socialism? The interests of the parties may differ, but they all believe in socialism.

Theoretically, socialist society is the most humane, the most democratic, the most prosperous, and the most reasonable of all societies. It subsumes the good points of all human forms of society (including capitalist society), yet casts off their corruption and other manifestations of backwardness. Although socialist society has its imperfections, the development of socialism is a continuous process toward perfection. So people wish to see this type of social system realized. Under a socialist multiparty system those who want to change the nature of society will get nowhere, for a multiparty system is itself a kind of equilibrium. To sum up, a socialist multiparty system is definitely feasible, not to say necessary.

Seventy years have passed since the first socialist state was founded in October 1917. However, all those countries practicing socialism have been left far behind by the capitalist countries. They are on the whole unprosperous and undemocratic. No wonder some people call socialism "social feudalism," that is, a step backward for human civilization.

Today most of the parties in power in socialist countries have begun to wake up. From the Soviet Union and Eastern Europe to China and Vietnam, a wave of reform has surged. This is an apt comment on socialism's failures. However, the Eastern European reforms have already been going on for two to three years, and China's for more than ten: and though they are not without their achievements, new problems (e.g., inflation and corruption) constantly emerge. Some people have become dispirited. They are bewildered, and are beginning to doubt socialism itself and to turn blindly to the worship of Western capitalist civilization.

Why does reform in the socialist countries produce so many annoying problems? Probably because it is not sufficiently thoroughgoing. China, the Soviet Union, and the countries of Eastern Europe have all reformed their economies, but the political system remains the same. So the sluggish pace of political reform acts as a brake on the reform of the economy, which in the long run is unable to develop smoothly. To overcome the widespread difficulties and dangers facing the socialist countries, we must reform the political system—there is no other way forward.

The key to reform is democracy. Without it, corruption cannot be eliminated and the economy cannot develop smoothly. But under a system of political centralism, democracy can only be granted by those in power—by the party in power. Although this party can grant democracy, it can also take democracy away. Democracy still lacks an effective safeguard. So the realization of democracy is wholly dependent on political pluralism, the best and the most reasonable form of which is the socialist multiparty system.

The superiority of a multiparty system is self-evident, yet some people may worry whether or not one can be realized in China. As long as the Communist Party maintains firm control of state power, it will never spontaneously let go of its privileges, so this worry is not unfounded.

But people hardly want things to carry on as they are. That goes for the Communist Party too. The corruption also perplexes the Communist Party, which finds it hard to take the necessary steps. People are becoming more and more dissatisfied, so the Communist Party too is becoming restless. This large-scale student movement has alerted it to the danger. So the conditions in China for realizing a socialist multiparty system are gradually ripening.

If we establish a new party now, even if we declare it to be socialist, the Communist Party will see it as a rival and close it down. It would inevitably be suppressed as an illegal or reactionary organization. So, are we impotent? No, there are still things we can do. For example, we can try to win over the existing democratic parties and make use of their legal status. Not everyone in them wants to be tightly controlled by the Communist Party. Let's promote their independence. With the people crying more and more loudly for democracy, some of these democratic parties may declare their independence. If so, the Communist Party will find it hard to declare them illegal. The worst it could do would be to cut off their funds. But if they relied on the support of the people and got help from patriotic Chinese abroad, funds would be no problem for them.

The comrades in the democratic parties also believe in socialism, they too are socialist parties. The emergence of an independent democratic party would pave the way to a socialist multiparty system in China. There is hope for democracy in China, there is hope for China's modernization!

May 12, 1989

I welcome anyone to probe further into this, or to argue against it.

DOCUMENT 51

A Letter to the People

Citizens of the Republic! Compatriots! Beloved Fellow-Students! Communist Party Members! Officers and Men of the People's Liberation Army!

Grief-stricken and indignant, we have for you an absolutely incontrovertible piece of news: General Secretary Zhao Ziyang has been recalled from office and Li Peng is in charge of the Politburo; moreover, Li Peng has decided to take harsh measures against the students tonight. This is roughly how it happened: On May 13 Zhao Ziyang proposed at a meeting of the Standing Committee of the Politburo the immediate rejection of the *People's Daily* editorial of April 26. On May 15 Zhao decided to go to Tian'anmen Square to make his personal views known to the public, but he was stopped by the Central Committee on grounds of Party discipline. On May 16, at a meeting that Deng Xiaoping also attended, Zhao made six proposals: (1) Reject the April 26 editorial; (2) he himself would take responsibility for the publication of that editorial; (3) the NPC should set up a special body to investigate "official speculation and profiteering" by the children of senior cadres, including his children; (4) make public the personal history and background of every cadre above the rank of vice-minister; (5) make public the income and welfare perks of all senior cadres; and (6) abolish the special supplies and other perks available to senior cadres. These proposals were rejected. On May 17 a plenary session of the Politburo narrowly decided that Zhao should step down and Li Peng should take over in the Politburo. Martial law was imminent. Suddenly the darkness that China knew after the suppression of the April 5 movement of 1976 was again about to descend.

But times change. History can never repeat itself exactly. According to reports, Wan Li resolutely supported Zhao and called a meeting of the Vice Chairmen of the NPC, which decided unanimously to reject this decision of the Politburo. Li Peng then threatened Wan with Party discipline. According to another reliable report, the Structural Reform Commission and nine other ministries or commissions have already decided to stage sit-ins and go on hunger strike. In view of the seriousness of these developments, we issue the following urgent calls to all sectors of the population:

(i) under no conditions resist violently or shed blood;

(ii) stage a national strike of workers, students, teachers, and traders;

(iii) the People's Liberation Army is made up of the sons and brothers of the people: we should not slaughter one another.

We fervently demand:

(a) an immediate meeting of the NPC to dismiss Li Peng;

(b) an immediate special National Congress of the Chinese Communist Party to decide on the election of a General Secretary and to put an end to the practice of "holding court from behind a screen" and to gerontocratic politics.

Citizens! Compatriots! Dear students! The Chinese nation is yet again in crisis, the Republic and the Chinese Communist Party face a life-and-death choice. Let us act at once! Let us resist resolutely by non-violent means!

Some Cadres in Central State Organizations
May 19, 1989

DOCUMENT 52

Preparatory Program of the Autonomous Federation of Workers of the Capital

SINCE mid-April, in the patriotic and democratic movement led by the students, most Chinese workers have already voiced their ardent democratic wish to take part in political affairs. At the same time they have recognized that they lack an organization to represent their aspirations. So in our view there is a need for an autonomous organization that speaks and acts for the workers. To that end we are preparing to set up an autonomous federation of workers of the capital. We propose the following program for it.

1. This organization should be a completely independent, autonomous, and democratically constituted body in which workers participate of their own free will. It should not be under the control of any other body, and it should coexist on the basis of equality with other mass organizations.

2. The fundamental aim of this organization should be to base its political and economic proposals in the aspirations of the great majority of workers, and not simply to act as a welfare organization.

3. It should assume the function of supervising the Chinese Communist Party.

4. In public and collective enterprises it should have the right to take all legal and effective steps to supervise its lawful representatives and to guarantee that the workers are the true masters of these enterprises; in other (kinds of) enterprise it should ensure workers' rights and interests by negotiating with the bosses or by adopting other legal measures.

5. This organization should, within the confines of the Constitution and the law, guarantee all its members' legal rights.

Preparatory Committee of the Autonomous Federation
of the Workers of the Capital
May 21, 1989

DOCUMENT 53

Workers' Declaration

THE working class is the most advanced class. We must be the main force in the democratic movement.

(According to the Constitution) the Chinese People's Republic is led by the working class. We have the right to chase away all despots.

Workers know better than anyone the role of knowledge and technology in production. So we will never permit anyone to harm the students, who are nurtured by the people.

To destroy dictatorship and autocracy and to promote the country's democratization is a duty that we must not shirk.

The source of our strength is unity; firm conviction is the source of our success.

In the democracy movement, "we have nothing to lose but our chains, and a world to gain." [A quotation from the *Communist Manifesto*, 1848.]

Preparatory Committee of the Autonomous Federation
of the Workers of the Capital
May 21, 1989

DOCUMENT 54
_____

Open Letter to the Students from an Army Veteran

Beloved Students, Townspeople:

As an army veteran, I greet you! Over the past weeks, I have silently watched your struggle. I want to remind you: you have already won a string of unimaginable victories! I cannot publicly stand up for you, but I do want to say a few things to you.

(1) Strategy

There is no way that a small number of troops can dispose of hundreds of thousands of people in Tian'anmen Square. Martial law has already been in place for a couple of days, but no action has been taken against the Square because there are too few soldiers or police in the city. What's more, soldiers are educated differently from police. It would be hard for them to point their rifles at the people. There is no way that they could handle ten million Beijing citizens united by a common hatred.

(2) Tactics

(i) Road intersections: It is marvelous and quite unprecedented for the masses spontaneously to intercept military vehicles in the way they have. Under no circumstances retreat, even if you hear that one or two other detachments have already advanced from elsewhere. For one or two detachments can achieve nothing by themselves. There is no way that they could carry out operations on the Square or enforce martial law and military control. So if you hold out at the intersections, victory is yours. Every intersection needs a stable system of command. If things are unorganized, this must be changed.

(ii) Breaking troops into pockets: This is an old military trick that the people can use against its main practitioners. If you are fully prepared, let two-thirds of the troops pass through your blockade and hold one-third back. Do the same again at the next intersection. In this way you will soon have broken the head of an organic army or division from its tail, so that its various parts can no longer act in unison. At that point, the troops' morale and combat strength will have been broken.

(iii) Firing rifles and tear gas: To do this into a crowd of more than one hundred thousand will create chaos and many casualties. You must warn army leaders that whoever gives the order to do so will be tried by a military tribunal and sentenced to death. Even if Beijing can be brought temporarily under control by massacring the people, can the same be done in dozens of other large cities? We have too few troops for that.

(iv) We must trust in the basic quality of the people's army and do painstaking ideological work among them. Don't just tell them to keep out of the city: tell them to turn their guns round and stand on the side of the people.

I wish the people of Beijing victory!

An army veteran, May 22, 1989

DOCUMENT 55

Smart Thieves' Voice

This letter, sent to *Beidazhi sheng* (Voice of Beijing University), a radio station founded by the Beijing Students' Autonomous Federation, was broadcast on the night of May 24, 1989. During the democracy movement there was a widely remarked improvement in social morale and behavior that the letter graphically illustrates. Thieves at Xidan Market in Central Beijing went on strike for ten days and instead worked hard at blocking military vehicles.

Townspeople, Students:
You have been hard at it and must be exhausted! We are a gang of thieves, but we are going on thieves' strike in your support!

Townspeople, don't worry, go ahead and support the students. That bastard Li Peng is bound to fall, he's a crook. We're no good at talking, we'll leave the students to do that.

Smart Thieves' Gang

DOCUMENT 56

Provisional Statutes of the Autonomous Federation of Workers of the Capital

ARTICLE 1: MEMBERSHIP

All workers and employees, active or retired, and all labor unions and autonomous labor unions belonging to enterprises or other units in our city that support our aims and tasks may register to join our organization. Individual workers and employees who are members and collective members (labor unions and autonomous labor unions) have the right to give up their membership of our organization. Members must pay their dues according to the regulations.

ARTICLE 2: OATH

Members must abide by the following oath: "I will freely observe the state's Constitution and laws and the discipline of this organization, and I will work tirelessly and determinedly to defend all the interests of the workers."

ARTICLE 3: CONGRESS

1. The congress of this organization is sovereign; it must be regularly convoked by the executive. If the standing affairs committee or one-fifth of the membership so propose, the executive shall convoke an emergency congress.

2. Our statutes and any amendments to them require the support of two-thirds of the members.

3. Members of the executive must be proposed by ten members and must receive the votes of at least half of the membership of the federation.

4. Members of the executive can be recalled if a proposal is made by ten members and supported by at least half of the membership.

5. If ten members sign a motion it must be put to congress by the president for discussion and decision.

ARTICLE 4: STANDING COMMITTEE

The standing committee is made up of representatives of labor unions and autonomous labor unions from enterprises and other units that participate in our organization. Its organization and powers are stipulated in the statutes governing the standing committee.

Article 5: The Executive

1. The executive is constituted by between five and seven members elected by the congress.

2. The executive elects a chairperson and two vice chairpersons. The chairperson chairs and convokes meetings of the executive; the vice chairpersons help the chairperson, and act as chairperson when the chairperson is absent.

3. The executive executes resolutions of the congress and of the standing committee and attends to day-to-day affairs. Resolutions of the executive must be arrived at according to the principle of subordination of the minority to the majority.

4. When necessary the executive can set up this or that administrative organ.

May 28, 1989

DOCUMENT 57

Lin Xiling

Statement

On June 7, 1989, Lin Xiling (see Document 10) addressed a rally in Paris in solidarity with Chinese workers and students. These are excerpts from her speech.

At the root of the recent events in China is the discontent of the students and workers with the ruling bureaucracy. The corruption is unbearable. The great bulk of the workers receive extremely low wages, while state functionaries are paid very highly in addition to their hidden privileges. The root cause of the current revolution is not unlike that of the 1949 revolution. It is a revolution against the oppressive sectors of society.

The current Chinese leaders are attempting to open the road to capitalism. There is no democracy, no freedom. Some people in France say, "It is not yet capitalism." For my part, I think there is too much capitalism. What the workers and students are doing in China is what you did in 1789—the revolution.

The demonstrations were peaceful. The brutal response by the government is what compels us to make a revolution. Shame on the Chinese government, which is an enemy not only of the Chinese people but of people throughout the world. We hope that you will aid us in the struggle against this regime. Long live internationalism!

DOCUMENT 58

WANG FANXI
Statement

This statement by Wang Fanxi (see Documents 14 and 20), an exiled leader of the Chinese Trotskyists, was read out at a meeting of Chinese students in Leeds, England, shortly after the June 4 massacre. It was broadcast on Independent Television's Channel Four.

TO MY deep regret, poor health prevents me from attending your meeting today. But I will add my voice to the universal protest against the abominable crime committed by the authorities in Tian'anmen Square.

I was an early member of the Chinese Communist Party. I joined it in 1925 and was expelled in 1930 because I disagreed with and opposed policies dictated by Stalin from Moscow and carried out by his Chinese followers. Among those expelled was Chen Duxiu, founder of the Chinese Communist Party and inventor in 1919 of the slogan "Science and Democracy."

Outside the Party I continued my activities as a socialist and I remain such, though I am now too old to do anything and am living in retirement.

Looking back, I won't say that the Chinese Communist Party under Mao and his followers has never done anything good for China. That would be untrue. Over the last fifty years or so the Party has done many good things alongside a lot of very bad things. The recent massacre in Beijing is the gravest crime they have ever committed.

We must oppose the regime, raise our voice in protest against it, fight against it, and call for its replacement. Such a brutal regime must be replaced!

The question is, how and by what should it be replaced? Some people accuse the students of conspiring to restore capitalism to China. I don't believe it. What they want is socialism with democracy. That's what I want too. If capitalism were restored, China—especially its toiling people—would be even worse off than today and would probably turn into a neo-colony.

June 9, 1989

DOCUMENT 59

An Eyewitness
The Massacre in Tian'anmen Square

This eyewitness account of the Tian'anmen Square massacre appeared in *Wenhuibao*, one of Hong Kong's two pro-Beijing, pro-Communist dailies, so it deserves to be taken seriously. The editor of this newspaper, Li Zisong, was a member at the time of Beijing's NPC. In the past he had toed the Beijing line, but the massacre was too much for him to stomach, so he and his newspaper went independent. (Now it is back under Beijing's control, Li and others having left to found a new publication, *Dangdai*.) This account of the massacre was in part corroborated by some reports but is at odds with others. Several Western journalists present during the students' withdrawal say that there was no mass slaughter in the Square itself, though a few did die there and perhaps as many as a thousand were massacred along nearby approach roads. The extent and location of the massacre is a matter for research: this eyewitness account is an important document of the incident, though not necessarily true in all respects and almost certainly exaggerated by the author's grief, shock, and anger. It was edited for *Wenhuibao* by Zhao Hanqing on the basis of a telephone call from Beijing on June 4.

I AM a student at Qinghua University. I am twenty years old. I spent last night sitting on the steps of the Monument to the Heroes of the People. I witnessed from start to finish the shooting and suppression by the army of students and citizens.

Many of my fellow students have already been shot dead. My clothes are still stained with their blood. As a lucky survivor and an eyewitness of the events, I want to tell peace-loving and good people across the world about the killing.

Frankly speaking, we knew early on in the evening that the troops intended to suppress us. Someone whose status I can't reveal phoned us at four o'clock in the afternoon. (The call was to a neighborhood phone station in an alley near the Square. The person in charge of the phone fetched us to receive it.) The caller told us that the Square was about to be invaded and cleared. We went onto the alert. After a discussion we took some measures. We did our best to alleviate contradictions and avoid a bloodbath.

We had twenty-three submachine guns and some incendiary bombs that we'd snatched from soldiers during the previous two days. The "Autonomous Students' Union" called a meeting and decided to return these weapons forthwith to the martial law troops to show that we intended to "promote democracy by non-violent means." Last night on the rostrum at Tian'anmen Square beneath the portrait of Chairman Mao we liaised with troops about this, but an officer said that he was under higher orders not to accept the weapons. So the negotiations failed. At around one o'clock in the morning, when things had become really critical, we destroyed the guns and dismantled the bombs. We poured away the petrol so that it wouldn't fall into the wrong hands and the authorities couldn't point to it as "proof" that we were out to kill soldiers.

After that the Union told everyone in the Square that the situation was extremely grave, that bloodshed seemed inevitable, and that they wanted students and citizens to leave the Square. But there were still forty to fifty thousand students and about one hundred thousand citizens determined not to go. I too decided not to go.

The mood was incredibly tense. This was the first time we'd ever experienced such danger. I'd be lying if I said we weren't afraid, but everyone was psychologically braced and tempered. (Some students, of course, didn't believe that the troops would actually shoot to kill.) In a word, we were imbued with a lofty sense of mission. We were prepared to sacrifice ourselves for China's democracy and progress. That was something worth doing.

After midnight, after two armored cars had sped down each side of the Square from the Front Gate, the situation became increasingly serious. Official loudspeakers repeatedly blared out "Notices." Dense lines of steel-helmeted troops ringed the Square. Despite the darkness, you could clearly see the machine guns mounted on top of the History Museum. There was not the slightest attempt to hide them.

We students crowded round the Monument to the Heroes of the People. I carefully estimated the crowd. Roughly two-thirds were men, one-third were women. About 30 percent from universities and colleges in Beijing. Most were students from other cities.

At four o'clock sharp, just before daybreak, the lights in the Square suddenly went out. The loudspeakers broadcast another order to "clear the Square." I suddenly had a tight feeling in my stomach. There was only one thought in my head: the time has come, the time has come.

The hunger striker Hou Dejian [a Taiwan pop singer who had been working on the mainland] and some other people negotiated with the troops and agreed to get the students to leave peacefully. But just as they were about to go, at 4:40 A.M., a cluster of red signal flares rose into the sky above the Square and the lights suddenly went back on again. I saw that the front of the Square was packed with troops. A detachment of soldiers came running from the east entrance of the Great Hall of the People. They were dressed in camouflage. They were carrying light machine guns. They were wearing steel helmets and gas masks. (By the way, at around six o'clock on the afternoon of the 3rd, while we were negotiating with officers of a regiment at the west entrance to the Great Hall of the

People, their commander told us that they were simply relief troops, and that when the time came it would probably be Sichuan troops that confronted us. This commander guaranteed that he wouldn't open fire on the students. Maybe the troops rushing out now were Sichuan troops.)

As soon as these troops had stormed out, they lined up a dozen or so machine guns in front of the Monument to the Heroes of the People. The machine gunners lay down on their stomachs. Their guns pointed toward the Monument. The rostrum was behind them. When all the guns were properly lined up, a great mass of soldiers and armed police wielding electric prods, rubber truncheons, and some special weapons of a sort I'd never seen before suddenly rushed us. We were sitting quietly. There were two differences between the troops and the armed police: their uniforms were different, and so were their helmets. The police's helmets were bigger than the troops' and had steel flaps going down over the ears. The soldiers and the policemen started flailing their clubs violently about us. They split our ranks down the middle and opened up a path to the Monument. They stormed up to its third tier. I saw forty or fifty students suddenly spurt blood. Armored troop carriers and an even greater number of troops that had been waiting in the Square joined the siege. The troop carriers formed a solid blockade except for a gap left open on the museum side.

The troops and policemen who had stormed the Monument smashed our loudspeaker installations, our printing equipment, and our supply of soda water. Then they beat and threw down the steps the students still occupying the third tier. We'd stayed put all along, holding hands and singing the *Internationale*. We'd been shouting, "The people's army won't attack the people!" The students packing the third tier had no choice but to retreat under the blows and kicks of such a large body of men.

While this was going on, the sound of machine guns started up. Some troops were kneeling down and firing. Their bullets whizzed above our heads. The troops lying on their stomachs shot up into the students' chests and faces. We had no choice but to retreat back up onto the Monument. When we reached it, the machine guns stopped. But the troops on the Monument beat us back down again. As soon as we had been beaten down, the machine guns started up again.

The dare-to-die brigade of workers and citizens grabbed anything that would serve as a weapon—bottles, pieces of wood—and rushed toward the troops to resist them. The Union gave the order to retreat to positions outside the Square. It was still not yet five o'clock.

A great crowd of students rushed toward the gap in the line of troop carriers. The heartless drivers closed the gap. Thirty-odd carriers drove into the crowd. Some people were crushed to death. Even the flagpole in front of the Monument was snapped off. The whole Square was in massive chaos. I'd never thought my fellow students could be so brave. Some started to push at the troop carriers. They were mowed down. Others clambered over their corpses and pushed too. Finally they managed to push one or two carriers aside and open up a gap. I and three thousand other students rushed through under a hail of fire. We ran across to the entrance to the History Museum. There were just over a thousand of us left.

There were large numbers of citizens in front of the Museum. We joined up with them. Seeing how bad things were, we immediately ran off to the north in the direction of the Gate of Heavenly Peace. But we'd only gone a few steps when rifle fire broke out from a clump of bushes alongside the road. We saw no people—just the bursts of fire from the gunbarrels. So we turned and ran off south in the direction of the Front Gate.

I was running and weeping. I saw a second batch of students running off under machine-gun fire. I saw lots of people lying on their stomachs on the road that we were trying to escape along. We were all crying—running and crying. When we reached the Front Gate we were suddenly confronted by a batch of troops who came running toward us from the direction of the Gate. They came running out from the direction of Zhubao Market. They didn't open fire. They were armed with big wooden staves. They beat us furiously. A large crowd of citizens came pouring out of the Front Gate. They clashed violently with these troops. They protected us while we escaped in the direction of Beijing Railway Station. The troops pursued us. It was five o'clock. Dawn was breaking. The gunfire on the Square seemed to have died down a little. Later I met a fellow student at the International Red Cross. He told me that at five o'clock the last group to escape had broken out. The machine guns continued to rake the Square throughout the entire period, for twenty minutes or so.

I'll never forget another student from Qinghua, a man from Jiangsu, who was shot and wounded but still carried on running with us. He was determined not to give up. As we ran along he touched me on the shoulder and said, "Could you please support me for a bit?" I was already supporting two physically weak women students, one on each arm. I could do nothing for him. I put him down on the ground. The crowd trampled over him. There's no way he could have survived. Look, this is his blood on my back. Half his body was covered in blood.

I will never forget my fellow students being mowed down by machine guns. Others selflessly and with complete disregard for all danger dragged away the corpses and tended to the wounded. Women students took off garments to make bandages for people's wounds. Soon some were almost naked.

After we'd run off to the Railway Station, I and two other students went back to the Square. By then it was half past six. A great crowd of citizens surrounded the Front Gate. I followed them further into the Square until I got to the Mao Zedong Memorial Hall. Lines of armored troop carriers blocked the way. Troops formed a human wall. I went to the side of the road and climbed a tree. I could see soldiers on the Square putting the corpses of the students and citizens in plastic bags, one corpse to a bag. Then they piled them up under a big canvas.

I met a student from my department. He'd escaped in the second batch. He told me that a very large number of people had died. The troops still weren't letting ambulances of the International Red Cross enter the Square to help the wounded. I and this student hurried off at once to the International Red Cross First Aid Center at Peace Gate. We saw many casualties being taken there by trishaw. The doctors told me that an ambulance trying to get into the Square had been shot at and set on fire. I saw students there from the second, third, and fourth batches of escapees. They said that many students who had fallen to the ground wounded were still lying on the Square.

At around 7:20 A.M. I went back to the Square for a second time. I asked what was happening. I particularly questioned a group of a dozen or so elderly people. They said that corpses were lying in long rows on the pavement round the Square and that the troops were hanging up sheets of canvas so that the citizens could not see them. They said that lots of trucks had driven into the Square and taken away the wounded, they didn't know where to.

At about half past seven the troops on the Square suddenly launched gas canisters at these people. A large group of soldiers charged us. I ran back to the Railway Station. On the way I saw students from the first and second break-outs, all crying.

The Union assigned us Beijing students the job of escorting students from outside Beijing to the Railway Station. I took them to the waiting room. I was hoping to put them onto trains, but a railway official said none were running. There was nothing for it but to leave the station. We were besieged by a great crowd of citizens who wanted to take the students to their homes and hide them. They were sad. They were all crying. The people of Beijing are truly good, they are truly good.

How many died? I don't know. But I firmly believe that the day will come when the people get revenge.

Am I pessimistic? No, I'm not. I've seen the heart of the people, I've seen their true mettle, I've seen the hope of China. Some of my fellow students died, even more are bleeding from their wounded bodies. I am a lucky survivor. I know how I must live my life henceforth. I cannot forget my fellow students who have died. I know that upright people throughout the world will understand us and support us.

DOCUMENT 60

Chai Ling
Account of the Beijing Massacre

Chai Ling became famous as a leader of the Autonomous Union of University Students on Tian'anmen Square. In 1989 she escaped via Hong Kong to the USA, where she has been active in the democracy movement. This message, here slightly condensed, was smuggled out to Hong Kong's Christian Industrial Committee and broadcast on Hong Kong television on June 10, 1989.

IT IS four o'clock on the afternoon of June 8. My name is Chai Ling. I commanded the student headquarters in Tian'anmen Square. I am still alive. I think that I best qualified to say what happened in the Square between June 2 and June 4. It is my duty to tell the truth to everyone in China and abroad.

At about ten o'clock on the night of June 2 a police car ran over four pedestrians, three of whom died. Then some soldiers began distributing guns, uniforms, and other equipment to townspeople and students who stood in their way. We took these things to the Public Security Bureau and got receipts for them. At ten past two on the afternoon of June 3 crowds of soldiers and police at Liubukou and Xinhuamen started beating up students and civilians. Some students standing on top of vehicles began to chant, "The people's police love the people, they do not beat the people." A soldier ran out and kicked one of the students in the stomach. The soldier shouted, "Who the hell loves you!" and hit him on the head with a stick. The student fell to the ground.

Let me explain where we were. We had a broadcasting station in the Square that broadcast news about the hunger strike. We used it to direct students' actions in the Square. Of course there were other students there too, for example, Li Lu and Feng Congde. We constantly received reports of student and townspeople being beaten and injured.

Things got worse between eight and ten o'clock that evening. We received at least ten reports of attacks on people. At around seven we called a press conference for Chinese and foreign reporters, but few foreigners attended, probably because their hotels were under army control. We told the meeting that our only slogan was "Down with Li Peng's puppet regime."

At nine o'clock all the students in the Square stood up, raised their right hands, and vowed: "I hereby pledge, in the name of the democratization and prosperity of the motherland and in order to prevent its exploitation by a handful of plotters and the loss of 1.1 billion Chinese to white terror, to defend to the death Tian'anmen Square and the Republic.

Heads may fall, blood may flow, but the Square must not be lost. We will fight to the last young life."

At ten o'clock, the Square set up Democracy University, with deputy commander Zhang Boli as its president. Many people warmly applauded this step. Meanwhile, reports flooded in about the increasing tension. While people near the Goddess of Liberty statue at the north end of the Square were applauding the establishment of Democracy University, blood was flowing on East and West Chang'an Avenue. The butchers of the Twenty-Seventh Army used tanks, assault guns, and bayonets on anyone who shouted a slogan or threw a stone. Dead bodies lay in pools of blood. The clothes of the students who came to headquarters to tell us what was happening were stained with the blood of their fallen comrades.

Our aim had always been nonviolence. No few students, workers, and townspeople had come to tell us that it was time to meet force with force. Some male students were particularly incensed. We had to keep reminding people that our demonstration was peaceful and that the price of peace is sacrifice.

Hand in hand and shoulder to shoulder we walked toward the Monument to the heroes of the People singing the *Internationale*. There we sat down, to await death. We realized that we were caught up in a conflict of love against hate, not of force against force. We knew that if we were to give up nonviolence and try to arm ourselves against the machine gunners and tank drivers, the tragedy would be even greater. So we just sat there quietly, awaiting the moment of sacrifice. Headquarters began broadcasting the song "Descendants of the Dragon." We sang with tears in our eyes. We embraced each other and held hands, for we knew that the end had come. It was time to die for the nation.

There was a young fellow named Wang Li. He had written his will. I don't remember its exact wording, but I do remember him saying: "There was this insect. Whenever I moved my foot to crush it, it would freeze." He was only fifteen, but already he was thinking about death. Citizens of the Republic, do not forget the children who fought for you.

At around two or three o'clock the next morning, on June 4, we were forced to give up our headquarters under the Monument. I walked round the Monument to rally the students, who sat there quietly. They told me that they would sit there whatever happened, and that they would kill no one. I reminded them of an old story. "One billion ants lived on a mountain. One day the mountain caught fire and the ants had to leave. They massed in a giant ball and rolled to the bottom. Those on the outside died, but most survived. Fellow students, we are the outside layer. Only by dying can we ensure the survival of the Republic."

We sang the *Internationale* again and again. Finally the hunger strikers—Hou Dejian, Liu Xiaobo, Zhou Duo, and another—could stand it no longer. "Children," they said, "don't sacrifice yourselves." We were all extremely tired. They went to negotiate with the soldiers and found an officer who was in charge of the martial law command. They told him that we would evacuate the Square if the army guaranteed us safe passage. We consulted the students, and decided to leave. But as we were preparing to go, armed and helmeted soldiers stormed up to the third level of the Monument, thus breaking their word. They gave us no time to communicate our decision to the students. Our loudspeakers were destroyed. They even fired at us on the Monument, the Monument to the Heroes of the People. Most of us left, crying. Onlookers shouted at us not to cry, and we answered that we would be back, for the Square was ours.

We only discovered later that some people still had illusions in the government and the army. They thought that at worst they would be removed by force. Some were asleep in their tents. The tanks ground them to pieces. According to some people, two hundred students died. Others put the figure at four thousand. I don't know who is right. But I do know that at least twenty to thirty members of the autonomous workers' federation died, on the edge of the Square. According to reports, soldiers flattened the tents with tanks and armored personnel carriers, poured gasoline over the bodies, and set fire to them. They later washed the Square to remove evidence of the killings. Our Goddess of Liberty statue was also crushed.

Arm in arm, we walked round the Chairman Mao Memorial Hall toward the south. There we saw several thousand armed troops. We shouted that they were "dogs" and "fascists." Heading west, we saw large numbers of troops running toward the Square. Students and townspeople shouted at them, "Dogs, fascists, beasts!" But they continued to run as quickly as they could toward the Square.

As we passed Liubukou, where the first bloody battle had taken place on the afternoon of June 3, we from headquarters walked in the front line. There was debris and garbage everywhere. On Chang'an Avenue we saw fire-razed trucks, broken stones, and other evidence of fierce fighting, but no corpses. We later learned that while the fascists at the front were shooting the students, others were coming up from the rear to collect the dead and wounded and throw them onto buses and trishaws, so that the wounded died of suffocation. They did their best to cover up the atrocity.

We intended to go back to the Square, but bystanders told us not to. "Children," they said, "don't you realize they have guns? Don't return to the Square just to die." We then decided to go west from Xidan. On the way I saw a mother weeping. Her child was dead. We also saw the corpses of four townspeople. Everyone we met was crying. One told us, "Is that why I bought state bonds? So they could make bullets to kill children and innocents?" Later reports showed that they'd really staged a massacre. They'd fired rockets at houses along Chang'an Avenue, killing children and old people. What were their crimes? They had not even shouted slogans. A friend told me that he saw tanks crush to death a small girl who was waving her arms at them, and that two students he was holding hands with were shot dead, one after the other.

We met a woman looking for her son. She told us his name and said that he had been alive the day before. Is he still alive today? Wives were looking for husbands, teachers for students. Posters on public buildings were still calling for support for the "correct" policies of the Central Committee. We tore them down and burned them. The radio kept announcing that the troops had come to Beijing to "quell a handful of rioters and restore order in the capital." Were we rioters? Put your hand on your heart and think of us young students sitting together arm in arm around the Monument: were we "rioting" while we peacefully awaited our executioners? If the soldiers are animals, what do you call those who sit in front of the cameras and mouth lies? As we left the Square a tank charged after us firing teargas and knocking down students and grinding them to pieces. Who were the "rioters"?

We walked on, with masks over our faces because of the teargas. How can we bring back those who were sacrificed? They are gone forever.

Our return to Beijing University spelled the end of the nonviolent protest that we had started on May 13 as a hunger strike and later changed into a sit-in. Later we heard that at ten o'clock on the evening of June 3 Li Peng had issued three orders: the troops could shoot, army vehicles could drive into the Square at full speed and take it before dawn on June 4, and leaders and organizers of the movement should be killed.

Friends, this frenzied government of puppets is still moving troops into Beijing and is still ruling China. Massacres are still going on in Beijing and throughout China. But the night is darkest just before the dawn. From this frenzied fascist crackdown a real people's republic will be born. This is a critical moment for the Chinese nation. Compatriots, citizens of conscience, awake! Final victory will be yours. Yang Shangkun, Li Peng, Wang Zhen, Bo Yibo—the days of your regime are numbered. Down with the fascists! Down with military rule! Victory to the people! Long live the Republic!

DOCUMENT 61

Y ANG L IAN
The Square

IN THIS confession, you are distanced from June, distanced from that person. Each person lives by informing on himself, so that person with the same body and face as yours did not come out of the gray brick building where you live, pause at the end of the alley, look about, and then turn into the road where you often stroll. Walk. Subway station, flower stalls, rusty iron railings, a row of locust saplings, the ground covered with green specks and brilliant white flowers. In this season you should just stand there smelling the fragrance of the flowers. Behind all this, the sky becomes more and more blue. You are used to walking slowly along this road, on your way to the Square.

But you were not in the Square. In the confessions, everyone testified that they were not there. In June there was no one in the Square.

You must write about someone wearing your face and name who did not leave the house. You are to find evidence to verify that your emotions had been paralyzed long ago and that your thinking had never gone past the brim of your hat; and moreover that your heart is locked behind sets of window frames, buttons, and rib bones so that it is soundproof and impregnable to aerial attack.

It is absolutely certain that this person had not been running about in the Square, slipped over, called for help, or heard the dull thud of bullets striking bodies. Black night was hacked open and trembled with searing wounds. You crawled over half of a mangled face, a single eye was staring at you, transforming you with its stare into a black and red marsh. It is absolutely certain that no one had lived in, crowded together in, nor died here. In June the Square did not exist. Summer and the strings of locust flowers are all hallucination.

This other person is as silent as a word, does not know the Square, and keeps walking along the wall, the wall streaked with ash and dirt. In the front, at the back, and on both sides four rows of teeth bite into you. A big mouth spits you out and you fall asleep. But you still dream; in bed you risk dangers in safety and caressed by flies you awaken. Everyone testifies: day and night you stay in this little courtyard, snail-like you say nothing, have a table against the door. This small house built of skeletons does not open windows even in spring. You are afraid of the wind and so always pull your skin tightly around yourself.

So you too are an accomplice in slaughtering the month of June. You had to write and you wrote: This year there was no June. The Square did not exist in June.

By getting another sheet of paper, the screams recede into the distance. By writing yourself up as someone else, you are able to go on living. As you write each stroke, with your own hand, you erase one month from your life. You become light, feel empty inside; that person has gone. The Square of before the wrong words were written everywhere has already been torn to bits. Scraps of paper fly everywhere. Flutter down. Locust trees have always had white leaves.

December 2, 1989

DOCUMENT 62

Open Letter to the Chinese Communist Party

This letter, sent from Paris on the anniversary of the June 4 massacre, was published in *Chaoliu* (Hong Kong). It is here slightly abridged.

TODAY is June 4, 1990, and we are exiled in France. This day last year many of our fellow students died for their convictions, while your prestige reached its lowest point since you came to power.

Originally we hoped for dialogue with you, but by committing the June 4 massacre you pushed us into a position of fundamental antagonism. China's economy is worse off than it was before June 4. The policy of "improving the economic environment and rectifying the economic order" has led to stagnation, and the living standards of the people have steadily declined. Outward appearances of calm and stability have been unable to dispel the people's hostility to the government. Corruption and privilege, which the students opposed, have not been eradicated but have even grown. The government has had to resort to antiquated propaganda like the "campaign to learn from Lei Feng" as a means of thought control and to the greatest measure of intimidation since the founding of the PRC in order to maintain temporary peace and security. The people, having lost confidence in government and state, try by every means possible to flee the country. The crises that led to the 1989 people's movement, crises that the government could not resolve, and the problems raised by the students in their dialogue with the government last year continue to persist and have reached ominous proportions. Even so, in recent months you have adopted some new attitudes, and we have particularly followed your policy on scholars and students.

On May 10 Jiang Zemin declared that you are no longer arresting students who participated in last year's movement. Recently you freed Dai Qing and others—211 intellectuals who took part in the movement—and said that of the 331 persons still under investigation, only 42 are students. According to Li Ruihuan, "Generally our policy toward those in exile is to try to win them back and restore solidarity, and to encourage them to return. We will not let the door shut; there shall be a home for them to return to." As students in foreign exile, far away from our parents, this is a problem that constantly concerns us.

Although these measures of relaxation are mainly meant to please the West and to dispel hostile feelings among the Chinese people, we note them with great interest. Before discussing the problem of "returning home," we must ask where we agree and where we disagree with this government. If we cannot reconcile ourselves with it and with society, history may decree a further spell of exile. But neither you nor we want calamity to befall our country. We believe that the overwhelming majority of Party members still want China to progress and free itself from poverty.

Where we differ is that we no longer place our hopes in a centralized system of one-party dictatorship, nor in the current socialist system. This system has been the main obstacle to the rise of the Chinese nation. On this point we have gone much further during our year in exile. The 1989 people's movement generally hoped that the Communist Party would institute its own reform, but the massacre showed that ending one-party rule is China's only way forward. We are not saying "down with the Communist Party," but we oppose its dictatorship and those who insist on keeping it.

Today the world trend is identical with China's historical trend. Those who now want China to stay independent of the world trend should think again; we hope that China will never experience another utopian tragedy.

Whether we seek common ground or oppose one another absolutely will be determined by the future development of Chinese politics. However, we fervently hope that the conditions will soon mature for our "return home." They are as follows:

1. Since some of you welcome our homecoming and rule out a "settlement of accounts," legally we should no longer count as criminals. So are we still "counterrevolutionaries" and "rioters"? If we can return as non-criminals, then the students still locked up in jail are also non-criminals, and they should be freed. So before we return home, you must release all the students, including Wang Dan, Guo Haifeng, and Yang Tao, jailed in connection with the 1989 movement. Otherwise we will neither trust you nor feel safe.

2. If we return, will the organizations we set up at Beijing University and at various provincial universities still be illegal? We shall only return to China after the autonomous federations have been reevaluated and their "illegal status" rescinded.

3. Deng Xiaoping told Schmidt that "the main cause of the political incident of 1989 was bad behavior at all levels of the Party; the widespread incidence of corruption within the Party caused general dissatisfaction among the people." Here Deng no longer speaks of the students as the main problem but of the movement's social causes. There is a certain connection here with the objectives that we ourselves pursued. The difference now is that we view things more broadly. We believe that the critical cause of the general discontent was the one-party system. A solution that looks merely at corruption in the Party is perfunctory and not radical. Hence the failure of Li Peng's economic retrenchment over the last two years. We hope that you will rethink the lessons of this and reconsider the causes of the social and economic crisis.

Recently an official said that retrenchment has been halted and that a price reform will be instituted, as advocated by Zhao Ziyang; we welcome this. On the student question, we hope that you will reconsider the origins of the student movement and its value for China's future. In a report, Jiang Zemin emphasized the role of young intellectuals in the state, saying: "Youth is that part of society that shows greatest vitality; . . . the twenty-first century will be your century." For our part, we will truly activate the "vitality" of all intellectuals and young students and encourage their trust in the state. At present, many think only of getting abroad. So the main thing is to reconsider and reassess the 1989 people's movement.

Yang Hao, Liu Wei, Wuer Kaixi, Wang Longmeng,
Peng Ming, Fang Li, and Lei Kai

CHAPTER SIX

THE INTELLECTUALS' CRITIQUE

DOCUMENT 63

Su Shaozhi
Proposals for Reform of the Political Structure, 1986

Su Shaozhi was until early 1987 director of the Institute of Marxism-Leninism-Mao Zedong Thought at the Chinese Academy of Social Sciences. He strove to loosen up and renew Chinese Marxism and was interested in the relevance for China of the political experiments in Eastern Europe in the 1980s. He left China shortly after the June 4 massacre. Selections of Su's writings are available in English in Su Shaozhi, *Democratization and Reform* and *Marxism and Reform in China* (Nottingham: Spokesman, 1988 and 1993).

THE ongoing economic structural reform urgently calls for the simultaneous reform of the political structure and the regeneration of ideology.

We began to reform the economic structure after the Third Plenary Session of the Eleventh Central Committee. The reform has been carried out step by step and is successful. But the economic reform has not been combined with political, social, and cultural reforms. The new economic system and the old one are at present in a state of equilibrium and deadlock. The measures adopted to tackle problems that have cropped up in the course of the reform are basically those of the old system. The political structure and ideology are unprepared and offer no guarantee for in-depth reform. The economic reform is increasingly becoming more than an "economic" question. It is being obstructed by political, social, and psychological factors.

Modernization is not limited to the "four modernizations," which modernize the material world. Modernization should include modernization of the political structure, social and cultural modernization, and ideological modernization. True modernization means the simultaneous modernization of the structured and the man himself. China needs modernization, but not only the "four modernizations."

The influence of the vestiges of feudal autocracy in the ideological and political fields is the principal obstruction to China's reform and modernization today.

China is a country with a history of two thousand years of feudal autocracy. For a long time China was a unified feudal autocratic empire. The brief existence of the Republic of China on the mainland and its particular nature failed to weaken feudal autocracy. After liberation, vestiges of feudal autocracy still remained to a considerable extent in China. The task of eliminating the influence of the remnants of feudal autocracy in the ideological and political fields has not been completed.

Privileges are a concentrated expression of feudal autocracy in society today. The symptoms of privileges in political and social life are the so-called "unhealthy practices." Bureaucracy engaging in trade through privileges, appointing people by favoritism, establishing a network of connections, and nepotism are all connected with privileges. "Unhealthy practices" are by no means the outcome of opening to the outside world; the latter is at worst only one of the external causes of the former. Privileges in the ideological and cultural fields are expressed as cultural despotism. "Putting labels on people," "swinging the big stick," "making things hard for somebody by abusing one's power," "stirring up political storms," are all not unconnected with privileges.

Feudal autocracy gives birth to privileges. The existence of privileges has lowered the prestige of the Party in power, hurt the reputation of Marxism, and quenched the enthusiasm of the masses for construction and reform.

The adverse impact of feudal autocracy proves that it is necessary to reappraise the question of the stages of social development in China today.

Socialist revolution can occur and win victory before the social productive forces have reached very high levels of development, but a socialist society cannot be built in its complete form before these forces have reached a certain basic level. Practice in China has forcefully proven this thesis. If New Democracy had been more fully developed and the transformation of the means of production had been carried out in more steady steps, the situation would have been different today. The reform in ownership and the emergence of the various sectors of the economy at the present stage show that it is not unreasonable to say that we are "making up for lost lessons." China is now at the initial stage of socialism, or "the early stage of socialism" as the Yugoslav theoretician Aleksandar Grlickov put it. Many socialist countries, including the Soviet Union, are reassessing the stages of social development. This is an objective stand, seeking truth from facts. It has profound significance for both methodology and practice.

The mentality of "peasant socialism" should be studied and criticized. It is necessary to study the objectives of China's traditional peasant revolutions, the causes of their rise, and their influence today. It is also necessary to recall and examine the progressive aspect as well as the backward and conservative aspect of the slogans, demands, and programs raised during the period of the New Democratic Revolution and the period of socialist revolution (including the Cultural Revolution). History cannot be separated from the present, and today is linked with tomorrow. It is the responsibility of the theoreticians to discover the connecting links so as to define clear objectives for the political reform.

An in-depth study would be worthwhile, on why things imported from abroad have become distorted in China under the influence of feudal autocracy. For example, the principle of distribution according to work and the bonus system are in themselves good things aimed at encouraging the enthusiasm of producers for work. But there is now the phenomenon of "indiscriminate distribution of bonuses." Bonuses are in essence part of surplus products; increased bonuses can only come from increased production. There should not be any "indiscriminate distribution."

For another example, the principle of commodity production has been introduced in the economic reform to shatter the ossified structure of over-concentration of power. It also is a good thing. But under feudalistic influences, there appeared the phenomenon of the children of senior cadres engaging in trade. This is no ordinary trade, but trade by the privileged. There is the danger of the formation of "capital of the privileged." This again is a distortion.

Again, the way Mao Zedong did things in the socialist period, particularly the theory of "continuous revolution under the dictatorship of the proletariat" he put forward in his later years, and the practice of the Cultural Revolution are also a kind of distortion. These things were a distortion of Marxism and of the image of socialism.

This distortion is not unconnected with feudal autocratic ideas. Finding out facts about distortion, finding out how things are distorted, and analyzing the reasons for distortion are today important topics for political and cultural discussion.

The Stalinist mode and its traditions is another obstinate malady that exists side by side with feudal autocratic ideas. When Stalin talked about dictatorship, he emphasized only the aspect of suppression and gave no attention to or even negated its democratic aspect. He maintained that the class struggle in socialist society would steadily intensify as socialist construction gained victory. He placed himself at the apex of power, encouraged the cult of the individual, and used his power indiscriminately. He crudely intervened in ideological and cultural life, acting as the "supreme authority" and umpire in historiography, linguistics, and economics. He ossified and turned into dogmas the doctrines of Marx and Lenin which are endowed with the spirit of criticism. Stalin's practice and the way he dealt with facts and theories were a distorted form of Marxism, a distortion resulting from the influence of the autocratic ideas and residues of the Russian tsars.

We began to be deeply influenced by Stalin's theories and practice as early as the 1930s. In China's political reform it is necessary to eradicate not only the pernicious feudal autocratic influence, but also the influence of some of Stalin's theories and practices.

"Democratic centralism" as a concept should be discussed. Marx made no mention of it. The concept was put forward by Lenin under the conditions of the revolution in Russia. It was later distorted with the emphasis laid solely on centralism. "Democracy" under the guidance of centralism means that it is not the people who are making decisions, but someone else making decisions for them. The term translated as "democratic centralism" should be translated simply as "democratic system" to distinguish it from bureaucratic centralism, feudal centralism, and capitalist centralism. Our centralism must be built on the basis of democracy.

There is a problem of understanding to be solved. Who is the subject force in a socialist society? The people or the leaders? The leaders are not clear about this question, nor the masses or even ourselves. Such ideals of a feudal society as "a sagacious emperor and righteous ministers" and "upright lords" often manifest themselves in our discussions and thinking today. Some people have been elected people's deputies. But from their speeches we can see that they often do not think first of all that they are responsible to the people. Instead, they express thanks for the "trust" their superiors have placed in them or for the "concern" of their leaders for them. Such phrases as the promise by those above to "listen attentively" to the opinions of those below, or talk of "promoting" cadres, and people's deputies "studying" reports on the work of the government, are all indications of the same problem.

Democratization is our political ideal; it should be guaranteed by our political system and elucidated in our political philosophy and political culture. Only the interests of the people are above all else.

Party leadership means leadership in the political line, principles, and policies. It does not mean the Party running everything.

First of all, the Party and the government should not be combined into one, turning government authorities into Party authorities. The division of work between the Party and the government should be made specific. [See exactly the same point made thirty years previously by Huang Shaohong in Document 7.] For example, "the system of the factory director taking responsibility," as it has been clearly stated, is different both in reality and in concept from "the system of division of labor with the factory director taking responsibility under the leadership of the Party committee."

Second, the relationship between the Party and the law should be made clear. Which comes first? The law or the Party? There can be only one first. It cannot be a case of both the law and the Party coming first. The Constitution and the laws are formulated by the people's deputies. The Party is to serve the people. Therefore, the Party should conduct its activities within the bounds of the law and the Constitution. Nobody is permitted to overstep the Constitution and the laws. It is therefore self-evident that the legislative organs and judicial organs should be independent. This is a topic in the reform of the political structure.

Third, the relationship between the Party and the mass organizations is not one between the "prime mover" and the "conveyor belt." The mass organizations are links between the Party and the masses. But "links" are not "conveyor belts." They are not part of the machine. They can only be understood as bridges between the Party and the masses, otherwise the mass organizations will become part of the Party organization. The mass organizations should represent the interests of their masses and should have independent rights. The relationship between the Party and the mass organizations should be one of mutual cooperation, supervision, coordination, and promotion.

Life in a socialist society should not be one of monotony and great uniformity, but varied, rich, and colorful. There are many different strata, circles, and groups. We should not only see the traditional differences between the working class and the peasantry, but also see the different strata, circles, and groups which have become increasingly distinct and active since the economic reform.

Economic interests in a socialist society are also many and varied. Two men doing the same work may have different interests and different incomes as a result of differences in skill and physical family conditions. As this is true for individuals, it goes without saying that the same is true for classes, strata, interest groups, and social groups. We acknowledge that the common and long-term interests of the whole people are the same; we also acknowledge that the immediate and specific interests of the different groups of people are not the same. it is necessary to understand, care for, and coordinate the different interests.

Political interests in a socialist society are also many and varied. The different economic interests are manifested in politics—through the people's congresses, the mass media, and decisions and laws, leading to diversification in political interests.

We should respect objective conditions and facts and we should pay attention to what is required by objective facts in the reform.

It must be acknowledged that as real life progresses, the theoretical structure of Marxism begins to become inadequate and must be supplemented and developed.

For example, studies in social psychology are absent in the traditional

Marxist theories. Today, both in theory and in practice, there has yet to be found a satisfactory answer to the question "what is the motive force of social development in socialism?" According to traditional theories, as soon as the proletariat and other working people gained state power, they would become "masters of their own destiny" and their enthusiasm for production would "erupt like a volcano." But a volcano cannot erupt continuously without cease; a volcano erupts only sporadically. We cannot expect the masses to engage themselves in the arduous cause of construction for a prolonged period of time with the same revolutionary fervor as they had immediately after liberation. It is therefore necessary to study social psychology and the motive forces of development. Until an answer to this question is found, it is impossible to discover the reason why labor productivity and production efficiency in socialist countries for a long period of time lagged behind those of the developed capitalist countries.

Marxist methodology also needs to absorb critically the methods of modern systems theory and other scientific methods. Only then can it help us to grasp the progress of reform in all its complexity and variety and understand the constantly changing external world.

Marxism also needs to develop its theories of the state, classes, and nationalities. Under new conditions, it is necessary to study not only the class nature of the state, but also its social character. In the new society, the old exploiting classes have disappeared and new social strata have emerged. The classical definition of "classes" has to be reconsidered.

Only by developing Marxism can we persist in Marxism.

Theory and practice should be combined, and ideals and realities unified, in the reform of the political structure.

Marxists are idealists. Marx looked upon the future society as "a coalition of free men," a new social community free from all forms of alienation. What we are after is socialist democracy, a genuine people's democracy. The aim of the reform is to unbind the talents, the creativeness, and the spirit of progress of every person.

Marxists are also realists. We should fully foresee the difficulties and limitations of the political structural reform and realistically and tactfully deal with all kinds of contradictions and problems, temporary compromises, and necessary retreats. The Constitution has made extensive stipulations concerning people's democracy. We should strive to turn into reality the rights to democracy and freedom given by the Constitution and correct and eliminate all factors that are not consistent with the spirit of the Constitution. We cannot expect to have all our wishes realized overnight; we can only promote the political reform in firm and steady steps. We are heading toward modernization and democratization. The two cannot be separated. We have made a good start since the Third Plenary

Session of the Eleventh Central Committee, but it is far from perfect. China with its heavy historical burdens will inevitably meet with setbacks on its road toward modernization and democratization. But this is the direction of history and it cannot be reversed.

DOCUMENT 64

YAN JIAQI
The Theory of Two Cultural Factors

Yan Jiaqi was until 1989 the youthful director of the Institute of Political Science at the Chinese Academy of Social Sciences. He campaigned for a more participatory form of politics and for checks and balances on the leadership. Yan settled in Paris after 1989 and became a leader of the Federation for a Democratic China. He later moved to the USA. See Introduction, note 63, for references to other English translations of Yan's work.

THE fierce criticism directed against "humanism" in the early 1980s befogged China's intellectual life. This inspired me to think deeply about the "factors that constitute the culture" of a country and a people. For a long time now, ideology in China must be "Marxist" or "in keeping with Marxism" before it can be disseminated. In order to propagate "humanism," some thinkers have started to advocate "Marxist humanism," though some "authorities in the matter of theory," intent on monopolizing the truth and posing as the defenders of "Marxism," declare "humanism" to be a "bourgeois ideology" and lash it mercilessly. In fact humanism preceded Marxism and is a precious achievement of humanity as a whole. On January 17, 1986, I wrote in an article that any country or nation embodies "two kinds of cultural factors," one being the "traditional indigenous culture" and the other being "common culture, which transcends national boundaries and belongs to the whole of humankind." This latter is the product of a rise in the level of people's perception and the development of skills in the administration of society; as a result of the growth of national, international, and global intercourse, its specific weight in national culture is increasing daily. "Variety" is culture's basic characteristic, and the growth of cultural intercourse will never do away with cultural difference on a world scale: "secondary cultures" in every shape and form will be with us forever. The differences in national and international concepts of value, level of perception, and skills in the administration of society have created, and continue to create, the differences in national and international culture. On December 17, 1986, I published an article in which I said that in the vast and boundless world of thought, besides "Marxism" there are all sorts of natural sciences and social sciences as well as art, religious thought, and rational and irrational kinds of thinking. Today, in the twentieth century, we are no longer in the period of the Reformation: there is no need to treat the "second kind of cultural factor" (a product of the progress of human civilization) as a "development" or "component part" of Marxism, nor is there any need to wear the overcoat of "Marxism" in order to propagate such ideas. In world mathematics, chemistry, physics, politics, economics, and sociology are many forms of thought that are scientific and a component part of spiritual civilization; they need no Marxist dress to justify their propagation. We can only talk of "Non-Marxism" insofar as we are concerned with what Marxist researches. In fact, not only are the theories of natural science "outside Marxism" but so too are many social science theories (since their object of inquiry is different). This was on the eve of the "anti-liberalization" campaign. In the article I criticized those methods that on the pretext of "protecting the purity of Marxism" reject "common cultural factors that belong to humankind as a whole."

Historically, China—a country closed to international intercourse—was unwilling to admit the existence of "common cultural factors." Only after its defeat in the Opium Wars did it begin to admit that "science and technology" are "common cultural factors," but it still refused to admit the existence of other such factors. "Chinese learning for the essence, Western learning for application" is a reflection of this outlook and the "theory" behind China's resistance to culture from abroad. "The idea of 'common cultural factors,'" I wrote in this article, "has been denounced time and again in China. This is one of the main reasons why the backward elements in China's traditional culture have been preserved for such a long time. Phrases like 'protecting the purity of Marxism' are a refurbished version of the theory of 'Chinese learning as the essence.'" Some people firmly believe that "humanism" and "Marxism" are opposites, and that as a worldview, humanism is bourgeois ideology. But to my mind humanism is a common cultural achievement of humankind as a whole that transcends boundaries between countries and peoples. Humanism means putting people and human value first. Life, nature, love, honor, knowledge, talents, freedom, and happiness are all things that people value. From a humanist perspective, respecting people and people's value is to admit the rationality of "cherishing life and nature," "pursuing love and honor," "valuing skills and knowledge," and "longing for freedom and happiness." Second, humanism places "human nature" and the "common human essence" above people's social differences. Humanism does not deny that differences exist within society and between people, nor does it regard everyone in society as united. It recognizes that people are divided into nobles and commoners, educated and uneducated, merchants and craftsmen, and so on; and that there are all kinds of differences between people's social station, thinking, character, and behavior. Even so it places humankind's common essence above these social differences. Humanism does not preach universal love, but on the contrary condemns and opposes everything that runs counter to human nature. It does not treat everyone equally without distinction, nor does it believe that all people have an equally noble character. It extols and cherishes life and nature, it pursues love and honor, it values knowledge and ability, it longs for freedom and happiness. It even extols those who are imbued with the spirit of self-sacrifice and mercilessly castigates all those who are hypocritical, ignorant, conceited, and corrupt. Victor Hugo says that "higher than absolutely correct revolution is an absolutely correct humanism." So humanism not only stresses people and people's value and speaks highly of freedom and happiness, but it puts human nature above social difference, above class oppositions, and even above revolution. Humanism too is a common cultural factor belonging to the whole of humanity, regardless of frontiers." I published this article because I firmly believe that China's progress will be in direct proportion to the extent to which it opens up to the outside world and recognizes and accepts the "common cultural factors" of human civilization.

DOCUMENT 65

FANG LIZHI
Problems of Modernization

Fang Lizhi, expelled from the Party along with Liu Binyan and Wang Ruowang in January 1987 after the fall of Hu Yaobang, was professor of astrophysics and first vice-president at Hefei's University of Science and Technology. He is a well-known and outspoken reformer, and a hero of the Chinese student movement. After the Tian'anmen massacre he sought sanctuary in the U.S. Embassy and was eventually allowed to travel to England, ostensibly for medical reasons, where he worked at the University of Cambridge. He later moved to the USA.

The following is a condensation, approved by Fang, of an interview with him published in Hong Kong.

THE prediction that the working class will dig capitalism's grave has been proved wrong. So has Lenin's idea that imperialism is capitalism in its decadent stage. Today's capitalism is different from that described by Marx in his day. It has realized its defects and adjusted accordingly. Since the depression, Europe has changed rapidly. Here at least I feel that Marxism is outdated. Marx's theories cannot describe today's capitalism. Some of his fundamental economic ideas are extremely inaccurate.

Poor service and inefficiency do not define capitalism. Capitalist society stresses politeness: market economies emphasize gaining people's confidence. An enterprise or service company cannot survive merely by cheating and deceiving.

Our present ill health is produced not by bad capitalist practices blowing in through the open door, but by the evil legacy of feudalism. Weber showed that European capitalism originated in the Protestant countries. Protestantism advocates discipline and trust. Developing a market economy is not of itself bound to produce unhealthy tendencies, despite what some people say. That argument is simply a justification for those who want to pursue a monopolistic and conservative closed-door policy. Not only capitalism emphasizes monetary relationships. Yes, capitalism has many defects, but compared with feudalism it is progress. True, it emphasizes making money, but people will only be able to profit exorbitantly for a short while, for competition acts as a brake. Money extorted by landlords and aristocrats disappeared into private pockets, but the capitalist must reinvest the bulk of his profits to increase the rate of reproduction and thus win even bigger profits. So viewed objectively, he raises the level of society's productive forces. His property may seem privately owned, but actually its functions have been socialized. The capitalist cannot do as he pleases and follow his every whim, for society restrains him.

Does true socialism exist? In my opinion, Marx's socialism was utopian. What the Soviets are now doing is also not socialism. Most "socialist" countries are backward countries practicing a highly centralized form of political and economic totalitarianism.

Marx had many expectations, but few materialized. He exposed capitalism's shady side and the suffering caused by the exploitation of the working class—which was true in his time. But his conclusions were not necessarily right, and his theories were quite crude.

Take East and West Germany, North and South Korea, Shanghai and Taiwan. The former are all failures, both economically and socially. Today we admit that we have failed and that we are at a "primary stage of socialism," while in the past we boasted about "catching up with America and overtaking England." Compared with then, our present attitude is progress. If we are now at the "primary stage," when will we reach the last stage? Nor do we have a model to follow. We are "groping for stones on which to cross the river." China's problems may look big, but actually they are not. Our aim is modernization. By now many countries and territories have modernized. For the first country it was probably hard to do so, but it was less so for the next, and today we can get "helpful advice from others" and follow models. Just like the atom bomb—the first scientist to make one got the Nobel Prize, but now anyone studying high-energy physics can grasp the principles of its manufacture. It is the same with modernization. If we refer to or repeat what others have done, we can get it right. Japan has made the grade, Thailand is edging forward, Singapore has got to the top, even Taiwan has succeeded.

What China does will have Chinese style, but we cannot include among the objectives of modernization "Chinese character." The criteria for modernization are universal. All developed countries have certain characteristics in common, even if they also have their special features. In both America and Japan the per capita GNP exceeds $5,000, more than 30 percent of the people have had higher schooling, and the political system is democratic and multiparty.

Inflation is hard to avoid at a certain point on the road to development. In Brazil inflation is almost 100 percent. Greece and Turkey too have serious inflation, as does Taiwan. But there are definite limits to the suffering: if it is such that people starve and can't go on any longer, that is a period not of hardship but of death and ruin. There has been no announcement of the rate of inflation in our country. Foreigners ask me how far Chinese will put up with high inflation before a crisis develops. I reply that we are already in a crisis, it is simply that so far no trouble has broken out. Supposing our inflation is 20 percent, then in world terms we are exceptional. All countries that restructure their economies suffer inflation, but some overcome their difficulties. For example, Taiwan has done so almost without anyone noticing.

Commodity prices do not rise simply because of the open-door policy. The social unrest in Poland, for example, is due partly to rising commodity prices and partly to a shortage of goods; it would be wrong to say that it was due to the reform of the social system. Why do commodity prices in China rise? Partly because of adjustments in the prices of agricultural products and of industrial raw and semifinished materials and fuel, though in certain other countries with monopolistic industries prices have also risen repeatedly and at more or less the same rate. Financial deficits directly affect currency circulation. I recently visited Sichuan, where people in the mint are working under enormous pressure. The press turns twenty-four hours a day, and even administrative staff have to help out "at the front." They fear that commodity prices will skyrocket. Some factors behind the deficit—for example, high-rise buildings and offices—are investments without value.

Another sensitive issue is military spending. The arms race drains the nation's strength. Even the United States and the Soviet Union find arms expenditure intolerable. China is a poor country, even less capable of fighting a foreign war. The deficits caused by war are senseless.

Wastage too can drive up prices. To take an extreme example, in the Philippines prices rose due to the Marcos clan's unbridled squandering and embezzlement of the nation's assets while deficits hit state finances year after year. Does the same happen in China? I have no idea how much money people in high places waste. One leading cadre's family has six cars, including one to take him to the office, one for the lady of the house, one to take the kids to school, and one to take amah shopping. With the country so poor, how can we possibly afford such things? Does Marx say that leading cadres need luxury cars to rush round in? That leading cadres right down to local level should hold large banquets and invite guests at public expense? A "bird's nest soup and shark's fin" dinner at the Jiaoyutai costs several thousand yuan, enough to feed someone for several years. Now they're proposing a limit of "four dishes and one soup," but even one dish—for example a ten-inch plate of sea cucumber or a dish of fried prawns—can cost 250 yuan in some restaurants. According to a journalist, one senior official's week-long trip to Jiamusi cost 200,000 yuan. Who pays for all this? The common people. The U.S. Congress recently criticized Reagan's excessive expenditure as one cause of the country's fiscal deficit. Will our leaders here in China publicly account for what they spend? I doubt it.

We used to speak of the Guomindang's four big families, and how they made such a mess of the economy. Today it is more like four hundred families. And how much have they salted away abroad? Some of their money comes from privately earned commissions, that is, bribes. If this leads to a deficit, the burden of inflation will be shifted onto the shoulders of the people, which is criminal.

Taiwan's economy is still more advanced than ours. So why not emulate Taiwan? If emulating America and Europe is "complete Westernization," why can't we learn from Taiwan, which is after all Chinese? Taiwan is not ideal, but it certainly runs its economy better than we run ours. Since we are bold enough to designate Hainan Island as even more "open" than the special economic zones, why not be bolder still and find somewhere to test the Taiwan model? If America is a friendly country, how can Taiwan, populated by Chinese, be "hostile"? Some people would rather praise the United States than praise Taiwan. We changed our opinion of America and the Soviet Union—why not revise our view of the Guomindang? To learn from foreigners is not disgraceful, but to learn from fellow Chinese is. We should look to practical results—they are the real test of truth. Taiwan has changed over the last decades. Once the Guomindang was corrupt and evil, but now it has changed for the better. In certain respects it was compelled to change, for otherwise how could it have survived on that small island? So we must now revise our view of the Guomindang.

Apart from satisfying one's vanity, being an official has material attractions. People who wield great power can use it to get rich. Even if they don't directly take the initiative to do so, their underlings will figure out their intentions and do what's necessary. Our officials come under very little pressure. By all means give them prestige and money, but also put pressure on them and properly prescribe their responsibilities. Western managers bear heavy responsibilities: if they lose money, out they go. But Chinese cadres have iron rice bowls. If they neglect their duty or make mistakes, at most they will have to write a self-criticism or transfer to another unit.

The ownership system is basic, for it determines many things. We practice a so-called planned economy, based on public ownership. However, that does not mean ownership by the whole people (at least not from the people's point of view) but ownership by a small group of people. It is even more private than private enterprise, and what's more it's free from all competition. In fact there is no real free market in China (save for vegetables). Everything else that you can squeeze a profit from is controlled by the state. We don't compete on grounds of quality or technology but we depend instead on other factors—we even use social connections to get supplies.

The Chinese interior has abundant resources. For example, Anhui supplies most of Shanghai's coal needs. But the more coal Anhui produces the more money it loses, for the price of coal is kept low, unlike that of industrial imports from Shanghai. How then can prosperity on the coast help develop the interior?

So everyone curses everyone else and everyone thinks they are being short-changed. I don't just mean intellectuals, who will probably never be well-off. I mean workers, who are cursing publicly, and peasants, who are complaining that it doesn't pay to raise pigs. Prices are fixed too rigidly, and each group lacks normal channels for its products and the chance to compete freely. You do what the plan tells you to do, and then you get your money, and that's it. The two systems—the planned economy and the market economy—are insufficiently coordinated.

China started economic reform ten years ago. The first five years (mainly in the agricultural sector) were successful: the fewer the controls, the greater the success. The peasants were enthusiastic about producing. But the last five years have been less satisfactory. Urban reform and industrial and commercial reform failed, for they inevitably involved politics. Our supreme leader has every intention of reforming the economy, but never politics. He is for half and half: open up the economy and even institute a system of contracts, but don't let go of politics. From Wei Jingsheng through Wang Xizhe, Bai Hua, and Liu Binyan, right down to the movement against spiritual pollution, his line on this has been quite clear.

If our young people go the way of progress, what's wrong with that? What's wrong with changing color if it helps society forward? I am optimistic about China's future, for we have opened up and there can be no turning back. Even if we turn back briefly, we'll soon open up again. Veteran workers are speaking out, so are intellectuals. "Rectifying" people is no longer easy. People were ordered to write articles during the campaign against bourgeois liberalization, but who did? No one wants to be controlled. Students now criticize leaders by name. Who would have dared do that in the past? That shows that China is now freer.

DOCUMENT 66

WANG RUOSHUI
In Defense of Humanism

Wang Ruoshui, who has written extensively about socialist humanism and alienation and is known to some as "the Party's conscience," was dismissed as deputy editor in chief of *People's Daily* in late 1983, during a campaign against "spiritual pollution." This is a condensation of an article dated January 1983.

THERE is a ghost haunting China's intellectuals: the ghost of humanism. Over the past three years, more than four hundred articles have been written discussing the problem of "humanity," and quite a few of them have explored Marxist humanism. That it has evoked such strong interest is not just a reaction to the ten years of turmoil (during the Cultural Revolution): it is also an expression in our new era of the need to build a socialist society with a high degree of culture and democracy. But some well-intentioned comrades reject any humanist slogan, on the grounds that humanism is unorthodox.

The main reasons they put forward are: humanism is an ideology of the bourgeoisie; humanism discusses humanity as something abstract; and humanism was early on denounced and abandoned by Marx. So they use Marxism to oppose humanism, instead of using Marxist humanism to oppose bourgeois humanism. They do not just disavow specific forms of humanism, but negate it as a fundamental principle. In this article, then, I shall defend humanism in general and Marxist humanism in particular.

"Humanism is an ideology of the bourgeoisie." If this means that humanism was the ideology of the bourgeoisie, then it is a statement of historical fact not open to dispute. But if it means that humanism can *only* be an ideology of the bourgeoisie, then I challenge it. We must never confound the two meanings; the second cannot be deduced from the first.

Materialism too was an ideology of the capitalist class (and even of the slaveholder class and the feudal class), but that did not stop materialism from becoming the worldview of the proletariat. Can we say the same of humanism? First we must look at its inner meaning. If humanism (like individualism) is essentially and inexorably linked with the bourgeoisie, then it can only be a bourgeois ideology; otherwise it will not be thus restricted. "Humanism" is a word of foreign origin, and many Chinese have only a vague and inaccurate idea of its meaning. There are many schools of humanism, each with a different interpretation, but there is one that is generally recognized.

The word "humanism" originally referred to the main ideological theme of the Renaissance (humanism in a narrow sense, also called "humanitarianism"), but it was later broadened to embrace concepts that have humans as their main purport, that is, human value, human dignity, human interests or happiness, and human development or freedom. Humanism is a long-standing and well-established trend of thought that in the Western world has existed for at least six hundred years. Since the Renaissance, we have seen the humanism of the Enlightenment, utopian socialist humanism, Feuerbach's humanism, and various shades of modern humanism. The concept "humanism" is derived from all these sources. Why do so many schools of thought call themselves "humanist"? Because they all acknowledge a common principle: the value of human beings.

Many comrades are perhaps not accustomed to the term "value of human beings," but everybody will be familiar with the words of Mao Zedong: "Of all things in the world, people are the most precious." Does that not put the highest value on human beings? True, Mao did not use the term "value of human beings," but that is only a difference of terminology. I shall now show that Marx had already used the term in a positive sense.

Many comrades mistrust the term "value of human beings" because they feel that affirming "human value" means affirming "the value of the individual," which makes them think of individualism. But it is not an affirmation of individualism, any more than affirming that "people are the most precious" is. During the development of humanism, some forms of it have borne the stamp of individualism, but others have carried connotations of universal love and altruism. Feuerbach propounded universal love between human beings; his humanism opposed selfishness. But Max Stirner, Feuerbach's contemporary and the founder of anarchist individualism, was firmly opposed to humanism. This shows that there is no cast-iron link between humanism and individualism, and that "the value of human beings" does not equal individualism. We are advocating collectivism; collectivism is the opposite of individualism, but it is not opposed to the value of human beings, correctly understood. A collective is made up of individuals. If one individual or a group of individuals in a collective is without value, in Marx' view that collective is illusory and alienated (capitalist countries are collectives of this sort). The value of the individual can only be realized within a collective.

Some comrades may admit the slogan "revolutionary humanism," but only in connection with such matters as healing the wounded, rescuing the dying, and treating prisoners of war leniently. They insist that we should not broaden its meaning and expand the sphere of its application. And here lies a problem. In the modern world healing the wounded, rescuing the dying, and treating prisoners of war leniently are international norms. Although these norms are repeatedly violated, international public opinion has always condemned such violations. If we restrict the practice of "revolutionary humanism" so narrowly, we will be unable to distinguish it from bourgeois humanism. What makes humanism revolutionary is not the humane treatment of the wounded or of prisoners of war, but its use of revolutionary means to realize human value. We cultivate the fields for the revolution, we work for the revolution, we do everything for the revolution. But for what is the revolution? Revolution is a means, not an end. We work for socialism and communism, for the interests and happiness of the people, for the liberation of all humanity. That is the meaning of revolutionary humanism.

It is a pity that during the "great cultural revolution" we counterposed "revolution" and "humanism." People thought then that since humanism was not revolutionary, the revolution must not concern itself with humanism. So the "capitalist-roaders," "revisionist elements," and "monsters and demons" of those days were treated even less humanely than prisoners of war.

The reason people view humanism as part of bourgeois ideology is because they believe that it merely opposed feudalism. Yet historically it has played a role against capitalism too. The originator of utopian socialism, Henry More, was a believer in humanism. In the eighteenth century, champions of the French bourgeois enlightenment raised the slogan of "freedom and equality" on the basis of humanism and in opposition to feudalism. In the nineteenth century, British and French utopian socialists seized this weapon, turned it around, and used it against capitalism. They exposed the hypocrisy of bourgeois "freedom" and "equality" and propagated true freedom and equality. A society that conforms to humanist norms is socialist. Speaking of the relation between French materialists and utopian socialists in the eighteenth century, Marx said that Fourier, Owen, Dezamy, and Gay treated the materialist doctrine as real humanism and as the logical foundation of communism and developed it further.

Marx criticized Feuerbach's humanism, but he never radically negated it. Rather, he advanced it to a new stage. Likewise, he criticized Feuerbach's materialism, but he never radically negated materialism: instead he developed Feuerbach's intuitive materialism into practical materialism. Feuerbach said that "humans are humanity's highest essence." He criticized the theological view that "God is humanity's highest essence" and instead showed that "God is nothing but the essence of humanity." Feuerbach believed that it was not God who created humans, but humans who created God, by projecting their own nature onto him, that is, by alienating their own nature. The problem is that Feuerbach regarded humans only in the abstract and saw their essential nature as reason, will, and affection.

Religion depreciates human value, but does only religion do that? Humans need the opiate of religion because the real world is full of misery and alienation. After exposing religious alienation, we must expose the alienation of real life. We must criticize all social relations that humiliate, enslave, forsake, and despise humans. Since these forms of alienation are not just figments of the imagination but lived reality, they cannot be overcome by relying only on "weapons of criticism"; we still need the "criticism of weapons," that is, revolution. We must rely on that class for which inhuman conditions have reached the limit: the class that must liberate all humanity to liberate itself, that is, the proletariat.

Marx proceeds from the idea that "humans are humanity's highest essence" to the necessity of revolution. He establishes a link between humanism and violent revolution. This is revolutionary humanism or proletarian humanism. Both Marx and Feuerbach place humans highest, and recognize no essence above them. But Feuerbach opposes illusory superhuman forces only in the ideological field, while Marx opposes the social relations that degrade humans to an inhuman level. Marx arrives at this revolutionary conclusion because of his firm grasp of real humanity, social humanity.

In 1844 Marx pointed out that productive life is the life of the species, and that the activities of the human species are characteristically free and conscious; which is where humans differ from beasts. But alienated labor under private ownership is forced labor, done merely to subsist. In 1844 Marx was still a young man. Did he later discard his humanism? The mature Marx's *Communist Manifesto* criticizes "transforming the dignity of human beings into exchange value" and "leaving no bond between human beings other than naked interest and unfeeling 'cash transactions.'" "In bourgeois society, capital possesses independence and individuality, but the individual operator has neither independence nor individuality." Marx and Engels pointed out that under communism the free development of each individual will be the condition for the free development of all.

Capital, a representative work of the older Marx, indignantly and at great length exposed capitalist exploitation, both physical and mental, of the workers and showed how large-scale industry turns the worker into an appendage of machines; it also exposed the pitiful fate of women and child workers. Marx further developed his idea of "alienation of labor" and expounded the doctrine of surplus value. Of human nature, he said: "We must first study general human nature, and then the changes in human nature that have typified each era." He believed that in communist society workers would live their material lives "under conditions most adequate to their human nature and most worthy of it," and "will begin that development of human power that is its own end, the true realm of freedom." This shows that Marx all along connected proletarian revolution and communism with questions of human value, dignity, emancipation, and freedom. This is the most thoroughgoing humanism.

"Humanism" is simply a word for various systems and trends of thought that emphasize human value. We must not confuse general humanism with the forms that humanism has taken in specific historical phases. Marxism is not identical with humanism, but it does include humanism. We propound Marxist humanism (socialist humanism, revolutionary humanism), just as we propound Marxist materialism.

Today, in the age of socialist modernization, we need socialist humanism. Humanism implies resolute rejection of the "all-round dictatorship" and cruel struggle of the Cultural Revolution. It rejects cults of personality that degrade the people. It firmly upholds the principle of universal equality before truth and the law, personal freedom, and personal dignity. It opposes the feudal concept of ranks and privileges, capitalist money worship, and the treatment of people as commodities or tools, and it demands that people be truly regarded as human beings. It sees people rather than socialist production as the goal, and aims to build up and develop a new type of relationship grounded in mutual respect, mutual concern, mutual assistance, and friendly cooperation as an embodiment of socialist civilization. It opposes bureaucratism, which ignores people, and extreme individualism, which strives for personal gain at others' expense. It promotes the human element in socialist construction and sees the workers as masters of their own affairs and creativity. It stresses education, the nurturing of talents, and the full development of humanity.

Is socialist humanism not already present in our practice? Is it not continuously developing? Why treat it as strange and alien?

There is a ghost haunting the vast expanse of China.

"Who are you?"

"I am humanity."

DOCUMENT 67

WANG RUOWANG
On Political Reform

Wang Ruowang, a critical writer expelled from the Party in January 1987 along with Fang Lizhi and Liu Binyan, criticized the increasingly autocratic Deng Xiaoping for becoming more and more like Mao Zedong. Wang refused to sign his notice of expulsion, and asked how he could be expected to break off a relationship that had lasted decades and in which he still believed.

Wang was arrested in July 1989 (at the age of seventy) and detained for "counterrevolutionary propaganda and incitement." Released without charges in October 1990, he was subject to constant police surveillance and harassment until August 1992, when he was allowed to travel to the USA. He soon became active in the China Alliance for Democracy.

This is a condensation of an interview with Wang Ruowang by Chen Yige, published in Hong Kong.

"POLITICAL DEMOCRATIZATION" means direct elections, general elections, the separation of the powers of the three branches of government, parliamentary politics, and a variety of political organizations—political parties and public groups—to run freely and on an equal basis in elections. All constitutions safeguard freedom of speech, the press, assembly and association (including by political parties), and so on. This is an achievement of the bourgeois revolution, one that has survived centuries of practice and any number of ups and downs. Many countries have benefited from it and suffered from the lack of it. The proletarian party rose to power on opposition to autocracy and one-party dictatorship: and will meet its end as a result of one-party rule and personal dictatorship.

Mao Zedong, constantly worried that a film or novel might bring down the Party and the nation, kept a close watch on literature, art, and propaganda. Though he acknowledged that the Chinese Communist Party too would ultimately perish, he did not see that it was precisely his willfulness, his despotism, and his use of violence against all dissidents and opposition (imaginary class enemies) that reduced a huge party to a mere name for eight years and lost the nation its place in the world.

Capitalist nations practice multiparty politics and allow communist parties to exist. Both the First and the Second Internationals had their headquarters in Western Europe. Never has a proletarian party succeeded in seizing power in a Western European country. Only in countries that practiced one-party dictatorship or drove the Communists underground—first Russia, then China—did Communists successfully seize power. Each victory had its unique characteristics, but both countries were still at the pre-capitalist stage of economic development and lacked a democratic political tradition. This favored the growth of one-man rule and personal autocracy.

Bourgeois democracy has proved to be an intelligent system of political leadership. It successfully regulates class conflict and gives all parties the right to compete freely on an equal plane, an advantage absent from socialist countries under proletarian dictatorship. Indeed, socialist countries view such a system as reactionary.

The fierce confrontation between the two camps lasted many years. Strangely, the socialist camp under Stalin allied itself with Hitler on the eve of World War Two while befriending the Japanese military in the East and signing a mutual non-aggression treaty with them. Did Stalin fall for the "National Socialists'" espousal of socialism and consider them fellow travelers? There is no evidence of this, though politically both countries rejected bourgeois democracy and practiced one-man dictatorship. In China, Mao followed in their footsteps. In the Soviet Union Stalin's atrocities were exposed and compared to Hitler's. In China the Cultural Revolution, personally launched by Mao, was referred to as the "Gang of Four's fascist dictatorship."

In the first few years after the proletarian revolution, both China and the Soviet Union were a picture of prosperity, brimming with hope and vitality. As soon as the worker-peasant regime had consolidated its position, however, it turned its guns on Party veterans, intellectuals, and rich peasants. The same thing has invariably happened after every peasant uprising throughout history. After seizing power, the leadership of the Communist Party went down its predecessors' beaten track.

Marxism-Leninism aims to smash the bourgeois state machine, create a brand-new regime based on proletarian dictatorship, and reject democracy and the rule of law, both of which have been effective in capitalist countries. Whoever proposes preserving and absorbing the good things in Western democratic politics is branded a rebel, an opportunist, a revisionist, and an advocate of bourgeois liberalization and class compromise.

Marx first talked in reference to the Paris Commune about the proletariat seizing power. Neither the Russian nor the Chinese Revolution was proletarian. Neither the Russian nor the Chinese proletariat became master of the state, which even runs the trade unions. In order to create the artificial appearance of proletarian rule, the Communists invented the idea of one-party rule and equated it with proletarian dictatorship. After all, Article 1 of the Constitution of the Chinese Communist Party states that the Party is the vanguard of the proletariat, so the Communists can argue that the leadership of the Communist Party equals proletarian rule. In Mao's words, this is to destroy first and construct later: without destruction there can be no construction. What the new socialism destroyed was bourgeois democracy: what it created was an absolutist system of personal centralization. The Communists, just emerging from a successful revolution, were pragmatic people. Told that they must not use building materials from the capitalist world in the new socialist edifice, they dug up the guillotines and crosses from the Czars' prisons and the frozen wastes of Siberia, while the Chinese Communists unearthed nail boards and torture racks in the Great Northern Wilderness. Despite shortcomings here and there, bourgeois democracy and the rule of law effectively curb personal despotism, prevent policies that harm the nation and the people, and check violations of human rights. In destroying bourgeois democracy, the Communists destroyed the electric mousetrap whose purpose is to punish self-indulgent rulers and gave ambitious and corrupt officials a blank check.

Economically, the Communists went in for state ownership of industry and commerce and for agricultural collectivization. To enforce these egalitarian ideals—which bore no relationship to reality—they needed a highly centralized form of iron-fisted politics. The result was a political system whose sole administrative methods were coercion, commandism, and draconian laws aimed at the slaughtering of innocent people. This is what proletarian dictatorship is all about. Economic destruction led to impoverishment and social decline. Add one-party dictatorship and life tenure for top leaders, and all you can do is wait for the dictator to breathe his last. By riding roughshod over human rights and impoverishing the people, the dictator naturally arouses popular dissatisfaction, which only serves to increase his paranoia. So he calls for the intensification of proletarian dictatorship. He tries to eliminate all art, literature, newspapers, and publications that articulate public opinion and discontent, and he even investigates street gossip, diaries, and personal letters. Stalin unleashed the most brutal purges to eliminate counterrevolutionaries. He saw an enemy of the people behind every bush. As for Mao, he talked about class struggle and uninterrupted revolution, conducted a literary inquisition, fabricated charges, and launched a string of political movements against intellectuals and veteran Party cadres. This only deepened the conflict between the people and the ruling party.

Khrushchev rose to power after Stalin's death, hopeful that reform would turn the situation around. But before long he was overthrown by Stalin's cronies. This shows that without radical surgery to the political system, partial liberalization will not last long and cannot prevent a counterrevolutionary comeback. Khrushchev kept the one-party system and even let the KGB (which later overthrew him) carry on as usual. Gorbachev, who came to power after the death of Brezhnev, had learned from Khrushchev that he must start by restructuring the higher echelons of power and by extensively democratizing political life. In China too the reformers had to wait for Mao to die before they could begin to act. If we do not destroy one-party rule and proletarian dictatorship at the root, an enlightened ruler and incorruptible officials will be of no avail.

As a veteran Party member, I am relieved and delighted to see that the Party has turned back from a blind alley. I have prepared the public for the economic reform that has been under way for the past two years. But my personal experience over the past ten years suggests to me that the new leadership is conniving at leftist conservatism. Another chronic problem is the failure to overhaul a political system suited exclusively for one-party dictatorship. This can only help corrupt officials, profiteers, and cadres to get rich at public cost and steal the fruits of reform. These two basic errors have bred widespread resentment against the government among intellectuals and urban and rural residents.

The Central Committee is aware of the seething anger and the crisis. The problems can be summed up as galloping inflation, lax Party and government discipline, a failure to enforce orders, and a failure to make orders effective. The Central Committee must run the Party and the bureaucracy strictly, step up supervision, and intensify political and ideological work. Its general principle: "Improve the economic environment, restore economic order." Missing is a willingness to tackle the key issue of political reform.

General Secretary Zhao Ziyang and Premier Li Peng have told Party members that "our Party welcomes you to speak your mind and express your opinions freely." Let me make two points here.

First, price reform without other changes is like an "isolated unit piercing deep behind enemy lines." So too is any attempt to improve the economic environment without first cleaning up the political system engendered by one-party dictatorship. Imagine relying on corrupt structures (which fail to enforce orders or are ineffective in enforcing them) to check corruption. The economic environment has several dimensions. It is closely related to political democratization and to management, for example ending inequality of pay between physical and mental labor, disseminating scientific achievements, ensuring that workers are satisfied, guaranteeing citizens' rights and freedoms, stabilizing prices, distributing wealth more equitably, ensuring peace of mind, and making officials and cadres serve the public rather than bully it.

Second, why has corruption run rampant? Five years of rectifying the Party have not worked. Can we overcome corruption simply by sending out work teams, investigation teams, supervisors, and price inspectors, like under Mao? Whenever we discover corruption, we zoom in on one or two blatant cases and punish the culprits amid much fanfare, instead of working to eliminate the breeding grounds of corruption, bribery, waste, and abuse. The result is either that corrupt officials lie low for a while until the alert is called over; or a few small fry are netted while the big fish stay at large; or members of the investigation team get caught up in complex networks of "personal relationships," confuse right with wrong in their report, and even fabricate charges. Since the imperial commissioner is sent by the Central Committee, no one dares voice dissent even when innocent people are accused. This has gone on throughout history. No one can guarantee that each and every inspector will be incorruptible.

The Chinese Communists have always loved to hear eulogies. People who write about corruption come under attack, and their works are banned or revised. For example, Liu Binyan was expelled for exposing corruption and violations of the law that victimized innocent citizens. This suggested to everyone that the Chinese Communist leaders shield the corrupt and cover up evil. Intellectuals who speak out from a sense of justice come to grief, so bad people become even more arrogant and the public's trust in the Party is vastly diminished. When healthy trends are not promoted, evil trends will prevail. Before 1985, the press was not even allowed to use the word "corrupt" (save with reference to the bourgeoisie, Hong Kong, and Taiwan).

The people judge your actions today in the context of what has happened and what will happen. When corruption first appeared, some people sounded the alarm. You ignored them and even criticized them. It was not until the running sore spread to your forehead and pierced your bones that you cried, "Corruption is indeed the scourge of the Party and the nation."

What dissatisfies most is the Party's habit of saying one thing and meaning another. The *National Day* editorial, "Our strength lies with the masses," explains that the Party is aware of the extent of public alienation. But on the same day, October 1, the Public Security Bureau set up permanent substations and offices in colleges and universities. This shows that the authorities no longer trust faculty and students and have made them targets of the dictatorship. They put forward a revolutionary idea only to belie it through their own actions. Xinhua News Agency explained that the police action was meant to step up law and order, protect the students, and ensure a stable and united learning environment, but this was mere newspeak. The real reason was to forestall and suppress the unrest simmering beneath the surface in the universities. Chinese people have become disaffected because they have been told so many official lies.

What plagues the Central Committee and the State Council most these days is that orders are not being carried out and prohibitions fail—a sign that government and Party are becoming paralyzed. The root of the problem is the leadership's failure to honor its word, together with the constant policy changes. Not knowing "what the policy is," people report that orders cannot be carried out and prohibitions cannot be enforced. This failure to carry out orders and enforce prohibitions is not necessarily bad. In many cases, it is because the lower levels are resisting wrong orders and instructions.

Then there is the phrase "stability and unity." Don't take it at face value. It is a weapon, an excuse to preserve the old order. Stability and unity is an auspicious phrase, synonymous with "The country is prosperous and the people live in peace." Stability and unity are agreeable to reactionary rulers, emperors, and generals everywhere. Things are looking grim, the people are panicking, they don't know when and what disaster may hit them. Greedy oppressive officials are in cahoots, while the base of society lacks all stability. Still this is a kind of "stability and unity." Even our campuses are no longer a haven. They must be guarded day and night by the military and the police, as stable and united as sheep in a pen. Stalin ruled the Soviet Union for thirty years, during which there was endless eulogizing and a sea of red banners, singing, and dancing. Before they were shot, veteran cadres who had confessed to false charges under torture wrote praising Stalin's immense kindness. Was this not also a kind of stability and unity? In China over the past ten years frequent measures—invariably preceded by loud calls "for stability and unity"—have been taken against democracy, humanism, and freedom of speech, assembly, and association. People concerned and brave enough to speak out are branded "unstable."

"The spectators see the chess game better than the players." The "players" are the officials, who sitting in their golden armchairs have everything they want. This determines their position, their viewpoint, their horizon. They have "lost their way and yet know not the errors of their way." They balk at delegating authority and relinquishing power. They are unwilling to return government to the people.

In the initial stage of reform, there were loud calls to "smash the iron rice bowl." Seven or eight years later, many bowls have not been smashed, mainly because the "golden armchair" has not been overturned. So after a while the reforms stalled. This sheds light on the psychology of those who try to avoid overhauling an obsolete and corrupt political system. It also explains why meetings, discussions, and efforts to solicit opinions from democratic figures and experts came up with either irrelevant measures or ineffective policies that emphasized the incidental instead of the fundamental.

The road is clearly open. The problem is that privileged officials would rather take the beaten track. Scholars, experts, and think tanks may draw up a closely reasoned action plan, but as long as the old feudal-monarchical or Mao-style political structure is not revamped, we will end up with just a handful of documents for future generations to marvel at.

Let's analyze another anomaly, namely political dissent. The hostility toward political dissidents shows that none of the Party's policies is scientific or democratic, let alone carefully considered. Under Mao, dissidents were called rightists and locked up. (Actually many of them were not really dissidents at all.) Under Deng Xiaoping, they were called "bourgeois liberalizers" rather than rightists. Just when Moscow was rehabilitating Sakharov and freeing more than five hundred dissidents earlier exiled to Siberia, Beijing declared that "it had found three new dissidents."

You might answer that these mistakes belong to the past, but actually things have got worse over the last two years. Here are two short excerpts from an internal speech. They vividly illustrate the way in which top leaders think:

> Student unrest has harmed development. Countries that grow quickly are characterized by a fair measure of political stability, centralization, and democratic development. Only in a socially stable climate can we develop the economy. Only under the highly centralized form of rule imposed by the allied occupation forces did West Germany and Japan transform their prewar military economies into market economies. Asia's four little dragons (Hong Kong, Singapore, South Korea, and Taiwan) all achieved economic take-off amid social stability ensured by a highly centralized political system. In Turkey and Brazil, the economy took off when military rule was imposed. With Pinochet on the way out, there is now talk in Chile of establishing a Pinochet regime without Pinochet. So anything that harms social stability will hinder economic take-off and the introduction of democracy. Political unity and social stability must be preserved.

And again:

> Pay for intellectuals and prices are perennial issues. In the past, the press was rigidly controlled. When controls were relaxed, it behaved sensitively. Intellectuals and the press take these matters too seriously, mongering in doom and gloom. . . . The editor-in-chief of *Pravda* said that the Soviet press is freer than China's. That is not necessarily true.

Those quoted do not mince words, which makes their statements all the more authoritative. Their only purpose in this exercise in international comparison is to resist democratization and to justify personal dictatorship and military rule. They even glorify this hogwash as a "law."

During Pinochet's sixteen years of rule in Chile, he violently overthrew Allende (the legally elected president), dissolved parliament and imposed martial law, killed large numbers of innocent citizens, rounded up oppositionists in concentration camps and exiled them to desolate islands, turned football stadiums and abandoned mines into makeshift jails, and arrested 130,000 people and exiled 10,000 in the first three years alone. Why include Chile in the honor roll of stability and unity? Either through ignorance, or because our rulers have lost their proletarian conscience and sense of justice.

A capitalist market economy does not necessarily conflict with the interests of a dictator. In Germany under Hitler business was as usual, and the armaments industry expanded spectacularly. Under Chiang Kai-shek, China was plagued by domestic trouble and foreign invasion, but private commerce and industry flourished. Prisoners in concentration camps turn out exquisite handicrafts that are sold on the export market. That the people can afford color televisions, motorcycles, and refrigerators does not necessarily mean that they are happy, free, and in control of their destiny.

This reminds me of two recent popular sayings: "Pick up the rice bowl and eat meat. Put down the chopsticks and curse." The first sentence means that people are now adequately dressed and fed. The second, that they resent social injustice, political corruption, and the lack of personal freedom. What these two statements show is that the economy is expected to take off under centralized military rule and without democratic freedoms. This is the birdcage economy (and birdcage politics): every day I feed you worms and millet so that you can sing my praises. You can flap your wings and fly about, but you can never fly away. Nor should you envy the world outside. Why are you complaining? Haven't I left you enough free space? If you don't behave, I will pull down the cover and let you rot in darkness.

The Chinese Communist Party is accelerating its own demise. It is in a terminal crisis. Why must a nation and a state suffer when one party degenerates? In a multiparty state, a party may go downhill, alienate the people, and lose public support. Its members may drift away and its organization may atrophy, but it will not influence national politics or the normal operation of the economy, for when party and politics are separated, voters will reject it. The lives and property of an entire people should not depend on one party or on the personal whims of one leader. After the Republic of China was set up, the nation's destiny was hostage to one party, the Guomindang. After Chiang Kai-shek fell, the Chinese put their destiny in Communist hands. This too put them at the mercy of one individual.

The Chinese Communist Party is a huge organization that does not lack clear-headed and healthy forces. Even at the top not everyone is benighted. After a decade of reform a new and economically powerful bourgeois-democratic stratum has emerged. All China's neighbors—Burma, South Korea, the Philippines, Taiwan, and the Soviet Union—are in the process of reforming or revolutionizing their economies or their political superstructures. The wholesale Westernization (capitalist economy and parliamentary politics) of Japan and Singapore is a shining example that exerts a powerful pressure on and greatly appeals to China.

The Party can only hope to live to a ripe old age if it sees the light, puts national interest before party interest, and performs radical surgery on itself. It must first clarify the purpose of reform. Is it solely to enrich the people (or some of the people)? That would be to confine ourselves to the economic sphere. Is it to protect Party interests and the purity of Marxism-Leninism? But there can be no special party interest above national interest. Yes, the productive forces must be developed, but if production relations and the superstructure are not reformed, the development of the productive forces will be nothing more than an empty phrase.

Now that we have called for the separation of party and government and for clean government, the expenses of the Party (including the Central Committee) should come not from the national exchequer but from Party dues (plus a fixed subsidy that the government gives to each political party). In the past, the Party's expenses were met by the government. This corrupted Party officials and turned the Party into a bloated bureaucracy. By introducing a multiparty system, we will stop all this. Even more important, we will greatly reduce the burden on the people. The Party leadership must be directly and democratically elected. There must be no designated candidates. There should be more than one candidate in Party elections below county level.

I am all for the "waterfront pavilion getting the moonlight first" (i.e., letting those who are well positioned reap the benefit first) as a way of learning everyone's strong points. Look around at your neighbors. Do you see something worth copying? If so, copy it. If something helps to develop the productive forces and to build democracy, borrow it. A Soviet newspaper advocated adopting the Swedish model. A Beijing newspaper says that the Shenzhen Special Economic Zone should copy the Hong Kong model indiscriminately. These are examples of the "waterfront pavilion getting the moonlight first."

Wherever the rigid model of socialist public ownership obtains, people live in destitution. The country is backward and there is widespread discontent and bitterness. We must summon up the courage to throw out this insidious model. So what if we have to start small on a tiny piece of land? It is at least better than the birdcage economy. China, being poor, must learn from the advanced democratic countries. It is surrounded by ready-made success stories. It costs not a penny in royalties to copy other people's systems of management and politics. All you need to do is forget that the Party leaders are 100 percent correct and that socialism is excellent.

What concerns me most is reform of the political structure. Yes, Shenzhen should copy the Hong Kong model lock, stock, and barrel. But as long as Shenzhen is under a dictatorship or a group of people who are able and ready to intervene, it matters little what civil service it sets up. The mainland has introduced democracy and enterprise management from the advanced countries, but they have never worked. Because of the ruling party's arbitrary intervention, efficiency has failed to improve. So though it is a good idea to set Shenzhen aside as a laboratory for reform and to compete with neighboring Hong Kong, the changes happen only at the bottom, not the top. Two attempts to develop Hainan Island both failed dismally; much was said but little was done. The same has happened to Shenzhen, Zhuhai, and Xiamen. The root cause is the political syndrome. For example, Hainan Island planned to publish a private newspaper but the idea was killed by the Central Committee.

Gorbachev's reform strategy is worth emulating. The Soviet Union is a socialist state. It shares some history with China. Its and China's power structures stem from the same source. Its bureaucracy is more entrenched, its leadership is more deified, and its leftism is more corrupt and insidious than China's. Reform in the Soviet Union is much more difficult than in China, and it trailed China by six or seven years. To make economic reform work in three to four years is difficult. Yet Gorbachev's strategic plan got off to a good start. He stated the ideological case for reform clearly. He explained the urgency of reform and exposed conservative efforts to obstruct it. So Gorbachev set clear goals for reform and explained that ideological struggle was inevitable. He also rectified the political system from the top down, unlike in China, where we restructured the bottom but not the top. He emphasized glasnost, encouraged the public to participate in decision-making and to criticize and debate freely, and relied on intellectuals to unshackle the media. He stopped at nothing to expose Stalin's brutal massacre of large numbers of old Bolsheviks, and he rehabilitated all those who had been wrongly accused. We too rehabilitated the wrongly accused, but we shielded those who trumped up charges (I don't mean those people who blindly carried out orders and committed minor offenses), thus perpetuating the idea that the violation of human rights is not shameful.

What makes Hong Kong worth emulating is its economic model and its business and industrial management. The Soviet Union too is a "waterfront pavilion," but its planned economy, its collective farms, and its rigid one-party system have lost their luster. The two areas that Gorbachev addressed—unshackling the media and exposing Soviet history's dark side—are exactly those that China did not address. So China has suffered setbacks and wasted six or seven precious years of reform. Our spokesman thinks nothing of this "waterfront pavilion." According to him, it "is not necessarily true" that "the Soviet press is freer than China's." But China's press, radio, and television are notorious for their lack of freedom and monotony. Why argue with facts?

I support Sun Yat-sen's "one world" idea. To realize it, we should adopt a multiparty system like in Britain, France, Germany, and the United States. One advantage of such a system is that it will promote peace talks and cooperation between the mainland and Taiwan, for who can quarrel with Sun Yat-sen? To reject the multiparty system is to put Party interest first and to perpetuate the Party's decline. Multiparty rule is the political basis for modernization, and a surging global trend.

DOCUMENT 68

LIU BINYAN
The Bureaucratic Paradise

Liu Binyan, one of China's most distinguished writer-journalists, was born in Changchun on February 7, 1925, and joined the Communist Party in 1944. Mao criticized him in 1957 for his "contentious nature" and he was expelled from the Party. In 1958 he was sent to work in the countryside, whence he returned in 1961 to resume work as a journalist. In 1969 he was sent away for labor reform and not rehabilitated until October 1976. In 1980 he became a reporter on *People's Daily*. As a realist, he advocates "truthful writing." As a Marxist and revolutionary, he emphasizes freedom. He was expelled from the Party a second time in January 1987 along with Fang Lizhi and Wang Ruowang, and now lives in the U.S. The following are excerpted from his book, *China's Crisis, China's Hope*, published in the USA in 1990.

MANY Americans and other westerners are of the opinion that the failure of Mao's experiment is a failed experiment of socialism and Marxism, thus constituting the essential failure of socialism and Marxism themselves. But Mao actually failed because his policies contravened the tenets of socialism and were in direct opposition to Marx's fundamental socialist policies. Marx never advocated socialism without freedom or a socialism that runs counter to concepts of humanism. Instead, Mao placed the people in a subordinate, passive role as soon as the new nation was founded, reserving the dominant role for the Party and the bureaucracy. For forty years Mao admonished the people to sacrifice their todays for a brighter tomorrow, to sacrifice their human values and freedom in the name of economic construction. As a result, all the todays have been sacrificed, and tomorrow is farther away than ever; the people have offered up their freedom, sometimes their very lives, but economic construction is in shambles. If Mao had implemented one-tenth of the precepts of the Paris Commune, there would not be such an enormous, impotent, and corrupt bureaucracy in China today.

DISREGARDING history and the modern experience of foreign countries, the Chinese Party established a system of control over a nation of nearly a billion people based upon its experiences in military control, in which a given area might be abandoned at any time. It is not a complex system: political fealty to the Party is the prime consideration in appointing an official, far more important than abilities or cultural level; the reinstatement, promotion, or demotion of an individual is invariably determined by how an official is to carry out the orders of the Central Committee; no consideration is given to whether the results will benefit or harm the local populace or people throughout the country.

Ever since the founding of the nation, or even earlier, during the civil war, there has been a tendency among Chinese officials to resort to coercion or, stated differently, lean to the left rather than to the right. This is something Mao Zedong knew very well, and he punished many cadres for it, but still he regarded it as a means to get things done, a work ethic. In China, the word "left" has unique implications above and beyond those it carries in other countries: it implies merciless and ruthless treatment of others. One ruthlessly attacks others in the class struggle and mercilessly exploits people's labor in production and construction, taking all their blood, sweat, and tears.

THIS unique position of the Chinese bureaucracy has created a special temperament among its members. Since these officials have become docile tools of the Party, and since their fate lies in the hands of their superiors, they maintain fealty only to these superiors, which in the long run forces them to implement policies and measures that are unreasonable, that violate their consciences, that are sometimes even inhumane. Over time their emotions grow numb; their senses of justice and of right and wrong gradually wither away. I have used the phrase "moral and political emasculation" to describe this phenomenon. Another reason for the symptom is that once a person becomes an official, he knows he is assured a good life so long as he commits no major mistake. The lifestyles and living conditions of these people differ greatly from those of ordinary citizens; they have their own troubles and their own joys. As a result, many of China's bureaucrats display attitudes of indifference: unlike most people, who sympathize with suffering and grow indignant over injustice, they no longer seem to experience normal human emotions.

PEOPLE who come out on top in internal Party struggles, who not only survive but continue to climb the ladder, can be categorized as people who know how to trim their sails in any political wind, who seize opportunities to benefit themselves, cater to their superiors, are ruthless with the people, engage in merciless struggles and extortion, and attack others with extreme cruelty. Their opposite numbers, humanists and true Marxists, find promotion or even survival in the Communist Party extremely difficult. This has led to a sort of anti-obsolescence process, the exact opposite of the struggle for survival in nature; on China's political stage, the race goes not to the fittest, but to the least fit. Today there are two kinds of people who flourish in the Communist Party: the mediocre (those we would call political hacks) and the opportunists (those with wild political ambitions).

CHINESE society still does not function under the rule of law. Incidents of malfeasance by officials are rising at the rate of 40–50 percent a year, but few offenders come under criminal investigation, since large numbers of officials are restricted only by Party or administrative discipline. There is, in addition, a self-preservation mechanism built into the bureaucracy. The Communist parties of China and the Soviet Union differ greatly. China has ancient feudal traditions that deeply affect interpersonal relations: bloodlines, family lines, and geographical origins have created a system of common interests that unites many members of the Communist Party, forming them into factions or parties within the Party. Power struggles within the Communist Party and struggles among factions seldom occur over major political principles or theoretical differences, as is true in the Soviet Communist Party. It is fair to say that the majority of the power struggles in China arise over personal interests. The same is true at the middle and lower levels, where all sorts of networks have been established since the Party first came into power. These officials pass their authority back and forth—not in the abstract, but as perquisites of authority or the opportunities authority provides, such as employment, promotion, Party membership, transference of census registration from the countryside to the city, and so on. Back and forth it goes: I'll help you by providing an opportunity; you help me by providing some commodities. The bureaucrats' children often intermarry, establishing a blood relationship or what is called a kinship relationship. There are also relationships that go back in time, such as place of birth or schooldays, all of which lead to extremely tight networks.

BASED on figures revealed by Mao Zedong in a 1957 speech, there were at the time 1.8 million officials throughout China. There are now 27 million. This figure may seem inflated, but according to a reporter who made a survey of five provinces in 1987, the ratio of nonproducing employees to workers in factories is often one out of three, sometimes even one out of two.

THERE are, in my view, two reasons for this state of affairs. First, since the Communist Party came to power it has, in contravention of the Marxist theory of a gradual withering away of the state following the establishment of authority by the working class, handed more and more social responsibilities over to the Party and government instead of to the people. A look at the growing ranks of officials shows that the people have become an increasingly passive component in the society and could not conceivably become the masters of the country. Second, prior to 1979, working for the government as an official was the only path open to personal development without courting disaster; since then, this has become the path not only to safety and convenience but to profit as well.

AN impoverished country like China is made even poorer by the cost of supporting the bureaucracy, particularly the upper echelons, who enjoy a standard of living that is sometimes higher than that of many officials in foreign governments. Their modest salaries are supplemented by perquisites equaling several times that amount. These people constantly receive valuable gifts from their hometowns, from places where they have worked, or from people or organizations for whom they have done favors. Since they receive more food than they can eat and more things than they can use, they trade off the excess to build up a surplus of goodwill and increase their network of connections. Meanwhile, they have established an international reputation of gross inefficiency and incompetence. Abandoning modern communications media, they prefer the more comfortable methods of agricultural villages, holding meeting after meeting to promote work. How many people are lodged in Beijing's official guest houses at any given time to attend meetings in the capital? Forty to fifty thousand. A national meeting on the chemical industry was held in Shandong province in 1988, at which an incredible sixty thousand were in attendance. Railroad officials complained that there were not enough trains to handle the increased load.

THE Chinese Communist Party believes that Chinese history entered a new age in 1949, signaling the end of a bureaucratic class once and for all; there would be no more "official" ranks. In fact, there was a time when the word "official" no longer existed; officials were all known as "revolutionary cadres." But in less than a decade, contradictions between the bureaucracy and the people caused grumblings in the cities and the countryside, and within two decades even Mao himself was talking about a "bureaucratic class." Today this clique, or stratum, has become the least restrained and richest segment of China's population. Mainland China has become a bureaucratic paradise. The picture that has emerged is almost comical. On the one hand, the political representative of the bureaucracy, General Secretary Zhao Ziyang, announced in 1987 a "clean government" directive to stamp out corruption within the Party and the government; on the other hand, in 1988 members of the bureaucratic stratum, high and low, who had a firm grasp on their special privileges, initiated an unprecedented plundering of the Chinese economy, arrogating billions in public assets to themselves. While the government worried about having sufficient funds to purchase farm products from the people, the profiteering bureaucracy, controlling tens of billions of RMB, engaged in illegal commerce. While the government sold fertilizer, diesel oil, and pesticides to the peasants at controlled prices, the bureaucrats withheld commodities to raise the price and reap staggering profits.

APPENDIX

🌿

SOURCES OF THE TEXTS

LISTED below are bibliographic references for the documents in this volume. Many of the original sources are rare items. The following abbreviations are used:

(a)   The document has been edited and abridged from a longer text, but the central points of the argument have been retained.

(e)   The text has been edited for style, but not significantly changed.

(ex)   The document comprises edited excerpts from a long article or book. In these cases, where possible we provide references to a more complete English version.

(i)   The document is an integral translation of a text.

JPRS   *Joint Publications Research Service (Translations on People's Republic of China)* (Hong Kong: U.S. Consulate General).

MZZH   Xianggang Zhongwen daxue xueshenghui (Chinese University of Hong Kong Student Union) (eds.), *Minzhu Zhonghua* (Democratic China), (Hong Kong: Xianggang Zhongwen daxue xueshenghui, 1982).

SCMP   *Survey of the China Mainland Press.* (Hong Kong: U.S. Consulate General)

ZGMY   Shiyue pinglun chubanshe (eds.), *Zhongguo minyun yuan ziliao jingxuan* (Selected source material from China's people's movement), (Hong Kong: Shiyue pinglun chubanshe, 1989).

ZMY   *Zhongguo minzhu yundong* (Hong Kong). Articles from this bulletin were translated into a rough English version and published in bulletins bearing the same volume and number under the title *Monthly Bulletin on the Chinese Democratic Movement* (Hong Kong: Chinese Democratic Movement Resource Center).

Document 1   WANG SHIWEI: Wild Lily

Wang Shiwei, "Yebaihehua" (Wild Lily), *Jiefang ribao* (Liberation Daily), in two parts, March 13, 1942, p. 4 (pt. 1); March 23, 1942, p. 4 (pt. 2). (i)

Document 2   WANG SHIWEI: Politicians, Artists

Wang Shiwei, "Zhengzhijia, yishujia" (Politicians, artists), *Guyu* (Spring Rain) (Yan'an) vol. 1, no. 4, February 17, 1942. (i)

Document 3   DING LING: Thoughts on March 8 (Women's Day)
Ding Ling, "Sanbajie you gan" (Thoughts on March 8), *Jiefang ribao*, March
9, 1942, p. 4. (i)

Document 4   LUO FENG: It Is Still the Age of the *Zawen*

Luo Feng, "Haishi zawende shidai" (It is still the age of the *zawen*), *Jiefang
ribao*, March 12, 1942, p. 4. (i)

Document 5   Forum of Democratic Parties and Groups on the Rectification
Movement
SCMP no. 1543, June 4, 1957. (e)

Document 6   Symposium of Scientists
SCMP no. 1541, June 2, 1957. (e)

Document 7   What Is the Fundamental Cause of the Trade Union Crisis?
SCMP no. 1551, June 16, 1957. (a)

Document 8   LUO YUWEN: Distressing Contradiction
SCMP no. 1551, June 16, 1957. (e)

Document 9   Liu Binyan and Tai Huang: Rebellious Journalists

Renmin ribao (People's Daily), July 20, 1957; *New China News Agency*,
August 7, 1957. Translated by JPRS. Also adapted in Roderick MacFarquhar, *The Hundred Flowers* (London: Stevens and Sons, 1960), pp. 73–
76. (e)

Document 10   LIN XILING: Excerpts from a Speech Made at a Debate Held at
People's University on May 30, 1957

Lin Xiling, "Zai renmin daxue wuyue sanshiride bianlunhuishang de fayan"
(Speech made at a debate held at People's University on May 30, 1957), in
Beijing shi xuesheng lianhehui (Beijing Students' Union) *Kan! Zhe shi
shenme yanlun?* (Look! What kind of talk is this?), June 14, 1957; also in
MZZH, pp. 8–14. Translated in Dennis J. Doolin, *Communist China: The
Politics of Student Opposition* (Stanford: The Hoover Institution on War,
Revolution and Peace, 1964), pp. 30–42. (ex)

Document 11   On the New Development of "Class"

Anonymous wall poster, Beijing University, May 28, 1957. In Beijing shi
xuesheng lianhehui, *Kan! Zhe shi shenme yanlun?* Translated in Doolin,
Communist China, pp. 43–44. (a)

Document 12   HEAVEN, WATER, HEART: Democracy? Party Rule?

Heaven, Water, Heart (ps.), wall poster, Beijing Normal University, June 6,
1957. In Beijing shi xuesheng lianhehui, *Kan! Zhe shi shenme yanlun?*
Translated in Doolin, *Communist China*, pp. 49–50. (e)

Document 13   I Accuse, I Protest

Anonymous wall poster, Qinghua University, June 2, 1957. In Beijingshi xuesheng lianhehui, *Kan! Zhe shi shenme yanlun?* Translated in Doolin, *Communist China*, pp. 60–67. (a)

Document 14   WANG FANXI: Seven Theses on Socialism and Democracy

Shuang Shan (pseudonym for Wang Fanxi), "Cong Chen Duxiude 'zuihou yijian' shuoqi" (On Chen Duxiu's "last views"), in *Sixiang wenti* (Some ideological questions), (Hong Kong: n.p., 1957), pp. 5–6. (ex)

Document 15   NIE YUANZI: What Have Song Shuo, Lu Ping, and Peng Peiyun Done in the Cultural Revolution?

Nie Yuanzi and others, wall poster, Beijing University, May 25, 1966. In *Renmin ribao*, June 2, 1966, "Beijing daxue qi tongzhi yizhang dazibao jiechuan yige yinmou" (A wall poster by seven comrades in Beijing University exposes a conspiracy), p. 1. Translated in *Peking Review*, vol. 9, no. 37, September 9, 1966, pp. 19–20. (e)

Document 16   Red Guard Statements, 1966–1967

Articles selected from *Renmin ribao*, August 26, 1966, and *Yangcheng wanbao* (Guangzhou) August 27, 1966. Translated in SCMP no. 3776, August 1966, pp. 6–9 and 19–20. "On Collective Boarding Schools," translated in Victor Nee, *The Cultural Revolution at Peking University* (New York: Monthly Review Press, 1969), pp. 75–84. (a)

Document 17   "Revolutionary" Power-holders

Mao Zedong, wall poster, August 5, 1966, "Paoda lingsibu" (Bombard the headquarters), in *Renmin ribao*, August 5, 1967, p. 1. Translated in *Peking Review*, vol. 10, no. 33, August 11, 1967. (i)

Proclamation of the Guizhou Proletarian Revolutionary Rebel General Headquarters in *Peking Review*, vol. 10, no. 7, February 10, 1967. (e)

Document 18   SHENGWULIAN: Whither China?

Shengwulian, *Zhongguo xiang he qu?* (Whither China?), in MZZH, pp. 31–50. Translated in The 70s (eds.), *The Revolution is Dead, Long Live the Revolution* (Hong Kong: The 70s, 1976), pp. 180–200. (ex)

Document 19   LI YI ZHE: On Socialist Democracy and the Legal System

Li Yi Zhe, wall poster, Guangzhou, November 1974, "Guanyu shehuizhuyi de minzhu yu fazhi" (On socialist democracy and the legal system), in *Zhonggong yanjiu* (Taiwan), vol. 9, no. 11, November 1975, pp. 45–98. A complete translation is in Anita Chan, Stanley Rosen, and Jonathan Unger (eds.), *On Socialist Democracy and the Chinese Legal System: The Li Yizhe Debates* (Armonk, N.Y.: M. E. Sharpe, 1985), pp. 31–86; also in The 70s (eds.), *The Revolution is Dead*, pp. 251–83. (ex)

Document 20   WANG FANXI: On the "Great Proletarian Cultural Revolution"

Shuang Shan (Wang Fanxi), *Lun wuchanjieji wenhua da geming* (On the great proletarian cultural revolution), (Hong Kong: Xinda chubanshe, 1974), (text dated 1967). Translated in The 70s (eds.), *The Revolution is Dead*, pp. 74–106. (ex)

Document 21   WANG XIZHE: Mao Zedong and the Cultural Revolution

Wang Xizhe, "Mao Zedong yu wenhua da geming" (Mao Zedong and the great cultural revolution), *Qishi niandai* (The Seventies), no. 133, February 1981. A complete translation is in Chan, Rosen, and Unger (eds.), *On Socialist Democracy*, pp. 177–260; also translated by Anthony Kwok (Hong Kong: Plough Publications, 1981). (ex)

Document 22   YI MING: China: A History That Must Be Told

Yi Ming, *Renminzhi sheng* (Voice of the People), July 8, 1979. (a)

Document 23   WEI JINGSHENG: Democracy or a New Dictatorship?

Wei Jingsheng, "Yao minzhu haishi yao xinde ducai?" (Do we want democracy or a new dictatorship?), *Tansuo* (Explorations), Special Issue, March 1979; also in MZZH, pp. 192–96. Translated by John Scott and Pamela Barnsley in *Harper and Queens*, March 1980. (e)

Document 24   Interview with Xu Wenli

"Siwu luntan zhaojiren Xu Wenli da jizhe wen" (Interview with Xu Wenli, Convenor of the *April Fifth Forum*), *Xuexi tongxun* (Study Newsletter), Beijing, October 1980; also in MZZH, pp. 286–99. (ex)

Document 25   XU WENLI: A Reform Program for the Eighties

Xu Wenli, "Cujin gengshen bianfade jianyishu" (Proposals to push forward political reforms in the 1980s), Autumn 1980, MZZH, pp. 300–304. (e)

Document 26   EDITORIAL BOARD, *RENMINZHI LU*: A Statement of Clarification

Renminzhi lu bianjibu (People's Road, Editorial Board), "Shishide dengqing" (Clarification of facts), ZMY vol. 1, no. 7, August 1981, pp. 4–5. (e)

Document 27   COMMENTATOR, *ZEREN:* Democracy and Legality Are Safeguards of Stability and Unity

Zeren pinglunyuan (Duty Commentator), "Minzhu, fazhi shi anding tuanjiede baozhang" (Democracy and legality are safeguards of stability and unity), *Zeren* (Duty) no. 3, January 16, 1981; also in ZMY vol. 1, no. 4, April 1981, pp. 8–9. (e)

Document 28   GE TIAN: A Guangdong Youth Forum on Wall Posters

Ge Tian, "Guangdong qingnian zuotan wu zhong quan hui" (A Guangdong youth forum on the Fifth Plenary Session of the CCP Central Committee), *Shiyue pinglun* (October Review), Hong Kong, no. 42, 1980, p. 9. (ex)

Document 29   GONG BO: The Wind Rises from among the Duckweed: Elections at Beijing University

Gong Bo, "Feng qi yu qingpingzhi mo: 1980 nian Beijing daxue xuesheng qu jingxuan renmin daibiao zongshu" (The wind rises from among the duckweed: how Beijing University students held elections for delegates in 1980), *Sixu* (Train of Thought), no. 1; also in ZMY vol. 1, no. 3, March 1980, pp. 2–3. (e)

Document 30   HE NONG: Election Scandal in a Rural Commune

He Nong, "Zhongguo yige nongcun gongshe xuanju yinqide fengbo" (Election scandal in a rural commune of China), *Fengfan* (Boat's Sail) no. 1, December 1979; also in ZMY vol. 1, no. 3, March 1980, p. 10. (i)

Document 31   ZHENG XING: The Election Movement Is in the Ascendant

Zheng Xing, "Zhongguo gedi gongren canjia difang xuanju" (Workers in many areas participate in local elections), *Zeren*, no. 3, January 14, 1981; also in ZMY vol. 1, no. 3, March 1980, pp. 7–9. (e)

Document 32   The Student Movement in Hunan

"Qunian Hunan xuesheng yundong shikuang" (The real story of the student movement in Hunan last year), *Renminzhi sheng* (Voice of the People) no. 6, 1981; also in ZMY vol. 1, no. 8, November 1981, pp. 10–12. (a)

Document 33   CHEN DING: Youth Disturbances in China's Far West

Chen Ding, "Xinjiang saoluan shijian zhenxiang" (The truth about the disturbances in Xinjiang), *Zhengming* (Contention), Hong Kong, May 1, 1981, pp. 20–24. (a)

Document 34   Advertisement: Modern Clothes

"Shizhuang guanggao" (Advertisement for modern clothes), (Beijing wall poster), printed in *Siwu luntan* (April Fifth Forum), no. 8, April 1, 1979, p. 26. (i)

Document 35   FENGFAN: The Reawakening of the Chinese Working Class

"Zhongguo gongren jiejide xin juexing" (The reawakening of the Chinese working class), *Fengfan*, no. 1, December 1979; also in ZMY vol. 1, no. 3, March 1980, p. 1. (a)

Document 36   FU SHENQI: In Memory of Wang Shenyou, Pioneer of the Democratic Movement, Teacher, Comrade

Fu Shenqi, "Wang Shenyou lieshi yong chuibuxiu" (The hero Wang Shenyou will never be forgotten), September 1, 1980. In MZZH, pp. 363–68. (e)

Document 37   Interview with Yang Jing

Guanchajia (Observer), (Hong Kong), no. 42, May 20, 1981. Translated by He Fu. (e)

Document 38   XIAO RUI: Eyewitness Account of the Arrest of Liu Qing

Xiao Rui, "Liu Qing beibu jingguo mudu ji" (Eyewitness account of the arrest of Liu Qing), ZMY vol. 1, no. 7, August 1981, pp. 12–13. (e)

Document 39   THE FAMILY OF LIU QING: Liu Qing Is Innocent!

Liu Qing jiashu (The family of Liu Qing), "Liu Qing wuzui, gongan wangfa" (Liu Qing is innocent, the Public Security Bureau is breaking the law), ZMY vol. 1, no. 3, March 1980, pp. 11–12. (e)

Document 40   LIU QING: Sad Memories and Prospects: My Appeal to the Tribunal of the People

Liu Qing, "Leisangde huigu yu panwang—wo xiang shehui fating konggao" (Sad memories and prospects: my appeal to the tribunal of the people), *Qishi niandai*, no. 10, 1980, pp. 56–66. Another version is in Liu Qing, *Yuzhong shouji* (Prison manuscript), (Hong Kong: Baixing ban yuekan chubanshe, 1981). A complete translation is in *Chinese Sociology and Anthropology*, vol. 15, nos. 1–2, Fall/Winter 1982/83, pp. 3–181. (ex)

Document 41   Women Are Human Beings Too

Wall poster, December 1980, Beijing University. Translated by Anita Rind and Murray Smith. (e)

Document 42   China and Solidarnosc

Qingdao *Lilun qi* bianjibu shelun (Editorial comment, Theoretical Banner, Qingdao), "Guanliao tequan jieji tongzhide sangzhong" (The death knell of the rule of the privileged class of bureaucrats), *Lilun qi* (Theoretical Banner), (Qingdao), February 1981; also in ZMY, vol. 1, no. 4, April 1981, pp. 14–15. Translated by Matthew Crabbe. (e)

Document 43   Proposal to Resign from the Party and Prepare an "Association to Promote China's Democracy Movement"

Renmin daxue bufen gongchandang yuan jiaoshi (Some lecturers at People's University, Communist Party members), "Tuichu gongchandang, chouzu 'Zhongguo minzhu yundong cujinhui' de changyi" (Proposal to resign from the Party and prepare an "Association to Promote China's Democracy Movement"), ZGMY, vol. 1, p. 63. (i)

Document 44   Letter of Petition

Beijing daxue xuesheng chouweihui (Preparatory Committee of Beijing University Students), "Qingyuanshu" (Letter of petition), ZGMY, vol. 1, p. 80. (i)

Document 45   REN WANDING: Speech in Tian'anmen Square

Ren Wanding, speech, April 21, 1989. In *Minzhu qiang* (Democracy wall), (Hong Kong), no. 9, 1989. Translated in a different version, *China Soul* (London), February 1991. (a)

Document 46   A Worker's Letter to the Students

Anonymous, Beijing Normal University, April 28, 1989, "Yige gongren zhi xueshengde xin" (A worker's letter to the students), ZGMY, vol. 1, p. 33. (i)

Document 47   A Choice Made on the Basis of Conscience and Party Spirit: An Open Letter to All Party Members

Anonymous wall poster, People's University, April 28, 1989, "Liangxin he dangxing mian qiande jueze: zhi guangda dangyuan di gongkai xin" (A choice made on the basis of conscience and Party spirit: an open letter to all Party members), ZGMY, vol. 1, p. 59. (i)

Document 48   Hoist High the Flag of Reason

Beishida zhiye gemingjia (A professional revolutionary at Beijing Normal University) "Juqi lixingde qizhi" (Hoist high the flag of reason), ZGMY, vol. 1, p. 73. Translated by Angus Pearson. (i)

Document 49   Where I Stand

Anonymous wall poster, "Wo biaotai" (Where I stand), Beijing Normal University, April 30, 1989, ZGMY, vol. 1, p. 62. (i)

Document 50   YANG XX: The Socialist Multiparty System and China

Anonymous wall poster, "Shehuizhuyi duo dang zhi yu Zhongguo" (The socialist multiparty system and China), People's University, May 19, 1989, ZGMY, vol. 1, pp. 47–48. Translated by Angus Pearson. (i)

Document 51   A Letter to the People

Zhongyang guojia jiguan bufen ganbu (Some cadres in central state organizations), "Gao renmin shu" (A letter to the people), ZGMY, vol. 1, p. 60. (i)

Document 52   Preparatory Program of the Autonomous Federation of Workers of the Capital

Shoudu gongren zizhi lianhehui choubei weiyuanhui (Preparatory Committee of the Autonomous Federation of Workers of the Capital), "Shoudu gongren zizhi lianhehui choubei wangling" (Preparatory Program of the Autonomous Federation of Workers of the Capital), ZGMY, vol. 1, p. 30. (i)

Document 53   Workers' Declaration

Shoudu gongren zizhi lianhehui choubei weiyuanhui, "Gongren xuanyan" (Workers' declaration), ZGMY, vol. 1, p. 30. (i)

Document 54   Open Letter to the Students from an Army Veteran

Yiwei lao junren (An army veteran), "Yiwei lao junren zhi xueshengde gongkaixin" (Open letter to the students from an army veteran), ZGMY, vol. 1, p. 43. (i)

Document 55   Smart Thieves' Voice

Anonymous letter, "Shentoumende xinsheng" (Smart thieves' voice), ZGMY, vol. 2, p. 68. (i)

Document 56   Provisional Statutes of the Autonomous Federation of Workers of the Capital

"Shoudu gongren zizhi lianhehui linshi zhangcheng" (Provisional statutes of the Autonomous Federation of Workers of the Capital), ZGMY, vol. 2, p. 42. (e)

Document 57   LIN XILING: Statement

Lin Xiling, text of speech to rally in Paris, June 7, 1989. (ex)

Document 58   WANG FANXI: Statement

Wang Fanxi, text of statement to Chinese students in Leeds, England, June 1989. (i)

Document 59   AN EYEWITNESS: The Massacre in Tian'anmen Square

Wenhuibao, Hong Kong, June 5, 1989. (e)

Document 60   CHAI LING: Account of the Beijing Massacre

Chai Ling, message broadcast on Hong Kong TV, June 10, 1989. (a)

Document 61   YANG LIAN: The Square

Yang Lian, *The Dead in Exile*, translated by Mabel Lee (Kingston: Tian'anmen Publications (P.O. Box 4100, Kingston ACT 2604 Australia), 1990), pp. 22–23. (ex)

Document 62   Open Letter to the Chinese Communist Party

Yang Hao et al. "Open Letter to the Chinese Communist Party," *Chaoliu* (Hong Kong), no. 40, June 15, 1990, pp. 12–13. (a)

Document 63   SU SHAOZHI: Proposals for Reform of the Political Structure, 1986

Su Shaozhi, "Zhengzhi tizhi gaige chuyi" (Proposals for reform of the political structure), *Dushu*, no. 9, 1986, pp. 3–7. English translation in Su Shaozhi, *Democratization and Reform* (Nottingham: Spokesman, 1988), pp. 161–69. (i)

Document 64   YAN JIAQI: The Theory of Two Cultural Factors

Yan Jiaqi, "Wode sixiang zizhuan" (The autobiography of my thought), *Xinhua wenzhai*, 1989, vol. 1, pp. 130–37. (ex)

Document 65   FANG LIZHI: Problems of Modernization

Interview with Fang Lizhi by Liang Shuohua, *Mingbao yuekan* (Hong Kong), no. 271, July 1988, pp. 15–24. Full English translation in JPRS, October 3, 1988. (ex)

Document 66 WANG RUOSHUI: In Defense of Humanism

Wang Ruoshui, "Wei rendaozhuyi bianhu" (In defense of humanism), in Wang Ruoshui, *Wei rendaozhuyi bianhu* (Beijing: Sanlian shudian, 1986), pp. 217–33. The article is dated January 1983. Full English translation in JPRS, October 3, 1988. (a)

Document 67 WANG RUOWANG: On Political Reform

Interview with Wang Ruowang by Chen Yige, in *Jiushi niandai* (Hong Kong), no. 227, December 1988, pp. 65–75. Full English translation in JPRS, April 12, 1989. (a)

Document 68 LIU BINYAN: The Bureaucratic Paradise

Liu Binyan, *China's Crisis, China's Hope*, translated by Howard Greenblatt, (Cambridge, Mass.: Harvard University Press, 1990). (ex)

INDEX

Note: When a whole text is cited, references to page numbers are in *italics*.

"Advertisement: Modern Clothes," *227–28*
African students in China, 54
agriculture
 collectivization of, 52–53, 176, 204, 319
 fantasies in, 176–77
 1957 criticism of practices in, 88–89
 1958–1962 drop in, 177
 women tractor drivers in, 86
 See also peasants
agro-socialism, 159–61
Ai Qing, 9, 13
Aksu (Xingjiang), 222–26
alienation, 21, 157, 314–16, 321
Amnesty International, 26–27, 135, 240, 247
anarchism, 112, 195, 313
Anhui, coal of, 311
Anti-Japanese Writers' Association, 11
antipolitical politics, 42
Anyang (Henan), 186
April Fifth Forum (Siwu luntan; periodical), 26, 185, 234–35, 239, 242–45, 248, *259*, 262
April Fifth Movement. *See* Tian'anmen Square (Beijing)—1976 demonstrations in
Arrow and Target (Shi yu di; Yan'an wall newspaper), 11
artists, 23, 24
 in Wang Shiwei's "Politicians, Artists," 75–78
 See also Yan'an Forum on Literature and Art
Asia Watch, 180
Asiatic mode of production, 160
Association to Promote China's Democracy Movement (APD), *264–65*
Autonomous Federation of Workers. *See* Workers' Autonomous Federation (WAF)
Autonomous Union of University Students, 286, 291

Bacon, Francis, 273
Bai Hua, 311

bankrupt firms, 193
Banner of Theory (Lilun qi; unofficial journal), *259*
Baoding (Hebei), 186
Baoshan Iron and Steel Works, 172
barber shops and hairdressing salons, 109, 111, *113–14*
Beijing
 boarding school for children of cadres in, 116
 Cultural Revolution in, 125
 dissidents in, 26
 Gorbachev in, 30
 influx of people into, 22–23
 1979 disorders in, 24
 numbers lodged in guest houses of, 330
 thieves of, *282*
 Wang Shiwei in, 9
Beijing Commune, 31, 57
Beijing Municipal Party Committee, 105
Beijing No. 2 Middle School, Red Guard statement from, *109–11*
Beijing Normal University, 265, 270
 "Hoist High the Flag of Reason," *271–73*
 1957 wall poster at, 99
 1989 wall poster at, *274*
 Red Guards' statement on boarding schools for children of cadres, *115–20*
Beijing opera, 84n.1
Beijing Student Union, 95
Beijing Students' Autonomous Federation, 282
Beijing University, 180, 265
 Cultural Revolution wall poster from, 104–8
 in Hundred Flowers, 15–16, 98
 "Letter of Petition," 266
 1980 elections at, *202–10*, 237, 257
 radio station of, 282
Beijing Youth (Beijing qingnian; publication), 213, 239
Bernstein, Eduard, 48
"Big Disturbance Must Be Made at Qinghua University, A" (Red Guards), *111–13*

big-character posters
  in Cultural Revolution
    discouraged by Beijing University offi-
      cials, 106–7
    hairdressers' support of, 113
    Mao's "Bombard the Headquarters,"
      120, *121*
    by Nie Yuanzi, 104–8
    "Proclamation of the Guizhou Prole-
      tarian Revolutionary Rebel General
      Headquarters," *121–24*
    See also wall posters
birdcage economy, 324
"black hands," 44
Bo Yibo, 175, 294
Boat's Sail (Fengfan; unofficial journal),
  211
    "The Reawakening of the Chinese Work-
      ing Class," *228–29*
Bohai II disaster, 172
"Bombard the Headquarters" (Mao's
  poster), 120, *121*
Brazil, 323
Brecht, Bertolt, 37
Brezhnev, Leonid, 137, 185, 319
Bukharin, Nikolai, 48, 161
bureaucracy
  Cultural Revolution's attack on, 17, 20,
    32, 124–34, 146, 148, 150, 163, 164,
    179
  democracy movement's opposition to,
    21, 33, 95, 100, 170–71
  democratic parties' criticism of, 85–88
  elections manipulated by, 210, 213, 215–
    21, 230, 237
  Hu Feng's opposition to, 14
  Hundred Flowers campaign against, 14,
    15, 150
  Liu Binyan on, *327–31*
  Mao as representative of, 152–54, 162
  opportunists in, 166, 171–73, 329
  in Poland, 259–62
  in post-capitalist society, 157
  ranks in, 73–75, 95–96
  reform process and, 189
  rice bowl of, 49
  size of, 329
  in Soviet Union, 74, 152–54, 172, 185
  Wang Fanxi on, 101–3
  at Yan'an
    Mao's campaign against, 8, 9
    Wang Shiwei on, 70–71, 73–75, 76

"Bureaucratic Paradise, The" (Liu Binyan),
  327–31
Burma, 324
Bush, George, 33

CAD (China Alliance for Democracy), 59–
  60, 317
cadres
  arrogance of, 179
  "bean-cake," 89
  children of
    business interests of, 301
    collective boarding schools for children
      of, *115–20*
    privileges of, 108, 141
  in Cultural Revolution, 126
  problems of promotion of, 87–88
  ranks of, 73–75, 95–96
  reform opposed by sections of, 206
  retired, benefits for, 193
  "rubber," 89
  of true proletarian authority, 132, 133
  See also Communist Party, Chinese
capitalism
  "abnormal" stage of, 148–49
  call for new interpretation of, 16
  changing nature of, 307–8
  Cultural Revolution attacks on, 109–10,
    126
  dangers of Chinese restoration of, 285
  democracy movement and, 41–42, 48–
    49, 59–60
  Deng's attitude toward, 53
  as dying system, 134
  in "four small dragons," 48–49, 323
  good and bad features of, 308
  intellectuals' support of, 43–44
  Li Xiling on, 284
  making comparisons with, 97
  multiparty system under, 276
  radical reformers and, 40
  as social-Fascist, 18
  socialist lag behind, 304
  state
    in China, 158–59
    Lenin's theory of, 176
  See also entrepreneurs
capitalist roaders, 7, 20, 108, 109, 115–16,
  119, 128, 133, 136, 139, 140, 147, 149,
  159, 161, 173, 314
  dictatorship over, 129
  Lin Biao as one of, 138

Carter, Jimmy, 187
Chai Ling
  "Account of the Beijing Massacre," *291–94*
  background of, 291
Chang Sucheng, 89
Changsha
  in Cultural Revolution, 125
  1980 student movement in, *217–21*
  1989 dissidents in, 25
Chaoliu (Hong Kong publication), 296
Chen Boda, 18, 134, 179
Chen Ding, "Youth Disturbances in China's Far West," *221–27*
Chen Duxiu, 4–5, 11, 101, 285
Chen Erjin, 21
Chen Lü, 247
Chen Qichang, 9, 12
Chen Shu, 114
Chen Shutong, 85, 87
Chen Xitian, 201
Chen Yi, 125
Chen Yige, 317
Chen Yiyang, 134–35, 200
Chen Yizhi, 59–60
Chen Yun, 30, 176
Cheng Yulian, 114
Chiang Kai-shek (Jiang Jieshi), 6, 9, 54, 94, 101, 142, 272, 324
  Mao's driving out of, 167–68
Chile, 323
"China: A History That Must Be Told" (Yi Ming), *175–80*
China Alliance for Democracy (CAD), 59–60, 317
China Association for the Promotion of Democracy, 85
China Democratic League, 85, 86
China Focus (periodical), 40
China Spring (1979–1981), 19, 21–29, 32, 157–262
  Wang Shiwei's ideas in, 4
China Watch (journal), 48
China Workers' and Peasants' Democratic Party, 85
China Youth (journal), 16, 95
Chinese Academy of Sciences, 265
Chinese Academy of Social Sciences, 265, 299, 305
"Chinese Declaration of Human Rights, The," 268
Chinese People's Political Consultative

Conference (CPPCC), 191, 194
  democratic parties' criticism of, 86
  Fifth, 189
  Sixth, 190, 192
Chinese Women's Study Association, 207, 257
"Choice Made on the Basis of Conscience and Party Spirit: An Open Letter to All Party Members, A," *270–71*
Chongqing (Sichuan), 1989 protests in, 32, 51
Christ, Jesus, 21
Christiansen, Flemming, 227
Ci Xi (Empress Dowager), 272
cities
  influx of people into, 22, 32, 53, 221
  1990s prosperity of, 60
class struggle
  in Cultural Revolution, 126, 132–33
  desire for special privileges covered up by idea of, 86
  falsification of doctrine of, 176
  Wang Xizhe's prediction of, 173
clothes
  Cultural Revolution condemnation of, 190, 111
  1979 "advertisement" for, *227–28*
coal, 125, 311
collective leadership, 86
  Mao's assault on, 160–61
collectivism, 313–14
command economy, 58, 159, 160
communism
  democratic, 151
  Mao's attempt to build, 160–61, 177, 205
  in one country, 151
  possibility of one-step realization of, 132, 133
Communist Manifesto (Manifesto of the Communist Party), 112, 281, 315
Communist Party, Chinese
  Bolshevization of, 4–7
  Central Committee, 160, 161, 170, 172, 189, 202, 217, 221, 274, 294, 320, 321, 326, 328
    in Cultural Revolution, 105–8, 110, 112, 114–16, 122, 147, 163–64
    force threatened against Tian'anmen Square students, 270–71
    1957 protest against, 99
    Tai Huang's letter to, 93–94
  Central Secretariat, 190

Communist Party, Chinese *(cont.)*
  collusion of government and, 86–87, 98,
    102, 159, 207, 272, 302
  confidence of people lost by, 274
  Congresses of
    Eighth, 178, 186
    Ninth, 165, 177
  conservatives in ("the left"), 39, 58
  corruption in, 34–35, 50, 52, 179, 180,
    205, 264, 276, 277, 296, 320–21,
    330–31
  democratic parties' criticism of, 85–88
  democratic tradition of, 7, 33–34, 47,
    177, 178
  Fang on lack of success of, 43
  first dissident of, 13
  first independent opposition to, 31
  future of, 55–56, 59, 60, 324–25, 327
  GMD 1930s policy against, 54
  as guiding power, 191
  increasing paralysis of, 321–22
  intellectuals always dominated by, ix–x
  legitimacy of, 17
  masses' revolutionary supervision over,
    140
  members' reregistration suggested for,
    191
  moderate reformers in, 39–40
  1989 proposed resignation of intellectu-
    als from, *264–65*
  non-party people looked down upon by,
    87
  old men as leaders of, 97–98. *See also*
    Gang of Elders
  privileges of cadres of, 90, 93, 94, 117,
    126, 141–43, 179, 187–88, 260, 268–
    70, 273, 276, 296, 300, 330
  wastage, 310
  Zhao Ziyang's call for investigation,
    278
  radical reformers in, 40
  Stalinism of, 5–7, 152–55, 158, 185, 194
  Wang Yizhe's 1981 support for, 174
  women's work not considered important
    by, 86
  See also cadres
Communist Youth League, 95–96, 195,
  200, 201, 222, 227, 229, 230
Constitution
  elections in, 99, 183–84
  human rights in, 197, 246, 304
  Four Great Freedoms deleted, 24–25,

  28, 171, 200, 202, 207, 209, 216,
    217
  freedom of correspondence, 195
  judicial process, 240
  Li Yi Zhe on, 137–38, 142–45
  Xu Wenli's proposals, 192
  1957 criticism of, 99
  1970 draft, 139
  Party as vanguard in, 318
Contention (Zhengming; periodical), 202,
  337
contradictions
  in capitalist vs. communist countries,
    148–49
  Mao on, 15, 91
  after socialism is established, 98
  in trade union movement, 91, 92, 96–97
corruption
  in Party, 34–35, 50, 52, 179, 180, 205,
    264, 276, 277, 296, 320–21, 330–31
  Beijing University students' call for in-
    vestigation, 266
  of Zhao Ziyang, 40
  in PLA, 39
counterrevolution
  call for end of concept of, 269
  Constitutional rights equated with, 99,
    197
  Cultural Revolution's struggle against,
    109, 121–22
  freedom of speech and question of, 207
  number of people executed for, 98
cronyism, 35
Cultural Revolution, (1966–1976), 7, 17–
  21, 104–55, 301
  army in, 17, 18, 36, 124, 127–30, 164,
    165
  August Local Revolutionary War, 128–
    30, 132, 133
  beginning of, 162
    Nie Yuanzi's poster, 104–8
  Central Cultural Revolution Group, 127,
    147, 165–66, 179, 232
  democracy movement and, 27, 28
  dual nature of, 174–75
  February Adverse Current, 127–28
  as genuine mass movement, 175, 178,
    180
  gun-seizing in, 128, 130
  humanism implies rejection of, 316
  January Revolutionary Storm, 124–27,
    132, 133

Li Yi She's analysis of, *134–45,* 157, 166, 173, 200
Mao on need for another, 30
1989 Tian'anmen occupation compared to, 31–32
positive legacy of, 32, 158, 168–69
September Setback, 130–31
Wang Fanxi's analysis of, *145–55*
workers' 1989 support for, 51
See also Mao Zedong—in Cultural Revolution; Red Guards
culture, two factors in, *305–7*
Czechoslovakia, 259

Dada, 21
Dai Qing, 4, 296
Dangdai (Hong Kong newspaper), 286
"Declaring War on the Old World" (Red Guard statement), *109–11*
democracy
Chen Duxiu on, 5
China's lack of, 6, 144, 181
economic, 102
economic obstacles to, 186–87
exhausted by long wars, 6
as fifth modernization, 180
genuine, 207
Lenin's denial of value of, 101
Li Yi Zhe on, 141–43
Mao's attitude toward, 164
market economy and, 35
mass, 138
middle class needed before, 44, 60
1980s Party support for, 31
Party should learn from, 16
in Party tradition, 7, 33–34, 37, 177, 178
people's, 99, 144, 155
proletarian, 261
sea power and, 43
socialism and. *See* Socialism—democracy and
Swedish-type, 61
workers' concept of, 58
Yan'an support for, 10–11
Zhao's attitude toward, 45–46
"Democracy, the Fifth Modernization" (Wei Jingsheng), 180
"Democracy and Legality Are Safeguards of Stability and Unity" (Commentator, *Zeren*), *196–99*
democracy movement
bureaucracy and, 170–71

chances for victory of, 39
Chinese democratic parties should be won over by, 277
foreign contacts of, 180, 185, 194–96
generational division of, 45
history of, 59
1978–1981, 19, 21–29, 32, 59, 169–70
of 1990s, 59–61
not a political party, 57–58
proposed Association to Promote China's Democracy Movement (APD), *264–65*
supported by the rehabilitated, 19, 20–21
See also journals, unofficial
"Democracy or a New Dictatorship?" (Wei Jingsheng), *180–84,* 248
"Democracy? Party Rule?" (Heaven, Water, Heart), 99
Democracy Wall
of 1957, 15
of 1979, 22–24, 27, 28, 59, 186, 197, 206–8, 227, 268
Hu Yaobang and, 267
sale of Wei's trial transcripts, 240, 244, 248, 250
democratic centralism, 161, 302
democratic parties (in People's Republic), 13, 16, 29, 275, 276
1957 forum of, 85–88
proposed democracy movement's winning over of, 277
as puppets, 99
Democratic Youth group, 158
Deng Tuo, 106, 107
Deng Xiaoping, 16, 35, 134, 174
as behind-the-scenes manipulator, 272
consultative style of, 7
Cultural Revolution and
denounced, 17, 104, 108, 115, 117, 119, 164
he cannot be blamed, 24
democracy movement and, 21–24, 28, 32, 170
trumpet pants attacked, 227
Wei Jingsheng's denunciation, 181–84
economic strategy of, 34, 48–49, 53–54, 311
1976 disappearance of, 167
1989 Tian'anmen occupation and, 29–30, 38, 278
his later statement of causes, 298
use of troops threatened, 270–71
personality cult opposed by, 178

Deng Xiaoping (cont.)
  reforms of, 32, 34–35
  as scientific socialist, 232
  students' opposition to, 41, 57
  succession to, 55
  Wei Jingsheng's imprisonment supervised
    by, 180
Diaoyu reefs and islands, 54
dictatorship
  class, 16
  Deng Xiaoping's, 182–84
  feudal social-Fascist, 136–39
  mass, 126
    armed, 129–31
  one-party, 273, 275, 297, 317–20
  people's democratic, 99
  of the proletariat, 123–24, 129
    danger of Communist bureaucracy,
      157
    democracy and, 101–3
    Li Yi Zhe on, 142–43
    Mao dynasty disguised as, 158–59
    one-party rule equated with, 318
    people's democracy needed for, 144
    Wei Jingsheng's "incitement to over-
      throw," 181
  Qin Shi Huangdi's establishment of, 271–
    72
Ding Ling
  background of, 9, 78
  in Yan'an, 8, 11, 83
  "Thoughts on March 8 (Women's
    Day)," 78–82
"Distressing Contradiction" (Luo Yuwen),
  92
divorce of wife for political backwardness,
  79–80
"dog-beating team," 224–25
dogmatism, 96, 169, 170, 172–73
Dong Zhongshu, 138, 156n.9
Doolin, Dennis J., 95
dress shops, 109, 111
Dreyfus case, 240
Duty. See Responsibility

East Germany, 275, 308
Eastern Europe
  Communist reform in, 277
  end of Stalinism in, 55, 59, 61
economic growth
  by command, 58, 159, 160
  dangers of, 49

economic centralism and, 323–24
  before Great Leap Forward, 176
  political democracy and, 207, 238–39
economic readjustment, 238–39
economism, 122, 123
education
  in boarding schools for cadres, 115–20
  low level of, among peasants, 187
  Mao's dictum on, 118
  Party's rejection of reform in, 264
  proposed reform in, 193–94, 207–8, 266
  See also specific universities
egalitarianism
  as aim of utopian socialists, 176
  Communist ideals of, 319
  in "Wild Lily," 73–75
"Election Movement Is in the Ascendant,
  The" (Zheng Xing), 213–17
"Election Scandal in a Rural Commune"
  (He Nong), 210–13
elections
  at Beijing University (1980), 202–10, 237
  call for parties to compete in, 273
  in Chinese Constitution, 99, 183–84
  of democracy movement activists, 237
  Hunan student protests against, 217–21
  Liberation Daily's attack on, 197–99
  Mao on, 164
  "particularities" vs. "generalities" in,
    209
  in Party, reform proposed, 325
  people's mandate only created by, 184
  in proletarian dictatorship, Wang Fanxi
    on, 102
  in rural commune, a scandal, 210–13
  Su Shaozhi's critique of, 302
  by workers, 213–17, 229–30
  Xu Wenli's critique of, 190
Engels, Friedrich, 112, 160
entrepreneurs
  as new class, 34–35
  state-owned capital deposited overseas
    by, 56
  See also capitalism
Eurocommunists, 188
exchange of revolutionary experiences, 20,
  31, 137
existentialism, 20
Explorations (Tansuo; publication), 180,
  181, 248
"Eyewitness Account of the Arrest of Liu
  Qing" (Xiao Rui), 239–44

families, separation of workers from, *228–29*

Fang Li, 298

Fang Lizhi, 29, 36, 43–48, 59, 61, 62
  background of, 307
  "Problems of Modernization," *307–12*

Fang Zhiyuan, 206, 207

fascism, 96, 134, 148, 294, 318
  social, 18, 136–39, 197

FDC (Federation for a Democratic China), 59–60

federal system proposed, 191

Federation for a Democratic China (FDC), 59–60

Feigon, Lee, 33, 51

feminism
  Ding Ling's essay on, 78–82
  See also women

Feng Congde, 291

Feng Youlan, 67n.72

Fengfan. See Boat's Sail

Fertile Soil (Wotu; unofficial journal), 237

feudalism, 96, 117–19, 128, 136–37, 140, 144, 177, 190, 272, 308
  humanism as opposition to, 314
  of Party, 232, 299–302
  revival of, 180
  social, 277

Feuerbach, Paul von, 313–15

Finance Ministry, 125

five-year plans, 87, 176

Follow Chairman Mao and Move Forward Bravely Amid the Great Wind and Waves (Wang Shenyou), 231

forced labor *(juyi)*, 254, 255

Four Clean-ups Campaign, 205

Four Great Freedoms, 24–25, 28, 171, 200–202, 207, 209, 216, 217

Four Modernizations, 166–67, 172, 191, 195, 229, 245, 299

four powers, 191

Four Principles, 194–96

Fourier, Charles, 314

France, democracy movement in exile in, 59, 284, 296, 305

free competition, 20

free enterprise, 21, 57

freedom of association, 137, 197

freedom of belief, 191

freedom of correspondence, 195

freedom of speech, 50, 99, 137, 197, 207
  Hu Ping on, 237

intellectuals' call for, 15
  in proletarian dictatorship, 102
  wall posters and, 216

freedom of the press (freedom of publication), 25, 30, 50, 137, 195, 197, 207, 236, 246, 266
  abolition of autocracy as prerequisite for, 273
  draft ordinance for, 209
  in proletarian dictatorship, 102

Friedman, Milton, 43

frontier, resettlement of people to, *221–27*

Fu Shenqi, 25
  background of, 229–30
  "In Memory of Wang Shenyou, Pioneer of the Democratic Movement, Teacher, Comrade," *229–34*

Fu Yuehua, 245–47, 253

Fudan University (Shanghai), 237

Gang of Elders, 30, 33, 39

Gang of Four, 24, 28, 135, 157, 169, 174, 177, 183, 188, 195, 197–98, 201, 206, 232, 318
  downfall of, 22, 54, 162, 171, 196, 233, 240
  trial of, 26–27

Gansu, Yumen strike in, 97

Gao Ju, 105

Gao Yunpeng, 108

Ge Tian, "A Guangdong Youth Forum on Wall Posters," *199–202*

Germany, Stalin's policy in, 155

ghosts and monsters, 122

Gittings, John, 54, 60

GMD. *See* Guomindang

golf, 270

Gong Bo, "The Wind Rises from among the Duckweed: Elections at Beijing University," *202–10*

Gong Ping, 213, 214

Gongren ribao. See Workers' Daily

Gorbachev, Mikhail, 42, 319, 326
  in Beijing, 30

Gramsci, Antonio, 48

Great Britain
  Mao's desire to catch up with, 160
  Wang Fanxi in exile in, 285
  See also Hong Kong

Great Leap Forward, 7, 17, 104, 160, 161, 176, 205

Grlickov, Aleksandar, 300

Guanchajia. See *Observer*
Guangdong
 in Cultural Revolution, number killed
   and imprisoned, 136
 Four Principles warning by government
   of, 194–96
 1980s economic growth in, 38
 "Guangdong Youth Forum on Wall Posters, A" (Ge Tian), *199–202*
Guangming Daily (Guangming ribao;
   newspaper), 218
Guangzhou
 in Cultural Revolution, 108
 proposals of hairdressers, *113–14*
 democracy movement in, 25, 194
 Li Yi Zhe poster in, *134–45,* 157, 166,
   173, 200
Guardian (London newspaper), 54, 60
Guizhou, big-character poster from, *121–
24*
Guo Haifeng, 297
Guo Hongzhi, 134–35
Guomindang (GMD), 9, 10, 191, 268, 274
 Communist united front with, 12
 Li Fen killed by, 59
 making comparisons with, 97, 310
 1930s anti-Japanese policy of, 54
 in People's Republic, 190
 possible comeback on mainland by, 56–
   57
Guomindang Revolutionary Committee,
85
Guyu. See *Spring Rain*

Hai Rui, 107
Hainan Island, 54, 310, 326
hairdressers. *See* barber shops and hair-
 dressing salons
Han Chinese, 55
Hangzhou, in Cultural Revolution, 128
He Defu, 213–14
He Ming, 105
He Nong, "Election Scandal in a Rural
 Commune," *210–13*
He Qiu, 25
Heaven, Water, Heart, "Democracy? Party
 Rule?" 99
Hebei
 elections in, 214–17
 resettlement of peasants from, 226–27
Hegel, G.W.F., 97
Heilongjiang, resettlement of peasants to,
227

Henan, resettlement of peasants from, 226–
27
Heraclitus, 15
Heshang. See *River Elegy*
Hinton, William, 49
Hitler, Adolf, 148, 155, 318, 324
"Hoist High the Flag of Reason," *271–73*
Hong Kong, 48, 54, 95, 321, 323
 capital moved out of China through, 56
 Diaoyu campaign by, 54
 as model for China, 326
 news of Tian'anmen massacre in, 286,
   291
 Red Guards' denunciations of, 109–11
 Shenzhen's competition with, 325–26
 support of democracy movement in, 33,
   59, 158, 194–96
 Trotskyists in, 135, 145
Hong Kong University, 196
Hongdou. See *Red Bean*
Hou Dejian, 287, 292
housing
 cadres' privileges in, 188
 call for reform in, 269
Hu Feng, 14, 15
Hu Ping, 46, 202, 203, 207, 237
Hu Qiaomu, 11
Hu Shi, 47
Hu Yaobang, 29, 41, 219, 220, 267, 271,
307
 Beijing University students' support of,
   266
Hua Guofeng, 24, 29, 184
 in Cultural Revolution, 125, 127
Huanan Teachers' College (Guangzhou),
201
Huang Shaohung, 85, 86–87
Huang Sungchun, 114
human rights
 Chinese rightists' desire for, 62
 leftists' disregard of, 328
 Li Yi Zhe on, 135–38, 142–45
 as 1989 theme, 268
 in prisons, 240, 250–57
 radical reformers and, 40
 Xu Wenli on, 187, 192
Human Rights League (Human Rights Alliance), 240, 247, 253, 266, 268
humanism, *305–7, 312–16*
Hunan
 in Cultural Revolution, Shengwulian's
   "Whither China?" *124–34*
 1980 student movement in, *217–21*

Hunan Medical School, 219
Hunan Teachers' Training College, *217–21*
Hundred Flowers campaign, (1957), 6–7,
    13–17, 27–28, 82, 85–103, 159–60, 179,
    259
    Wang Shiwei's ideas in, 4
Hungary, 55, 275
    1956 anti-Communist rising in, 14, 28,
        94, 159, 259
hunger strikes
    by Hunan students, 219–20
    of Shanghai students in Xinjiang, 224
    at Tian'anmen Square, 30, 44, 291, 292
Huntington, Samuel, 45
hybrid corn, 88

"I Accuse, I Protest" (wall poster), 100–101
Ibsen, Henrik, 84n.3
imperialism, 47, 67n.72, 122, 128, 134
    as decadent stage of capitalism, 307
"In Defense of Humanism" (Wang
    Ruoshui), *312–16*
"In Memory of Wang Shenyou, Pioneer of
    the Democratic Movement, Teacher,
    Comrade" (Fu Shenqi), *229–34*
individualism, 20, 151, 180, 195, 197, 313
    anarchist, 313
individuality, respect for, 207
inflation, 34, 50, 268, 269, 309, 320
Institute of Marxism-Leninism-Mao
    Zedong Thought, 299
intellectuals
    critique by, 299–331
    encouraged to reveal themselves, 3
    in Hundred Flowers, 13–17, 176, 179
    in 1980s, 43–44, 46, 48
    Liu Shaoqi and, 161
    Mao's dislike of, 14, 41, 150
    as members of working class, 14
    1989 proposed resignation from Party
        by, *264–65*
    in 1990s, 60, 61
    Party's domination of, ix–x
    reform supported by, 206
    Tian'anmen occupation and, 30
    today's split among, x
    who remain abroad, 187
    in Yan'an, 8, 11, 13, 17
    See also literature
International Red Cross, at Tian'anmen
    Square, 289, 290
Internationale (song), 41, 144, 218, 267,
    288, 292

irrigation, 160
"It Is Still the Age of the *Zawen*" (Luo
    Feng), *82–83*
Italian Communists, 188

Japan
    Chinese Communist loss of sovereignty
        to, 54
    Diaoyu reefs and islands occupied by, 54
    economic takeoff of, 323
    May Fourth Movement and, 53–54
    Westernization of, 324
Ji Dengkui, 201
Jiang Jieshi. *See* Chiang Kai-shek
Jiang Mingdao, "What Is the Fundamental
    Cause of the Trade Union Crisis?" *89–
    91*
Jiang Qing, 18, 84n.1, 104, 124, 127, 131,
    162, 165, 171, 177, 179, 231, 253
    after the fall of Lin Biao, 165–66
    trial of, 26–27
Jiang Zemin, 40, 60, 296, 298
Jiangxi, in Cultural Revolution, 128
Jiefang ribao. See Liberation Daily
Jin Jun, 158, 162, 173
Jin Zhixuan, 85, 87–88
Jinggangshan, 168
Jinwangdao, Mao's summers at, 100
Joravsky, David, xi
journalists, foreign, police attack on, 241
journals, unofficial, 25, 157, 185, 194–96,
    199
    democracy movement and, 235–36
    National Committee to Save Liu Qing,
        240
    National Federation of, 196, 229, 235
judicial system (legal system)
    call for improvement in, 158
    Communist Party as superior to, 24,
        302–3, 329
    Constitutional requirements for, 240
    in Cultural Revolution, 138
    democratic parties' call for establishment
        of, 87
    proposed independence of, 191
    socialist legality in, 15, 26
    in Soviet Union, 98
    in trial of Gang of Four, 26–27
    Wei Jingsheng's questions on, 184

Kang Sheng, 12, 18, 104–5, 179, 231
Kang Youwei, 189
Kautsky, Karl, 48

Khrushchev, Nikita, 137, 159, 161, 169, 172, 173, 185, 205, 319
killing a chicken to scare the monkeys, 36
Kissinger, Henry, 188

labor unions. See trade unions
law
  definition of, 139
  See also judicial system (legal system)
Lee Ou-fan Lee, 42
Lee Teng-hui, 33
"leftists," 39, 62, 153–55, 175, 205, 328
  See also ultra-leftism
legal system. See judicial system
legislative power, 191, 210
Lei Feng, 256
Lei Kai, 298
Lenin, Vladimir I., 4, 44, 101, 124, 159, 302, 307
  vanguardism of, 170
Leopardi, Giacomo, 3
"Letter of Petition" (Preparatory Committee of Beijing University Students), 266
"Letter to the People, A," 278–79
Lhasa (Tibet), martial law in, 36
Li Anjiang, 251
Li Boqiu, 85–86
Li Fen, 3, 9, 69–70
Li Kenong, 12
Li Kouzi, 88
Li Lu, 291
Li Min, 201
Li Peng, 30, 35, 37, 45, 57, 62, 282, 294, 298, 320
  calls for removal of, 278–79, 291
Li Ruihuan, 297
Li Xiannian, 125
Li Xingchen, 108
Li Xiuren, 89
Li Yi Zhe, "On Socialist Democracy and the Legal System," 134–45, 157, 166, 173, 200
Li Zhengtian, 134–35, 145, 200, 202
Li Zicheng, 168
Li Zisong, 286
Liang Heng, 217–19
Lianshanbo, 168
Liberation Daily (Jiefang ribao; newspaper), 71, 197–98
Life (Shenghuo; unofficial journal), 195, 200
Lin Biao, 17, 26, 161, 173, 178, 179, 231
  death of, 164–65

Li Yi Zhe on System of, 135–41, 143–45
  Mao's letter of criticism of, 165, 177
  movement to criticize Confucius and, 166, 174
Lin Xiling, 15–16
  background of, 94–95
  1957 speech at People's University by, 94–98
  Paris statement by, 284
Literary Gazette (Wenyibao), 17
literature
  in Hundred Flowers, 15
  Jiang Qing's 1967 speech on, 131
  of 1979 democracy movement, 23
  "scarred" ("of the wounded"), 19–20
  Yan'an Forum on, ix, 11
  Yan'an writers on, 8–9
  usefulness of zawen, 82–83
  See also artists
Liu (commune secretary), 211
Liu Binyan, 29, 40, 44, 46–48, 61, 307, 311, 321
  background of, 327
  "The Bureaucratic Paradise," 327–31
  "Foreword," ix–x
  Mao's attack on, 14, 17, 327
  1957 denunciation of, 93
  on speculation in China, 56
Liu Guokai, 200
Liu Qing, 25, 158, 185, 192, 236–37
  account of detention smuggled out by, 240, 247–57
  background of, 239–40
  "Eyewitness Account of the Arrest of Liu Qing" (Xiao Rui), 239–44
  "Liu Qing Is Innocent!" (the family of Liu Qing), 244–46
Liu Qingyang, 85, 86
Liu Shaoqi, 7, 17, 175, 178, 204, 206
  in Cultural Revolution, 137
  denounced, 22, 104, 108, 115, 117, 119, 120
  Mao's desire to oust him, 18, 152, 164, 202
  democratization sought by, 159, 161
  Li Yi Zhe on, 136, 140, 141
  rehabilitation of, 200–202
Liu Wei, 298
Liu Xiaobo, 292
Liu Xijian, 211–12
Liu Zhongyang, 217
Liu Ziyun, 127, 129
Long March, 5–6

Long Shujin, 127, 129
Look! What Kind of Talk Is This? (Kan!
Zhe shi shenme yanlun?; pamphlet), 95
Lotus Temple labor camp (Shaanxi), 254–57
Lu Dingyi, 13, 108, 115, 117, 120, 178
Lu Ping, 104–8
Lu Xun
on politics and literature, 8, 12
Wang Shiwei on, 77
zawen of, 82, 83
Lukács, Gyorgy, 48
Luo Feng
background of, 82
"It Is Still the Age of the *Zawen*," 82–83
Luo Kejun, 249
Luo Ruiqing, 98, 178
Luo Xinguo, 252
Luo Yuwen, "Distressing Contradiction," 92
Luxemburg, Rosa, 48

Macao
democracy movement in, 195
Wang Fanxi in, 101
Mai Mao, 251
Mao Zedong
ambitions of, 150–51
in Cultural Revolution, 17–20, 122, 137–38, 162–69
"Arm the Left," 130, 156n.3
"Bombard the Headquarters" (poster), 120, *121*
cited by Shengwulian, 127–28, 132–34
"Great Helmsman," 124, 147
his desire for the oppressed to rise up, 32, 124
Nie Yuanzi poster, 104–5
praised, 105–8, 110, 111, 115
promotion of production called for, 123
"to rebel is justified," 108, 110–11
use of Red Guards, 146–52, 163, 164
Wang Xizhe's essay on, *157–75*
death of, 167, 319
on democracy, 99, 144
Deng Xiaoping's praise of, 182
despotism of, 317, 319
on early Chinese Communism, 4
on education, 118, 119
flattery of, 178
humanism of, 313
in Hundred Flowers, 13–16, 27–28

invoked by 1989 protestors, 32
leaders' reliance on prestige of, 86
Li Yi Zhe on displays of loyalty to, 135
"On the Correct Handling of Contradictions among the People," 15, 91
on the need for new Cultural Revolution, 30
1927 report on peasant movement by, 217
on overthrowing political power, 109
as peasant leader who intended to become emperor, 157–59, 162, 168
personality cult of, 156n.8, 160, 177
privileges of, attacked, 100–101
Red Book of, 17
Stalinist variant developed by, 5–7
on starting a prairie fire, 4
on sugar-coated bullets, 116–17
Tai Huang's letter to, 93–94
"Talks at the Yan'an Forum on Literature and Art," ix, 11
workers' support of, 49, 50
Xu Wenli's assessment of, 186
in Yan'an, 8, 10, 100
"Mao Zedong and the Cultural Revolution" (Wang Xizhe), *157–75*
Mao Zedong thought
in Cultural Revolution, 106, 108, 113, 114, 116, 120, 124, 134, 147, 150
Lin Biao System as, 138, 140
Liu Shaoqi and, 159, 201
questioning of, 173, 188, 191, 232
Mao Zhiyong, 220
Marcos, Ferdinand, 54, 309
Marx, Karl, 112, 160, 160
humanist writings of, 14, 21, 48, 61, 312, 315
Marxism
critical school of, 48
humanism and, *305–7*, 314–16
intellectuals' abandonment of, 43
Mao's attitude to, 159, 168, 205–6, 301, 327
as outdated, 307, 308
rethinking of
after Cultural Revolution, 20, 48, 61
in 1980s, 48
problems involved, 303–5
after Tian'anmen occupation, 61
social psychology absent in, 303–4
students' abandonment of, 46
summed up in "to rebel is justified," 110–11

Marxism *(cont.)*
    of Wang Shenyou, 231–32
    Wei Jingsheng's opposition to, 180
Marxism-Leninism, 153, 188, 191, 219,
    272, 318
masses, the
    in Cultural Revolution, 126, 128, 129
    Mao's concept of, 7, 10, 17, 138
    need for leadership of, 106–7
    Party's estrangement from, 93
    "the people's eyes are bright and clear,"
        149
    question of relationship of Party to, 303
    revolutionary supervision over Party by,
        140
    See also trade unions
mathematics, middle-school textbooks in, 89
May Fourth movement, 4, 16, 29, 53–54,
    267–68
    science and democracy as goal of, 30, 53,
        285
May 7 Directive, 129
medicine, Soviet, 96
Medvedev, Roy A., xi
Meng ("bad element"), 212
Meng (brigade official), 211–13
middle class, as prerequisite for democracy,
    44, 60
military, the. *See* People's Liberation Army
Ming Dynasty, 168
modernization, 23, 28, 39, 41, 214, 299
    China's need to follow models of, 308–9
    democratization cannot be separated
        from, 304
    the fifth, 180
    integrated, 191
    rural, 53
    in Third World countries, 45–46
    See also Four Modernizations
Montesquieu, Baron de, 21
More, Henry, 314
Mu Changqing, 25
multiparty system
    in capitalism, 317
    needed in China, 326–27
    socialism and, 275–78
Mussolini, Benito, 169

Nameless Association, 25
Nanfang ribao. See Southern Daily
National Day (periodical), 321
national nihilism, 47

National People's Congress (NPC), 191,
    194, 272, 273
    Third, 272
    Fourth, 139–44
    Fifth, 189
    Sixth, 190, 192
    Standing Committee of, 190
new authoritarianism, 45
New China News Agency (Xinhua News
    Agency), 88, 93, 266, 321
New Democracy, 300, 301
Nie Rongzhen, 38
Nie Yuanzi, 120
    background of, 104–5
    "What Have Song Shuo, Lu Ping, and
        Peng Peiyun Done in the Cultural Rev-
        olution?" *105–8*, 120, 121
Nietzschean superman, 20
Nixon, Richard M., 145
North Korea, 308

Observer (Guanchajia; Hong Kong publica-
    tion), 234
old book stalls, 109–11
"On Collective Boarding Schools for Chil-
    dren of Cadres" (Red Guards), *115–20*
"On Political Reform" (Wang Ruowang),
    317–27
"On Socialist Democracy and the Legal Sys-
    tem" (Li Yi Zhe), *134–45*, 157, 166, 173,
    200
"On the 'Great Proletarian Cultural Revo-
    lution'" (Wang Fanxi), *145–55*
"Open Letter to the Chinese Communist
    Party," *296–98*
"Open Letter to the Students from an Army
    Veteran," *281–82*
Organic Chemical Factory (Beijing), 213,
    214
Ou Yangshan, 219
Owen, Robert, 314

Paris Commune, 124, 125, 127, 130, 132,
    164, 170, 231, 318
patriarchy, 139, 140
peace, smashed by Party, 100
peasants
    democracy movement and, 60, 187
    economic condition of
        in Cultural Revolution, 143
        Li Yi Zhe on need for incentives, 143–
            44

new exploitation, 35
1950s improvement, 98
in 1989, 52
1990s problems, 52
rice bowl mentality, 49
as instinctively socialist, 159
after liberation, 176
Mao supported by, 32
plans for resettlement of, 226–27
proposed popular assemblies of, 193
redress of wrongs demanded by, 22
reform supported by, 206
steel-making by, 160
Peking Review (periodical), 120, 121
Peng Dehuai, 161–62, 165, 177, 178, 205
Peng Ming, 298
Peng Peiyun, 104, 106
Peng Zhen, 162, 219
People's Commune, 125, 126, 129, 130, 132–34, 160, 176
People's Daily (Renmin ribao; newspaper), 3, 30, 31, 105, 108, 121, 147, 243, 270, 278, 312, 327
People's Liberation Army
  business investments of, 39
  corruption in, 39
  in Cultural Revolution, 17, 18, 36, 124, 127–30, 164, 165
  like fish in water, 128
  in 1989 Tian'anmen occupation
    assault and massacre, 30, 36–38, 279, 286–96, 297
    letter on defense problems of students, 281–82
    martial law, 281
    plea that army not be used, 279
    threatened use of army by Deng, 270–71
  politics and, 37–39, 191–92
  recommended changes in, 192
  Soviet army copied by, 96
  spending by, 309
people's power, 42
People's Road (Renminzhi Lu; unofficial journal)
  "A Guangdong Youth Forum on Wall Posters" (Ge Tian), 199–202
  "A Statement of Clarification," 194–96
People's University (Beijing)
  Lin Xiling's 1957 speech at, 94–98
  in 1989 movement, 33, 42

"Proposal to Resign from the Party and Prepare an 'Association to Promote China's Democracy Movement,'" 264–65
wall posters, 270–71, 275–78
permanent revolution, 151
Philippines, 309, 324
  fall of Marcos in, 54
Pilgrimage to the West (Xiyouji; by Wu Cheng'en), 237
Pinochet Ugarte, Augusto, 323
Plekhanov, Georgi, 44
plows, useless, 88–89
poets, 23
Poland, 55, 275, 309
  1956 anti-Communist rising in, 14
  Solidarity movement in, 29, 39, 57, 229, 238, 239, 259, 265
police
  in arrest of Li Qing, 239–44, 250–53
  in colleges and universities, 321, 322
  use of reeducation through labor by, 254–57
political democratization, definition of, 317
political prisoners
  Liu Qing's account, 240, 250–57
  1989 petition for release of, 44
  Xu Wenli's proposed release of, 192
  See also rehabilitations
"Politicians, Artists" (Wang Shiwei), 75–78
post-capitalist society, 157
pragmatism, 47, 172
prairie fire, 264–98
  Mao's saying on, 4
Princeton China Initiative, 48
prisoners
  categories of, 254
  See also political prisoners
private owners, monetary interest to, 95
"Problems of Modernization" (Fang Lizhi), 307–12
"Proclamation of the Guizhou Proletarian Revolutionary Rebel General Headquarters," 121–24
professional revolutionaries, 170, 273
"Proposal to Resign from the Party and Prepare an 'Association to Promote China's Democracy Movement,'" 264–65
"Proposals for Reform of the Political Structure, 1986" (Su Shaozhi), 299–305
public ownership, meaning of, 311
public security. *See* police

Qin Jiwei, 38
Qin Shi Huangdi, 151, 271
Qingdao (Shandong), 259
Qinghua University, 265, 286
  1957 wall poster at, 100–101
  Red Guards' statement at, *111–13*
Qingyuan (Hebei), elections in, 214–17

Radio Broadcasting Administration Bureau, 125
railways
  ministry of, 125
  students allowed to pass by, 220–21
ration coupons, 176
Reagan, Ronald, 62, 310
real estate markets, 56
"Reawakening of the Chinese Working
  Class, The" *(Fengfan)*, 228–29
rectification movements, 8, 10, 85–88, 179,
  237–38, 312, 320
Red Bean (Hongdou; unofficial journal),
  195
Red Cross, 86. *See also* International Red
  Cross
Red Flag (Hongqi; periodical), 233
Red Guards, 17–20, 22, 23, 27, 28, 179
  Mao's suppression of, 169, 231
  Mao's use of, 146–52, 163, 164
  published statements of, 108–20
    "A Big Disturbance Must Be Made at
      Qinghua University," *111–13*
    "Declaring War on the Old World,"
      109–11
    "On Collective Boarding Schools for
      Children of Cadres," *115–20*
  students of 1989 compared to, 31–32
  Wang Fanxi's analysis of, 146–52
  Wang Yizhe's 1981 opinions on, 174
  Western confusion about, 145
reeducation through labor (rehabilitation
  through labor; *laojiao),* 254–57
"Reform Program for the Eighties, A" (Xu
  Wenli), *189–94*
reform through labor *(laogai),* 251, 254–
  55
reformism, 126, 206–7
regionalism, 38
rehabilitations
  after Cultural Revolution, 18–19, 21–24,
    166, 200, 327
  after Hundred Flowers, 17, 21, 27, 78
  of Li Yi Zhe, 135

1989 calls for, 266, 269
  of Wang Shiwei, 12–13
Ren Wanding, 51, 192, 247, 249
  background of, 266–67
  "Speech in Tian'anmen Square," *266–69*
Renmin ribao. See People's Daily
Renminzhi Lu. See People's Road
Renminzhi sheng. See Voice of the People
Responsibility (Duty; Zeren; unofficial jour-
  nal), 25, 229, 337
  "Democracy and Legality Are Safeguards
    of Stability and Unity," *196–99*
revisionism, 149–51, 167, 175, 179, 275
"rice bowls," 49
"rightists," 62, 153–54, 159–60, 176, 177,
  264, 323
  Hundred Flowers and, 16–17, 179, 205
Rind, Anita, 257
River Elegy (Heshang) TV series, 43–44, 46
"Running into difficulties" (article in
  Yan'an newspaper), 71–72

"Sad Memories and Prospects: My Appeal
  to the Tribunal of the People" (Liu Qing),
  247–57
Sakharov, Andrei, 323
science, 30, 47
  idealism in, 88
scientists, 1957 symposium of, 88–89
sea power, democracy and, 43
secret coordination, 195
sectarianism, 85–86, 96, 153
separation of powers, 191, 207, 317
September 5 Directive, 130
Serge, Victor, 217
"Seven Theses on Socialism and Democracy" (Wang Fanxi), *101–3*
sexual inequality, Ding Ling's attack on, 8
sexual love, 20
Shaanxi, Lotus Temple labor camp, 254–57
Shandong, resettlement of peasants from,
  226–27
shangfang movement, 22
Shanghai
  Cultural Revolution in, 162, 169
  as economic failure, 308
  elections in
    factories, 213, 229–30
    universities, 213, 237
  1980 dissidents in, 25, 186
  rusticated youth from, 222–26
  WAF in, 52

Shanghai Commune, 164
Shanghai Motor Factory, election in, 213
Shanghai Trade Union Council, 89
Shanxi
    dissidents in, 228
    election scandal in, *210–13*
Shaoguan (Guangdong), dissidents in, 25
Shenghuo. See *Life*
Shengwulian, 173
    "Whither China?" 32, *124–34*
Shenyang (Liaoning), Japanese 1931 seizure
    of, 54
Shenzhen Special Economic Zone, 325–26
Shi Jinsheng, 255–56
Sichuan, Chinese mint in, 309
Singapore, 48, 309, 323, 324
Siwu luntan. See *April Fifth Forum*
Sixteen Points, 112, 114, 119
Sixu. See *Train of Thought*
"Smart Thieves' Voice," 282
Snow, Edgar, 177
social fascism, 18, 136–39, 197
socialism
    China now at initial stage of, 300, 308
    "with Chinese features," 54, 275
    class contradictions after, 98
    democracy and, 187, 196, 206
        Wang Fanxi on, 101–3
    dissidents' current opinions on, 59–61
    economic interests in, 303
    feudal, 157, 232, 233
    free peasantry and, 52–53
    humanitarian, 186
    many strata in, 303
    multiparty system in, *275–78*
    in one country, 151
    peasants as reservoir for building, 159
    praised by Lin Xiling, 97
    radical, 15–16
    utopian, 176, 314
    world victory of, 134, 151
Socialist Education Campaign, 229, 230
socialist legality, 15, 26
"Socialist Multiparty System and China,
    The" (Yang XX), *275–78*
Solidarity movement (Solidarnosc; Poland),
    29, 39, 57, 229, 238, 239, 259, 265
Song Shuo, 104, 105
Song Yixiu, 108
Song Yuxi, 163
South Korea, 48, 308, 323, 324
    authoritarianism of, 46

student demonstrations in, 54
Southern Daily (Nanfang ribao; news-
    paper), 195
Soviet Union
    aid to China by, 176
    bureaucracy in, 74, 152–54, 172, 185
    collapse of, 59, 61
    Cultural Revolution denunciations of,
        111, 117, 122, 134
    democracy movement group in support
        of, 239
    dissent in, 21–22, 186
    Gorbachev's strategy in, 326
    judicial system in, 98
    killings in, 101
    literature in, 11
    privileges of cadres in, 141
    show trials in, 12, 101
    as source of dogmatism, 96
    textbooks of, in China, 89
    uprising of minority nationalities in, 222
spiritual pollution, 29, 33, 311, 312
Spray (Langhua; unofficial journal), 200,
    201
Spring Rain (Guyu; Yan'an periodical), 75
Spring Thunder (Red Guard paper), 108
stability and unity, 322, 323
Stalin, Joseph, 4, 5, 7, 11, 12, 98, 146, 149,
    151, 170, 185, 322
    critique of policies of, 301–2
    Khrushchev's denunciation of, 159, 176,
        178, 232
    Lenin responsible for crimes of, 101
    Mao and, 168
    popular dissatisfaction and paranoia of,
        319
    as representative of bureaucratic central-
        ists, 152–54
    whether "left" or "right," 153
Stalinism, 10
    of Chinese Communism, 6–8, 149, 301
State Council, 189, 190, 191, 221, 236,
    245, 321
"Statement of Clarification, A" (Editorial
    Board, *Renminzhi Lu),* 194–96
steel-making by peasants, 160
Stirner, Max, 313
stock markets, 56
Stone Company (Stone Group), 34, 60
strikes. *See* workers—strikes by
struggle, criticism, and correction (trans-
    form), 112, 149

"Struggle for the Class Dictatorship of the Proletariat, The" (Wang Xizhe), 157
"Student Movement in Hunan, The," 217–21
students
  African, 54
  "democratic salons" of, 29
  in Hundred Flowers, 15–16
  "mahjong faction" among, 42
  1979 demonstrations by, 23
  1986–1987 movement of, 29, 268
  1989 control of Beijing by, 30
  1989 Tian'anmen Square occupation by, 29–32, 41, 57–58. See also Tian'anmen Square
  in Red Guards, 17, 20, 23
  rustication of, 221–26
  at Yan'an, 71–72
  See also Beijing University; other universities
studios, photographic, 109–11
Su Ming, 217, 218, 221
Su Shaozhi, 48, 60
  background of, 299
  "Proposals for Reform of the Political Structure, 1986," 299–305
Su Wei, 57
Su Xiaokang, 43–44, 46
sugar-coated bullets, 116–17
Sun Yat-sen, 272, 326–27
Sweden, 275
system of rites, 139–43

Tai Huang, 1957 denunciation of, 93–94
Tai Songsi, 88
Taiping uprising, 168
Taiwan, 48, 135, 191, 308, 309, 321, 323, 324
  democracy movement and, 59, 65n.40, 268
  Diaoyu campaign by, 54
  as model for mainland, 56, 310
  Progressive Party in, 268
Taiyuan (Shanxi), demonstrations at steel works in, 228–29
Tan Zhenlin, 125
Tansuo (Explorations; publication), 180, 181, 248
Tao Sen, 217–21
Thailand, 309
Thatcher, Margaret, 43, 62

"Theory of Two Cultural Factors, The" (Yan Jiaqi), 305–7
thought reform, 14
"Thoughts on March 8 (Women's Day)" (Ding Ling), 78–82
Three Anti's campaign (1951–1952), 178–79
"Three-Family Village," 105
Tian Cheli, 206
Tian'anmen Square (Beijing)
  in Cultural Revolution, 164
  1976 April Fifth demonstrations in, 22, 59, 167, 169–70, 174–75, 181, 183, 185, 201, 230, 232, 267
  1989 occupation of, 29–37, 54
  antipolitical politics of students, 42
  army assault and massacre, 30, 36–38, 279, 286–96, 297
  army assault threatened, 270–71
  arrests following, 30, 37, 296, 297
  defense plans for students, 281–82
  entrepreneurs' support of, 34
  explanations for, 33–34
  feigned compliance afterwards, 58
  Goddess of Liberty (statue), 292, 293
  headbands of students, 54, 67n.87
  hunger strikes, 30, 44, 291, 292
  martial law, 38, 281
  number massacred, 36
  as prairie fire, 4
  Ren Wanding's speech, 266–69
  students attempt to turn guns over to army, 286–87
  students' mistrust of intellectuals, 44–45
  thieves' strike in favor of students, 282
  use of pedicabs and motorbikes, 34
  worker participation, 30, 32, 33, 49–52, 57, 269–70, 279–81
  "A Worker's Letter to the Students," 269–70
  Zhao's visit to Square, 30, 278
Tibet, martial law in, 36
Tito, 21, 162, 259
trade unions (labor unions)
  contradictions between administrations and, 91, 92
  independence from Party proposed, 268–69. See also Workers' Autonomous Federation
  1957 criticism of, 89–91

Train of Thought (Sixu; students' journal), 202

Trotsky, Leon, 21, 153, 162

Trotskyism, 63n.9, 101, 135, 285
Wang Shiwei accused of, 9–12, 75

Turkey, 323

ultra-leftism (extreme leftism), 126, 134, 143, 153, 155, 165, 176–77

Union Research Institute (Hong Kong), 95

United Front Work Department, 85

United States
Chinese Communist rapprochement with; predicted, 145, 155
Cultural Revolution denunciations of, 122
democracy movement in exile in, 59, 291
freedom of the press in, 273
worship of, 96

Urumqi (Xinjiang), 223

vanguard, 170, 318

Vietnam, 24, 277

Voice of the People (Renminzhi sheng; unofficial journal), 25, 157, 175, 195, 200
"The Student Movement in Hunan," 217–21

voting. *See* elections

WAF. *See* Workers' Autonomous Federation

Walesa, Lech, 26, 262

wall posters
Deng Xiaoping's banning of, 171, *199–202*
Deng Xiaoping's early statement on, 170, 202
in elections, 210, 216
of 1957, 98–101
of 1989, *270–71, 274, 275–78*
"On Socialist Democracy and the Legal System" (Li Yi Zhe), *134–45,* 157, 166, 173, 200
"Women Are Human Beings Too" (Zhang Ailing), *257–59*

Wan Li, 279

Wan Runnan, 60

Wang Dan, 297

Wang Dongxing, 169, 170, 201

Wang Fan-hsi. *See* Wang Fanxi

Wang Fanxi, 4, 9–10, 12

background of, 101, 285
"On the 'Great Proletarian Cultural Revolution,' " *145–55*
1989 statement by, *285*
"Seven Theses on Socialism and Democracy," *101–3*

Wang Juntao, 203–7

Wang Li, 292

Wang Longmeng, 298

Wang Ming, 10–12, 152

Wang Ruoshui, 48, 61
background of, 312
"In Defense of Humanism," *312–16*

Wang Ruowang, 29, 36, 44, 46, 47, 307
background of, 317
"On Political Reform," *317–27*

Wang Shenyou, Fu Shenqi's memorial piece on, *229–34*

Wang Shiwei
background of, 7–10
Dai Qing's study on, 4
execution of, 3, 12
Liu Binyan compared to, 17
"Politicians, Artists," *75–78*
rehabilitation of, 12–13
trial of, 11–12
"Wild Lily," ix, 9, 11, 12, *69–75*
text of, *69–75*

Wang Xizhe, 21, 25, 46, 59, 194, 200, 311
background of, 157–58
Li Yi Zhe poster of, *134–45,* 157, 166, 173, 200
"Mao Zedong and the Cultural Revolution," *157–75*
"The Struggle for the Class Dictatorship of the Proletariat," 157

Wang Yifeng, 214–17

Wang Zhen, 30, 43, 219, 226, 294

warlordism, 37–38

Washington, George, 272

Weber, Max, 308

Wei Jingsheng, 23, 29, 44, 46, 62, 192
background of, 180–81
"Democracy, the Fifth Modernization," 180
"Democracy or a New Dictatorship?" *180–84,* 248
free enterprise sought by, 21, 59
as issue in Beijing University election, 207, 209

Wei Jingsheng (cont.)
    Liu Qing's prison meeting with, 253
    trial of
        Liu Qing asked to be Wei's lawyer, 249
        publication of transcript, 239–50
        severe sentence, 24, 28, 171, 180, 186,
            248
Wei Rongling, 252–53
Wenhuibao (Hong Kong newspaper), 286
Wenyibao. See Literary Gazette
West Germany, 308, 323
Westernization
    intellectuals' support of, 43–44, 46–48
    of Japan and Singapore, 324
    Taiwan as alternative model to, 310
"What Have Song Shuo, Lu Ping, and Peng
    Peiyun Done in the Cultural Revolu-
    tion?" (Nie Yuanzi), 105–8, 120, 121
"What Is the Fundamental Cause of the
    Trade Union Crisis?" (Jiang Mingdao),
    89–91
"Where I Stand," 274
"Whither China?" (Shengwulian), 32, 124–
    34
"Wild Lily" (Wang Shiwei), ix, 9, 11, 12,
    69–75
"Wind Rises from among the Duckweed:
    Elections at Beijing University, The"
    (Gong Bo), 202–10
women
    proposed four-hour day for, 193
    trained as tractor drivers, 86
"Women Are Human Beings Too" (Zhang
    Ailing), 257–59
Women's Association, 86
Women's Day, Ding Ling's essay on, 78–82
women's liberation, 207
workers
    bonuses for, 301
    democracy movement and, 58, 60, 61,
        268–69
    in 1979–1981, 25–26
    distribution of weapons among, 124
    economic condition of, 49–51
        Li Yi Zhe on need for incentives, 143–
            44
        1950s improvement in life, 98
    proposed reforms, 193
    safety wanted by workers, 49, 58
    elections by, 213–17, 229–30
    "floating class" of, 49
    human rights for, 192

during 1989 Tian'anmen occupation, 30,
    32, 33, 49–52, 57, 269–70, 279–81
self-management by, 193
    in Cultural Revolution, 125
single, 228–29
strikes by
    Jiang Zemin on danger of, 60
    Yumen oil field, 97
See also trade unions
Workers' Autonomous Federation (WAF),
    51–52
    massacre of members of, 293
    Preparatory Program of, 279–80
    Provisional Statutes of, 283–84
    "Workers' Declaration," 280–81
Workers' Daily (Gongren ribao; news-
    paper), 89
Workers' Dare-to-Die Brigades, 51, 288
"Worker's Letter to the Students, A," 269–
    70
Workers' Picket Teams, 51
writers. See literature
Wu Cheng'en, Xiyouji, 237
Wu De, 201
Wu Han, 162
Wuer Kaixi, 33, 298
Wuhan (Hubei), dissidents in, 25, 26

Xia Jianzhi, 108
Xia Shen, 203, 206, 208
xiafang program, 21, 22
Xiamen (Fujian), 326
Xiangshanzhuang brigade (Shanxi), 210–
    13
Xiao Jun, 8, 9, 11
Xiao Rui, "Eyewitness Account of the Ar-
    rest of Liu Qing," 239–44
Xinjiang
    resettlement of peasants to, 227
    rusticated Shanghai youth in, 222–26
Xu (Zhongshan teacher), 200
Xu Wenli, 26, 158, 239, 262
    background of, 185–86
    1980 interview with, 185–88
    "A Reform Program for the Eighties,"
        189–94
Xu Xiangquan, 38

Yan'an, 5–13
    democracy at, 177
    Ding Ling's essay on women in, 78–82
    intellectuals in, 8, 11, 13, 17

"little devils" at, 74
wall newspapers at, 10–11
Yan'an Forum on Literature and Art, ix, 11, 75
Yan Jiaqi, 43, 44, 46, 59
background of, 305
"The Theory of Two Cultural Factors," 305–7
Yan'an Literary Resistance Association, 75
Yang Hao, 298
Yang Jing
background of, 234
interview with, 234–38
Yang Keming, 108
Yang Lian, "The Square," 295–96
Yang Peikuai, 206, 207
Yang Shangkun, 30, 38, 64n.23, 294
Yang Tao, 297
Yang Xiguang, 173
Yang XX, "The Socialist Multiparty System and China," 275–78
Yangcheng wanbao (Guangzhou publication), 108
Yao Wenyuan, 162
Yi Ming, "China: A History That Must Be Told," 175–80
Yi Zhongxun, 195
youth
official definition of, 222
today's attitude of, 41–43
See also students
"Youth Disturbances in China's Far West" (Chen Ding), 221–27
Yu Louke, 163
Yu Zhonghai, 255–56
Yuan Renyuan, 219
Yuan Shikai, 272
Yue Zhengping, 251, 252
Yugoslavia, 55, 238
Yumen (Gansu), 97
Yuquanshan, Mao's vacations at, 100

Zafanolli, Wojtek, 189
zawen, 70, 82–83

Zeren. See *Responsibility*
Zhang Ailing, 207
"Women Are Human Beings Too," 257–59
Zhang Boli, 292
Zhang Bosen, 125, 127, 129
Zhang Chunqiao, 26, 169, 253, 164
Zhang Guotao, 152
Zhang Manling, 203
Zhang Pinghua, 125
Zhang Wei, 203, 204
Zhang Wenhe, 240, 247, 253
Zhang Wentian, 161
Zhang Xifeng, 22
Zhao Hanqing, 286
Zhao Zhengyi, 108
Zhao Ziyang, 43, 55, 60, 238, 298, 320, 330
corruption of, 40
political and economic ideas of, 58, 61, 62
possible reemergence of, 40
Tian'anmen Square occupation and, 30, 35, 38, 45–46, 278–79
Zheng Xing, "The Election Movement Is in the Ascendant," 213–17
Zhengming. See *Contention*
Zhongguo qingnian bao. See *China Youth*
Zhongnanhai (Beijing), demonstrations at, 22–23
Zhongshan University (Guangzhou), 195, 200
Zhou Donglin, 256
Zhou Duo, 292
Zhou Enlai, 14, 35, 50, 93, 164, 173, 176, 186, 201, 206, 258
in Cultural Revolution, 124, 125, 127
Cultural Revolution Group's attempt to overthrow, 166–67
death of, 167, 267
as first Chinese, and then Party member, 271
Zhu Yuanzhang, 168
Zhuhai (Guangdong), 326
Zinoviev, Grigori, 12

Gregor Benton is Professor of Chinese Studies, and
Alan Hunter is Lecturer and Senior Research Fellow, both in the
department of East Asian Studies, University of Leeds, England.
Benton's previous book was *Mountain Fires: The Red Army's
Three-Year War in South China, 1934–1938* (California). With
Chan Kim-Kwong, Hunter is the author of *Protestantism in
Contemporary China* (Cambridge).